Casebook of
Marital Therapy

THE GUILFORD FAMILY THERAPY SERIES
Alan S. Gurman, Editor

Casebook of Marital Therapy

EDITED BY

Alan S. Gurman
University of Wisconsin Medical School

The Guilford Press
New York   London

PRINTED IN THE UNITED STATES OF AMERICA

This book is printed on acid-free paper

Last digit is print number   9 8 7 6 5 4 3

Library of Congress Cataloging-in-Publication Data

Main entry under title:

Casebook of marital therapy.

   Bibliography: p.
   Includes index.
   1. Marital psychotherapy—Case studies.   I.   Gurman,
Alan S.
RC488.5.C37 1985   616.89   85-9778
ISBN 0-89862-062-7
ISBN 0-89862-466-5 (paperback)

TO MY FAMILY
Gerri, Jesse, and Ted

Contributors

W. Robert Beavers, MD *Southwest Family Institute, and Department of Psychiatry, University of Texas Health Science Center, Dallas, Texas*

Insoo Berg *Brief Family Therapy Center, Milwaukee, Wisconsin*

John Byng-Hall, FRCPsych *Institute for Family Therapy (London), and Family Therapy Program, Tavistock Clinic, London, England*

Evan Imber Coppersmith, PhD *Department of Psychiatry, University of Calgary Faculty of Medicine, Calgary, Alberta, Canada*

Steve de Shazer *Brief Family Therapy Center, Milwaukee, Wisconsin*

Henry Grunebaum, MD *Harvard University Medical School, and Department of Psychiatry, Cambridge Hospital, Cambridge, Massachusetts*

Alan S. Gurman, PhD *Department of Psychiatry, University of Wisconsin Medical School, Madison, Wisconsin*

David Kantor, PhD *The Family Center, and The Kantor Family Institute, Cambridge, Massachusetts*

Florence W. Kaslow, PhD *Department of Medical Psychology, Duke University Medical College, Durham, North Carolina, and Florida Couples & Family Institute, West Palm Beach, Florida*

Michael E. Kerr, MD *Department of Psychiatry, Georgetown University School of Medicine, and Georgetown Family Center, Washington, D.C.*

Gayla Margolin, PhD *Department of Psychology, University of Southern California, Los Angeles, California*

David J. Moultrup, MSW, LICSW *New England Center for the Study of the Family, Newton, Massachusetts, and Private Practice, Arlington, Massachusetts*

ix

William C. Nichols, EdD *Department of Psychology, University of Detroit, and Private Practice, Birmingham, Michigan*

M. Duncan Stanton, PhD *Department of Psychiatry, University of Rochester School of Medicine and Dentistry, Rochester, New York*

David C. Treadway, PhD *The Institute at Newton, Newton, Massachusetts, and Private Practice, Cambridge, Massachusetts*

Preface

I have been teaching and supervising marital and family therapy for over a decade, and have been doing it a good deal longer than that. I have attended dozens of clinical workshops, demonstrations, and lectures on family therapy over the years, and have led a fair number of them myself. I have read more books and journal articles than any sane person should be allowed. But, of all this "exposure" to the theory and practice of marital and family therapy, only a very small proportion of it has exposed me to systemic treatment as it is practiced on a day-to-day basis. Like a novel, all of psychotherapy has a beginning, a middle, and an end. The predominant opportunity I have to experience the full course of therapy is in my own clinical work, with an additional smattering of families treated by trainees under my supervision. Such a pattern of exposure to therapy is representative of what is true for most family therapists (indeed, therapists of any ilk), but it is also misleading. Edited videotapes, oral accounts of therapists' personal experiences in their work, selectively published case vignettes, role playing, and the brilliant one-session-only demonstration by a workshop leader who will never again see the family or couple he or she has interviewed, help us to get partial glimpses of the complexity that is family therapy. As useful as such glimpses may be for refining or learning certain technical skills, they ultimately are not as instructive as slow, long looks. Family therapists brought the television camera and the one-way mirror into the arena of psychotherapy and thereby made the experience more open to public scrutiny than it had ever been, but so much is necessarily left unseen.

Until a few years ago, only a handful of published full-length case studies of family therapy existed, and only one book (Papp, 1977) was devoted entirely to such presentations. Opportunities for family therapists to experience vicariously the inevitable vicissitudes of the unfolding of treatment have arisen more recently with the publication of two additional volumes of full-length case studies of families in therapy (Coleman, 1985; Kaufman, 1984). Yet, in all three books, very little attention has been devoted to the treatment of marital problems. This is especially ironic because, despite the appropriate emphases in the field on multigenerational and ecological perspectives on marital and family life, face-to-face work with couples probably accounts for a major portion of most family therapists' clinical practice time. This is not to say that marital problems cannot or should not be treated with multigenerational and ecological awareness and sensitivity, or even with the direct participation of only one partner to the relationship. It is to say that much marital work focuses its attention on the dyadic dimension.

Perhaps a major reason why the lion's share of public attention of family therapists has been directed at clinical problems other than those in the marital domain grows out of the history of the field. Family therapy unfolded largely in the context of treating major psychiatric disorders, especially schizophrenia, of adults and families with symptomatic children and adolescents. The origins of marital therapy, by contrast, lie in the fields of so-called marriage counseling, a professional movement that evolved quite apart from what most of us think as the mainstream of the family therapy movement, and, in the largely psychodynamically oriented practices of the earliest marital therapists. In the 1980s, of course, it is rare to find colleagues who dub themselves "marriage counselors," and with a more refined appreciation of systemic dynamics than existed even a decade ago, most of us now view "marital therapy" as but one possible expression of the idea that relational boundaries exist where they are drawn. Still, the marriage counseling movement evolved independently of mainstream family therapy, and the psychodynamic predilections of the early marital therapists reflected the types of theorizing from which many of the early, and most of the more recent, family theorists sought to differentiate themselves. Given these two historical facts, it is hardly surprising that marital therapy, even as currently practiced in all its diverse fashions, *publicly* remains the ambivalently valued stepchild of the family therapy field.

This volume, then, was conceived as a means of letting family therapists and students of family therapy into the consulting room during courses of therapy focused on marital difficulties. Contributors to this *Casebook* were encouraged to present a completed case that was representative of the kinds of problems they frequently deal with in their practices, and in which their way of working with such problems could be made clear. Moreover, contributors were cautioned not to select a "star" case, that is, one in which everything went "according to the book." In brief, these colleagues were discouraged from taking up the understandable and predictable temptation to show how gifted they are in their work.

What emerges here, then, are full-length case studies of marital therapy with a wide range of presenting problems treated by a diverse number of therapeutic approaches. Some of the therapies were of very long duration; some were very brief. Some therapies included individual sessions in addition to conjoint interviews; others included interviews with family members other than the marital couple; and two courses of therapy described here included only one spouse. Some presentations reflect consistent adherence to a given "school" of therapy, whereas others reflect persistent efforts to integrate the principles and practices of two or more "schools."

Though we all like to have, and perhaps need to have, professional heroes and heroines whom we can simultaneously admire (we may learn from them) and despise (they unwittingly embarrass us with their charisma), few of our sessions with couples and families, and even fewer full courses of therapy, could ever qualify as "modern classics" of conceptual and technical brilliance. Umbarger (1983) has aptly and honestly noted that "beyond the initial interview lies the dogged, usually undramatic, process of bringing about the changes that seem needed" (p. 99) and that most of what is ultimately therapeutic for the couples and families who seek our help takes place in the "muck and mire of the middle phase of our work" (p. xiii). Contributions to this *Casebook* reflect, indeed underscore, this middle-phase reality. What is revealed are the reflections and actions of thinking and caring experienced clinicians. Just as these cases describe moments and periods that were telling and forward moving, they also describe stretches of motionless redundancy. Just as they portray the therapist's exuberance and confidence, they also portray the therapist's hesitation and confusion. In other words, taken together, these full-length case studies convey the everyday ups and downs of clinical practice with couples. While all the couples described here undoubtedly profited from their experiences with their therapists, some clearly profited more than others, and certainly none left therapy problem-free, wrapped in a cloak of marital ecstasy and bliss. Since therapists are mere mortals, hardworking and reasonably effective, some readers may find such an assessment disappointing; most, I think, will find it reassuring.

In the final analysis, learning to be an effective therapist with couples does not come about by attending workshops, by receiving countless hours of supervision, or even (perish the thought!) by reading this *Casebook*, though each of these pieces will help. Effective therapy comes about by some uncertain mixture of raw natural talent and unteachable genuine caring, honest and frequent appraisal of one's own deficits and refinement of one's skills, and thousands of hours spent in the actual practice of therapy. I hope that this *Casebook* will encourage the reader to sustain a lifelong pursuit of therapeutic excellence.

ALAN S. GURMAN
Madison, Wisconsin
February 1985

References

Coleman, S. (Ed.). (1985). *Failures in family therapy*. New York: Guilford Press.
Kaufman, E. (Ed.). (1984). *Power to change: Family case studies in the treatment of alcoholism.* New York: Gardner Press.
Papp, P. (Ed.). (1977). *Family therapy: Full length case studies*. New York: Gardner Press.
Umbarger, C. C. (1984). *Structural family therapy*. New York: Grune & Stratton.

Contents

*Casebook of
Marital Therapy*

Chapter 1
Resolving Distance Conflicts

John Byng-Hall, FRCPsych

Intimacy and Autonomy: Mutually Supportive or Undermining?

Many marriages may seem too close and suffocating at times; at other times they may feel too distant and remote. Spouses need to know and heed these signs. If they do, there will be periods of intimacy, safe in the knowledge that it will not become too intrusive. Interspersed with these will be periods of greater autonomy that are also protected by the knowledge that the relationship will not be allowed to become too tenuous and that the other person will be available when closeness is needed—a safe base to which to return.

An adequate marriage can be described in this way. A creative marriage is one in which fresh discoveries are made in the to and fro of daily contact. In the safe, familiar, warm setting of intimacy, two imaginations fire each other off to find new experiences of each other. When separate, each can be independent, although exploration may be fostered by an inner imaginary dialogue with a spouse who, it can reliably be anticipated, will be interested. An ongoing sharing of some of the new ideas can bring freshness into the intimacy, thus rejuvenating the relationship. An increasing depth of both intimacy and autonomy can then develop with each phase complementing and adding to the other.

1

Sometimes, however, the safety thresholds shift in the opposite direction. For instance, anxiety about intimacy may increase, and the safety threshold may be pushed so far away that the relationship cannot sustain itself through intimacy. When that happens, periods of separation will often be filled with anxiety, e.g., "Will my partner be off because we are not getting through to each other?" The threshold beyond which it feels unsafe will then be drawn in closer to keep an eye on things. Attempts may be made to curb autonomy. As these two thresholds converge, the "too close" and the "too far," the potential movement within the relationship may diminish until eventually the marriage becomes stuck at a particular distance, the proverbial "ten-foot pole" marriage. If either of the partners turns away from the other, cues are set up that will pull them back. If they turn toward each other and try to achieve some intimacy, however, the barriers will go up, and they will push one another away.

Very frequently, the thresholds continue to travel in opposite directions so that they eventually overlap; the point at which the couple are far enough away to be free of anxiety about intimacy is now so distant as to make them feel constantly insecure. This system is called the too close–too far system (Byng-Hall, 1980, 1981) and is potentially very uncomfortable, with constant attempts to get closer coexisting with struggles to escape. This creates a cybernetic system of mutual positive feedback, which will escalate if unchecked into a systems "run-away" until the relationship itself breaks down. For instance, clinging provokes pulling away, which intensifies the clinging, thus provoking pulling right out. Clearly, this is incompatible with everyday life, and various mechanisms come in to halt the escalations. For instance, one partner may become symptomatic, say the husband becomes alcoholic, in which case intimacy is probably reduced, but he is also incapable of managing on his own, and so he needs his wife. Alternatively, the wife may become agoraphobic, in which case the husband has to stay nearby; on the other hand, her intense anxiety interferes with intimacy. In each case, the symptom removes the distance conflict by becoming the reason both for staying together and for the lack of intimacy.

Other people may be recruited to regulate the distance. I have discussed (Byng-Hall, 1980) how a child's ambivalence about his parents' relationship can become the distance regulator in the relationship. A child naturally wants his parents to stay together but also wants them not to be so close that he cannot get in between them to get something for himself. When parents start an escalation, they may find that one of their children acts to disrupt intimacy but also behaves in a way that brings them together if they get too far away. This may provide such relief that the child's ambivalence is given positive feedback. The child's contradictory feelings are then amplified, while the parents' approach–avoidance conflict decreases. It is hardly surprising that the child often becomes symptomatic. The symptom itself then tends to become the regulator of the parental distance; for instance, they have to come together as mother and father, which is a nonintimate form of sharing, in order to cope with the child's problem. Since I am a child psychiatrist whose main interest is in family therapy, much of the marital work that comes my way is of the latter, initially child-centered, variety.

Aims of Therapy

The main aim of therapy is to change the thresholds of anxiety about distance, thus freeing intimacy and autonomy to function again. I aim to give the couple new experiences of closeness and distance in the session. I explore the effect that certain interactions have on the distance within the relationship. In this way, new meanings for what is happening are found and a new epistemology centered on distance is built up.

As the therapist, I model the capacity to move in and out, creating closeness and intimacy at one time and moving out to gain the wider perspective of understanding and reflection at other times. I see maintained change resulting from the couple's learning to use this to-and-fro exploration to solve problems during therapy and hence having it as a tool for the future. Thus, I want the couple to start finding their own solutions during therapy.

I anticipate that I will be drawn into the same distance conflict as the couple at some point. At the engagement phase, I will be working fairly quickly and freely, often using proximity to generate intensity. I know that this will expose me to the trap of their relationship and that my willingness to be close will almost certainly be used to triangle me into the role of distance regulator. This will develop into an impasse in which the therapist–couple system reaches a new homeostasis. I know that I will have to spot when this is happening and then find my way out. Although this will be unique and specific to each family, the distance conflict is likely to become manifest at a countertransference level in the following general form: I want simultaneously to get more intensely involved, to force them to change, but also to get farther away by discharging them, especially as the symptom is often better now that I have taken on some of the distance-regulation function previously undertaken by the symptom.

If I can find some understanding of that particular distance conflict, I am then in a better position to help them resolve it. The final stage is handing back the management of distance regulation to the couple.

Mr. and Mrs. A.

Mr. and Mrs. A. were referred by a behavior therapist who had been helping them with sexual difficulties. Intercourse had virtually stopped, and when it did occur, premature ejaculation followed. The therapist had become aware that there was no change in the sexual difficulties and that there were many personality problems. What is more, their only son, George, age 13, was beginning to produce symptoms. The therapist felt that the problem would be better handled by someone who was also able to work with families.

The referral letter gave me the following information: The wife, Anne, was 37 years old and worked in the personnel department of a large airline. She was brought up in the East End of London by working-class parents; she left home after a row with her parents at age 16 and now had very little contact with them. She was an only child. Bob, her husband, age 40, was also an only child. He had arrived in London with his parents, who had emigrated from New Zealand 15 years earlier; he was a successful accountant. Anne is robust and forceful, while Bob is quiet and polite. The family lives next door to Bob's parents.

Engagement and Exploratory Phase

In the first session, which lasts up to 2 hours, I like to get a picture of the problem and of what the couple want done about it. I move on fairly swiftly to ask for a description of how they met and what it was that attracted them to each other. I then take them in detail through their marriage, or how they came to live together, trying to assess what the original marital contract was based on and what elements were not negotiated properly at that time. I do this in the first session not so much to glean information—I could do that any time—but because it is a powerful way of joining. I join them through the emotional experience of telling and being told what is likely to be their most moving story. What is more, the couple are rejoined through their shared memory of a time when they were coming together. This can produce a surge of warmth and tenderness that I will need if there are now powerful distancing mechanisms at work. Sometimes the intensity of the hostility in the session is such that that they will not allow me into that area. I will ask them whether it is divorce counseling I am really being asked for. In that case, I will ask questions about the future: Are they contemplating separation? Who will go where? Who will keep the children? Who will miss whom and what most? And so forth. If a separation is imminent, then nothing is lost; indeed, time may be saved in avoiding pseudo joining games when the real direction is toward separation. If there is still a potential future in the relationship, this contemplation of going "too far away" can generate energy in the opposite direction—energy that can be used by the therapist.

Anne and Bob started by confirming the referring psychologist's picture of the problem. They then told me the following story: They had met at a tennis party, and Anne had been particularly impressed about how Bob was very much at ease with his parents and how nice his parents appeared to be. Anne had seemed to Bob to be a very independent-minded young woman. Within 3 months of meeting, Anne became pregnant, and they agreed to get married. Everything was fine until the wedding day. Bob helped his father with some leaking plumbing just before the wedding. After the reception, Bob delayed his departure on the honeymoon by 3 hours in order to help his parents sort out the mess that the leaking pipe had created in the house. It suddenly dawned on Anne that Bob was still completely tied to his parents and was very little attached to her. The couple had planned to live with Bob's parents until they had saved enough to go and live on their own. I asked Bob whether Anne had been successful in helping him to grow away from his parents, something that has to happen when a new family is created. Bob was noncommittal, but Anne looked interested and went on to say that after the wedding, she set about trying to wrest Bob away from his parents and fought with her in-laws. Bob, she said, remained unchanged. After George's birth, she became deeply depressed. She cried as she remembered this.

During this description, which was mainly given by Anne, it was clear that she was describing something that touched her emotionally, whereas Bob seemed unmoved.

I enjoy stories; they fire my imagination. No doubt my fascination is evident to my clients. I listen intently, nodding in response to what they say, asking questions, showing sympathy when painful experiences are remembered and generally showing that I have empathically joined them in their memory of the past. I am, of course, not passive in this. By the questions I ask, I also give new directions to the story, throwing new light on the experience. For instance, neither Anne nor Bob had seen Anne's fights with her in-laws in terms of a developmental struggle before. Questions are my most frequent intervention, and they are congruent with helping the couple find their own solution. The joining of imaginations that occurs in storytelling when each imagination il- luminates the other provides one example of creative intimacy. Clearly, I had reached Anne and she me, but Bob and I had not contacted. All my attempts to involve him led to rather dry, obsessional recounting of detailed facts, leaving my imagination merely contemplating the reason for some people becoming accountants. Clearly, I had to find another way.

Experiential Use of Space

I decided to explore the changes in their relationship experientially in the second session. I asked Anne and Bob to show me how the marriage had evolved. I asked them to stand up and move toward each other and meet. Bob stood still, looking at Anne, while she walked up to him. I said that I would represent his parents. When asked where his parents would be, he placed me behind him but also facing toward Anne. I asked them what happened at the wedding, while I grabbed hold of Bob's jacket and pulled him toward me. Anne pulled away on Bob's jacket sleeve, and for a while all the tension between Anne and her "in-laws" was channeled through Bob's jacket. Bob himself was totally unmoved (in both senses) and was not experiencing any tension. I commented on this and how Bob seemed to get away with it. Anne agreed that it was very irritating. She and I found ourselves tugging even harder, until his smart jacket started ripping. The grip was changed somewhat to avoid further damage, and I made the comment that the real contact was between Anne and her "in-laws." Bob was hardly involved.

We used a pillow to represent the arrival of George. Anne cradled "George" in her arms and then sank down to the floor, crying. This is how it had been, she sobbed. I asked what happened to George, and Bob picked up the pillow and gave it to me, saying that his mother and father looked after him. Bob told me that the tension between Anne and the in-laws had changed totally because they now took Anne into the bosom of the family and looked after her like a sick child. Meanwhile, in the session Bob stood to one side, looking somewhat spare. Anne agreed that she then became very close to her in-laws. This completed the reframing of meaning of the contact between the two families, her first version of which was that it was Bob who was totally tied to his parents. Toward the end of the session, I asked the couple to explore how they might like to have managed the situation given a second chance. Instead of the in-laws pulling Anne up from the floor, Bob did it himself. When Anne was standing again, they put their arms around each other while facing each other, in an embrace. I left them there until they became restless; they also noticed that there was now no room for George. They then turned sideways, linking arms, standing side by side. Each now had a hand available for George. They said that this felt better and that being in a total embrace felt uncomfortable. Now Bob was fully alive and involved in the therapy. They sat down and discussed together how they might be close but also have some separateness.

I do not frequently use family sculpting (Simon, 1972) with couples as I did here. Usually, there is sufficient intensity generated by touching people's imagination. I felt frustrated by my lack of contact with Bob, and I remembered the previous therapist's lack of movement with him. Sculpting is a good way of bypassing an intellectual defense. I discussed elsewhere some of the principles behind using sculpting to resolve distance conflicts (Byng-Hall, 1982a). One principle is to explore both the experience of being left out, separated, or "too far," as well as being "too close." Bob was left out in the sculpt, and later Bob and Anne were embracing each other in a "too close" position. The mistake that many therapists make is to be so delighted that the couple finally gets together that the problem inherent in that very proximity is ignored, in which case distancing behavior may go on after the session. A therapeutic opportunity is also lost.

Use of History

In the third session, I drew a genogram to explore the relationships one generation back. Anne's parents used to argue openly with each other but would be united when it came to disciplining her. Father was a tough, rough-and-ready builder. Mother was a soft-spoken, kindly Irish lady who overtly gave in to her husband but secretly wielded most of the power. They had enormous ambitions for Anne. When she showed some academic prowess, her parents planned for her to go to a local college. However, when she started going out with a young Polish motor mechanic, her father flew into a rage and with the support of her mother threw Anne out of the home. She described in vivid detail how her father threw her suitcase out the window after her. Anne became stubbornly independent and determined to succeed academically. She worked her way up to and into university. She had hoped that this would be a ticket back to her parents' favor, but they refused to support her at the university, saying instead that she should come home and go to the local college, as originally planned. I commented that Anne was taught by her family that you have to be either totally obedient to the sexual mores and precise academic dictates of your parents or you must leave home forever. Soon after finishing her university course, Anne met Bob.

In contrast to Anne's family, where conflict was made specific and overt, Bob's family remained covert in the way that it handled distance confict. His father was a distinguished librarian in a well-known academic library. He was overtly in total control of the family. Bob's mother was covertly influential, and in practice her unspoken wishes prevailed. Against this unspecified but ever-present female threat, Bob and his father set about creating a male intellectual bond. As Bob grew older their relationship became increasingly like the all-male intellectual club that his father retreated to in the evenings. Bob developed a very brilliant mode of debating with his father in which he could, at an intellectual level, spar with him. The moment he became assertive in terms of independence and coping on his own, however, his parents joined together in thwarting it, and Bob colluded by becoming awkward and incompetent. That particular family system largely remained unchanged until the present. The picture of Bob's family together now was of Bob being quiet and diffident, doing what he was told, but with an occasional exciting intellectual male debate taking off and soaring away into the clouds, while his mother made the tea.

Tracing the history farther back places the meeting of the couple in its historical context. It was now possible to invite the couple to make sense of how they got together and what happened. My style is to create a sense of exploration. I do not find this difficult because, indeed, it is fascinating. Once again, I see the most powerful joining maneuver as being one in which the imagination of the couple joins with the imagination of the therapist. This allows for a blend of intense closeness generated by the sense of exploration in the context of being at a safe distance. It is as if the therapist and the couple can look back and observe unfolding history. In this way, the couple learn at times to take a meta-position vis-à-vis their own relationship. By being able to reflect, they can modify their automatic responses. This is, I consider, a more useful experience than one in which only the therapist remains meta to the marital interaction as can happen in either an interpretive mode or one in which the therapist uses an outside team to make hypotheses as in the Milan model of therapy (Selvini Palazzoli, Boscolo, Cecchin, & Prata, 1980).

I invited Anne to think about what it meant to come into Bob's family. To her, Bob's intellectual ability, encouraged rather than fettered by his parents, was something that even now she could find engaging. Bob could be brilliant without being overtly rebellious; that was reassuring for her. It only dawned on her later that the price for this was being eternally bound to his father. "I suppose that was a real contrast to my upbringing." I asked Bob what he found important in Anne's relationship to her parents. "It was her independence that intrigued me." He found Anne's open criticisms of his mother and father disconcerting but unusual. I suggested that perhaps Anne had expressed his rebellion for him. She went on to say that she had demanded that they should get their own flat and leave his parents' home. He said, "I suppose I was not ready for that, but anyway Anne's depression forestalled that." I commented that perhaps Anne's depression had a function in that case. Bob said, "It certainly brought Anne closer to my mother." I commented that Anne's new family gave her a chance to be looked after, something impossible in her own family. Anne said, "But when I grew out of that and no longer wanted to be so close to them, I found that Bob was still tied to his parents' apron strings. I think that's when I became increasingly upset about Bob's lack of drive, especially sexual drive."

When using a genogram I follow certain principles. I help to alter the meaning given to history. I call this "re-editing family mythology"

(Byng-Hall, 1979). I find out which stories have been told repeatedly and hence have become family legends (Byng-Hall, 1982b). I do this because I see family legends as stories that, although about the past, enshrine family rules about how things should be done now. If Anne had her clothes thrown out the window by her father and was banished from home for having the wrong boyfriend, this could be a powerful message to George about choosing girlfriends and about clothes. If the legend is told with scorn, it will mean one thing; if told seriously, it can mean the opposite.

Another important principle is to ask for stories about how people got on with each other, not about individual characteristics. This generates information about interaction that is in the same mode as the therapy in the room. I also write down the legends on the genogram. It is fascinating to go back later to see how the details of the stories change as the couple's epistemology changes during treatment. At a later telling, Anne included details of the row with her father. After a shouting match about leaving her filthy clothes all over her bedroom floor, she had stormed out of the house. Her father had stuffed her offending clothes into a suitcase and thrown them after her. Anne added, "I suppose we were both needing to get away from each other." This episode now had a very different meaning from that given in the original story. The legend had been reedited.

In the third session, we explored what followed Anne's recovery when she no longer played a connecting function to Bob's family. I asked what the family preoccupations were following this. There was considerable anxiety about George. He had wet his bed until age 10 and also had developed many physical illnesses. Anne could now go to her mother-in-law to ask for help with this problem. I noted that George had now become the distance regulator for the whole family. In the sessions, George was discussed in an increasing way, so I asked them to bring him in for a few sessions.

Detriangulating Children

George proved to be an engaging boy who clearly enjoyed the role of truculent adolescent, which he played with considerable gusto and variation. He entertained his parents with pithy comments. At other times, he lay back in his chair, making a great show of being bored or sullen. Every now and then he would reveal that he had taken everything in by coming in on his father's side against his mother. His stretched-out legs always seemed to be either touching or about to touch his father's feet. I commented on this bond, and Anne flew into a rage about how the two males ganged up against her. We explored how George appeared to be the one taking an active role in this bond but that this disguised the fact that Bob was constantly setting George up. He had invited George to sit in the chair that was facing his. He had also had his leg stretched out toward George. Somehow, nobody noticed that. Then I commented that George was doing a service to his father by rebelling against his mother on his father's behalf. I thought that this also helped Anne, who could get very angry with George, instead of experiencing her full fury directed at her husband. I said to George, "I think you are doing a grand job acting as a lightning conductor to your parents' anger. You are somehow sensitive to the fact that they are both anxious that a major row might lead to a split." Linking this to the past, I pointed out that Anne was anxious because a row had led to a split in her family and that Bob's family was even more frightened about this, to the extent that all rows were blocked so that no splits or even separations ever happened. We went on to explore how both Anne and Bob had been subtly used by their parents in attacks on each other. George was now sitting up and was fascinated to hear this discussion. He was quickly pointing out similarities between this family and both previous families. From this moment on, he became a useful therapeutic ally. Several times I found myself using him as a co-therapist but then had to remember that this was colluding with his role as a parentified child. I worked on how he had become his own grandfather and spent his time bossing his own parents about. He did not like this much because he saw his paternal grandfather as a silly old fusspot.

In the next session, George came in angry and proceeded to be very rude to his mother. I demanded that his parents take responsibility for this, and I worked, using structural family therapy techniques (Minuchin & Fishman, 1981) to ensure that Bob disciplined George. Anne kept on subtly undermining Bob's authority. For instance, when Bob did finally become angry with George, she disqualified this by repeating her demands that Bob should discipline George, as if nothing whatsoever had happened. I pointed out that George attacked his mother and so rebelled openly for his father, but that George's rebellion on behalf of his mother was much more subtle. By remaining on an

equal footing to his father, he provided continuous proof that his
father was not in charge. I commented that the price for this was that
the potency of fathers tended to be undermined by their wives and
children. I pointed out to Anne that Bob's lack of drive was what she
had complained about. I suggested that she should try and keep out
of Bob's attempts to discpline George. I helped her to do this by
interrupting her and making her move out of the family circle. Bob
did become much more assertive with George, and Anne was very
slowly able to acknowledge that he was effective. This session proved
to be the turning point in the detriangulation of George from the
marital problem. George, having joined for four sessions, dropped
down to attending every fourth session and later dropped out almost
entirely with only an occasional family session.

Mutual Maintenances of the Distance Conflict

In the next marital session I explored the mutual service that the
couple did for each other's distance conflicts. Bob had been complaining
that he had wanted their relationship to be closer, whereas Anne had
insisted on going to another bed in a separate room. I said that I
thought Anne did a service for Bob by keeping herself apart, making
Bob feel that he really wanted more intimacy. This protected him
from his anxieties about intimate contact and from his fear of being
swallowed up by Anne. Bob, in his turn, did a service to Anne by
continually pursuing her, which protected her from her awful dread
of being thrown out by a man, something she had experienced from
her father. In the following session, the theme of cleanliness was
pursued. Anne said that Bob sabotaged their sexual life by keeping
himself dirty. She complained that his clothes were always scruffy and
filthy. He did not wash enough, and he knew this upset her. Bob
remained puzzled about this; he did not think he was dirty. Certainly
in the sessions he appeared to be neatly dressed and clean. Something
about Anne's intensity of reaction to this issue suggested that it had
historical origins. I asked about her father's cleanliness and what emerged
was that her father came home filthy dirty from work, immediately
had a bath, and put on clean clothes. This marked the transition from
being at work to being with the family. This was in contrast to Bob's
father, who came home from work late and took his suit off, putting
on something informal and relaxed. The way in which clothes and

their cleanliness had diametrically opposite significance for each spouse was now clear. Anne was enormously relieved to have understood this. The intensity of her feelings about the topic still needed some further exploration, however. She described how she was often given the job of washing her father's dirty clothes and how she was disgusted by them. I commented that the intimacy of her father's dirty clothes had probably been too much and that she had developed a disgust reaction to clothes, which reminded her of the intimate contact with skin. I also reminded her of her father's disgust with her dirty clothes. Nevertheless, despite this understanding, she remained preoccupied by dirty clothes. Bob made the comment that he had a distinct impression that Anne liked him to be a bit dirty in some sort of odd way, despite her protest to the contrary. We could see now that dirty clothes were acting as distance regulators. They prevented intimacy through disgust, but they fascinated nevertheless.

Impasse Phase

By now, the marital relationship was much less hostile. I had managed to detriangulate George and was firmly entrenched as the distance regulator in the marital relationship. They were well engaged in therapy and had been using my interventions in a creative way. I knew from experience that I would be recruited into the homeostatic mechanisms of the marriage at some point. This usually happens somewhere between the fifth and the seventh session, although sometimes earlier or later. However, here I was at the tenth session, and therapy was still apparently on the move. I decided that perhaps my theorizing was wrong or that somehow I had circumvented the danger either by my very clever structural work with George or later with my clever understanding of the marital interaction, which somehow had enabled me to be in a safe meta-position to the interaction. The couple were now saying that they were ready to work on their sexual relationship. I said that I thought I could help them with the problem of premature ejaculation. They said that their previous therapist had told them that that problem was relatively easy to solve. I arranged to treat the sexual dysfunction, using Kaplan's (1974) techniques. I set up the first session to plan a sensate focus, and they accepted instructions in a way that would suggest that things were going to go well. At the next session, everything had reverted to its worst possible state. They had not been able to do anything in which they had been instructed. Anne had retreated to her room and refused to allow Bob in; they had had some of the worst rows for years. They said that what I was asking them to do was superficial, whereas their problems obviously involved more complex things to do with their personalities. I felt that perhaps they were right and that I should postpone this series of sessions and continue work in the way that had been more effective. In retrospect, I can now see that I put them in a "too close" position before they were ready.

I made a number of more complex interpretations about how the symptoms were a manifestation of the distance conflict. I tried using clever metaphors that incorporated the image of premature ejaculation. I traced parallels between their social interaction and the pattern of their sexual interaction: how he came to a conclusion before she had even engaged properly in the discussion, and so on. I started to use myself as an alter ego. I stood behind each member of the couple, speaking for each spouse in turn. In this way all the anger and the complexities of the transactions emerged much more powerfully and clearly. Over a period of six sessions I became increasingly active and increasingly in command of the situation. The only problem was that absolutely nothing happened. I now had to recognize that I was in an impasse. I switched to a strategic mode. I explored the function of the symptom in terms of the way it affected the distance between the couple. I think I did this quite well and accurately. Having done this, I suggested that the symptoms fulfilled such an important function that they should continue in the same way for the time being. Nothing changed. Since the beginning of the impasse phase I had tried many of the techniques that had been successful with other couples. Apart from the overt resistance to sensate focus, the couple accepted all my interventions with respect and gratitude, giving me a feeling that I had at last "cracked the nut."

I began to realize that I was now more a part of the couple system than I could perceive. In one session, I took a break in the middle and tried to write down some of the dynamics. This did not seem to get me further. Again, this maneuver is frequently successful for me when I am stuck. Following this session, I had some spare time and thought to myself that there must be something that was staring me in the face. What was the unusual particular behavior on my part in this case? It suddenly struck me that I was repeatedly behaving as if

I had just cured or was just about to cure this very difficult couple and that despite the evidence to the contrary, I continued to make the same assumption in the very next session. This was omnipotence. I had recently contributed to a chapter on the supervision of therapy in impasse (Byng-Hall, De Carteret, & Whiffen, 1982). In that chapter I had explored the idea of an overlap, that is, that impasse happens when therapeutic behavior overlaps or is similar to aspects of the behavior of the family. It must, I realized, be the omnipotence of the couple that was overlapping with my therapeutic omnipotence and had led to the impasse. This thought was enormously relieving. I mused on the fact that within the family the repeated theme was omnipotence laid low. This was also repeated in the sexual transactions. I was also now locked into the family. I persisted because I was always about to cure them, but as nothing changed I could never leave.

In the next session, I discovered that George had presented a problem again. This is quite a common occurrence when some marital work is not being successfully handled and where a child or another member of the family has been triangled in as a distance regulator in the past. The therapist is then no longer entrusted with the role of distance regulation, and the triangled member gets back into the act. On this occasion, George was helpful in the symbolism that he used; he broke into his grandfather's house with one of his delinquent friends and stole one of the rare first editions that his grandfather had in his private library and that was a family heirloom. I received the message loud and clear that it was a three-generation problem; I reflected on the fact that my policy is to involve all members of the household. Normally, I would include grandparents who live next door as being in the same household. Somehow, once again my omnipotence had interfered with normal practice with the assumption that I could resolve this marital problem without any help from anyone else.

If I had been seeing this couple in a different setting where consultants were available, I might have asked a colleague to do a consultation for me. On the other hand, it was quite likely that I would not have done so because that was not congruent with the omnipotent position that I was adopting. I consider that resolving the impasse will always involve time taken looking at any personal overlap of attitudes, blind spots, etc., and that for every family or couple it is unique. In some couples it is easier to unravel than in others. A consultation with

someone else can be very helpful. On the other hand, it is beholden
on teachers such as myself to devise ways in which therapy can be
done on one's own. My students often have to practice solo after
graduating.

In the rest of the session following their report of George's mis-
demeanors, I explored the theme of omnipotence. Anne seemed to
be the one who was the more sure of herself in the session. She would
often talk as if she knew the answer, telling Bob what he should do.
Bob would usually accept her complaints, but it was noticeable that
he would often do this with a slight smile at the corners of his lips. I
said I thought that perhaps Bob actually had the last laugh because
inside he could see so clearly through everyone's game and perhaps
privately felt very triumphant. He seemed somewhat relieved that I
had spotted this. He admitted that much of the time he was scornful
of other people's attempts to do things. Anne commented that at work
he was recognized as supremely successful and competent; despite
this, he appeared always to be all fingers and thumbs and making a
mess of things. His greatest triumph came through fooling people
into thinking that he was incompetent, whereas, in fact, he was fully
in control of the situation. I said that I thought he must have felt very
triumphant when I had been thinking I had been doing such good
work but actually I had not been touching the problem. The omnipotence theme obviously overlapped somehow with Anne. She also felt
the same triumph over her parents; not only had she foiled them by
surviving despite being thrown out, but she had succeeded even better
without them than she did with them. The anger behind this triumph
was very clear. Now I suggested the couple were continually able to
triumph over each other. Every successful move could be undermined
in the subtlest of ways. The meaning of the premature ejaculation was
explored in this way too. Each could triumph: Anne by having greater
full-blooded sexuality and Bob by beating her to the post and simultaneously depriving her of achieving her orgasm. In planning to bring
in the grandparents to the next session, we discussed how Bob would
have to avoid giving the feeling that he was going to triumph over
his parents in the very act of asking for their help. This was something
that he had perfected over the years, and Anne, of course, had helped
him to continue the same game.

I asked them to convey my invitation to the grandparents to come
to the session to help us in the work and to tell them that while they

were here it would be useful to consult them about the family history. I have discussed elsewhere (Byng-Hall, 1982c) the way in which I work with grandparents by treating them with considerable respect as having expertise in the family history. In the session that included both grandparents, as well as George, Anne, and Bob, the main theme was the distance-regulation function of George's behavior. It started with a historical review of George's life. He had been the person to bring the parents together in the firt place. Later, he had held his parents together, as well as linking them with his grandparents, keeping the whole family united in one household. The recent episode also fulfilled the same function with the additional dimensions that George's behavior had linked me into the whole system. I congratulated George for this incredible feat of linking everyone to everyone else. I was now, however, more aware of the potential for fueling George's omnipotence, so I then explored with him just how much he was ruining his life in the process, which was less glamorizing. I then shifted the spotlight away from his role and on to a joint business venture Bob ran with his father that also acted as a distance regulator. They never quite let it flourish, thus ensuring that Bob's father could never afford to retire, while Bob himself had to spend many extra hours in the evenings with his father, working on the project.

We discussed openly how Anne had wanted to take Bob out of his parents' household and set up a separate house. I explored this in the context of family cultures: Anne's family expected a total break between generations, whereas Bob's family had stayed in the same household or at least in the close vicinity over many generations. In this discussion, Bob's mother emerged as a warm, loving person who said that secretly she had agreed with Anne that the family should go elsewhere. Her own family was much less tied to one other. She went on to share with Anne just how upset she had been when Anne had been so depressed and how concerned she had been for George as a small child during Anne's depression. Finally, both grandparents suggested to Bob and Anne that they should look for somewhere else to live. I jokingly said to Bob and Anne that perhaps they would block the power of the parents' suggestion by doing something that would make it impossible for them to move. I looked at George and said that I was sure he could help out in some way by being a problem. I said this with a twinkle in my eye, and the joke was appreciated. Bob's father did complain that the couple seemed to be very dependent on them. The problem of distance had now been reframed from that of Bob's parents keeping the couple trapped to that of a failure of the couple to become independent.

Following this session, the couple seemed to relax considerably, and I reduced the number of sessions to fortnightly and then monthly. Each session would start with a catalogue of catastrophes. I learned not to accept this as a triumphant defeat of the work that I had done because the overall pattern showed improvements. I also learned not to expect too much. In this way, the cycle was broken in which therapeutic enthusiasm repeatedly led me up the garden path, only to be dashed by failure to make sustained changes—a sort of therapeutic premature ejaculation. Eventually the couple decided that things were going as well as they could expect and decided to stop coming for therapy. In the final session (the twenty-first), the review revealed satisfactory changes in many ways. Each member of the family was getting on with his or her own life tasks. George was not in any trouble and was making better friendships, although his school work was less satisfactory than his parents hoped for. Of course, they all encountered difficulties, but the important change was that autonomy was now being supported, not sabotaged. Sexual intimacy had not improved very much, although occasionally it had been more satisfying. The relative failure of their sexuality, which had never been satisfactory, was, however, no longer being used as a battleground for controlling each other. The creative intimacy of discussion had increased. They were also back in the same bed.

I was left with a question: If I had finally tackled the sexual dysfunction, would I have been drawn back into the trap of trying to solve their problems for them, with predictable consequences, or could I have now been successful? Who knows. The fact is that they were not now asking for help with that problem, and it would have gone counter to the task of handing responsibility back to them.

Another way of looking at the question is that the sexual dysfunction continued its function as a distance regulator. It enabled them to remain together with the idea that they could finally have a fulfilling relationship some time in the future—which indeed remains a possibility—and simultaneously protecting them from their remaining anxieties about overcloseness.

They had drawn me into the middle of their "frustrating because forever overpromising" experience. I had resolved this for myself by first understanding our shared core of defended omnipotence expressed by "I can promise to resolve this difficulty—except that they/he/she will not let me." Once this was understood, I was free to expect less, and to be less anxious about the anger when promises were not fulfilled. This enabled me to leave them without having completed the perfect cure and, in the period leading up to termination, to work with them on developing more realistic expectations of themselves and each other.

All this represented a step toward the resolution of the midlife crisis.

References

Byng-Hall, J. J. (1979). Re-editing family mythology during family therapy. *Journal of Family Therapy, 1,* 103–116.

Byng-Hall, J. J. (1980). The symptom bearer as marital distance regulator: Clinical implications. *Family Process, 19,* 355–365.

Byng-Hall, J. J. (1982a). Dysfunction of feeling: Experiential life of the family. In A. Bentovim, A. Cooklin, & G. Gorell Barnes (Eds.), *Family therapy: Complementary frameworks of theory and practice* (Vol. 1). London: Academic Press.

Byng-Hall, J. J. (1982b). Family legends: Their significance for the therapist. In A. Bentovim, A Cooklin, & G. Gorell Barnes (Eds.), *Family therapy: Complementary frameworks of theory and practice* (Vol. 1). London: Academic Press.

Byng-Hall, J. J. (1982c). Grandparents, other relatives, friends and pets. In A. Bentovim, A. Cooklin, & G. Gorell Barnes (Eds.), *Family therapy: Complementary frameworks of theory and practice* (Vol. 2). London: Academic Press.

Byng-Hall, J. J., & Campbell, D. C. (1981). Resolving conflicts in distance regulation: An integrative approach. *Journal of Family & Marital Therapy, 7,* 321–330.

Byng-Hall, J. J., De Carteret, J., & Whiffen, R. (1982). Evolution of supervision: An overview. In R. Whiffen & J. J. Byng-Hall (Eds.), *Family therapy supervision: Recent developments in practice.* London: Academic Press.

Kaplan, H. S. (1974). *The new sex therapy.* New York: Brunner/Mazel.

Minuchin, S., & Fishman, H. C. (1981). *Family therapy techniques.* Cambridge, MA: Harvard University Press.

Selvini Palazzoli, M., Boscolo, L., Cecchin, G., & Prata, G. (1980). Hypothesizing–circularity–neutrality: Three guidelines for the conductor of the session. *Family Process, 19,* 3–12.

Simon, R. M. (1972). Sculpting the family. *Family Process, 11,* 49–58.

Chapter 2
Couples Therapy, Crisis Induction, and Change

David Kantor, PhD

In this chapter I describe an approach to the treatment of couples (and families) that I call *structural-analytic therapy*. Although I think of it as a family theory, and one that is systemic, it makes special reference to couples and the individuals who make up the couple system.

The theory's orientation is a developmental one. Family system development, the theory holds, is largely a function of couple system development. This is true, it contends, under many and varied family circumstances, for example, in developmentally skewed families (i.e., certain one-parent families), in systems occupied by "odd couples" (an unmarried woman who adopts a child and coopts her own mother as a child-raising "partner"), in families that have experienced natural life-cycle accidents (a divorced woman and her adolescent son, or a widowed mother and her grown son), as well as in the natural couple relationship.

Families differ, the theory continues, in their organization, in how they define their goals, in how they establish and defend their boundaries, in the rules and strategies they devise for reaching their goals, and in what they do with deviants who break the rules. Out of the integration of all these processes is defined the ultimate task that all families, without exception, face: the responsibility for evolving a *model* (Kantor & Lehr, 1975) or *paradigm* for guiding their members through the ordinary and extraordinary exigencies of life, a model for construing and dealing with realities within the family and between the family and its external environment.

For their actual or working models or paradigms, families draw on three pure family types: *open*, *closed*, and *random* (Kantor & Lehr, 1975; Kantor, 1980). Implicit in each pure type but central to its developmental course are the rules for how *change* is to take place. Roughly, in the random system, change occurs spontaneously, in discontinuous leaps; in the closed system, change occurs in a gradual, more continuous evolutionary pattern; in an open system, change may occur through both means, the family shifting its change mode in response to shifting pressures within the family and within the environment.

That families differ, and the systematic *ways* in which they differ, is the key to the therapy associated with structural-analytic theory. Most therapists make passing reference to the fact that families differ and then proceed to describe interventions that in no way take into account the supposed recognition of difference. Suddenly the difference disappears, and all families become one. In contrast, structural-analytic therapy attempts to hold on to the fact that families differ. A technique that works with a closed family may not work with an open family. The therapist's techniques and his or her client families are in an interactive, not a linear, relationship.

Structural-analytic theory, still laying claim to being systemic, focuses also on the individuals who join together to form a couple system. Together, over the course of time, the partners share responsibility for the model-building task, cooperating when they can, fighting when differences prevail, both courses being intrinsic to "normal" family development. Indeed, *competition for control over the family's model* is a major source of both conflict and creativity in families. In these key family matters, in these couple struggles, individual developmental constructs play a crucial role, one such being a small subset of internalized images that I call *critical identity images* (Kantor, 1980). Because these special images contain the formats for how individuals are to behave in relationship structures (since they are, simultaneously, dilemmas from past and formats for future family structures), they are *systemic*. From this is derived a basis for the claim that a theory can be both systemically and individually oriented. Needed, however, to justify this claim is a bridging concept that links individual with other (the systemic) levels of family organization. Examination of the internal organization of many critical images reveals that within their structure (and they have a distinctive structure) are the seeds of most of the relationship structures (one level), the patterns and processes that a family evolves (another level), and the model or paradigm that informs and oversees those patterns (yet another level) of system organization.

That the *genetic code* for any developing couple and family system can be found (*a*) in the specific structure of each individual's small set of critical identity images and, more specifically, (*b*) in how the structural elements of each partner's images (present and "missing") interact with the other's to form system structures is a discovery that is crucial to structural-analytic theory and therapy. The conceptual linchpin of the discovery is that *the image and its structure contain the genetic formats for the systemic perceptions and behaviors each person uses in ongoing intimate relationships*. If correct, structural-analytic theory sheds much light on how what happens does, in fact, happen when a couple set out on their developmental journey—a journey through which the couple carry on their individual and collective backs a model-building task heavily weighted with unaddressed dilemmas from the past that lie waiting to be addressed in intimate relationships.

Building the model itself is a moving, changing, dynamic, evolutionary, and sometimes revolutionary process. En route to its completion, an unending assignment, couples and their families face a series of developmental tasks or dilemmas.

Because each partner is informed by the image called into play by the task to address it in his or her own way, these tasks are inherent sources of growth and conflict. When conflicts arise, the system can enter a period of temporary developmental crisis. The successful resolution of such crises enhances the family's capacity to deal with future events, conflicts, and crises. The failure to resolve one of these crises results in a more chronic breakdown in the family's problem-solving mechanisms. Eventually, some individual or a part of the system will suffer, either in the form of a symptom or in a crippling repetitive sequence. This is a way of saying that when couples or families come for therapy, they are usually facing one such developmental crisis.

Where is the therapist in all this? Structural-analytic theory holds that there are three essential elements in the family therapy equation: the family, the technique, and the therapist. It maintains that you have to pay equal attention to all three. If you concentrate only on technique, then you have left out two-thirds of the equation. And that omission may very well do damage to clients. It holds that therapists must understand that they, their methodologies, and their client families are inextricably bound up in a system of interactional influence and that only by developing a clinical awareness of that cybernetic process can they hope to attain their highest possible levels of clinical performance. In support of this ideal I have developed a chart that requires me (and others I work with) to set down for the record what we know about our Boundary Profile, both its general features and those that might work for or against particular client systems. This chart on the therapist is included in the client's case folder. When we examine therapeutic process and assess outcome, we are able to describe interactive effects that take family, technique, and therapist into account.

In order to expand on these perspectives I follow a couple through a course of therapy. In keeping with the clinical emphasis of this volume, theory is subordinated to treatment matters. Because clinical decisions rely heavily on theoretical considerations in the structural-analytic approach, however, conceptual references are unavoidable.

Stages and Goals of Therapy

I conceive of therapy as taking place in three stages, each stage having its own goals that focus on system phenomena at different structural levels. In Stage 1, the goal is *change*, which here is defined as the relief of a symptom or the resolution of a problem. The aim is to accomplish this goal as economically as the therapist's available technology allows. Structurally, what we change is a pattern or a particular behavior that plays a key part in leading a repetitive couple pattern or sequence to an unfortunate outcome.

In Stage 2 the goal is *transformation*, the restructuring *of those root or foundation structures* that have been maintaining the symptomatic behavior or problematic couple sequence identified and addressed in Stage 1. What we transform are those internalized meaning structures that each partner has used as a basis for the part he or she plays in creating and maintaining the problematic sequence.

In Stage 3 the goal is *prevention*, the rechanneling of couple system development so that the couple is better equipped to deal with future crises. What is "prevented" is disablement in the next most vulnerable structure. That such endangerment exists is predicated on the hypothesis that through contamination effects, other structures—a child, for example—will be affected in the future by past systemic problems that remain unresolved for significant periods of time. Identification of the endangered person or relationship structure is based on information that surfaced in Stages 1 and 2 but that, properly, was not addressed at the time. For, once again, in this approach, unless otherwise indicated,[1] goals are always linked to stages and to the sequencing of change.

Goals, Stages, and the Sequencing of Change

In the structural-analytic approach a distinction is made between these goal-specific "stages" and the "sequencing" of therapeutic change. Sequencing issues must be made *within* each of the three stages as well as *between* them. So, for example, therapy in Stage 1 might resemble (and often does) brief therapy conducted in the strategic or structural mode. In brief therapies the goal is to change behavior rather than perspectives, a goal that guides or even constrains the therapist to elect and sequence techniques best suited to sudden, not gradual change. "Should a parodoxical maneuver precede an enactment or a homework assignment?" is a within-stage sequencing question, yet all three techniques are appropriate for reaching "change" goals of Stage 1. "Do I in Stage 1 do a genogram (which suggests to the clients that I am recommending perspective rather than change goals), or should I wait until Stage 2?" is a between-stage sequencing issue. According to structural analysis, perspective-giving techniques are more appropriate for reaching Stage 2 goals.

The Politics of Conscription

In effect, then, I am describing three change sets—one might even say three therapy programs. Who decides whether clients will do all three, and how is that decision made? Obviously, it is politic to say,

---

1. It is not always possible to follow the sequence of goals and stages as prescribed by theory. Some couples are unable to give up their symptoms or problems until after their foundation structures have been dealt with clinically. The decision to alter course is a difficult one. I have erred in moving too soon and not soon enough.

"Both." How? Obviously, "Through negotiation." Ludicrous, given the skewed power arrangement between therapist and client? Yes, but . . . Yes, but it is the therapist's job to be responsible ultimately for being aware of the factors that affect therapeutic decision making, two of which are key to the point I want to make. First, therapists must be aware of the general features of the theory of change they happen to buy into, with specific reference to its influence structures, that is, its ideas about how the power to *know* and *do* is distributed between client and therapist. Second, therapists must be aware of the general features of their Boundary Profiles, with specific reference to organized tendencies of need and action that attenuate their theories, often reducing their clinical effectiveness. One feature of my theory of change is that its success is to be measured in part by the client's being more empowered after therapy than before to affect his life and destiny in the world. One criterion of improvement is *knowing*: Does the client know more about the workings and sources of the particular relationship structures that he shares with others and that he brought into therapy for repair? Another is *doing*: Has the client expanded his behavior repertoire for dealing with these previously "stuck" structures?

Therapy is a microworld for these macro matters. A goal of structural-analytic therapy is a gradual transfer to the client of the power of the therapy to affect change through knowledge of how it works and through a shared role in decision making. A key feature of my Boundary Profile, however, is the *wish to be sought after for my competencies*. Only after years of thinking that I was offering clients a free choice to go on to Stage 2 or 3 or to end therapy at the completion of Stage 1 goals did I realize that the techniques I used and how I used them had the effect of a politically subtle process of conscription. Thanks no doubt to continuing work on my Boundary Profile, now more than in the past more of my clients elect to end therapy after Stage 1. Now I conduct my politics of influence more clearly. The power to exercise "the power to know and do" is more evenly distributed between me and my clients. The Gordons, the couple who serve as illustration, "decided" to complete the three stages of therapy.

Background

Marty and Emma Gordon are a middle-class professional couple; he a 32-year-old business administrator, she a 30-year-old guidance coun-

TABLE 2-1
A Model for Treating Couples: Stages and Steps in Carrying Out the Therapy Model

Stage 1. Resolving "the problem": change through symptom relief
   Step 1.   Engaging the system and establishing a working alliance
   Step 2.   Mapping the problem and testing the structure
   Step 3.   Inducing the first therapeutic crisis
   Step 4.   Consolidating the change
Stage 2. Transforming the structure: change through individual image work
   Step 5.   Mobilizing for retrenchment
   Step 6.   Unfolding and pinning down image elements
   Step 7.   Inducing the second therapeutic crisis
   Step 8.   Forging positive identity claims
Stage 3. Preventing future problems: Change through predicting (the involvement of)
             next most vulnerable structures
   Step 9.   Identifying the endangered structure
   Step 10. Discovering the couple's evolutionary model
   Step 11. Inducing the third therapeutic crisis and terminating the therapy

selor. They came for couples therapy on the recommendation of Emma's former therapist, with whom she had completed a 2-year course of individual psychotherapy. Married 9 years and childless at the outset of couples therapy, the couple complained of "incessant fighting and sexual problems."

Stage 1. Change through Symptom Relief or Problem Resolution

Step 1. Engaging the System

In too much therapy the engagement process, or initial boundary exchange, is identified only in retrospect. This may be a serious error, representing a loss of important information about the client interpersonal system, a loss of information about the therapist–client interpersonal system, a loss of leverage for change, and frequently a loss of the case. With certain client systems, therapy ends with the failure to engage. In other cases, engagement is made and seems to have succeeded, but in retrospect it can be shown that the therapy was already doomed to failure, the therapist unaware that the damage was done at entry. When blown up for purposes of study, how a therapist initially engages proves to be surprisingly important.

In my work I *deliberately use happenstance* to discover something about the interaction between their, and my, boundary characteristics. My antics at this time also serve to give clients information about me and how I work.

Typically, over the phone I try to minimize the boundary exchange because I rely a great deal on visual and kinesthetic information. Hence I work at engaging only if necessary. With some clients the phone conversation is more of a negotiation than it was with the Gordons:

COMMENT: *Emma phoned. I returned her call more than a week later (a bad habit). Pretending familiarity, Emma laughed. "Oh, it's you. I thought you'd never call. Are you afraid of pretty women? Don't answer! Marty, come to the phone. It's him." After introductions, Marty buffered: "She tries to scare everybody into line. Basically harmless, though." I hesitated to respond, when a quip would have been my custom. I got right to scheduling: "Well, I can see you two want to start your work before we even meet. I take full responsibility. I shouldn't have kept you waiting so long. It's a habit I can't shake. Has nothing to do with how I am after getting started."*

In the waiting room, I usually pick up the *getting started* process. Moving in quickly, my behavior often seems quixotic. In reality, it is deliberate. My intention is to convey the idea that I skip formality and get right down to work, a Boundary Profile feature about which students of mine complain, but clients rarely do. When they do, the event is worth attending. With the Gordons, I noticed that as I approached the couple, Emma's body rebounded and her eyes were thrown open. (Surprise?)

DAVID (*backing up, in a gesture of mock apology*): Is something wrong with me?
EMMA: You're bigger than I thought.
DAVID (*extending hand to Marty*): Will that work for or against me? (*After saying this, David notes that he'd made exactly the same deflective move as he did over the phone, without knowing why.*)
MARTY (*smiling, picking up on nuance*): I've never been able to figure things like that out with Emma, but you can check it out with her. She'll give you an honest answer, God knows.
DAVID (*to Emma*): Is he always as quick and as considerate?
EMMA (*smiling, casting one arm around her husband's waist, the other at his throat*): He is quick. He is considerate. But he gives other people more room than he gives me.
(*They proceed to the office.*)

By the time a couple is seated in my office, where of course the initial boundary exchange continues, I know a fair amount about them, and they know some things about me and how I do my work. The getting-started process is not an incidental or preliminary activity. It represents and sets off a complex, two-way communication, rich in information about therapist and couple Boundary Profiles and how these will interact to form structures that are not part of the official therapy process and often go unnoticed but that under certain frequently occurring circumstances have much more to do with the actual (which may not be the same as the "reported") outcome of therapy than the official process. I call these hidden patterns *forming structures*, as compared with *formed structures*, which are the official structures in the client system that the therapist identifies as needing repair or restructuring. While the forming structures occur throughout therapy, I pay special attention to them at the beginning of therapy and at critical junctures in each of the three stages of therapy because of their tendency to escape notice. Often they go underground, only to reappear at these crucial junctures in the therapy when they may be mistakenly identified as client resistances or therapist–client stucknesses; or, worse, where still unnoticed they do damage to a client system without the therapist even knowing the part he or she has played.

Step 2. Mapping the Problem

Mapping or diagnosing a symptom or problem in its system context is not something that happens and then is done with. When conducting a structural-analytic systems diagnosis, one derives not a fixed category but a description of an ongoing developmental process that is partly stuck, or developmentally derailed, and partly still evolving.

In a therapy that completed all three stages, assessment would continue through all three, gathering different information in each stage. In a brief[2] therapy intended to end after Stage 1, mapping the problem could be confined primarily to two activities: identifying the key ritual sequence, and isolating the couple's stuck psychopolitics for the purpose of making preliminary changes in these.

2. By "brief therapy" I mean therapy designed to reach its goals in a short period of time, between 8 and 10 sessions. This should not be confused with brief strategic therapy, which indeed does have such a goal. But therapists using other methods can also choose to do brief therapy.

In other words, a brief therapy not only does not require a thoroughgoing diagnosis but its goal of rapid change is probably dissolved by certain clinical maneuvers designed to gather system diagnostic information.[3] Hence circular questioning (Penn, 1982) is a more appropriate technique than the genogram (Bowen) for gathering systems diagnostic information in a one-stage brief therapy. In these circumstances I am even careful when using my own technique of sculpture (Duhl, Kantor, & Duhl, 1973) to confine myself to those applications that get the information without deep affectual involvement on the client's part, that allow me to remain at a more disengaged than engaged stance (Kantor, 1982; Kantor, Peretz, & Zander, 1984), and that avoid giving perspectives on the relationship between past and present.

Failing to observe these cautionary principles tends to confuse clients who might prefer brief therapy. Why? Because techniques conducted from an engaged position, which arouse and attend to affect and offer insights linking family history to present structures, induce the client's commitment to therapy.

When I saw Marty and Emma Gordon in couples therapy in 1979–1980, my thinking about the above matters was more intuitive than it is now and was therefore subject to possible conceptual as well as clinical error. Actually, in retrospect, the Gordons did seem to prefer a therapy geared more toward *transformational* than rapid *change* goals alone. Nevertheless, while believing that I was leaving open the option to elect a brief therapy, I did use at least one technique (i.e., the Time Line, a spatialization or sculpture technique described below) that helped to reinforce their commitment to a fuller therapy program.

Overviewing the therapy process notes in Stage 1 reveals that, among others, the following techniques roughly in sequence highlighted the mapping process.

1. *Position Claims.* Usually done in a first session, in this technique each person in turn is asked to name "the problem" from a "personal and biased position." If people soft-pedal, they are helped to amplify. If already off the scale, they are asked to recall two or three occasions when they were more (of whatever they are presenting). The technique is used mainly for getting at each person's explanatory system and at

---

3. Note that I do not draw sharp lines between activities associated with assessment and those associated with intervention. As with other systems therapies, a diagnostic maneuver *is* an intervention.

the images, themes, and psychopolitics embedded in their explanation of "the problem."

2. *Reasons for Not Changing.* This technique can be done any time in Stage 1. It is a confusion technique, which when done early in the sequence of change moves is usually associated with accounts by the couple about what they have done about the problem to date. Thus used, it resembles positive connotation. When done later in a sequence of moves, it is more like a constraint of change maneuver.

3. *Reframing.* This technique is done usually about midway in the stage, only after certain conditions are met. I rarely attempt to reframe the problem before (*a*) getting a profound sense of each individual's personal explanation of the problem and his or her own part in it; (*b*) gathering a solid enough base of information about the systemics of each person's contribution to the problem and view of the other person's contribution; and (*c*) making strong and very concretely conceived joining moves based on the above that give evidence of reaching each partner. A failure to fulfill these conditions may result in a failure to formulate a convincing and acceptable relabeling or a failure to convince and gain acceptance of an otherwise ingenious redefinition.

4. *Sculpture.* Since introducing the basic techniques of sculpture at the Boston Family Institute in 1967, I have developed a variety of spatializations, which I employ, usually sparingly, throughout a course of therapy. With the Gordons, I used two in Stage 1.

a. The Circle of Influence. Done early in Stage 1, this is a sculpture that quickly maps everything and anything the couple thinks might be contributing to "the problem." They race against (an arbitrary) time limit, throwing anything that comes to mind—events, people, objects, images, methaphors—into a circle circumscribing the available space or an agreed upon portion of it. After independently but simultaneously throwing into the circle all these influences, they are asked to comment on the relationships between and among these reciprocating system elements.

b. The Time Line. Two imaginary lines are drawn down the length of the room. Each partner travels his or her own Time Line, starting on one end with the beginning of their courtship. Along the line, as they proceed through time to the present they independently indicate the significant critical junctures, usually damaging events, sharing perceptives on some, differing on others, ignorant of still others. I usually heighten the affectual and meaning values of these events by asking them to add gestures and metaphorical postures that represent their private experiences at each juncture. This technique is better employed in Stage 2 than in Stage 1, for reasons cited above. I used it primarily as a diagnostic fairly early in the sequence of Stage 1 moves. This I now believe was an error.

5. *How does the problem work?* A more appropriate mapping technique for first-stage goals is the systemic hypothesis, a procedure used to identify the part each member of the family plays in maintaining the symptom or problem sequence. The hypothesis can be derived indirectly from the analysis of data or directly from a circular process between therapist and family members launched with the question, "How does the problem work?" The technique is used in early to middle Stage 1, at any time following *position claims* and before *reframing*.

6. *Researching the Problem.* Done at the end of a session at any time in Stage 1, this is a simple form of out-of-session task, or homework assignment. The couple are asked to observe themselves, to witness the redundancy and make mental or written notes on how it works in its various manifestations, sharing their findings with the therapist at the next session, not with each other between sessions. Researching the problem is used to test, strengthen, or activate the couple's bystanding capabilities—in simple terms, to give them some distance from the problem. If the task is completed, it serves as a good source of information for discovering *the key ritual sequence*, a basic part of the mapping assignment.

7. *Using the Structure to Test or Change the Structure.* This technique is a fundamental feature of structural-analytic therapy and, I believe, of all properly executed systems interventions. Its basic premise is that in order to change a system pattern you change its structure, sometimes the whole structure (as with a more paradoxical maneuver) or a part of the whole as a step in a sequence of structural changes. This technique has many guises. In a family where a father is a disabled and too-distant *bystander*, blocked from *moving* toward the symptomatic child by a mother who is detouring a fight with a grandmother, a move to get Grandma to provoke the fight with her daughter would be one such structural move. The technique, really an umbrella for a class of moves, is employed variously throughout the stages of structural-analytic therapy. It is particularly useful as a means for testing the "stuckness" of a disabled *psychopolitical* configuration, or relationship structure, whose part in maintaining the problem sequence has been identified.

The couple were having problems with intimacy; not only was sex infrequent and unsatisfactory but they were having trouble even "negotiating" lovemaking. Indeed they were having trouble culminating all but the simplest of shared experiences that required close cooperation. Dinner out? A disaster. A discussion about what to do about Emma's troubles at work? A disaster. An attempt by Marty to redesign their living room? A disaster. An unplanned visit by two friends? A disaster. Both wanted children in principle, but not in the existing climate. They talked about separating instead. It was hard to say whether sex as a problem preceded or followed the emergence of these other problems or whether that mattered.

Redefining the presenting problems in systems terms and in the language of structural-analytic theory and then narrowing these into a problem on which treatment could be focused is aided by an understanding of at least two concepts—the *four-player psychopolitical model* (Kantor & Lehr, 1975) and *three interpersonal target domains*. In particular, we need to know the characteristic ways the couple combine the "four-player moves" (mover, opposer, follower, and bystander) in forming stuck relationship structures and in which of the three domains (affect, power, and meaning) these stuck moves take place. From the above described techniques I was able, diagnostically, to discern the part that these structures played in the "key" problem sequence. (By the third session I was confident I had identified it.) In their impasse, Marty and Emma were fused at the interface of affect and power. During the escalation of the impasse, each retreated into the domain of choice: Marty safely using indirect power domain strategies to control Emma's affects or feelings, and Emma using escalating affects to control Marty's use of power.

The second thing the impasse reveals is the couple's stuck moves: Marty, a weak mover in affect and unable to follow Emma's strong affectual moves, ends up confused and withdrawn, a stuck and disabled bystander. Emma, a weak mover in power and unable to follow Marty's power moves, ends up with her feelings spiraling and out of control, an angry and disaffected opposer.

THE SEQUENCE

Looking at the moments in their repetitive interactional sequence from reported scenarios in their lives and from observed ones in the therapy, we can conceptualize the specific frames in the sequence. The first

frame can be seen when Marty makes a bid in affect (an invitation to
go to dinner, a sexual move). In Frame 2, Emma, responding instead
of following, makes a strong move in affect in her own style. In Frame
3, Marty, shifting from the affect into the power domain, attempts to
control Emma's strong affectual moves. In Frame 4, Emma, angrily distancing, further escalates her affect, challenging and opposing Marty's
determined controls. In Frame 5, retracting in the face of strong affect,
Marty weakly follows Emma's move, attempting now to join her in
affect. In Frame 6, an outraged, and sometimes outrageous, Emma
escalates the affect, sending it spiraling upward and out of control. In
Frame 7, a confused Marty, his hands and tongue tied in both affect
and power, retreats to the position of the disabled and stuck bystander.
With each of them now in their stuck positions of opposer and bystander,
the two of them polarized and steeped in despair, Marty and Emma's
conflict temporarily abates, yet is ready to recycle significantly when,
and only when, Emma once again invites Marty to try to reach her in
affect.

Before shifting to the next step in Stage 1 of structural-analytic
therapy, from mapping the problem to resolving the problem, it helps
to run a preliminary test, one that estimates the rigidity–flexibility of
the stuck psychopolitics by attempting to make preliminary changes
in their structure. (Incidentally, I use the information I get from such
tests as one diagnostic criterion for deciding whether, in *my* view, the
couple can do with a brief therapy program.)

The technique I used with the Gordons to run this test was one
of the class described above as "using the structure to change the
structure." In the session, the fifth, the couple had been going back
and forth on their issues.

MARTY (*complaining that his all too rare bids for intimacy are being rejected*): Well,
    um, she's not available all the time, sometimes I try and make an invitation.
    I make a small gesture and, ahh—look, I feel I'm a sexy person and
    ahh. . .
EMMA (*breaks in*): You are really amazing . . . you think you're a sexy person?
    Yes, our sex life stinks. You make an invitation, and I should be there,
    ready to perform, ready to give. I mean, it's not sex. (*Emma escalating.*)
    It's the feelings, Marty, you don't have any feelings. You don't, oh, you
    talk about your feelings, you don't feel anything. You don't know what
    it is to get angry, you don't know what it is to get sad. You're never in
    there with me, I can't even have a fight with you.

MARTY (*trying to tone down her affect but not with his words*): It's a little hard, Emma. It's a litle hard to show any feeling while you're all over the place.

DAVID (*interrupting the sequence, which by now is known to him*): Marty, let me ask you to try something. (*Turns to Emma.*) You like to play games, right? (*Emma nods and seems interested in David's move.*) O.K., Marty, play a game; gag her.

MARTY: What?

DAVID: Gag her. Use your handkerchief, use your tie; gag her and see what happens.

MARTY: David, you've got to be kidding.

DAVID: I'm not kidding. (*Turns to Emma, who starts to encourage Marty.*) You just hold it for a minute. (*To Marty.*) See what happens. Try it.

MARTY: You want me to do this now?

DAVID: Do it now.

MARTY (*visibly warming up to the game*): You want me to gag her? With what, my tie?

DAVID: With your tie.

EMMA (*pointing playfully to her mouth*): Right here, Marty.

MARTY: I love it. Here you go, Emma darling! David, you don't know how much I've wanted to do this. Let me tell you. (*Emma tries to talk, but David tells her to stay with the game.*) Wonderful! Just wonderful!

DAVID: Does that help?

MARTY: It certainly does! It certainly does!

DAVID: So, what do you want to say about your own feelings?

MARTY (*begging the question*): I would feel pretty free about saying anything that I felt like saying just now.

DAVID: Try one. Say one thing.

MARTY (*after a pause*): Emma, SHUT UP!

(*Emma applauds.*)

This maneuver, an attempt to change Marty's and Emma's stuck psychopolitics, is what some family therapists might call prescribing the symptom or a paradoxical intervention, and it probably is. But I would call it using the structure to change the structure.

The structure I am referring to, of course, is the couple's psychopolitical arrangement. In it Emma is an effective but overly strong mover in the affect domain and a strong opposer in power, especially in those contexts where preparation and planning are necessary, or, better still, where they are unnecessary for the goals of affect. Marty is an effective but overly undermining mover in power and a stuck bystander in affect, especially in those contexts where, spontaneously or unpredictably, emotions or feelings may spiral upward and out of control. Given this, Emma tended to see controls where there were none, and Marty tended to confuse violence and ecstacy, putting them both in the same category of overly strong emotions that are threatening and must be controlled.

In the gagging maneuver I directed Marty into a shared affectual experience with Emma, using control as a tool to realize, rather than eliminate, affect. The results were interesting. Emma revealed that she might follow in power if such controls were exercised in the spirit of play and were out in the open. Marty revealed that he was capable of moving in affect and of opposing more directly there if he could feel in control. I learned that their psychopolitics, in therapy at least, were more flexible than they first appeared, a mapping consideration of much importance. I knew something about Marty's and Emma's capacity for change and the direction that such change should take.

A CROSSROADS WHERE A MAJOR CLINICAL DECISION IS MADE

At this point structural-analytic therapists come to a crossroads. A decision must be made whether to attempt to change the structure (the crippling redundant sequence) through the use of direct or indirect techniques. Should the focus be on changing behavior to the exclusion of changing perspectives, or on changing behavior through the inclusion of perspective change? Should the techniques used be hands-on or ones exercised from a position of neutral detachment? The first options are inducements for longer therapy and eventual pursuit of transformation goals after change goals are reached. The second options are persuasions for brief therapy confined to the pursuit of change goals without direct therapist involvement in perspective change.

One's choice of technique is a crucial factor. But it is not the only factor.[4]

The use of positive connotation, playing dumb, symptom scheduling, prescribing the symptom, paradoxical injunctions, paradoxical prescriptions, and constraint of change are suited for interrupting the vicious positive feedback cycles and quickly resolving the presenting

---

4. At least one other factor is the therapist's Boundary Profile. I have observed in training many times, and in research on therapeutic process and outcome, therapists whose internalized personal theories and explanations get in the way of their trying to use a clinical approach that requires them to perform in ways that violate their profile requirements. They think and report that they are doing one thing; observed, they are doing another.

problem. Also useful are tasks, homework assignments, and enactments that remain in the present and are not too emotionally evocative. Enactments that invoke the past, genograms, various evocative sculptures, various forms of role playing, and corrective communication exchanges are less well suited for resolving the problem quickly. By judiciously combining techniques from both sets and paying careful attention to the sequencing of techniques, one leaves the option open to go either way, to give clients a say in the matter and make better matches between therapist, technology, and client characteristics.

When the decision is made that a second course of therapy is to follow the brief first course, I ordinarily include some form of cross-perspective image work among the techniques I use. The technique called *eliciting the couple's critical identity images* is the strictest formalization of image work. It serves as the high point of the third step in therapy in Stage 1 and as a transition to the transformation stage. If the decision is to complete the therapy at the end of Stage 1, I substitute a less impactful form of image work, perhaps a role play or a sculpture that draws on my already existing knowledge of the couple's images, followed by paradoxical prescriptions and confusion techniques designed to reinforce the behavior changes that result and to give the indirect message that the couple can complete work on their own, but not in further therapy. With the Gordons, I conducted Step 3 with the intention of eliciting their critical images.

Step 3. Inducing the Therapeutic Crisis

The objective in this phase is to give the couple a new "peak" experience, leaving them altered but in a way that defies logical description. Often the change is experienced as irreducibly magical, sensory rather than cognitive, even when, depending on the technique used, some cognitive or perceptual reassemblage results.

For the therapist seeking radical change in a stuck-couple system, it is frequently necessary to take the system by surprise. "By definition, revolutions are not linear," someone has said. What we want to accomplish is a psychological revolution in the service of systemic change.

How, then, is structural-analytic therapy different (in Stage 1) from other attempts to bring about radical and rapid change? Like the proponents of brief therapies, this approach is prorevolutionary insofar as it recognizes the need for paradigm shifts. Where it departs from others is in its insistence on the ascent of consciousness following the paradigm shift, even at the risk of slowing the revolutionary process down so that it becomes "re-evolutionized."

Both routes to change confront the couple's developmental crisis with a new crisis, the *therapeutic crisis*. Different schools of family therapy induce the paradigmatic crisis around particular issues: strategic therapists by circumventing and totally disarming the resistance; structural therapy by confronting the family's model with a new one; structural-analytic therapy by insisting that the seeds of the system's relationship problems lie within the self. When a structural-analytic therapist decides "at the crossroads" to take the route of rapid change without transformation, the paradigmatic crisis resembles those induced by strategic and structural therapists. If Stage 2 (transformation) work is elected, he is more likely to induce the crisis through the technique of eliciting the couple's critical images. Such crises do not represent breakdowns of the structures presented for change, but breakthroughs. Following the change is a new consciousness, a new perspective advancing the ideal that an enhanced human community with intimacy as its mainstay is possible and necessary.

I admit that this combination, change followed by the ascent of consciousness, is a hooker. It leaves the unmistakable dual message: "Settle for what *you've* got. It's pretty good after all." And, "If you really want it all, you've got more work to do." Our hope is that buying into both messages will drive couples sane, not crazy.

ELICITING THE IMAGE

In the seventh session with the Gordons I was presented with an unmistakably clear example of the ritual sequence. It followed in the session just preceding the example. It was a drawn-out account of the same battle fought at home and an extended run-through of the cycle in the session. In the home scene, Marty proposed that they take a vacation together, a practice they had discontinued for the past 2 years. Emma enthusiastically agreed, but counterproposed that they go to the Mardi Gras, instead of accepting Marty's idea for a more conventional and less expensive vacation. The cycle began, escalated, ran its course, and repeated itself I don't know how many times, and was taken up again in the session.

Because it is important for the moods and affects associated with the image to be fully present before eliciting the image, it is best that the couple replay the sequence directly in the session, rather than get it from indirect accounts. If they do not relive the crisis directly, the therapist may have to generate it or else wait. This was not necessary with Marty and Emma.

A complete documentation of the process would take us into prohibitive length. Instead, I now describe the procedure by weaving together direct transcription with summary and commentary.

COMMENT: *The intervention is made when the couple sinks into the depths of despair. The familiar vicious cycle is over, having just run its course. They are hit by the horror of having "been here so many times before."*

DAVID (*gets up, stands behind Emma with his hands on her shoulders*): Let me try something. (*Turns to Marty.*) I'd like you to consider just how you're feeling right now. . . . Go through all the experiences of your life and come up with some picture, some memory of an experience that is telling you how to behave and feel right now. . . . It can be a single event. It can be several events of a single kind. But it's a memory picture. It explains how you're feeling and how you've been behaving. It doesn't have to be one event. It can be many that you've culled from your experience and put together yourself—an experience of your life, and it's telling you how to behave and feel right now in the fight.

COMMENT: *Where the therapist positions himself, behind the partner and in full view of the targeted person, is important. The couple have just had a fight. They are alienated. Working with one may mean abandonment to the other. It is important to keep this partner involved. For, in the struggle, the mate being attended was "the enemy." Developing sympathy for that person's pain and gaining a new perspective on what is behind that person's hateful behavior are, while difficult, the key to change. By my physical contact (hands on shoulder) with the outwardly inactive partner, much can be communicated: "Stay involved!" "You are not forgotten." "Don't interrupt." "Isn't that something?"*

MARTY: I don't know. The feeling is something similar. It's an old feeling.
DAVID: What's the scene that comes to mind? What is the memory?

COMMENT: *A long search is not necessary. Usually the first thing that comes to mind is the "correct memory." There is no correct memory. The actual event remembered is rarely important. What I want to tease to the surface of awareness is the structure of the experience, a structure embedded in many events, not a single one, in interaction with elements in the partner's image. We want to surface that structure. Its elements, and how these interact with elements in the partner's image are the key to the system structure under the lens. Hence, when a client says, "I can't think of anything," I say, "Make it up." Whereupon I help construct the image. This is not a problem as long as my own images are kept where they belong.*

MARTY: Wrestling with my brother.

DAVID: What's going on? Just describe it. Try to see it and describe it.

MARTY: We used to wrestle. He used to pin me down and I used to get so angry. I can even get angry now thinking about it.

COMMENT: *Once a memory is located, the mood and affect structures of the image are close by. We want to explore these elements of the image structure. But there are other elements. The inexperienced therapist often spends too much time promoting expression of feelings, dwelling there, and missing important information.*

The context of the image is thoroughly explored for information about the internal structure of the image. An image has three structural elements: a thematic structure, an affect or mood structure, and an action structure. All three are explored, as in the transcript example.

DAVID (*later*): Who else is involved in the action that's in the memory picture? Who else is important in it?

MARTY: No, it's just Jerry and me. There's no one else.

COMMENT: *This question about the action structure of the image is at first almost universally misunderstood by clients. I am probing for* relationship structures. *I have psychopolitics in mind, for the psychopolitical moves that a person makes in the ritual sequence can be traced to moves in the image. Hence, I will continue:*

DAVID: Just Jerry and you were there physically. But thinking about other people important in your life at the time, who might somehow relate to the action, who else was involved in the issue? They're not there physically, but they're involved in the action

MARTY: My father. My father is a character in my head that somewhat goes with that memory.

DAVID: If you had to take him trom your head and put him into the scene, where would you place him?

SUMMARY: In this way we develop the idea that, structurally, Jerry, the brother, and the father are identical. Father is placed immediately behind Jerry, "approving Jerry's guardianship over me . . . stamping out my feelings." Mother is placed spatially in support of father.

COMMENT: *In the action structure of his image, Marty is punished for expressing himself, for making moves in affect. His brother opposes these moves, acting for their father. Mother is a disabled bystander. The importance of the action structure and of the* missing element, *the element, which, if present in the action, would have redeemed the experience, will be shown later.*

Our images serve as our basic references for our ideas about the world. More important, some of our images are the bases of the characteristic behaviors we manifest in our relationships with intimate others. This special subset of images are called *critical identity images*. Through the memory picture I elicited in the above therapy sequence, I was beginning to understand the critical identity image that Marty was using in his cyclical struggle with Emma. The "wrestling scene" he described (its structure, not the specific details) is an important foundation event or experience that is part of that image, an image that guides him and that he uses to regulate others in the expression of emotions. In his ritual struggle with Emma, Marty is making a claim about how this should be done — through the competent management of one's affairs. Emma, however, has her own ideas. She makes a competing claim, based on her own foundation experience and her own critical identity image.

(David now repeats the process, eliciting Emma's image. He stands behind Marty, with his hands on Marty's shoulders, and faces Emma, repeating the instructions.)

EMMA: I remember exactly. It was my dad. He invited us out to dinner. My mom was coming too. And he took us to Howard Johnson's. It was awful. It was terrible. Oh, it was so bad. (*Emma is vocally and visibly upset.*)

COMMENT: *When both partners' images are elicited in the same session, which is preferred, the one who follows gets a running start. Something may be lost in this. I was puzzled by Emma's upset, which continued over the next few minutes. This degree of emotional arousal was not explained by the material. Was my Boundary Profile involved? I thought not. What I did not guess at the time was that another memory, replicating the structure but more emotionally loaded, would be recalled down the line.*

SUMMARY: Emma was disappointed because she thought her dad was taking her "someplace really fancy." She had imagined going to a "fancy restaurant." What began to emerge was that she was protecting him. Her disappointment bordered on a lack of trust, which she acknowledged and then took back.

EMMA: It's like I didn't have a right to be, to be angry, because . . . my dad was, he was innocent in all this. I mean, he would have taken us fancy if we could afford it.

DAVID: In relation to what happened, just where would you place Mother? Very close? Alongside you? Between you and Dad?

SUMMARY: Emma establishes that her mother was a stuck follower and a disabled bystander to her father. Mother was an adorable dreamer, but not very useful in circumstances like these. When Emma went to Mother to complain or for solace, Mother's line was, "Oh, you must have been imagining it, dear." Mother, who could not subject her daughter to harsh realities, simply denied their existence.

DAVID (*tries to get Emma to imagine who else in her life at the time might be part of the structure of the image*): Is anyone else related to it?

EMMA: No, this was a kind of special thing, just me and my parents. My brothers, they're not related to this.

DAVID: If you *had to* put them in, where would you put them?

EMMA: They're not part of it.

DAVID: They just don't belong to this?

EMMA (*somewhat adamantly*): They don't belong to this picture. (*Emphatic.*) They're not there!

DAVID (*changing the subject*): Do you know what you were wearing at the time?

EMMA (*instantly cheering up*): Oh God, I can't believe you asked me that.

DAVID: Why?

COMMENT: *The thematic structure that emerged was* being disappointed and controlled by a man, whom you were supposed to trust but couldn't. *In the action structure that emerged, Father was a mover who promised more than he gave; Mother was a stuck follower to Dad and an unavailable bystander to Emma; Emma was an invited follower cum distrust, and henceforth in such contexts, a stuck opposer. In the mood and affect structure of the image, high hopes turn to disappointment, hurt, and sadness—and to anger that could not be acknowledged, except with Marty.*

SUMMARY: My exploration of the image ended soon after this exchange. Emma, who had a flamboyant air, even at age 9 picked over her wardrobe "a million times trying to figure out some outfit to go to this wonderful restaurant." Having dressed wildly for the occasion, her disappointment was heightened.

MARTY: You know, I could see how you could really get angry at me because it seems that you just couldn't get angry at your father.

EMMA: You know, I think you're totally right.

DAVID: Mixing up times and places and people.

EMMA: I guess so. I sure couldn't get mad at my father. (*Turns to Marty.*) And I sure don't have a hard time with you. (*She laughs.*)

Step 4. Consolidating the Initial Change

If I thought that therapy with the Gordons was going to end with a brief course, I would not have used the uncovering technique of eliciting images. Some technique designed to change the whole structure would have been preferred, an enactment technique that was richer in metaphoric than in concrete information, for example, or a sequence of confusion techniques aimed at confounding the couple's resistance to change. When rapid revolutionary change occurs, what needs accomplishing as soon as possible is a consolidation of gains. An economical way to do this is by predicting, with paradoxical intention in mind, that the change will probably not hold.

Stage 2. Transforming the Structure: Change through Individual Image Work

Marty and Emma Gordon were not going to end therapy after a brief course. With the uncovering of their images, they had a peak experience, and a "surprising" change was reported in the next session. This change has a combination of features. One part of the change is behavioral. What they did before to fuel the conflict, they now stop doing. What they seemed unable to do before, they now can do. Couples report that they "had the best week in a long time." Some say the best "ever." They speak of "second honeymoons." But along with this behavioral change, there is a new awareness, an ascent of consciousness. This part of the change is perceptual. It is based on the contemporary exposure of the two images, on a beginning understanding of how each partner's image elements interact with the other's, and on more than a hint of how the past has been filtering present happenings.

Changes brought about in this way are not expected to be stable. Many couples eventually retrench. For a retrenchment around their images and a replaying of the familiar stuck psychopolitics is just as common following the initial breakthrough as the breakthrough itself, even when the therapist has done an effective job in making the required preliminary changes in the couple's psychopolitics.

This is true because image work bites off a large chunk of couple territory. Through image work, underlying issues are named and faced, rather than bypassed as in a true paradigm shift. Change brought about in this way is not, in the final analysis, revolutionary. It is evolutionary. Even so, what needs accomplishing here, no less than in the above instance, is consolidation of gains. Here, too, we predict the retrenchment. Our intention is not paradoxical, however. We mean to imply rather directly that in order to do the transformational work of Stage 2 of structural-analytic therapy, the retrenchment is needed.

Step 5. Mobilizing for Retrenchment

Anticipating and mobilizing for retrenchments may well spell the difference between succeeding and failing to hold on to the goals of Stage 1—and between moving surely and more or less evenly toward the goals of Stage 2 and getting caught up in a therapy that drags on unnecessarily. In retrenchment, couples call on two tactics—they either develop "new" problems or return to the "old." In either case, they sink back into blame and despair. The experienced structural-analytic therapist is not distracted. His countertactic is to thank them for bringing in interesting new information for joint consideration and for helping all three of them get on with the real work at hand; or he chides them for boring him with uninteresting replays of tired scenes; or he reproaches himself for moving too fast or expecting too much.

Minor therapeutic struggles and crises sometimes ensue. Usually, however, couples are relieved either to be laughed at or pleased to enter into a new relationship with the stuff of their lives, one in which they experience and bystand with gradually increasing awareness.

Each time the therapist succeeds in isolating the retrenchment crisis and uses it to explore image elements that have fueled the ritual sequence, the couple gains more control over the repetitive pattern, suggesting not only that the initial change will hold and remain stable but that more significant change may yet come.

Step 6. Unfolding and Pinning Down the Image Elements

In this step, the structural-analytic therapist goes back and forth between active techniques designed to change specific substructures and waiting. "Waiting" does not mean being idle. During waiting periods the therapist gathers further diagnositic information, reinforces gains by direct or indirect techniques, and helps the couple focus on the structure being addressed. In ongoing therapy, couples tend to unfocus. They tend to introduce new materials as their personal winds blow. The therapist who follows these materials and shows interest in them without judging whether they (*a*) directly relate to his diagnosed structure; (*b*) require him to alter his diagnosis; (*c*) represent resistance or a systemic slowdown tactic on the couple's part; or (*d*) reflect his own unfocusing or the operation of his own Boundary Profile; may conduct an inefficient or uneconomic therapy or, worse, do damage to clients.[5] Nevertheless, some aspects of the pinning-down process cannot be rushed. Unpredictable events that come up in the couple's life, events that cannot be clinically solicited, are pivotal sources of information about each partner's image elements and how the elements interact. Three "waiting" sessions passed. In the fourth, one of these developments took place.

SUMMARY: Marty and Emma were in the throes of another battle. Emma had come up against a problem at work. Michael Davenport, the head of Guidance at the school where she worked as a counselor "has just been screwing me royally. . . . He's been very underhandedly coming down on me in ways that I cannot figure out what's going on." Her boss, Emma went on stridently to explain, first gives and then takes away her autonomy. Because of his "underhanded" tactics, she feels "boxed in" and powerless to do anything about it.

DAVID: What does all this have to do with Marty?
EMMA: Well . . . I'm going through some incredibly emotional experience at school, and I come home and tell Marty about it and he's nowhere. He hasn't been there. He hasn't been available. [*She means, of course, psychologically, not physically unavailable.*]

SUMMARY: Emma's proposed solution was to quit her job and go back to school for an advanced degree. Marty not only withheld support for the plan but demeaned it, which further incensed Emma. In the arguments before and now in the session, I saw that the fight was beginning to escalate into the old disastrous sequence.

MARTY: Emma, let's look at this sensibly. You've been working with this guy for how long? Let's—
EMMA (*talking over Marty, who has gone into his power-tinged rational routine*): You're doing exactly what this guy [Davenport] does and says: "Look, Emma, this is what you're supposed to do, this is the right way to do it."
DAVID (*interrupting Emma*): What's the next step? I mean, after you escalate your anger like that, what's the next thing that happens between the two of you? We already know the steps. We know the image.

COMMENT: *In this pinning-down stage of the therapy, allowing yet another escalation of the ritual sequence would not have been useful. In the session, I already had*

5. I would estimate that between 2 and 5 sessions were added to the 15 it roughly took to complete Stage 2 and that this inefficiency was due to my failure to observe carefully enough the principles just stated.

enough content and process to fill a chapter in a book. My aim here was to get whatever new information the episode had to offer and to work at cross-referencing image elements.

SUMMARY: Emma did not like my blocking off her story of the incident and her angry feelings toward Davenport and Marty. At the risk of being included with the "other men" as a manipulator, I drew her (and Marty's) attention from the episode itself to its "workings," and reminded them that they are familiar with their "little dance," with their "ritual" and with the image that prompts it.

DAVID (*to Marty*): Now in all this, what part do you play? What part are you playing right now?

MARTY (*hesitating, not following him*): What—what part do I . . .

DAVID (*turning to Emma*): What part is Marty playing? What part does Michael Davenport play? I mean, is he your father, disappointing you? (*Turns to Marty.*) Are *you* the father? (*Back to Emma.*) Who [meaning "in the image"] is he to you right now?

EMMA (*obviously struggling with something*): It's really striking, and it, it reminds me, I don't know where it fits in.

DAVID: Say it and we'll worry later about where it fits in.

EMMA: Well, this is something that happened when I was young. I don't know, it happened for a while, maybe I was eight or nine, something like that.

COMMENT: *My moves in the above interchange are quite deliberate. Their meta-message is: Let's get on with this. Fight if you like, but there is something more interesting than the fight. Let's get to work! Bystand a little! Follow the pattern, not the content! Play detective with me! Discover how each of you is enjoined and ruled by elements of your own image to act in ways that drive the other person crazy. Learn more about your own image elements and how, driven to get your partner to fill in the "missing element" or to play a part identical to an existing element, you are provoking him or her into existential despair or physical violence, because as he or she sees it, what you want is precisely what cannot be given because to do so would be to sacrifice the grounds for reality on which identity rests, or so each cannot but insist.*

EMMA: O.K. Umm, well I was, this is something that happened when I was young. I don't know, it happened for a while. Maybe I was eight or nine, something like that. And, I used to share a room with my brother. . . . And, umm, he used to come in, you know, we'd all be asleep and, umm, after everyone was sleeping he'd come into my room and he'd, umm, get his, he wouldn't get into bed with me, but he'd get his hands under the sheets and under the blankets and he'd start playing with me. And, ah, that was pretty bad, right? That's bad enough as it is, but, as bad as that is, worse than that was that I would go to my mother and I'd tell her, I'd tell her about it, I'd tell my mother what was happening and she—she didn't believe me. She didn't support me.

COMMENT: *Triggered by the events at work and home, Emma has recalled an incident, another example of the negative foundation event whose structure occupies the core of the competing image she is using in her struggle with Marty. Once again I note that structurally it is nearly identical to the restaurant scene. What is new is the expansion of the theme of disappointment with men to include sexual subject matter and the shift from merely being "led on" to being "bullied." Emma's irritation with me when, in exploring the action structure of her original memory, I asked "who else" was involved in the action now made sense. Also better understood was her upset over Michael Davenport and the language she used to express it: "underhanded," "coming down," etc. I could now see a basis for connecting her image to the problems she and Marty were having with their sex, and I could begin to track how these image elements connected with elements in Marty's image.*

DAVID: What did Mother do? What stand did she take?

EMMA: The stand she took was kind of "you made it up!"

DAVID: Uh, huh! It was all in your imagination.

EMMA: Uhm. That's right.

DAVID: So, let's see if we can track this a little bit better. So, Marty is . . . playing a lot of different parts. If we . . . take this new information and plug it into the image we're already somewhat familiar with, Marty is *disappointing*, and when he's doing that, he's Daddy. And Marty does have a way of, ah, certainly, Michael Davenport is doing something of a trip on you.

EMMA: He's trying to con me into something.

DAVID: As brother does in the image, and, as you say, often, Marty does with you in real life. So Marty is also—

EMMA: Brother.

DAVID: Yes, probably. But, look, who is Marty also?

MARTY: I'm also her mother.

DAVID: How so?

MARTY: Well, if Michael Davenport plays the part of laying the trip on her, then she comes and looks for support from me, and I don't give it. . . .

COMMENT: *With Emma and Marty working together smoothly, the above connections were sorted, refined, and deepened; the couple's awareness of the place that Emma's image had in their lives was expanded. The work of pinning down the elements of an image and of establishing structural links between an individual's past and present and structural symmetries between one partner's characteristic behaviors (as predicated on his own image) and key elements in his partner's image is, in my experience, among the more truly rewarding of all therapy experiences. In it, clients feel empowered, through the effort of sharing with the therapist both the challenges and the returns when new perspectives on old dilemmas are discovered. Becoming an informed collaborator with the therapist in the search for such linkages, symmetries, and complementarities gives clients an active part in the crucial task of accelerating the* transformation of negative foundation events into positive identity claims. *Being actively involved helps to speed up that all-important process.*

But I am sure that the clinically sophisticated reader will not be misled by the seeming ease of recognition and unfaulting cooperation shown by the couple in the above account. Recognizing connections between image elements is not the same as effecting the transformation of image elements. Nowhere in an ongoing (i.e., Stage 2) therapy process than in the realization of this task is there required more skill in sequencing techniques and in balancing (a) in-session vs. out-of-session; (b) direct vs. indirect; (c) awareness-raising vs. awareness-blocking techniques. Nowhere, moreover, is the therapist required to have more patience. And nowhere, finally, must the therapist be more on the alert for signs[6] that some feature of his or her Boundary Profile may be involved in the formation of "unnoticed structures," which invariably serve to delay the reaching of transformational goals.

Transformational change is a gradual process. It comes hard, not easy. Partners give and take back their commitment to such change. Some, unhappily, never trust enough to make the commitment in the first place. Intimacy for these couples is elusive. While I had clinically judged Marty and Emma capable of achieving the intimacy that they (like almost every couple) ostensibly wanted from therapy, the task was not easy.

SUMMARY: In the same session we have been examining, Emma marched steadily forward, gathering up new perspectives about present action structures; and thematic structures were linked to structural elements in her image. For example, how the structural equivalencies between Marty, on the one hand, and her father, brother, and Michael Davenport, on the other, oversensitized her to Marty's shifts from affect to power domain strategies, how those same shifts (which occur as a learned structural response to his brother's control over Marty's emotions) "undermine [her] competence"; how men in positions of hierarchical authority leave her feeling "misled," "oppressed," and "unable to mobilize effective counter-moves" when they exercise authority. In all this, Marty seemed to stand by. But, toward the end of the session, the following occurred.

6. One item in the Boundary Profile Chart, the detailed chart which structural-analytic therapists are encouraged to complete over their professional lifetimes (a current edition of which goes in each client's folder), refers to *Theme Sensitivities*. "Sexual coercion" is one such sensitive theme for many therapists. It is not one that "gets to me." But this did not excuse me in Emma's case. A lack of sensitivity to the significance that the theme held for her could have gotten me into a clinical trap. Later in Stage 2, the issue of sexual oppression arose for consideration. I had the option of dealing with it lightly or in depth. As a male therapist, I had to be sensitive to the option of not dealing with it altogether or recommending that Emma work with a female in individual therapy. As we shall see, I chose the latter.

MARTY: Yeah, David, you know, it all seems to make sense once we start working with it this way, but it still doesn't do anything for the way I feel about it. I mean, I don't like being put in this position. It all makes sense, but she still drives me crazy. She drives me nuts!

DAVID: And when you get driven nuts, what happens to you?

MARTY: I get paralyzed. You know, we've been through that I don't know how many times.

DAVID: And what does *that* have to do with *your image*?

COMMENT: *I imagined that Marty's response to Emma's productive in-session work on her image had the effect of undermining her. (I failed to check it out.) Perspectives were shifting. But action structures lingered on, still basically unchanged. Had Marty been farther along in the transformation of his own image, the theory holds, he would have been capable of a different response—of exercising a different psychopolitical option, that of* following *Emma's moves. Instead, functioning (as her mother did), he was a disabling* bystander, *indirectly opposing her bid to have her sense of reality validated and supported. His failure to fill in the "missing element" in Emma's image, by becoming a* bystander who validates an awful reality, *is Marty's way of giving notice that his own image and the behavior he was required by that image to deploy in current situations that aroused the image were the foundations of* his *reality and that these, when challenged, would not readily give way.*

In their ritual struggles people often feel victimized by their own hurtful experiences and threatened by their partner's, without being in touch with either. This is why, beyond merely revealing the image, the goal of structural-analytic therapy is to help each partner develop an appreciation of his or her own identity-forming images and then, of the partner's. Crucial for the realization of this goal is the process I have been describing, the sixth step, pinning down the image elements.

What organizes the therapist's attention and moves throughout this process is the above-mentioned tripartite structure of the image: (a) themes; (b) affects and moods; (c) action relationships. When the couple bring the pleasures and vicissitudes of their struggles into the therapy from session to session, the therapist is screening the materials through his understanding of the structure of their images, listening for consistencies and inconsistencies in these themes, affects, and actions, making this a more or less conscious process for which the couple gradually come to share the responsibility with the therapist.

What the therapist hopes for is that through his planned interventions in sessions and unplanned happenings in the couple's life, "breakthroughs" of two kinds will take place. First are further memories of foundation events that add important information about the structure of the image. Emma's in-session memory of her brother's sexual antics was such a breakthrough. The new thematic information it revealed explained, better than her earlier memory did, the sexual aspects of the couple's impasse. This was a breakthrough into a new perception of her image. *It did not concurrently entail a breakthrough into new action, the second kind of breakthrough. Marty did experience such a breakthrough. It occurred out-of-session, just before a resumption of therapy following a month-long winter break.*

SUMMARY: Marty reported at length and with the excitement of new discovery: He and Emma were invited to a party, a rather formal occasion. As was his way, Marty was dressed promptly in his three-piece suit and was waiting impatiently for Emma, "who was ensconced in the bathroom for 45 minutes, dressing." When she appeared, she was "decked out in this 1920s garb, right? Beads hanging off her, flowered hat, the whole scene." Her outrageous, flamboyant, custom-defying statement triggered Marty's familiar attempts at control: "It starts to build up, she starts to get angrier, the whole scene happens. I start getting into paralysis . . . when this thing comes into my head, which I had totally forgotten about. . . ."

COMMENT: *Marty proceeded to describe a new memory picture, a scene from the past in which after "playing house" with a little girl in the woods (they were about 7 or 8 years old), he is found out and, hiding and scared, is facing certain punishment from his father. Choosing a rather uncertain sanctuary as a hiding place, under a table in the living room, every moment of waiting to be found by his father and punished for his excesses is an ordeal of suppression.*

Notice, again, the structural equivalence between this and the "wrestling scene" he described earlier. What structural analysis shows is that what remains stable in the events that converge into a critical image is not the specific circumstance of the memory picture but the structural elements of that memory picture. During the preparty encounter at home with Emma, their ritual struggle beginning to escalate, Marty made a connection between his tendency to suppress excitement, fun, play, and passionate emotions in Emma with the suppression in him of behaviors associated with these same themes and affects by his brother and father; as a result, he was able to stop, not for the first time, but willfully, the escalating ritual pattern.

With this so-called breakthrough the image emerges into awareness during a ritual sequence. That is, Marty was able to change his behavior, not by conscious effort alone, but because he saw, for the first time in the heat of battle, where his behavior was coming from. The work of pinning down the image elements was finally paying off. What was noteworthy was that in the session itself, Marty was affectually freed-up. He was, in the theory vocabulary, becoming a mover in the affect domain, while Emma seemed to be doing some following and bystanding of his moves. But Emma was "not entirely convinced." Along with her qualified support, there persisted a subtle opposing.

We had a good idea already about the source of Emma's persistent opposing from other voyages into her past. While her parents were distracted by their struggles to make ends meet, Emma was being involuntarily subjected to prepubescent sex play by her brother. She felt powerless to oppose either brother or father, who had his own career—employment problems. Her mother, to whom she turned, was unable to respond to her plea for help in controlling either the boundaries of her body or her reality in connection with these assaults. Not surprisingly, Emma, who needed to put into perspective the effects of these intrusive sexual experiences on her ability to enjoy sex, was not easily going to accept her therapist's efforts to transform these negative foundation events into positive identity claims. Surely not without an attempt to keep control, as she was doing so successfully with Marty, especially in their sex. In an instance like this, the asymmetrical structure of therapist–client relationships, and the "skewed contracts" (Kantor, 1983) that obtain in the therapy situation, may work against therapeutic outcome unless that structure is openly monitored by all three participants. Emma, who seemed to be opting for a working system model based on the random *stereotype, might give a therapist who worked in the* closed *system style as difficult a time as she was giving Marty, whose preferred system model seemed to be* closed. *What I am leading to is this: Even as I largely ignore my own Boundary Profile issues as I describe in the next two steps the techniques I used to begin transforming the couple's images into positive identity claims, I am mindful of the part they played.*

The four steps covering the clinical work of Stage 2 refer, of course, to overlapping rather than discrete activities. This is especially true of the last three steps, where any claim of orderly progression may be misleading. Here is a useful way to explain it.

Once the work of *pinning down the image elements and their cross-image interactional effects* begins to pay off, the therapist's techniques can begin to serve transformational goals as well, and can be designed with those goals in mind. Somewhere along the line where techniques designed to reach the goals of transformation are beginning to achieve their effects, a crucial event will take place—the couple, but also the therapy itself, will face a crisis, typically the most serious crisis of all.

In resolving it the therapist often bumps into himself coming and going—holding his ground, backing up to do more "pinning down" of elements (often uncovering important new information) and moving on in forging the all-important positive identity claims.

Incidentally, I have been raising the question whether this second therapeutic crisis is *inevitable* in this form of therapy and *necessary* for maximum gains to take place. My hunch is that it *is*, and thus is raised the question whether it should be *induced* if it does not occur naturally. I suspect that it always is induced, that it is an inherent feature of the therapeutic process with couples, that therapists are unaware of this, and that they would do well to bring it under therapeutic control.

Step 7. Inducing the Second Therapeutic Crisis

In this crisis the couple question the basic premises of their relationship, doubting its validity, its reasons for existence, and its future. Curiously, the success the therapy has had in revealing the role the past has played in producing current relationship structures in large part accounts for the cataclysmic breakdown. "If the *past* plays a part so pivotal, what *are you* to me, and are *you* real, and do I love *you*, and did I *ever* love you?"

At this point in the therapy, the therapist is called on to do his best work and, incidentally, to pay most careful attention to those features in his Boundary Profile that might be inveighed, such as to bias the outcome of the crisis, leading to a premature or unappropriate end to the relationship or marriage, for the couple may talk of separating or of ending the therapy. One member may have an affair, or threaten to. Symptoms may return, exhibiting variations that make earlier expressions pale by comparison. In facing this crisis, as with earlier crises of change and retrenchment from change, the therapist must hold his ground.

Several considerations govern the choice of techniques: the need to give the couple some relief and some emotional (occasionally even physical) distance; the need to hang in there, going further in the exploration of the problematical, and, until now, usually only super-ficially addressed structure from the past that is causing both the psychological unrest and breakdown of the relationship; the client's resistance to facing this troublesome structure, leading to projection and blame; and enough basis in reality for the most troubled member to conclude that not the past but the present (the mate's performance) is what must be dealt with.

The Gordon crisis emerged, not from any dramatic incident, but from Emma's appearing to be visited by the profound realization that the men she loved had acted ignobly. At the peak of the crisis I responded with direct confrontations, an extra session, tasks that encouraged distance and tasks that encouraged more intense closeness. I backed off from a continued exploration of the couple's (mainly Emma's) image(s) only when persistence bordered on insensitivity.

Step 8. Forging Positive Identity Claims

When couple stability was reestablished, we continued with the process of accelerating the transformation of Marty and Emma's images into positive identity claims. The following techniques highlighted the pro-cess.

THE INTIMACY SCULPTURE[7]

Intimacy sculpture is a special application of family sculpture that focuses on the moves, rules, and distance-regulating mechanisms that couples use to attain or block access to intimacy, especially sexual intimacy. The technique has shown itself to be an economical way to pin down the repetitive sequence in which an impasse is embedded and to provide an opportunity to transform the stuck sequence into a more varied series of moves to enable intimate contact. The procedure is videotaped for replay to the couple. With the Gordons, it was used early in Stage 2 to establish the parameters of the problem and the directions for transformational change. Because such spatializations frequently "hit home" with dramatic impact, they are also a source of behavioral change. This variety of sculpture is direct rather than indirect. It uncovers feelings embedded in patterns and seeks to facilitate awareness. It sets the stage for, more than it achieves, behavioral change.

A STRAIGHTFORWARD HOMEWORK ASSIGNMENT: BE INTIMATE

Straightforward tasks frequently contain direct and indirect messages. First, they directly tell the couple what the partners already know. For example, Emma was instructed to make two (and "only two, not one, certainly not ten") "moves" toward Marty. The direct message was, "We all know that you rarely do." Next, such techniques indirectly try to influence the structure they are designed to address. For example, Marty was instructed to make no "*moves* of his own, merely to *follow.*" The indirect message was, "Since you are allowing yourself to be handcuffed, doing nothing, while whining, maybe *you* might try making some moves in affect." This out-of-session, direct–indirect technique is designed more to effect behavior than perspective change.

Doing the task, Emma did initiate intimacy, not twice but three or four times, and Marty followed. For example, after dinner one evening, Marty stayed around at Emma's invitation and just talked. Typically, he would have settled into some project or task. And once, Emma, after a long evening of pleasant talk, gave and then asked for a back rub, which led to lovemaking. So far, the homework "worked" rather well in its design to help Marty learn to follow Emma's moves

---

7. A technique I developed in 1976 with Dr. Arlene Katz. It is described in an unpublished manuscript (Kantor & Katz, 1980).

in affect (without shifting domains) and, without being explicit about this, encourage Marty to make moves of his own in this domain.

But when Marty, assuming license indirectly given by the task but not yet endorsed by Emma, made a strong sexual move on his own, Emma balked, introducing a problem that was to occupy the therapy for the next few sessions. What problem? The obvious transformational goal was for Marty to become a better mover in the affect domain and Emma a better follower in the power domain. But, should Marty move sexually, and specifically if he did so somewhat awkwardly (and he still did), precipitously, or without proper regard for Emma's sensitivity to invasion at her physical boundary, Emma might experience this bid as an invasive power move. Obviously, the couple was not yet out of the woods transformation-wise, its "breakthroughs" notwithstanding. I will mention three other techniques that were used to accelerate the transformation process.

THE LETTER-WRITING TECHNIQUE

The letter-writing technique is borrowed from psychodrama. It is a cathartic technique used specifically to uncover feelings that are systematically suppressed. Release of the feelings frees the "letter writer" to act differently, that is, to increase behavioral options in specific relationship structures that were previously rigidly limited and stuck. A direct technique, it leads both to behavioral and perceptual change when it succeeds. When used in couples therapy, the partner stands behind the seated "letter writer," who verbally addresses a person involved in his untransformed image. Marty wrote to Jerry, his brother. The partner (Emma), standing with hands on the writer's shoulders, can add lines she feels the writer is leaving out. This arrangement also carries an indirect intention—a restructuring of the partner's relationship to the other's image elements from an adversarial to cooperative one. As an enactment it can have a powerful transformational effect on the writer, the partner, and the structure they have created.

Marty's letter, spoken from sources of deep resentment long locked inside, came off like a stanza of moving verse. It ended: "I can feel it now, Jerry. I can feel the anger that you knocked out of me. I want to feel, Jerry. I want to feel as I felt when I was a kid. And I don't want your shadow or anyone else in this world to take it away from me anymore. Just get out, will you. Get out of my life. And stay the _____ out! Cause I'm going to live, damn it! I'm going to live in spite of you or all that stuff you did to me!"

VIDEO PLAYBACK OF LETTER SESSION

Marty and Emma watched the video playback of the letter-writing scene. With this technique, we were working toward the goal of changing the meaning of Marty's image. In the original, his feelings were freed-up along with the new behaviors they sponsored. Here, Marty was to gain some perspective on the image, its affectual elements, and its effect on current relationship structures; Emma was to increase her understanding and appreciation for Marty's image in order to envision new responses to his stereotypical behaviors.

"HOW IT WILL BE"—A SCULPTURE

In this simple spatialization, one partner directs the other in a *moving sculpture*, a metaphor-in-motion depicting change in the structure from "how it is" to "how it will be."

It is an evocative and kinesthetically imposing maneuver, one whose impact derives from the condensation of great bodies of meaning and experience into a brief and deceptively understated improvisation. It offers possibilities both for perceptual and behavioral transformation.

Emma scuplts her relationship with Marty by alternating between rage and fear toward him until she finds, with difficulty, some attempt at equality. She does this by nonverbally acting out the expression of her feelings toward Marty: first, by showing him her fist, to signify anger, then by covering her eyes and cowering away to demonstrate her fear. Then she stands up to try to ground them both in equality. The equality soon leads to Emma's leading Marty into play, by turning him, in what looks like a dance step, in which she leads.

In her simple spatialization, Emma made a poignant (nonverbal) statement about herself in the couple relationship. Through it she gained a more profound understanding of how her feelings of coercion with Marty connected with those she experienced at an earlier time with her brother and father. For Emma, the spatialization experience was a rehearsal for behavioral changes that took place in the weeks following its execution. Both for Emma and Marty, transformation was under way.

TRANSFORMATION TO WHAT?

I should have said, "transformation was once again under way." For if, as the theory contends, intimate couple relationships furnish a context for the development of individual identity, meaning here, the transformation of negative (as well as positive) foundation events into positive identity claims, then a system developmental crisis calls a halt to normal transformational process, for each partner and for the couple system itself.[8]

This transformational process is rarely complete. If an individual in an intimate relationship nears the complete transformation of one image, some other image struggle, possibly leading to another developmental impasse, should sooner or later take its place. It might be said that the person who has succeeded in transforming all of his or her significant foundation experiences, positive and negative, into positive identity claims is a fortunate person indeed. (He or she probably would approach what Abraham Maslow called self-actualization.) But what is a *positive identity claim*?

When I say that during their identity struggles, people confront each other with competing identity images, I mean that they confront each other with competing claims about reality and claims about identity. Identity claims tend to be active assertions of positive value. For instance, early in therapy, Marty and Emma had a fight without end about improving their living-room aesthetics, he wanting a sensible design with traditional furniture and color schemes, she an experimental design with colors that titillated the senses and furnishings meant to change with the seasons and their moods. Their world views differed. What was positively valued by one, threatened the other. They differed in their views as to how to manage in the world. Marty would feel good in insisting, "I know how to do things right and can help you get things done," while Emma would feel equally good in insisting, "I know how to have fun and can help you enjoy life."

While these competing claims are fiercely defended in the couple struggle, there remains something hollow and incomplete about them until the foundation events on which they rest are sufficiently transformed (in an intimate relationship) into a positive claim *that incorporates the negative features of the original experience*. When Marty's work on his image is near to completion, he might say, "I know so much about a family world in which unharnessed expression was considered dangerous and unproductive, and having suffered and reacted to that suffering by closing off my own expressions, and now having discovered that I really do have a choice in the matter, you can entrust to me the

8. Not in all areas, although sometimes this *is* the case.

complementary assignment of helping you check excess when you need to, and to get things done in an orderly way when this serves you and us." A transformed image is a derivative of its foundation event while reframing it into a positive form. This is what we mean by "forming over." The foundation image, including its painful aspects, are preserved. Only the meaning of the image and the constraints on the behavior as formatted by the original image are changed; transformed.

But if, as proposed, transformation is rarely completed even in a thoroughgoing therapy sequence, when does the therapy stop? I have not worked out the criteria for making this judgment. By the time the question has come up for serious consideration, the couple will no doubt have ideas of their own and, of course, the partners may frequently disagree. Once again, Boundary Profile issues arise. A couple who would continue longer than necessary, and who induct an easily seduced therapist, represent but one dangerous combination. There are others, obviously. All can be considered and monitored by the therapist who is aware of those Boundary Profile features that might be relevant to stopping therapy.[9] Clinical judgment will do the rest, in lieu of formalized criteria.

When in the therapist's best clinical judgment the couple have acquired a capability of continuing transformational work on their own, the time has arrived for *fixing the image* and moving toward the last stage of therapy.

I have found that in transformational work with couples, it helps both to crystalize and to punctuate the therapy process if the therapist fixes, that is, renders the elements more visible (as in a photographic developing process where a chemical fixer "sets" the positive photographic image).

Every therapist, I venture to say, not only has worked with clients' critical images (whether such image work was formally recognized and dealt with) but has "fixed" these images. When Milton Erickson tells a story whose structure he is suggesting as an alternative solution to the one the client brought in (Erickson, 1982), he is fixing an image. When Jay Haley spins out a tantalizing sexual metaphor as an indirect

9. Each therapist's personal explanatory system and formal clinical epistemology include a view as to how much effort to put into changing what does not work. Therapists' preferences for brief strategic versus historical transgeneration therapy probably reflect these differing Boundary Profile influences.

way of recommending a new course of intimate action for a shy parental couple, he is fixing an image (Haley, 1976). When Robert Gardner in his storytelling technique with children tells the child's story with an alternative outcome, he is fixing an image (Gardner, 1971).

By fixing an image we are anchoring the change already accomplished and/or the change desired in an experience that by its nature is hard to forget and is easily recalled. It seems to be in the nature of things that most people tend to lose hold of and forget the new perspectives and action prerogatives they have learned in therapy, especially when some new circumstance has rearoused the foundation event and its perceptual and behavioral proscriptions in its original forms. The tendency to revert to form is irresistible, except perhaps for individuals in couple systems who have done their transformation work long and well, and who faultlessly check whatever tendency the partner still has toward retrenchment. But in the therapy, doing something to fix the image helps.

I have found that in fixing the couples' images, dramatic use of metaphor helps. Different techniques can serve the purpose: psychodrama, for example, or a major sculpture. Of the two, sculpture suits the purpose better, especially if the proper format is selected. As I originally conceived it (Kantor, 1970), sculpture is to be seen as a more systemic tool than psychodrama, a technique for highlighting the individual–system interface. Psychodrama, because of its more or less fixed format, can be distracting, the couple getting so immersed in the emotional aspects of the experience that they lose hold of the structure in which these are embedded. Carefully executed, however, this and many other techniques can be used effectively to fix an image.

With the Gordons I experimented with an elaborate technique, the use of an artist to capture the couple's images in a visual metaphor (Kantor & Barnett, 1979). Because it is so specialized and costly, I will not detail the technique here; it would derail us. What matters is the purpose behind whatever image-fixing technique is used and what actually is done with it in therapy.

The major aim is to cement the image. All three participants should be free to interact during the rendering of the image, making connections between each partner's past and present and discovering crossover connections and relationships between the partners' image elements; all the while collaborating and creating the visual metaphor. In the course of fixing the image, each partner becomes an expert on the other person's image.

Importantly, a fixed image should first contain elements of the image bearer's past and future, dramatically metaphorizing the transformational work each individual has done and has to do, positively appropriating, rather than being engulfed by, hurtful foundation experiences and dilemmas from the past. Second, it should reveal the ties between the individual's past relationship structures and both present and future ones. The very definition of this assignment is by itself an intervention. In taking it on, Marty and Emma took their development as a couple into their own hands.

In Emma's fixed image, the key elements from the past included Emma, reaching out for reality support from her mother, who, dreaming of better times to come, remains distracted and unavailable, while the brother's invasive sexual explorations go unnoticed and the father, if anything, anchored too much in a difficulty reality, metes out mealtime services whose meagerness the family must deny.

In Marty's fixed image from the past the key elements from the past included Marty, the young boy, who, after arousing sex play, is being shamed, exposed, and psychologically beaten down by his father and brother, while his mother fails to speak out on his behalf.

In Emma's fixed image, the (transformed) future was represented by Emma as an on-stage entertainer, men at her feet, altogether in control, reconciled with her mother, whose denial of reality makes Emma's dream possible. In Marty's fixed image, the (transformed) future was represented by Marty, the man, standing apart from his family, traces of an erection barely concealed in his tightly tailored, smartly fashioned conservative attire, his back to his brother, who is pictured oversized but curiously disempowered by Marty's smugly smiling countenance.

Once the images are fixed, therapy can wind down. Usually, concluding that the images can be fixed means that most of the desired changes have occurred in the structure underlying the ritual sequence; that is, new psychopolitical behaviors have replaced ones that maintained the impasse, and, for each partner, there has been a change in the meaning of both images.

When a couple have made significant transformation change, as Marty and Emma did, little things that previously would have bogged them down or escalated into a major dispute no longer get in the way. Following the fixing of their images, Marty and Emma did report several instances in which they successfully negotiated circumstances that previously triggered their impasse. When trouble threatened, "recalling" the image had an attenuating effect, monitoring the would-be escalation.

No longer pursuers of their ritual struggle, the couple were freed to grow, individually and collectively. Where earlier the untransformed competing images resulted in a fusion of affect and power strategies, they did so now with far less frequency. More successfully facing the tasks of the *attachment* phase of development, they no longer needlessly implicated the other developmental sectors, like *industry*, and, we assumed, they would be able to move on with still other developmental tasks, like *inclusion*, which Marty and Emma had not dared to face until now.

At this time in the therapy, two things occur: The transformation of founding experiences into positive claims begins to accelerate, the couple doing most of the work by themselves; and therapy begins to wind down, the therapist insisting that the couple's fear of future retrenchment, while not unfounded, will succumb to the attenuating power of their own collaborating authority guided by the fixed image, which also is in their hands. At this time, incidentally, the therapist's thoughts turn to the "whether" and "how" of Stage 3.

The decision to wind therapy down at this time, to turn from considerations of present and past (Stage 2) to past and future (Stage 3) puts structural-analytic therapy at another theoretical–clinical crossroads. Having taken the transformational path at the earlier crossroads, settling that earlier contest of choice between awareness-giving and awareness-blocking techniques in favor of the former, the clinical choice here is less unnerving but no less serious. Embedded in the practical question, "Is the couple ready?" is a theoretically more insidious question, "Are the individuals in this couple system capable of sustaining the new system strategies they have worked out for themselves?"

Merely by taking this question on, the structural-analytic therapist comes face to face with his "purer" systems colleagues, many of whom might have argued that transformational work itself is *not* systemic. In this essay I have taken issue on theoretical grounds with these colleagues.

Clearly, the question above must be subjected both to conceptual *and* empirical test. My own clinical observations suggest that some individuals, psychologically disadvantaged by genetic or historical events, can and do challenge the stability of the systems of which they are a part. Such individuals are, in a word, more powerful than their systems.

Rather than play their assigned parts in their families' organizational structures, the system structures form around *their* otherwise hard-to-manage proclivities.

Now, it might be said that the genius of systems-oriented interpersonal therapy rests fundamentally on two principles: (*a*) that by *systemically* relabeling what others call individual pathology, symptomatic behavior can be eliminated or modified; (*b*) that by *paradoxically reversing* a system's problem-solving approach, conflicts in the system can be bypassed. Nevertheless, even the most zealously devoted systems clinician, who endorses and uses the pragmatically demonstrable wisdom of these principles, must still face up to those instances where they simply do not work or, even when they do, that the cost entailed, on some level other than the pragmatic, sheds dubious light on the value of the outcome.

With these considerations in mind, the question, "Are the individuals in the couple system capable of sustaining the newly formed structures?" is both more interesting and more difficult to answer. It behooves us, therefore, to investigate those factors that interfere with the hypothetically possible capability of the individuals in the couple system to realize their transformational goals in the therapy and following it.

Certain of these factors immediately suggest themselves:

1. One partner may enter the couple relationship having already done some of this transformational work, while the other has not (both the fact and the discrepancy mattering).
2. The task of positive transformation is more easily accomplished if the founding events of the critical identity image are positive rather than negative.
3. Some individuals seem to make *negative*, rather than positive, identity claims; falling into this category are the occasional suicidal risk and some people diagnosed as schizophrenics.

Put simply, some foundation events are more injurious to individuals than others. For instance, the mother of a developmentally skewed (a poor, systemically disadvantaged, "multiproblem") family, whom I see at the Family Center, was subjected as a child to continued sexual seductions and coercion by her father in a system where her mother's failure to acknowledge the deed matched the original betrayal. The damage to this woman was immense.

In the case of Emma, a similarly structured experience seemed to take a significant but lesser toll. She could form productive relationships with men; her need self-protectively to control men was considerably less entrenched and ritualized. But as therapy in Stage 2 neared an end, Emma was still trying to put into perspective the effects that her intrusive sexual experiences had had on her ability to enjoy sex as fully as she wanted, and the pressures they had put on a 9-year marriage that she now knew she definitely wanted to preserve.

Although intimacy, including sexual intimacy, was now within the couple's reach, neither Marty nor Emma claimed that they had arrived in sexual paradise. "Should the therapy," I asked myself, "be a context for further work on the image?" If yes, what techniques might help? Indirect techniques were ruled out. I had noticed that Emma, with her bent for whimsical spontaneity, responded well to indirect, aware-ness-blocking maneuvers, except when they touched the subject of sex too directly or deeply. She experienced these moves, I came to see, as manipulations that reproduced the very problematic structures we were attempting to neutralize.

Bringing the broader questions to Emma's attention, *she* decided to declare a break in the therapy before proceeding to Stage 3. She would consult a female therapist—one who was neither militantly feminist nor coopted into a field (psychology) that, dominated as it is by men, tended to be insensitive to the special requirements of some women's issues by ignoring them—and call for a resumption of the therapy when she felt ready.[10]

Not until she and Marty returned did I learn that Emma's consultation with a woman therapist lasted only two sessions. Instead of therapy, Emma, with her consultant's help, decided to take private ballet lessons with a woman who came recommended as one who would understand how this form of expression might more effectively get at the issues involved.

A woman mentor who validated Emma's struggle to come to terms with her own body and the sensitivity to invasiveness lodged there, a

10. In this matter I found myself "betwixt and between." Was this a clinical copout, a too-great readiness to endorse the women's movement? Was I not putting the couple at risk by sending one of the partners off for individual therapy *elsewhere* (a practice I knew to have splitting effects on the couple system when not done in conjunction with couples therapy)? Following work with these clients, I discovered through work on my Boundary Profile that a wish to protect women has created a tendency to withhold even my own best clinical skills, when even the question of their being hurt arises.

woman who might guide her into a freer use of that body in dance movement with its obvious intended extension to freedom of sexual expression—these, it seemed, constituted a nearly perfect structural correction to Emma's sexual dilemma.

In their return session, Emma came dressed in her leotards under a winter coat. Positioning Marty between us, she had him hold her coat by its stretched arms, a "curtain" that he would draw on signal when, moments later, she would perform her "3-minute improvisation." Playing with her *directoral controls*, she laughed, and Marty laughed with her, at the apparent analogies to their problem: "Not yet—not yet" when Marty's outstretched arms wearied. An explosive "Now" when she decided to begin her remarkably sensual dance.

When all three returned to the seriousness we knew we had to muster, Emma chose to understate the brilliance of her performance and all its meaning. Said Emma, soberly: "I still do 'it' better this way." From my vantage point, the cards were now more evenly stacked in the couple relationship. Emma, I found a way to say later, had climbed over a hurdle of sorts and was now better situated to work out the terms of her positive identity claim: "I am a woman who, having risen above the pain and ignominy and rage associated with an unacknowledged betrayal of my physical boundaries, is alert to the possibilities of oppression, sexual and otherwise, intended or unintended, real and fantasized, and can help men and women in their abuses of one another around these issues."

Stage 3. Preventing Future Problems: Change through Predicting the Involvement of the Next Most Vulnerable Structure

In Stage 2, the couple enlarged their awareness. In Stage 3, this enlarged awareness is extended. In Stage 2, the couple returned to their evolutionary course. In Stage 3, the couple discovers their own evolution. In Stage 2, the couple were helped to achieve major change in one previously problem-riddled area of their lives. In Stage 3 they discover that when you understand the change taking place in one major area, it is easier to make sense of other areas.

Structural-analytic therapy culminates with the couple's discovering their own evolutionary model. Crucial in this is the discovery that paradigmatic differences were involved in their impasse; that the present resolution of these differences is probably not permanent; that in the fallout from their struggles other aspects of their lives (structures and people) were probably affected; that the therapist and his theory represent not one but two more evolutionary models; and that these, too, are impermanent, changing, and no more sacred than their own.

In keeping with these principles, in Stage 3 structural-analytic therapists make *their* truths, *their* goals, *their* theory of change, and where necessary, *their* personal models, known. This allows couples to make a conscious assessment of these therapist persuasions as, *more in charge*, they face the decisions of their final phase of the therapy and take on the life tasks affected by the therapy.

In Stage 2, beginning with the pinning down of the elements, in which the couple are helped to an expanding awareness of *patterning* in their interactions and life experiences, the therapist begins to refer to his theory vocabulary, without formalizing the learning he hopes is taking place. For example, when Marty is recognizing on his own a pattern of interaction in the present based on an earlier experience and says, "You know, David, since you have been flashing on those *images*," he is showing the effects of an informal learning process. Also, when a therapist decides in Stage 2 to respond selectively to the life materials brought into the therapy by the couple, he can "explain" his selective attention either by direct or indirect means, as clinical contingency wills it. But, either way, he has the opportunity to reveal his theory vocabulary.

In Stage 3 the theory is more formally shared—not, of course, as a lecture but as a language that is consciously used by the therapist with increasing frequency while he is carrying out the other three steps of this stage, beginning with the rather important identification of the next most vulnerable structure.

Step 9. Identifying the Endangered Structure

Preventing the problem from extending to the next most vulnerable structure almost always requires an anticipation of how dilemmas from the past will affect future developmental tasks and dilemmas, individual and systemic, which involves predicting who will be involved in the endangered structure.[11] Emma and Marty predicted that a new problem

11. The simple formula for prediction is this: Given the workings of the impaired couple structure as we have come to know it, and given the behaviors of the people in

would evolve around *inclusion* issues, around having a child. They predicted that the vulnerable structure would occur around their different ways of getting things done; that control and protection were themes that would result in contention about handling simple child-rearing routines; and that the child primarily, but also they and their relationship, would be endangered, specifically, that issues of nurturance and intimacy (attachment) might get confused with issues of competency (industry).

The simplest technique for preventing symptom reoccurrence in the next most vulnerable structure is, if it is a person, to bring that person into the therapy, or to bring the therapy to the person, as Norman Paul does when he has couples play videotapes of key dramatic moments in the therapy to their children. Emma, role playing her still unborn child, was told, no holds barred, what was wrong with her mothering style.

My approach is similar but more specific. Here there is no child as yet. Anticipating its arrival, Marty and Emma were asked to imagine the struggles they would get into. Within moments, play slipped over into reality. They *had* the fight they *would* have. Referring to specific elements in their *fixed image*, they tracked the origins of the new pattern they were projecting. (Two years later, they came for a one-session consultation, babe in arms. A new pattern, recognized as such, had emerged. They wanted help in nipping it. Doing most of the work themselves, they roughed out its source, searching together for their separate images about inclusion and about the rights of infants.)

At this point in therapy, Steps 9 and 10 overlap. Efforts to prevent damage to future structures proceed best when the couple *discover their evolutionary model*.

Step 10. Identifying the Couple's Evolutionary Model

Central to all the therapeutic work of Stage 3 is the partners' *discovery of their own evolution* as a couple system. Earlier in this chapter I proposed

---

their lives, who appear to be implicated in the impaired structure, directly or indirectly? For instance, a couple invited their 17-year-old son to a session before ending their therapy in order to convey to him how their 20-year marital struggle may have limited his choices. Though their son was not "symptomatic," the couple felt (and I agreed) that his obsessive preoccupation with academic success was in part an unhealthy response to their avoidance of sex and intimacy and in part a healthy avoidance of triangulation. The couple predicted that their son might face a crisis in relationships when he went off to college.

that "the ultimate task of all families without exception is . . . the responsibility for evolving a model . . . or paradigm for guiding their members through the . . . exigencies of life, a model for construing and dealing with realities within the family and between the family and its external environments." Crisis, I said, is "the couple stalled in development." Their working model (i.e., the current status of their attempt to operationalize in everyday realities the paradigm or ideal family type they have internalized with other critical images) has broken down because of the emergence of competing images. Therapy of the kind described has as its ultimate goal putting the couple back on a developmental track. One of the best guides that a couple have for staying on track without serious derailment is the discovery of their own evolution, the key to how they grow as a system—or fail to.

Once a couple are faced with a new developmental task,[12] each of the individuals brings a new identity image into play, providing each partner with a perspective for viewing the situation (a definition of reality), a format for behaving in that situation, and a model of how the future would be if each could get the other to see and act according to one's own prescription (Kantor, 1980). If the images are compatible and do not have competing elements, no serious impasse will occur, and the system will evolve without crisis. If a crisis occurs, and it is resolved through natural or therapeutic means, the couple can move on.

Over the 9 years of their marriage, Marty and Emma had faced three of these tasks. They had done very well with *affiliation*. They had done fairly well with the tasks of *industry*, except when these got caught up with the tasks of *attachment*, with which they had failed until their breakthroughs in the therapy. Assuming that they avoid or resolve future impasses, they will complete all eight tasks and continue to grow through the life cycle of the relationship. Put simply, this means that they will develop more and more successful strategies for covering more situations, contingencies, and opportunities in the eight sectors. Growth, then, results in an increase of substantive richness and complexity and an increase in efficiency in conducting the system's affairs.

In structural-analytic theory, a system's growth occurs on four levels. At the *meaning level*, it grows from the accumulation and sharing

---

12. I have identified eight developmental tasks: attachment, industry, affiliation, inclusion, centralization, consolidation, decentralization, differentiation, and detachment.

of more and more images. Marty and Emma, having enriched each other around themes of attachment, know so much more about vulnerability and constraints on passion. At the *action level*, it grows from the couple's expanding their repertoires of behaviors. When Marty, in a home scene not reported above, throws off his tie, signaling to Emma that he will attend to her distressed emotions rather than go to a family dinner, he is not just *"moving in affect,"* he is communicating loyalty and affection with decisiveness, precision, and subtlety that previously were beyond his authority. At the *pattern level*, the system grows from the couple's evolving more and better strategies and sequences through which the goals of affect, power, and meaning are realized in expanding variation. Emma's sensual response in the just-cited scene is a token of a newly acquired strategic victory over long-standing barriers to the couple's intimacy. At the *model level*, the system grows as it drafts a more refined blueprint for patternings of perception and action, which then are carried out at the three previous structural levels,[13] a blueprint that, as it evolves from the successful resolution of imagistic difference, increasingly satisfies each partner's requirements in more and more situations that call for collective action.

The model level is where the system's rules and its rules about its rules are set down, rules that govern the couple's strategies and patterns, their actions and interactions, and their meanings and images. Whenever a couple are at a developmental impasse, their struggles will not only be over definitions of reality—how events are to be perceived and acted on—but over the very models that contain the meta-principles for such perceptions and actions.

I have identified three pure or ideal types (Kantor & Lehr, 1975) that individuals and couples use as paradigmatic frameworks for evolving their working system models—the closed, open, and random types. No value is placed on these terms. Each has a successful and flawed variety. They simply describe three different ways of regulating the boundaries, defining the goals, and prescribing the pathways to the goals of real-life family systems. When couples are struggling over whose definition of reality will prevail, they are at the highest level of

13. In structural-analytic theory, structure is seen as occurring at all four levels, not, as in much systems thinking, at the pattern level alone. This notion has great consequences both for theory building and for therapy. If, as the theory hypothesizes, "structures" at all levels are morphologically linked, therapists have more options to intervene and whole avenues of family experience are opened up for consideration.

system abstractness, struggling over which of these "typal designs" will be the basis for the system's working model.[14]

In their attempt to arrive at a model, Marty seemed to prefer a closed system and Emma a random system. For Emma, a straight line may be the shortest, but it is not the most interesting way to travel the distance between two points. For Marty, it is, in most matters. Marty and Emma play to different drummers. They respond differently to a surprise visit that requires them to change their plans for the evening. They have radically different ideas about how to decorate their living room, not only about what it should look like but how to go about the task. Their pathways to intimacy have different signposts and different things would happen at their destinations. These differences are the differences between the closed and random perspectives. Looking at the one crisis resolution we were priviledged to see them through, they appeared at the end of therapy to be approaching an open system perspective, which drew selectively from the closed design.

In the last phase of the therapy, Marty and Emma knew that they had risen above the crisis in attachment in their marriage. In the hope of avoiding a crisis over inclusion issues, I asked them to anticipate the *worst possible case*, a commonly practiced prophylactic technique. Once again studying the fixed image (the artist's rendering of their images),[15] they placed their as yet unborn child into the scene. Under

14. Will Lehr and I knew that in formulating these three pure typal designs we had conceptualized broad paradigmatic frameworks used by individual family members in their struggles to settle on an actual, collectively endorsed, working family model (Kantor & Lehr, 1975). We did not, however, carry forward the work of operationalizing the theory. David Olson (Olson, 1984) and David Reiss (Reiss, 1982) have done pioneering work in developing operational models of these and similar ideal family system typologies.

15. A note on the technique is called for. I have avoided making it focal in this presentation for at least three reasons. First, it is expensive, requiring on average a 3-hour preparatory session, time for the artist to complete the rendering on her own, and a 1- or 2-hour meeting in which the rendering is presented and, if necessary, modified. Second, other techniques (sculpture and psychodrama most prominently) are competitive in value. Third, it is specialized, requiring extra-therapeutic skills.

As it happens, Rosamund Zander, the artist who helped pioneer the technique, and whose contribution I gratefully appreciate, is both artist and psychotherapist. But I have collaborated with one other artist, also successfully. In recent years, I have used the technique sparingly, questioning whether its value warranted the effort. My current conclusion, based on followup with couples with whom it has been used, is that it is very much worth it. For, whereas subsequent events in the couple's life can dim the focus or power of the image, an actual rendering that can be materialized on call (which, I learned, is how the Gordons use theirs) cannot be dimmed or erased.

its current *random system rules*, they imagined fingerpaint on the walls, jelly in Marty's old books, a child engaging in sex at age 6 with his mother looking on. Under its *closed system rules*, they imagined shining glass and unblemished white enamel paint; Marty, at table, as an anthropomorphic grandfather clock, chiming a signal for dinner at the precise second; and a child tied hand and foot to his crib. The Gordons had discovered their own evolutionary model.

Step 11. Inducing the Third Therapeutic Crisis and/or
Terminating the Therapy

Before terminating the therapy, therapist and couple have the option of inviting briefly into the therapy figures from the past, such as parents or siblings who played key parts in the formation of the key critical images and therefore with the impaired structures the couple presented for treatment; or, if their physical presence is impossible or not essential, they can be dealt with through role play, sculpture, or psychodrama; or, if an out-of session technique is preferred, they can be dealt with through homework assignments or tasks. Here is an example of the third option:

SUMMARY: Marty and Emma decided to invite Jerry for dinner. Emma, they schemed, would dress up in one of her outrageous outfits. Marty, who in the past would be made "nervous" by such antics, would show obvious approval. Emma would also sexualize her behavior, a practice not unknown to her on past occasions involving Jerry and other "oppressors." Marty would more than approve; he would respond in kind. Jerry's predictable response (toward Emma, outright disapproval, disgust, or a studied "not noticing"; toward Marty, an attempt—which usually succeeded—to engage him in a coalitionary power move to suppress Emma) would be ignored.

COMMENT: *In the exercise, Emma and Marty are playing out their new relationship structure, one in which Emma's moves in affect are supported by Marty. The intentional use of altered couple patternings in situations that readdress old relationship structures is the principle of* isomorphic patterning *once removed. What the therapist did to affect changes in the couple they do to affect changes in other key relationships that are negatively patterned from past experience.*

The dinner succeeded in shifting the suppressive structure from a negative coalition of Marty and Jerry against Emma to a positive alliance between Marty and Emma, which Jerry must have experienced as a coalition against him. At my suggestion, therefore, Marty met alone with his brother with the intention, not of angrily confronting the brother (as in the letter-writing exercise), but of exploring how he happened to get trained in their family for his monitoring role. Not surprisingly, Jerry balked. But over the months following the end of therapy (I learned in the consultation session mentioned above), Marty persisted, meeting his brother for an occasional dinner, without Emma. What resulted was a surprise to both. Putting together fragments of previously unshared information, the brothers concluded that in the period under discussion their father was probably involved with other women and that their generous, nurturant, but effete mother had no interest in "rocking the boat." Father's wish to deflect from his own sexual excesses could account for his pattern of suppressing even normal expression in others and for his employment of Jerry as an aid in the enterprise.

Marty told me of these developments in the consultation session mentioned above, 2 years after therapy ended. That *he* persisted was fortunate. That *I* failed to persist during the therapy, that I failed to induce the third therapeutic crisis, is a key clinical issue.

Bringing a parent or other key figure from a childhood past into therapy is sometimes the most difficult thing an adult client can do. For many, the idea is shattering, raising specters of shame, rage, sadness, and fear. I have seen a 40-year-old male university professor and a 35-year-old female head of an advertising agency tremble and cry at the mere mention of it, the suggestion reinvoking the (often victimized) child within them. Such reactions are understandable when the themes surrounding their relationships with these figures from the past have profound arousal value, such as abuse, incest, or shameful secrets. But they occur around lesser themes as well.

At this juncture along the path of change, the traveler runs into another roadblock, and a crossroads. Blocking access to further progress is the ragged rock of childhood experience. "Whatever else may be true, mine is to obey." If I, the child, (is) (am) to have a place, (he) (I) must keep it. If I challenge, if the child becomes father to the man, he is no longer a child. The twin issue at the core of the rock is one of loyalty vs. betrayal and love gained vs. love lost.

In Stage 2, at the critical juncture we learn that the effects of discovering one's roots are not altogether sanguine, awareness of where we started raising questions about where we have come/gone and questions about the bases of our adult choice in intimate relationships. In Stage 3, at the critical juncture we learn that the effects of discovering the evolutionary map takes another toll. Awareness of our childhood dilemmas raises questions about the rights and benefits of growth. If I choose to grow, do I lose whatever love I have gained?

As in earlier stages, the crisis of change occurs naturally. The *process* takes care of itself. And again, if it does not, should the therapist induce it? My hunch, yet again, is yes. If the issue does not arise, or if it does arise but gets bypassed, look to a structure of resistance or denial at the therapist–client boundary interface.

I suspect that the rule in my own family against mentioning an absent father, who I failed either to reconcile with or confront before his death, qualified my otherwise confrontative style and filtered my power to reason clearly on the issue of Marty confronting, not his brother Jerry, who was after all a shield, but the father whom he shielded. Only in this writing exercise did this Boundary Profile feature come to light. I have added it to my Profile Chart. Is it possible that only now am I ready in my development of a clinical theory to begin thinking clearly on the delicate issue of therapeutically induced crises? I suspect also that a Boundary Profile feature, a tendency to help women keep their secrets, influenced my handling of Emma's reluctance to confront the key players in her critical image. Because I am more aware of this Boundary Profile feature, I was able to refer to it during the therapy.

Emma decided to delay tapping into impairing structures from her past that were still affecting her present life with Marty, most notably her brother's invasive sexual seductions and her mother's denial of the events. I was faced with Stage 3's clinical dilemma. Do I persist? Or do I drop it? With Emma, I dropped it. But not entirely, and not without realizing some further therapeutic gains that are consistent with the clinical goals of Stage 3.

In confronting Emma in this matter, three theories converged and clashed—my personal theory of families (still unfolding, as suggested), my clinical theory for doing family therapy (which, though more set, is also still unfolding), and Emma's (which the therapy was trying to put into *her* hands).

In this collision of perspectives, Emma's prevailed. Her idea was that she would gain more therapeutically if *she remained in control*, if *she* decided when and if and in what context to deal with her brother and parents. In session, she did a sculpture in which Marty alternately played brother and mother; and we talked. More awareness resulted. Emma's therapist's theory was out in the open. She *was* discovering her own evolutionary model. But Emma decided not to test out her capability for new behaviors face to face with family members. Resistance? Who knows. In any case, I acceded. My Boundary Profile? Who knows.

In order to resolve our theoretical debate, Emma and I agreed to disagree. The impasse, Emma pointed out, was a victory for her and therefore for me. "That's what you say you want, isn't it?"

Emma, I think, was right. The therapy was "working" because on the level of isomorphic patterning, Emma, not I, was tapping into an old structure to advance its transformation into a new one. In the therapy, she was in charge of her boundaries. She was even in charge of her male therapist, who was trying to impose his will on her.

References

Duhl, F. J., Kantor, D. & Duhl, S. (1973). *Learning, space and action in family therapy: A primer on sculpture*. New York: Grune & Stratton.

Erickson, M. (1982). *My voice will go with you* (S. Rosen, Ed.) New York: Norton.

Gardner, R. (1972). *Therapeutic communication with children: The mutual story telling technique in child psychotherapy*. New York: Science House.

Haley, J. (1976). *Problem-solving therapy: New strategies for effective family therapy*. San Francisco: Jossey-Bass.

Kantor, D. (1970). *Sculpture: The use of action, image and space in the assessment and treatment of families*. Unpublished manuscript.

Kantor, D. (1980). Critical identity image: A concept linking individual, couple, and family development. In J. K. Pearce & L. J. Friedman (Eds.), *Family therapy: Combining psychodynamic and family systems approaches*. New York: Grune & Stratton.

Kantor, D. (1982). Facing the hidden effects of doing therapy. In A. Gurman (Ed.), *Questions and answers in the practice of family therapy* (Vol. 2). New York: Brunner/ Mazel.

Kantor, D., & Barnett, J. G. (1979). *Images and identity: A videotape course on Dr. David Kantor's theories of couple and family therapy* (text and narration by D. Kantor; designed and directed by J. Barnett). Cambridge, MA: MIT Press.

Kantor, D. & Katz, A. (1980). *The intimacy sculpture*. Unpublished manuscript.

Kantor, D., & Lehr, W. (1975). *Inside the family*. San Francisco: Jossey-Bass.

Kantor, D., Peretz, A., & Zander, R. (1984). The cycle of poverty—where to begin? In J. C. Hansen (Ed.), *Family therapy with school related problems*. Rockville, MD: Aspen Systems.

Olson, D. *et al.* (1984). Circumplex model of marital and family systems: VI. Theoretical update. *Family Process, 22*, 69–84.

Penn, P. (1982, September). Circular questioning. *Family Process, 21*(2).

Chapter 3

Inside the Group

Henry Grunebaum, MD

Grau ist alle Theorie, and grün ist Lebens goldener Baum.
—GOETHE **(Faust, Part 1)**

A wise man once said that a man is rarely forced to confront himself so honestly as he does when he is with his wife. If that be so, then even more so, perhaps, in the circle of a couples therapy group. Jane and I came to the group acutely aware of "problems," but with only vague ideas of where trouble lay. We were sure that we were the only ones in the city of Boston with our particular patterns of conflict, our issues, our insensitivities, our incompatibilities. Tension lay not only in our fighting and not getting along despite our feeling that we loved each other, but was intensified in our feeling of isolation. Imagine our astonishment in the very first session when we heard another couple relate our fight of the last week as their own. The details were changed (not to protect the innocent—there never were any), and roles may have been reversed, genderwise, but there we were, and we hadn't even opened our mouths yet. The look we exchanged held the shock–relief we felt at being recognized. Here was this group of strangers who apparently had a good idea of what it was to fight with the person you love most. And all of a sudden, and gradually over time, I was to learn that that was not the worst thing in the world.

—JACK GOODHEART

When the invitation came from Alan Gurman to write this chapter, I found myself pleased and perplexed. What would I write about? I have always been somewhat baffled by the fact that so many of my colleagues seem clear and certain that they know how to treat their patients and the reasons why the patients improve. Personally, I have always been uncertain and unclear how it is that the people I see get better. They do seem to get better, they tell me that they are grateful that I have been their therapist, and they recommend me to their friends. But I have always felt somewhat at sea as to why the changes, which both I and they see, happen.

On the other hand, I have thought a great deal and written a good deal about why and how change occurs. Like many people who write about psychotherapy, I have tried to reason about it. For instance, it makes sense, as Neiberg, Christ, and I (1969) wrote 16 years ago, that couples who do not have marital problems or who do not wish to work on these problems should not be seen in couples therapy and that couples with problems who are committed to working on their marriage should be seen in conjoint psychotherapy. However, I have increasingly found myself believing that couples group psychotherapy is a more effective intervention than conjoint work. This particularly seems to be the case as the conjoint treatment continues, for as it goes on past 6 months to beyond a year, I seem to become part of the system despite my efforts to stay out, and find I am losing much of my earlier effectiveness. Yet why couples group psychotherapy should be effective continued to puzzle me, even though I was the co-author of an article that stated it was the treatment of choice for couples whose problems were enduring (Grunebaum, Christ, & Neiberg, 1969) and seemed rooted in their characters instead of arising out of a recent event or change in their lives. The problem of understanding change is all the more perplexing in a couples group, since one can know so little about what goes on in the minds and hearts of 8 to 10 other people. People who, in addition, go home from the group only to continue the discussions that had begun there. While one can ask an individual patient what his or her reaction to a previous intervention is, one can hardly do this with each member of a group.

This was my quandary when I received Alan's invitation. Now another influence came to bear, for over the last few years I have been engaged in a wholly unrelated series of clinical investigations. I have been the consultant to the clinical services of a large, rural, and typical state mental hospital where we have gradually become involved in psychoeducational groups for families of mental patients (McLean & Grunebaum, 1982). This enterprise occurred in part because while I first began to interview families of the patients, I was interested primarily in how the family had adversely influenced the patient, but gradually, after several hospitalizations, I found myself increasingly interested in how the patient had influenced the family (Grunebaum, 1984; Terkelsen, 1983). Out of this change of viewpoint, I find myself involved as a consultant with a group of parents of mentally ill offspring writing a book for such parents. Coincidentally, I had embarked on a series of studies of psychotherapy, all of which involved interviewing patients about their experiences. The first study was an investigation of the criteria that experienced therapists use in their search for a psychotherapist for themselves (Grunebaum, 1983a), and the second involved interviewing a series of therapists who had been patients in what they experienced as harmful psychotherapy (Grunebaum, 1983b). What all of these ventures have in common is that I have taken seriously, and as valid for them, the point of view of people who are not therapists but who are patients. The intersection of this series of experiences and the invitation has led to this chapter. I decided that rather than describe why I believe couples group psychotherapy is a helpful form of treatment, I would ask couples in my group about their experiences.

This decision was motivated not only out of scientific zeal but also out of some degree of laziness. I have always preferred to write with collaborators, and here was a new group of potential associates. The therapist's perspective on treatment is limited, for surely of no other intense and emotional relationship (which therapy is) would we ask only one participant to describe the experience. The reader of this chapter should be warned in advance that while the excerpts quoted are complete and uncensored, the couples who responded were those who had persisted in the group and were, therefore, those who found it useful. Now while there is an inherent bias in the members' point of view in the direction of positive responses, we should not be too troubled by this. Instead of psychotherapeutic treatment effectiveness being determined only by the patient's diagnosis, effectiveness results at least as much from the patient's enthusiasm and commitment to the particular treatment and particular therapists. In fact, Gurman (1977), in a comprehensive review of individual therapy outcome research, concluded that, if anything, the patient's experience of the therapist and the therapy is better correlated with outcome than are assessments of the quality of the therapeutic relationship as viewed by either therapists or independent judges.

The case to be described here is typical in the sense that the problems are ones I see frequently, that I often encourage couples to join a couples group, and that I enjoyed knowing and working with the Goodhearts. It is atypical in that I did not meet with either of them and their parents and that I asked them to describe their own experiences in the group.

Background

When Jack and Jane Goodheart came to see me, in the context of his having told her about an extramarital affair, it was on referral from his former therapist, whom he had seen in intensive psychotherapy in another state where he had held an entry-level job in hospital administration. Jack had sought psychotherapy for depression and still seemed to be somewhat down, although he felt he was somewhat improved.

Jack was a tall and solidly built man who spoke slowly and whose feelings seemed to move and change at subterranean depths, in striking contrast to Jane, who was shorter, lithe, and whose feelings darted about, shining through her eyes. During the first session, she wept openly; Jack took her hand and then put his arm around her and was obviously moved, tearing up a bit himself. When couples are able to reach out to each other physically, it is a good sign, and over the course of the therapy, not surprisingly, I came to care deeply about the Goodhearts, feeling like an older brother to him and like a father to her, for reasons that will become evident as the story evolves.

The Goodhearts related that during the 8 years of their marriage they had slowly grown apart, which both of them attributed to Jack's depression and his tendency to distance himself from Jane and from their daughter in order, he said, to study for an examination he needed to pass if he was to complete some graduate work he had embarked on. Jane, who worked part-time in a school and cared for their daughter, was an active and energetic woman who was deeply attached to her parents, who lived in a nearby state. She believed that Jack's problems were the source of most of their marital problems but was interested in "learning how to handle Jack better." At the time of the initial evaluation, Jack was 34 years old; Jane was 31; and they had a 3-year-old daughter, Sarah.

The Goodhearts described how they had met at a summer resort where Jack was a tennis instructor and Jane was one of his pupils. She had been attracted to him immediately and had set out to capture his interest. He was older, wiser, and she looked up to him and the seemingly straightforward and clear way that he was pursuing his career. At that time Jane had been in doubt as to her own direction in life, but as soon as the couple became involved in an increasingly committed relationship, Jane "found herself" and began to study actively to be a special needs teacher. That Jane thrived when she was involved with a man seemed natural, for she had always looked up to her father, who was an eminent member and much-respected leader of the community where she grew up. She described her mother as tending to put her father down, whereas Jane admired him unstintingly. On the other hand, she increasingly had come to see Jack as ineffectual in contrast. Jack had also grown up in a family with a very busy but very successful father and saw his mother as rather ineffectual. He was much surprised when his mother turned out to manage life very well after his father's death in his early 50s. But Jack also felt that he had to be a support to his mother and his younger sister.

The marital difficulties that the Goodhearts described had emerged gradually over the last 5 years. Jane had felt hurt and angry that Jack was increasingly distant from her and less and less interested in talking, doing things together, and being involved in their sexual relationship. Jack thought that Jane was a nag. It was depressing for him to be at home with a woman who complained so much, but who also seemed to enjoy her life apart from him. When she got angry, it was like a thunder shower—she swore and yelled but it was soon over and she was ready to make up at a time when Jack had just begun to know how angry he felt and was starting to glower. Both members of the couple related their coming to couples therapy at this time (for they had had my name for 18 months) to Jack's revealing a brief affair that he had had at work. Jane was furious and frightened by this episode; Jack was deeply humiliated and ashamed of his behavior—but also somewhat secretly pleased that he was that important to Jane.

After some evaluation interviews and discussion, I decided that this couple would gain much by being in a group. I believe that there are three essential questions to be answered during the evaluation:

1. To what extent are the problems marital and experienced as within the marriage; this determines if the treatment should be of the marriage.
2. Are both members of the couple committed to the marriage and to working on the problems; this determines if treatment is possible.

3. Are the problems acute and alien to the marriage or long standing, arising out of basic personality characteristics of both members; this determines if the couple should be seen conjointly
   or in a couples group.

A couples group would support both of them in their feelings that
they had unmet needs and would help them to see how others solved
problems similar to the ones that they found insolvable. Their difficulties
seemed to arise out of long-standing characteristics of each of them,
which had come to a head recently. They clearly cared a great deal
about each other, expressed their love openly, and wanted very much
to preserve their marriage and the integrity of their family, for they
both loved their daughter deeply and wanted to have more children,
since they felt they were "very good parents."

What Happens in a Couples Group

The Group as a Source of Hope and Universality

When the Goodhearts joined the group, they had in their very first
meeting two experiences that seem uniquely to occur in couples groups.
The first experience was described by Jack in the quote that began
this chapter, in which he related the impact of learning that his and
Jane's problems were not unusual. They were no longer as defective
and different because of the kind of fights that they were having.
Other married couples struggled with the same issues and were seemingly finding help in the group for such problems. Yalom (1975)
discusses the importance of the instillation of hope and universality
as 2 of the 10 curative factors operating in all therapy groups. The
opportunity to see that others have the same problems may be more
salient in couples groups than it is even in other therapy groups. No
relationship is more private than the intimate details of couples' lives —
how they express their affection, how they fight, and the little details
of everyday life that make up a marriage. Most people have had the
opportunity to observe closely only one marriage, their parents', but
this is seen through the eyes of a child. So most people know little
about how to be married, nor is it a competence easily learned. Dating
and courtship offer some anticipatory socialization, but much of the

learning remains for the couple to do on their own—the opportunity for much joy and pain.

The second experience, which occurred during the first meeting of the couples group that the Goodhearts attended, arose when Jane bitterly described her shock, despair, and rage at learning of Jack's affair. Jack sat there, anxious and embarrassed, not knowing how to reply. With about 10 minutes to go in the meeting, he, looking very distressed, said, "I suppose that I really have to say something about this." I commented that maybe he really did not have to reply yet if he was not ready. He looked quite relieved. Kama spoke of her sympathy for Jane, since she had been in a somewhat similar position about 8 years ago. At this point Kama's husband, William, said to Jack, "Maybe instead of your trying to answer Jane now, I can answer for you." He then went on to relate how he had felt sad and bereft when he had ended his affair. Being married was much less exciting than a new love, even though one knew that the excitement of a new love would eventually abate. One cannot really say to one's wife that one is grieving over an affair but it was true that one felt very guilty but also sad, and that these feelings were painful enough without having to deal with one's wife's anger. As much as one might feel good about trying to work things out anew, it sure looked like a lot of work at this point.

This experience of being understood by someone who has been through the same experience and who has learned something about it is of particular developmental significance in peer relationships. The consensual validation, empathy, and understanding of a peer are not readily available from a therapist. Therapists rarely share their painful experiences with patients. Thus, both Jack and Jane felt that they had allies in the group who had been through what they were going through and who would understand the help. This incident offers an example of the unique therapeutic impact of peer–peer comments. The leader's task, then, is to foster an atmosphere in which such comments are a natural part of the group—sometimes even the leader's comments are experienced as like those of a peer and not always those of the omnipotent–omniscient therapist of fantasy.

At a later meeting in the group, having recently described how he and Kama had handled his affairs of some years back, William once again dealt with the impact of affairs in a couple's life by confronting Jack. Jack had just described rather blandly how, since the ending of his affair, he had turned his attention to Jane. William said, "But having an affair is terribly exciting. You are guilty, and anxious, and thinking of it all the time. What has happened to that energy?" Jack said, that he was "putting the affair behind him, in a different compartment, and starting a new life." I commented: "Rather like having a wife in one compartment and a mistress in another." William, however, returned to his theme, saying, "How often do each of you think of the affair?" Jane said, "Often," and Jack said, "Maybe once a week." William continued: "I still think of mine often," which seemingly disturbed Kama not at all. "And I wonder what had happened to your excitement and energy," William went on. Jack said, he was "feeling more grown up." I commented that "being grown up does not mean that you should give up your zest for life and the playful child inside of you." In this meeting we see an evolution of William's interest in Jack and his understanding of what having an ending affair is like. In this first episode, he is more supportive; in the second, more confrontive. Group members seem to have great awareness of members' ability to tolerate confrontations and rarely act with other than sensitivity to what can be heard and accepted. I might add that during this meeting I almost said to the group, "I've really planted William here. He's a couples therapist incognito."

The Group as a Stage

The central work that the Goodhearts accomplished in their first year in the group involved a rebalancing of their marriage. For a number of months, Jack attempted to deal with the feelings that had led him to have an affair, and with Jane's anger, but gradually his depressive issues came to the fore, as did her needs to take care of him. Jane was the "strong" member of the couple, Jack the one with weaknesses, and this marital style was not described but rather enacted in the group. A group, as is capitalized on in psychodrama groups in particular, offers a stage for its members. They do not only describe what has happened; they enact it. In particular, this is often most evident when they are trying to help other members of the group. At these times their strengths and weaknesses often come to the fore. Jack tended to sympathize with the weak and those who hurt; Jane gave useful advice about how to solve the problems of others. It could be seen that Jack's ability to empathize and Jane's to solve problems, while a form of marital specialization that caused difficulties in their marriage, were also very useful in their lives and interaction with others, particularly at work.

How the issue of Jane's being "strong" and Jack's being weak can be dealt with in group is well illustrated by the following sequence: Jane, Lucy, and Adam were the first to arrive at a meeting, and after some general conversation about various minor matters had transpired, Jane said to Lucy, "I want to thank you for what you said at the last meeting; it really helped Jack." Lucy was somewhat baffled by the comment, and they reviewed the previous incident, which Jane felt had made it "easier for Jack to talk about his affair." After a bit, Jack arrived. When he had been caught up on the subject under discussion, I asked Jane why she had spoken for Jack. He then said, "I think I can speak for myself, I am a grown-up after all." Jane agreed, and the meeting went on to other subjects. After a while, Jack was explaining how his work was going. Adam asked him whether he found his supervisory responsibilities onerous, and Jane replied, "It's what he likes best about the job." I commented that she had done it again and speculated that she might feel that she had to "make things easier for Jack, since you worry if he is as committed to the group as you are, especially since at the last meeting he spoke about his finding it rather boring." Gradually, other members of the group began to comment on Jane and Jack's relating in this way. The impact on Jane is described by her as follows:

Stop Trying to Fix Things. After hearing Henry say this first and the others agreeing, I made an effort to let things be. When I no longer rushed in to fix situations, they just stayed the way they were. If I didn't say hello, Jack wouldn't, and there'd be no greeting. If I didn't invite him to sit with me, he'd sit in another room. If I didn't initiate, there'd be no conversation, no plans, no sex. On the first week of this plan, I thought, "What a jerk he is." Then I began to experience the relief of not carrying the "fix it" burden. I didn't withdraw, become unfriendly, or create problems. His passiveness was no longer supported or obscured and seemed to stand out more. Slowly he began to fill in the spaces a little. By the end of the third week he began to surprise me by making some suggestions for social activities, calling from the office more often, and not being depressed so often.

That reminds me of an earlier question–suggestion that was asked in the group: "Relax, let things happen. Don't think of Jack as sick, Jane the nurse." Whatever I was doing before must have been rather over-whelming, and it's clear Im not going to fix anything by force. I'm used to taking on most of the responsibilities at home so that he can just work. I've stopped doing that, and he has gradually taken on decisions concerning the appearance of the house, its maintenance, the discipline of our daughter, her appearance, major and minor purchases, his work needs at home (I no longer monitor Sarah's interruptions or noise, and he seems to manage), his health, food, and medications. It seems we both needed this change. Everything goes just as well as when I was managing it, just differently, and I don't care, since it means a lot less work for me. I like having him take on those responsibilities. They seem more appropriately allocated.

When we impatiently look for big signs of progess (everything fixed immediately), we remember the analogy of building a bridge and not putting more weight on it than it can bear. This has helped many times. It has helped us pay attention to the small, kind, fragile attempts at rebuilding the relationship. In measuring the recovery rate, I also remember your comment that "It took a long time to get to your present problems; it will take a long time to work out of them."

The Group's Provision of Multiple Perspectives

Early in the group, an example of the broadening of perspective that a couples group offers was useful to the Goodhearts. Kitty began to describe her anger at Paul because of his inability to make a decision. He seemed to dither about endlessly. The group explored the matter and learned that Kitty and Paul always strive for a decision that is right and logical. But when it comes to some decisions, Jim said, "There is no right or wrong decision," one just has to trust one's feeling. At this point, Jane said that she was just like Kitty and Paul, in wanting a "sensible decision," and experiences Jack as just like Kitty and Paul "in dithering about endlessly." Jack denied this, asserting that it just takes a little longer for him to know what he wants and that Jane is always in "such a hurry." At this point, Lucy surprised everyone by telling the group that "I made up my mind ten minutes after I met him that I was going to marry Adam" and that, in addition, they had bought their house "sight unseen from three thousand miles away." With glee she related how they had driven east with two small children, celebrating their wedding anniversary by splitting a pint of Jack Daniels in the small bathroom of a motel while the children slept. All the members of the group left feeling that there were different ways of making decisions and that there was no right or wrong way. Jack and

Jane, in particular, described that, after this, they had fought less and fought better.

One of the advantages of groups is that they can correct the leader, although, in general, they supported him in his perspective on the Goodhearts' marriage. I believe that in these days it is difficult for anyone to be sure that they are not reacting out of the perspective of their own sex and sexual stereotypes. And the fact that there are both men and women in equal numbers in couples groups and that there are people who disagree with me means everyone can find an ally and is a valuable corrective mechanism. Mel, for instance, commented that he and Mary had been in couples therapy with two separate therapists. In both these experiences he had felt very much blamed by Mary, and he and she were in a battle to have the therapist on their side, a battle that he inevitably felt he had lost. In independent conversations with the therapists, they had asserted that they had been quite aware of this problem and had endeavored to lean over to ally themselves with Mel. From Mel's point of view, however, their attempts had been unavailing, and he experienced himself as isolated and unsupported. He went on to say that in the couples group, he felt that he always had allies there, that somehow the issue of taking sides had never been a problem. In only one instance in my experience do I remember a group that turned strongly on a member. This was the husband in a couple who was both very demanding that his wife do things his way and psychopathic in his treatment of other people, using her and others solely to serve his own needs. When he finally became physically abusive, the group was united in feeling that his wife had to call the police or leave him or both.

While the Goodhearts were rebalancing their relationship, a life event occurred that fostered change in this direction, for Jane's father developed a rapidly progressing fatal illness. She found herself grief-stricken. Jack was able to be of much-appreciated support both to her and to his father-in-law, for whom he had great love. Such events as deaths and births are so common in the lives of members in couples groups that they are almost expectable. They afford an opportunity for everyone to examine their deepest feelings about life and to share these feelings with caring others. As the first year of group therapy drew to a close, the Goodhearts were more optimistic and seemed to have less painful moments and more fun.

The Group as Peer Socialization

At this point in the therapy, the Goodhearts were involved and committed members of the group. This meant several things. First, they
experienced other people of very different backgrounds as genuinely
helpful and caring. Jane described this experience as follows:

> Most often, if we entered calm, we would leave with that sense of calm
> disturbed in some essential way, whether as a result of what someone else
> had shared or by something we had decided on the spur of the moment
> to bring up for group discussion.
>   The same is true when we entered feeling distant and angry. The
> group really helped to distill from that anger important patterns and
> feelings that we would not have been able to understand on our own.
>   The group at times helped us with some very immediate, practical
> crises. What a tremendous gift! It was at those times when we could feel
> most sharply and keenly the benefits of being a part of a support group
> that is not afraid to be honest and loud and unfriendly and nonsupportive
> of our ways.

It has been of interest to me that over the years certain couples
have come to specialize in particular ways of helping other people.
Thus, during one period, Jack lost his position in a reorganization,
and another member of the group, Arthur, an older man in an executive
position in a large corporation, helped him to figure out what had
happened to him, how to cope with the experience, and how to find
another position. I remember contributing my own advice, suggesting
to Jack that he get his boss's permission to write a draft of a letter of
recommendation to be submitted to the boss. He was able to capitalize
on the advice he was being given, particularly that from Arthur, and
to reflect on his own contribution to his job difficulties. At another
time in the life of this group, a couple became specialists in helping
other couples solve their financial differences and how to organize a
budget—a specialty that arose out of their own experiences in solving
this problem.

Benefits in Extragroup Relationships

The second aspect to becoming members of a group was that there
were also opportunities for extragroup socializing. Often couples began,
as did the Goodhearts, by having supper together after the group,

which was usually the only time during the week when they were alone with each other. As another member of the group put it:

> An important part of our benefit from the group meeting derived from my wife and me having dinner together right after the group each night. This had three tangible benefits: (1) We had valuable (and otherwise seldom available) quality time together at a time when we had already "decompressed" in the group from the pressures of our normally hectic life. (2) Each of us had the chance to revisit some part of the dialogue from the group and figure out in a nondefending environment what points people in the group had been trying to make. Having my wife there allowed me to replay situations with her added insight. (3) We had time to revisit the comments highlighted by the therapist and more thoroughly absorb them.

This then evolved to sometimes joining another couple for supper. Finally, there were a number of times that the whole group got together socially. Jack wrote:

> A final impression. Many of the individuals in the group became close. Not necessarily socially, although there were the pleasant interludes of a group-wide summer afternoon party where we met the kids we'd heard about all winter, and the occasional after-session supper with one or two other couples. But the closeness developed primarily along lines of empathy—we *cared* with each other, even though we might not have chosen each other as personal friends otherwise, and we couldn't have told you the last name of a single couple in the group. In that shared empathy, I felt supported and valued as an individual, and admired as a couple with special qualities that exceed the mere sum of our two individualities.

In addition to the extragroup socializing, I make a practice of giving the members of my group the key to the office and expect that they will have meetings when I am unable to attend, except during the summer when we all take a break. I do not believe that extragroup socializing is acting out, but do believe that it should be discussed in the group. This view arises out of practical experiences, such as occurred when I was leading my first private group. I was dismayed on learning that the members of the therapy group were meeting for supper together, only to gradually change my view as I came to realize that for many of them, it was the only night during the week when they did not eat alone. As will be discussed later in this the chapter, I am convinced of the vital contributions of peer relationships to development, including adult development, particularly when early peer experiences have been wanting. For instance, many men in particular find it difficult to have close and sharing relationships with other men—they do not have a male confidant or good friend. This places added burdens on the marriage, and group therapy seems to make a unique contribution to change in this area. Such, at any rate, was the case with Jack, who reported increasingly comfortable collegial relations at work and even going to lunch with his friends—he had always dealt well with subordinates.

The Group as a Place for Changing and Learning

During the second year of the Goodhearts' stay in the couples group, several issues seemed to occupy them. The first was a continuation of work on the problem of who was the cause of the problem. In a critical session, when Jane said things were better because Jack had stopped "acting out," the group began to deal with this description. She described the meeting as follows:

> I personally had a very significant session of a couple of months ago. I spoke first and said that things have gotten a lot better lately because, in Jack's own words, he had stopped "acting out." That is, he consciously decided to try to stop being depressed or at least to stop venting and taking out his depression on me and everyone around him. However accurate or inaccurate that portrayal was, there were two problems with how it was presented. First, the group immediately took me to task for saying essentially that the "problem" was Jack and that he needed only to change to make everything okay. I protested that I don't as a rule think that, but in this specific case there was some validity to it. Second, the group pointed out that a lot was said by the fact that *I* opened the discussion and did not give Jack the chance to say that he felt better and to take credit for working so hard to improve things. It showed that despite my words, I was, in fact, taking Jack for granted and regarding him as the source of problems. What I relearned from this particular session was that often the *process* and the seemingly external small things are more important and revealing than the intellectual analysis that goes on within and outside the group. I think this realization—that the process, *how* things are said and presented, rather than solely the *content* of what is said—has been the single most important factor in the overall improvements in our relationship. Because we have both learned *how* to talk better and more effectively, we can talk more. The result is that things that once would have been big issues of discussion and argument are now settled before they get out of hand.

This part of the work dealt with Jane's perception of Jack as the problem with which she had to cope. Another aspect of the group work dealt with Jack's contribution. Jack was depressed, which made him seem weak and Jane seem strong in the marriage, but which also gave him considerable power. It was difficult to see much change in his position, but he gradually seemed to change. At a meeting early in the second year, he described that "at the last meeting Mary had said to me, 'You come across as a victim.' This really hurt but I think Mary was right. I have tried to think about how this happened, but I still don't know—maybe because I think Jane is powerful; she has become that way, and yet she often says that she wants me to share decisions more and even take the initiative."

At one meeting, Jack described an automobile ride they had taken at Jane's invitation. Jack accepted the offer, then he dithered about so that they left after a delay of about 3 hours. Once in the car, Jane, having looked forward to the date, eagerly began to talk only to realize gradually that Jack was depressed and unresponsive. She found herself wishing she had never gone for the ride and became depressed and angry herself. The group offered various thoughts on the matter that seemed to be going nowhere until Mel spoke up, forcefully telling Jack that he thought Jack was "manipulating Jane's feelings so that she was going up and down like a Yo-Yo." Mel did not exactly like the word "manipulate," but it seemed that way to him, and he wondered why Jane put up with it.

I was rather taken aback by the bluntness of Mel's comment and wondered how Jack would take it. In fact, he took it well, giving it considerable thought. I suspect if I had made the same comment, Jack would have been hurt and would have bridled at it. Comments such as this are not those of an expert, but of a peer whom one has had a chnce to see in pain and to help. In addition, group members often observe aspects of situations that I have overlooked.

The other central issue that the Goodhearts worked on in their second year of the group was their sexual relationship. They had heard other couples discuss sex but had been hesitant to bring up the fact that they almost never made love. Finally, the subject came up in a meeting with which I was quite dissatisfied. I felt that I had tried to explore all the reasons why Jack and Jane never had sex but that I had gotten nowhere. It seemed like there was an endless series of minor reasons why they could not. Sarah came into their room sometimes during the night, so they could not put a lock on their door; besides, Sarah slept in the room next to them, and making love would wake her. And though there was another room where Sarah could sleep, that could not be until they had fixed it up, and this couldn't happen because. . . . How useless can a therapist feel? For, in previous meetings, I had made various suggestions to no avail. Finally, I gave up, asking somewhat acerbically, "What are you waiting for?"

Jane later spoke about her thoughts about this meeting, saying, "It really does seem like a good idea to make love, to go out, to have talks and companionship." She felt that they had grown apart out of her anger and that if she did nothing about the situation, nothing would happen. It was not simply Jack's business at work; rather, she had to want sex, desire Jack, which increasingly seemed like a good idea, and not simply want to get pregnant again, although she did want another child. Love was more than procreation, although sometimes Jack said they had forgotten that.

The second year of the Goodheart's stay in the group ended and the third year began after what they both agreed was "the best vacation we have ever had." This year seemed characterized by three features: (*a*) a continuation of the discussion of sex; (*b*) dialogue about Jack's desire to leave Boston and take a sabbatical, and Jane's reluctance to do this; (*c*) the Goodhearts' new status as the senior couple in the group.

The Group as a Setting for Facing Ethical–Existential Issues

The first and second issues intersected in very meaningful ways, for as Jane came to agree that she could willingly leave Boston, leaving in particular a job that was very important to her, she also brought up her desire for another child. To some extent, she felt that by giving Jack what he most wanted, she was entitled to some reciprocity. Jack brought out that increasingly he felt that she was being demanding of him sexually and very dissatisfied if he was not interested. He said, "I am supposed to produce the plane tickets for our sabbatical and sperm in the same envelope." Jane said that this was only partly how she felt but that she really was interested in sex now, she desired him, had tried her best to seduce him, and that often, too often, he wasn't interested, he was too preoccupied with the departure now, as he had once been too busy studying.

The group began to explore two aspects of the situation. First, they clarified Jane's powerful belief that if Jack wasn't interested tonight, he never would be, and that she never would get pregnant, particularly since she had had a miscarriage before Sarah was born. These thoughts left her feeling hopeless and helpless, as she had when her father had died.

The group also discussed with the Goodhearts the ethical dilemma they faced. Does Jack owe Jane something for giving up things she wants and going on sabbatical with him, or does he just owe her something because they are married and should seek to give to one another? After a while, Jack said that really he did want another child also, but the feeling of being asked to produce one bothered him. It feels mechanical and unloving, and reminds him of his father, who wanted him to excel and was never quite satisfied with his grades. I was impressed once again how often the issue, projected on a partner, reflects feelings about the parent of the same sex, Jack's father, rather than the partner of the opposite sex. In addition, it is worth emphasizing how important issues of what is fair and equitable in marriages frequently arise in couples groups. A genuine dialogue on this subject between members of a couple is one of the goals toward which I strive. The ability to have such a dialogue seems to develop only after some time in treatment and is fostered by the various different solutions different couples arrive at, all with the common goal of fairness.

The discussion of such ethical–existential dilemmas, including the rehashing of previous affairs, has a unique quality in a group. Just as people get married "before God and this company," so, too, the group acts as a "company." Confessions and ethical commitments are not made only to a partner and a therapist; the former may be hurt or angry, the latter expected to forgive and foster understanding. The group, however, is the representative of humanity and will judge, expecting that some good must come out of the sharing of pain and that reparative action be taken. In this way, the group implicitly demands that people go beyond confession and understanding to deeds.

Perceptions of Outcome

In their last months in the group, the Goodhearts tended increasingly to be helpful to the other members of the group more than to bring up their own problems, except for a brief flare-up just before they left. They spoke warmly of the other members and were sad about leaving. As they departed, Jane wrote:

> Everything is not neatly tied up as we now depart for an overseas "sabbatical" full of unknowns. Many struggles and crises are ahead of us. We don't see ourselves as riding them as one would do waves. More accurately, we imagine ourselves sinking at times and being powerfully knocked about. But we do not sink deeply; we know how to emerge, and we have learned many useful skills as to how to "dry off" and continue.
>
> We have come to know ourselves better as individuals and as a couple. We have been forced to pay attention to the tender and to the ugly. In sharing our experiences with other couples. we have been opened up to the elements of our marriage that make us wonderfully unique and well suited, as well as to the elements that set us apart from others and from each other.
>
> These thoughts are incomplete. Our experience is incomplete. We have cried; we have made others cry. We have wounded, and we have been wounded by other's words. We have helped, and we have been helped. We continue to hate, to wound, to abuse, to distrust, and to be disappointed. But we have tapped an enduring kind of love and commitment that remains intact. We hope that we will continue, with our newfound skills, to pay attention and to persist. And we hope, too, that we will never allow that sometimes overattention to "how we are doing" keeps us from laughing at each other and ourselves, and enjoying even the imperfections, the raw edges, and most importantly, the process and challenge of sharing and building a mutual home.

At termination, I was impressed at the progress that the Goodhearts had made, but I cannot describe it nearly as eloquently as Jane did. They were much happier and functioned better as a couple. This seemed based on a sounder sense of who each of them was and what the other was like, without feeling that their differences were reasons for blame or shame. Loyalties to the past had been clarified and a dialogue about their ethical balance had been begun. The marital system was in better balance, and each of them had grown as an individual, becoming better able to be assertive in a competent and caring manner. Yet certain issues remained unresolved. For instance, at the beginning of the group, Jane had spoken of her need to nag Jack to fulfill his religious and community commitments, an area to which they both were deeply committed, Jane, in particular, because of her devotion to her father. At the end of the group she spoke with pride of Jack's work in that area and even wondered if he had not gone a bit too far in concerning himself with their religious community instead of having fun with her. In addition, Jane's need for immediate action and her feeling that postponement of needs was equivalent to never gratifying them remained, and Jack still had a depressive tinge that both made him responsive to the pain of other people and caused him distress at times. It is worth emphasizing that Jane's need for action had its very positive effects for the couple in that she was a mover and a shaper of events, and Jack's empathy for people's sadness and his responsiveness to them were also part of what enabled the couple to function well as an active and empathic pair. The very traits that caused the Goodhearts their difficulties, to a considerable extent, were the talents that enabled them to function well as people and as a couple.

The Members' Experience of the Leader

Clearly, I am not the same person to all my patients, and while Jane Goodheart, who had lost her father only recently, said:

> Our psychiatrist, our group facilitator, is a man we trust deeply and whose words we accept most of the time as true to our needs. His way of stepping back and giving us perspective on our relationship has been invaluable. He cares in a way that no other adult male in our lives cares, and we have treasured his caring, kind, and thoughtful manner. He has helped us to grow up and to care. His humor and sharing of his own personal experience has allowed us to relax a bit in our desperate, overly determined and conscientious efforts to get better and get closer.

Another member of the group who was finding it useful, but with whom I did not empathize so deeply or feel quite so close, stated:

> Our group leader took a very passive role in the group—seldom probing individuals and more often allowing other members of the group or (painful) silence to draw out individuals in the group. At first I found this disconcerting: I wondered why he wasn't more active in getting people to speak up. After a number of months in the group, I finally got fed up and decided I was tired of wasting my time and money and I was going to bring up a problem that was bothering me. It wasn't long after that that I realized the leader's style was aimed at having us take the responsibility for our problems. I found that I had to decide to bring up a problem

and that when I was ready, I was more likely to be at the point where I would listen to the feedback from the group.

Reflections on Technique

At this point it is appropriate that I should describe something about the way that I lead and think about psychotherapy groups. The characteristics of the leadership style are well described by Yalom (1975), who emphasizes the unusual therapeutic impact of comments by patients to each other rather than those of the leader. It also owes much to my readings in British Object Relations Theory and the influence of social workers with whom I have collaborated, particularly my wife, Judy, who have helped me to value support, caring, and playfulness by the therapist and who do not base their therapeutic approaches on the model of the cool, withholding, and relatively unresponsive therapist.

Finally, I have been involved in a series of reviews of the literature on peer relationships with a colleague that have led to an understanding of the special contributions of peers to adult human development and the unique opportunity afforded in group psychotherapy for correcting early and unfortunate peer experiences. And, indeed, while couples therapists do not as a rule inquire about their patients' history of peer relations and friendships, choosing rather to focus on early experiences in the family, it turns out that many of our patients have had very unhappy experiences with their age mates. Since a marriage is, above all else, a relationship between two peers, the ability to be a friend to one's spouse is vital.

I find the following scheme particularly useful in deciding on the focus necessary with any given couple. It is that marriage requires abilities in four areas: (*a*) coping with the world as an economic partnership; (*b*) the ability to love in an attachment, the structure of which is influenced by experiences with one's parents; (*c*) the ability to share and enjoy sexual relations; and (*d*) the ability to be a friend, which arises out of experiences with peers.

All of these theoretical perspectives converge in a leadership style that is warm, caring, and supportive. I endeavor to protect patients from attack, from revealing too much too early, and strive to maintain an atmosphere in which it is safe to show oneself and be oneself. I believe that the comments of the group members to one another are of great importance and that the statements I make are not more valuable, although I hope they are equally useful.

Couples group psychotherapy is different from other forms of group therapy in that pairs of people in enduring and emotionally central relationships are present in the group. At this point, it may be useful to the reader to delineate some of the perspectives on couples that I have found of particular value. When I came to write this chapter, I reread a chapter on couples group psychotherapy that Neiberg (1976) had written for a book (Grunebaum & Christ, 1976) I edited several years earlier. On rereading it, I was impressed by how many of the basic ideas I have delineated here are described there. In particular, he emphasizes those moments when one member of a couple reenacts and thus experiences his or her characteristic difficulties with a member of another couple, what Kantor (1983) has so aptly described as the "ritual impasse."

Early in my work with couples, I was much influenced by the writing of Dicks (1967) and continue to find the concept of projective identification valuable. The work of Boszormenyi-Nagy and Spark (1973) on the importance of intergenerational loyalty, and of the central human need to be treated justly and fairly (Boszormenyi-Nagy & Krasner, 1980), speaks to me personally and with equal force to the members of the group who seem to resonate to this point of view intuitively. A concern with fairness in interpersonal relationships is central to how most people live (Grunebaum & Grunebaum, 1980). Finally, the impact of experience in sex therapy, an interest in behavioral therapy, and extensive work with families has made me realize the importance of learning not only what people think and feel but also how they act, including their behavior in the group. While these three sources are perhaps central to my thinking about couples, I find that I have left out entirely the influence of psychoanalysis, which was the core of my training as a psychiatric resident and thus seems to me as ground rather than figure. It is what I always knew as a therapist, rather than what I have discovered and learned since then.

All of this leads to a style that is rather open. I tell the group what I think is going on with them as individuals and couples. I focus on relationships between members of different couples, but I rarely make whole-group comments. Bionesque comments tend to disorganize the group, and I am relieved that some colleagues (e.g., Malan, Balfour, Hood, & Shooter, 1976) have found that such Tavistock groups are experienced by patients as painful and unhelpful. I frequently suggest tasks or new options and inquire if they have been carried out. Sometimes these tasks are perverse and paradoxical, and the members tend to look on them with perplexity and humor and are likely to try them as an "experiment" rather than feel bound to do it. Finally, at times I discuss some of my own experiences in life.

What is the best name for this brand of couples therapy? Chasin and I (Grunebaum & Chasin, 1982) have dealt with this problem in a recent paper that presented a classification system of theories of family therapy. We suggest that information about couples or families can be seen from three different perspectives (historical, interactional, and existential) and that treatment proceeds from three approaches (understanding, transformation, and identification). Using this scheme, we demonstrate that different theories extract from experience different features for diagnostic emphasis and therapeutic intervention. It turns out that whatever approach a therapist employs, it can and must have effects in terms of all three. For instance, assigning a task may change behavior but also fosters identification with a taskmaster and teaches that actions are more important than thoughts. In the immediately preceding section, I indicated the importance in my work of projective identification, which arises out of historical forces and can be interpreted; of actual behavior, which must be observed and new actions fostered; and of existential–ethical concerns, which may be altered by new identification with the leader and group members. Thus, all three perspectives and approaches are important as ways of describing events. This should come as no surprise, since our thinking fractures experience, for thought is, perforce, linear and logical, while life and group leadership are interactive, dialectic, and unitary. Thus, I have no name for this kind of couples group psychotherapy.

However, I almost called this chapter "The Patchwork Quilting Bee." *Patchwork* is defined as a "collection of miscellaneous and incongruous parts," which, in *quilting*, are sewn into a useful and coherent whole that keeps one warm. A *bee* is defined as a "gathering of neighbors for work, competition, and amusement." This, it seems to me, is precisely what happens in a group.

Acknowledgment

I would like to acknowledge the contributions of the members of this couples group to this chapter.

References

Boszormenyi-Nagy, I., & Krasner, B. (1980). Trust-based therapy: A contextual approach. *American Journal of Psychiatry, 137,* 767–775.

Boszormenyi-Nagy, I., & Spark, G. M. (1973). *Invisible loyalties.* New York: Harper & Row.

Dicks, H. V. (1967). *Marital tensions.* New York: Basic Books.

Grunebaum, H. (1983a). A study of therapists' choice of a therapist. *American Journal of Psychiatry. 140:* 10; 1336–1339.

Grunebaum, H. (1983b). *Harmful psychotherapy.* Unpublished manuscript.

Grunebaum, H. (1984). Comments on "Schizophrenia and the family: Adverse effects of family therapy." *Family Process. 23:* 421–428.

Grunebaum, H., & Chasin, R. (1982, October). Thinking like a family therapist. *Journal of Marital and Family Therapy, 8,* 403–416.

Grunebaum, H., Christ, J., & Neiberg, N. (1976). Diagnosis and treatment planning for couples. In H. Grunebaum & J. Christ (Eds.), *Contemporary marriage: Structure, dynamics, and therapy.* Boston: Little, Brown.

Grunebaum, J., & Grunebaum, H. (1980, July). Beyond the superego. *American Journal of Psychiatry, 137,* 817–818.

Gurman, A. S. (1977). The patient's perception of the therapeutic relationship. In A. S. Gurman & A. M. Razin (Eds.), *Effective psychotherapy: A handbook of research.* New York: Pergamon.

Kantor, D. (1983). The structural-analytic approach to the treatment of family developmental crisis. In H. A. Liddle (Ed.), *Clinical implications of the family life cycle.* Rockville, MD: Aspen Systems.

Malan, D. H., Balfour, P. H. G., Hood, V. G., & Shooter, A. M. N. (1976). Group psychotherapy: A long-term follow-up study. *Archives of General Psychiatry, 33,* 1313–1315.

McLean, C., & Grunebaum, H. (1982). *Parents' response to chronically psychotic children.* Paper presented at the American Psychiatric Association annual meeting, Toronto.

Neiberg, N. (1976). The group psychotherapy of married couples. In H. Grunebaum & J. Christ (Eds.), *Contemporary marriage: Structure, dynamics, and therapy.* Boston: Little, Brown.

Terkelsen, K. (1983, June). Schizophrenia and the family: Adverse effects of family therapy. *Family Process, 22,* 191–200.

Yalom, I. D. (1975). *The theory and practice of group psychotherapy* (2d ed.). New York: Basic Books.

Chapter 4
A Part Is Not Apart: Working with Only One of the Partners Present

Steve de Shazer
Insoo Berg

When we were asked to contribute a chapter on marital therapy, we wondered at the distinction implied in the label. Is marital therapy somehow different from family therapy? If so, what is the difference? And if there is a difference, does this difference make a difference?

Since our practice and the practice of the Brief Family Therapy Center (BFTC) involve seeing individuals (people who live alone, half a marital pair, or one member of a larger family group), couples (married and unmarried, heterosexual and homosexual pairs), and family groups (two or more people, representing at least two generations or parents without the troublesome child), we found that the distinction between marital therapy and family therapy does not apply. A problem is a problem; the number of people (and their relationship to one other) whom the therapist sees to help solve the problem does not seem a useful distinction. This, of course, presupposes a strong belief in the systemic concept of wholism: If you change one element in a system, or the relationship between that element and another element, the system as a whole will be affected. At BFTC we tend to categorize cases according to the pattern of interaction between therapist and client. We had to give further consideration to whether, from our point of view, marital therapy could be distinguished.

Haley (1963) discusses the voluntary–involuntary nature of marriage, but this is no different from the voluntary–involuntary nature of family. In fact, the spouses are freer to go than either the parent or the minor child, so marriage might even be seen as more voluntary. The only criterion that seems to make a potential difference is that in "marital therapy" the relationship treated is that between two people of the same generation, whereas in family therapy the relationship of concern is often or usually between people of different generations. But does this affect the nature of the problems encountered or the nature of the solutions or the patterns of intervention–response?

A quick check of case records accumulated over the years at BFTC and some research we have been doing indicated that the nature of problems, the nature of solutions, and the patterns of intervention–response do not differ along the lines implied by this distinction. In fact, the process of therapy seems relatively constant across situations. The kinds of intervention messages used appear over and over, and the patterns of response appear over and over. *Marital therapy*, *individual therapy*, and *family therapy* do not seem to be separate classes of brief therapy.

In our view, the therapist needs to set the stage for the "cooperating" of client and therapist. The therapist needs to assume that the client is also interested in cooperating and, consequently, to build the therapeutic stance on the assumption that changing is inevitable, rather than difficult, as many models built on the concept of resistance assume. Of course, the particular way of cooperating can differ from session to session with the same client (de Shazer, 1982).

Brief therapists, as a group, tend to hold some rather simple, perhaps even simpleminded, notions about therapy. They tend to think that a problem should be approached in the most simple manner first. If that does not work, they collect some more information and then try the next most simple solution, as long as it is different from the first one. Simply stated, the rule is: If all you need is a screwdriver, do not use dynamite. Milton Erickson put it this way:

> What you—as a therapist—need to do is to try to do something that promotes a change in the patient—any little change. Because the patient wants a change, however small. And he will accept that as a change, and the change will develop in accordance with his own needs. It's much like rolling a snowball down a mountain side. It starts out a small snowball, but as it rolls down it gets larger and larger . . . and it starts an avalanche that fits the shape of the mountain. (Gordan & Meyers-Anderson, 1981, pp. 16–17)

Another simpleminded notion brief therapists tend to share is that therapy must be goal directed and that the more concrete and specific the goal is, the better (de Shazer, 1982; Weakland, Fisch, Watzlawick, & Bodin, 1974; Watzlawick, Weakland, & Fisch, 1974). Thus, both client and therapist can know when the problem is solved and the client has gotten his money's worth, and, therefore, therapy can stop.

Session 1

Mrs. Johns, in tears, called for an appointment on an "emergency" basis. She was feeling desperate and in a panic about her marriage. Our schedule premitted us to see her the same morning. Her problem, as she stated it, was that her husband frequently went out at night without her, stayed out as late as 4:30 a.m., or did not come home at all. This would happen particularly on his days off from his second-shift job as a detective on a small-town police force. He told her he was going out with his single friends, and she believed him. Up to this point, she had not suspected him of seeing other women, but she resented this behavior because it resulted in her being left alone. Whenever she expressed her resentment, her husband comforted her about their relationship and assured her that there was no problem. Consequently, she continued to accept his going out, and even kissed him and wished him a "good time" because she felt he would go out anyway, no matter what she said or did.

Meanwhile, she repeatedly stayed at home and suffered stomach pains, diarrhea, depression, crying bouts, headaches, and recently thoughts of suicide, which she rejected because of their two children, who were 4 and 6 years old. Her priorities were clear, however: She wanted this particular marriage and was willing to do almost anything to make it work.

Her own words best describe what finally brought her to therapy:

> What brought me to the climax in this last week? Well, I mentioned to you how I've noticed makeup on his clothes sometimes? On Tuesday, he came home and his shirt was washed in this area [around the neck and shoulder]. I confronted him about his. Well, that night he was at a party, and, he said, someone dropped chicken on his shirt. So, he washed it off.

Well, I'm assuming—I'm figuring this out—that there was makeup on his clothes and he decided to wash it off.

She was asked what she would do if she caught him having an affair. "Would you think about murdering him, or her, or both of them, or would you think about suicide?" She rejected all these expressions of anger and said that she hoped in that situation that they could talk things out and go on with the marriage. She was not angry at her husband, or even hurt, but she did feel deprived and felt he treated her unfairly. She was a good wife trying to be the ideal wife; in turn, he was not being the good husband, as she defined it, and he was not trying to match her ideal.

Mr. Johns had been out again the night before this session and she had not yet seen him that day.

THERAPIST: So, when he comes home today, what are you going to do?
MRS. JOHNS: That's it, I don't know what to do anymore. We've discussed it! We've argued! I have been standoffish, you know, very silent. I've tried that approach. And nothing works! I have noticed, nothing really works.

She had tried talking to him about it; she had tried passively accepting it; then she had talked to him some more. He was a man of few words, so he just sat there listening. Since nagging and suffering had not worked to keep him home, she now wanted to know what to do to change things. She wanted him to go out less often without her and more often with her. She clearly saw that any changes to be made were hers, since he thought everything was O.K. If she could not stop his going out, then she wanted to be able to accept his going out without becoming emotionally upset.

Consulting Break

Mrs. Johns seemed to be a likable, hardworking, dedicated young woman. In fact, if anything, she seemed too nice. As far as we could see, she would continue to be a doormat, despite her mild protests now and again. She saw that role as part of her job as "wife" and as part of the price she had to pay for this marriage. Although one might see Mr. Johns as the one "misbehaving," she blamed herself, at least to the extent that she could not find a way to make him behave. She also felt more hurt than angered by his misbehavior. Clearly, a classic example of the pursuit–withdrawal/withdrawal–pursuit situation. The more she let him know she did not want him going out, the more he went out.

Mr. Johns was a detective, and detectives love mysteries. This fact prompted the whole design of our intervention plan. Of course, it is common folklore that marriages need some mystery, but Mrs. Johns described herself as an open book. Therefore, we saw her detective husband as being out of a job. It was our idea that if Mrs. Johns could create a mystery, this would initiate some change in the pursuit–withdrawal pattern.

Although the structure of the intervention was clear to both of us before the start of the consultation, the question of how to implement it remained. The most encouraging aspect of her presentation was her repeated attempts to modify her behavior in hopes of modifying his behavior; this told us she would try more new behaviors. Primarily she wanted him not to go out alone, but she also indicated that she would be willing to accept his going out if she could handle this without the emotional cost she was now paying. Therefore we thought we would suggest new behaviors to her that were neither punitive nor pursuit behaviors but were just mysterious.

Intervention Message

THERAPIST: We are quite struck by your fairness and your patience and your having tried everything you can think of to try to solve this problem. But we think you haven't gone far enough.

What we would like you to do is—we don't want you to do anything about it yet—just give some thought to it and make a very careful plan of how you are going to carry this out. So, just keep it to yourself and don't talk to your husband about this. I assume he doesn't know you are here today?

MRS. JOHNS: No, he doesn't. He knew I was going to go for help, but he isn't sure when or whatever.

THERAPIST: We want you to keep it a secret.

MRS. JOHNS: O.K.

THERAPIST: The whole idea is to make it as mysterious as possible to him. Some of the ideas we have are these: Make an arrangement for your family or mother or friend to call the house periodically, and if your husband answers, have the caller hang up. When you are both home and he's likely to answer the phone. You might need a secret code or something.

MRS. JOHNS: Ah, O.K.

THERAPIST: Do you have someone who could do that for you?

MRS. JOHNS: Ah, I'll think about that.

THERAPIST: Well, that's just an idea. Another possibility is for you to send yourself flowers, with no note—

MRS. JOHNS: I know what you're getting at, that there's someone else in my life.

THERAPIST: But you're not going to make it very obvious. Just drop a hint. Don't make it too obvious. That's what we mean by careful planning. It has to be done over a long period. You can't do this all in a week or two. You have to be very subtle. After all, he's a detective. He knows how to put pieces, clues, together. So you have to outdo him on that. You can't give him too many clues at the same time. You have to drop hints one at a time, spaced out.

Another possibility is, when you know he's leaving that night and going to go out alone, you get all dressed up and go out before he leaves the house, not saying to him where you are going. Don't say anything about it. Not a word. Just make it as normal as possible.

MRS. JOHNS: And if he confronts me?

THERAPIST: Be as evasive as possible, very reluctant to give him any information about what he wants to know. Another possibility is for you not to be there when he comes home at four thirty in the morning.

MRS. JOHNS: That's a good one.

THERAPIST: Maybe have someone come and stay with the kids, or maybe you and the kids stay at your friends overnight after he leaves the house. So that when he walks into the house, you're not there. No note, nothing.

Another possibility is for you to collect some matches and napkins from bars, different bars. Just leave them around the house and let him find them by accident. The farther away the better—places he'd not expect you to go.

Generally, when you go out with him, act very preoccupied, as though your mind is elsewhere, and you're thinking about something else. When he asks what you are thinking, say "Oh, I'm sorry," and pretend everything is O.K. You can do that around the house, too. Act like you're thinking of something—a sly smile now and then.

You can't do these all at once. Otherwise it will be too obvious to him. You have to be sort of sneaky and calculated—subtle hints, one at a time.

We want you just to think about these ideas. You may not be ready to implement any of them, yet, but you ought to have carefully laid out plans that you're going to start with this, then add this, then that, slowly increasing the mysteries about you so that he can't put a finger on it. After all, policeman like mysteries. They get very curious and go after it more when they find there is something not quite fitting.

MRS. JOHNS: Those are good suggestions, sort of the opposite of what I've been doing.

The next session was set for 1 week later.

Session 2

MRS. JOHNS: I'm much better this week. Things have worked out well this week.

THERAPIST: How? What did you do right?

MRS. JOHNS: First of all, I suppose, in a sense, I've reached my goal. My husband did not go out this week!

THERAPIST: What!

MRS. JOHNS: Would you believe it! Two years this has been going on.

THERAPIST: How come?

MRS. JOHNS: I'll tell you what I did. I went home after last time, and it was really an emotional help talking. Although I was still upset, I was quiet. And the next day I was quiet, but it seemed as if the quiet—

THERAPIST: What do you mean, "quiet"?

MRS. JOHNS: I was—I'm kind of an open person and always talking. So when he came home, I had nothing to say. I was just aloof, not offering much information, although when he talked—

THERAPIST: You weren't crying or anything like that?

MRS. JOHNS: No, although that evening I did just go off by myself and I cried quite a bit when I was upstairs. And then I came downstairs—

THERAPIST: He didn't know you were crying?

MRS. JOHNS: No! I came downstairs and he said, "Oh, you've been sewing upstairs," and I thought, "We're really on different wave-lengths." He was so insensitive, especially at that time when he knew things were tense. The next day it continued. It seemed he was thinking I was angry. He was starting to get a little bit angry, following what I was doing.

THERAPIST: Being aloof?

MRS. JOHNS: Being aloof. All day I was kind of waiting. How was I going to handle this if he was going to go out? And that caused a lot of anxiety for me, even though I realized it was nice that I was able to have some control instead of just sitting back and waiting and being scared.

THERAPIST: Right.

MRS. JOHNS: This time I could sit back and say, "O.K., now if you're going out, I have my plan."

THERAPIST: You were not as upset, even though anxious.

MRS. JOHNS: I handled it much better. That was a real help.

THERAPIST: So, he didn't go out?

MRS. JOHNS: No! And that was a surprise. He could have. Monday, I decided that I was going to venture out. That was harder for me than I thought it would be. There was a lot of anxiety and thinking and planning. I left about a quarter to nine, and when I came up to him and I said, "I made plans for this evening," he was real surprised, but he just said, "fine." And I went out, and I came home about a quarter to one. That was very good, and he was real quiet. So all Tuesday, we didn't talk at all. He was kind of angry.

THERAPIST: He wasn't asking—

MRS. JOHNS: No! He didn't ask me. And that basically took care of it. Tuesday night . . . things got better. By Wednesday, we were starting to communicate. Now, my thought was, "should I go out again?" I did not.

This sense of control, the idea of having a plan, prevented her from getting as upset as previously with just the idea of his going out. Although her behavior might not have stopped him from going out, it did have that effect that week. Therefore, she had at least the illusion of controlling his behavior by having more control of hers. This successful change is enough to breed further confidence and further changes.

Fortunately, she realized that she would be unable to stop him from ever going out and that she would be quite satisfied if he just went out less often and she handled it better. She agreed that he was the kind of guy who was going to go out, and she was the kind of sensitive person who was going to react to his going out, sometimes more than other times. When he went out, however, no matter how upset she might be, she would now know that she had a plan. A relapse, then, might be defined as her just feeling bad when he went out without her having that sense of control over her part in the pattern.

Intervention Message

THERAPIST: We are very pleased with what you have done, particularly Monday night. That certainly turned things around: the beginning of turning things around—obviously, it's not all solved yet. One step at a time. And we are also glad that you have saved some of the other possibilities we've talked about for later so that you'll have them ready. If you need them, you can pull them out.

MRS. JOHNS: That's a good point.

THERAPIST: Now, we're thinking that it's not that he has taken you for granted so much, but it's more that he has kept you very, very interested in him.

MRS. JOHNS: True.

THERAPIST: You see, every move he makes, you're very interested in. All your energy goes into figuring him out.

MRS. JOHNS: That's a good point.

THERAPIST: We're also thinking that when it comes to mystery, he's a professional and you're an amateur. That's his job, to solve mysteries, so you have a lot to catch up with him on that score. He has much more advanced skills in keeping things mysterious and keeping you interested in him. Therefore, we think you have to catch up with him to make the marriage very interesting and mysterious. Perhaps you could think about some ways of getting him as interested in you as you have been interested in him. That will be the turning point, and we think marriages should have some mystery. Not everything should be open about everything when two people live together. If you can look back to when you were dating, part of the attraction is this unknown, the mystery about this person.

So, some of the suggestions we have are like, perhaps, you could insist that he go out one night, on his night off. And insist that he doesn't come home before one or two o'clock. He must stay out at least until one o'clock. He will not know what you are up to. That's something he's going to do anyway. We've talked about this. It's unrealistic to expect him not to go out at all. You might create the opposite reaction. You don't want it to backfire in your face by not having him go out at all because it doesn't sound like he's that kind of guy. He may feel cooped up, and that's not what you want either. So, when you decide what is a good night for you, insist that he go out on that night. You tell him in the morning. And don't tell him what you're doing when he's out. Be as mysterious as possible.

MRS. JOHNS: Should I leave that night, do you think?

THERAPIST: You can leave or not leave. Insisting he goes out will be such a shock to him.

MRS. JOHNS: That's excellent. That's even shocking me!

THERAPIST: The other things we've suggested, you may want to save yet for a while. If you need to, you can bring them out periodically, one at a time. As we said, the clues have to come one at a time. Too many at the same time will be too obvious.

What do you think, should we get together in one week or two, depending on how much control you have?

MRS. JOHNS: I don't think in a week it will be really necessary.

The next appointment was set for 2 weeks later.

Session 3

Mr. Johns had not gone out once during the 2 weeks, and Mrs. Johns felt much better. She knew they were playing a game, but she felt in control of the game. She was continuing to be aloof, was asking him fewer questions, and, most important, was not volunteering information. During this 2-week period, she discovered that she and her husband were really angry at each other.

She saw a different kind of tension developing around the house. In the past, the tensions had all been hers; now the tension was between them. She saw this as an improvement, even though she did not like the periodic arguments. Before, she had been nice on the outside but had felt that she was being torn apart inside. Now she was letting her anger out. This, she thought, confused him. When he did something she did not like, she let him know about it.

Things were going so well that a relapse of some sort could be expected and could, in fact, be predicted, particularly since Mrs. Johns had decided not to insist that he go out one night because things were going so well. It worried us that she might be overly confident that she had done enough to solve the problem.

Intervention Message

> We are impressed that the verbal communication between you and your husband is getting better and better—even though right now there are more arguments. But these arguments are a necessary step in making the marriage better. What you two are going through now might be called "creative confusion," a result of mysterious tension that leads to growth and change. Now, you need to prevent either an escalation of the arguments into fights or a return of the old pattern. As you know, he responds very well, and therefore you need to further the creative confusion by reacting to anything good or desirable he does with something equally good or desirable—when he least expects it, hours or days later.
>
> Once the creative confusion is over, then you can be the you you want to be—but not until he's confused to the point of cooperating with you the way you want things to be.

The next session was scheduled in 2 weeks.

Session 4

When Mrs. Johns returned from a camping trip with her daughter, Mr. Johns bought flowers for each of them, which was completely new behavior for him. However, the tensions between them continued for several more days until he asked her what the problem was. She told him, but he said that he had not known she was upset about his going out alone. They talked for more than 2 hours.

As a result, he promised to give her enough warning about his going out so that she did not have to *see* him getting ready and leaving. He did not keep this promise, however, which really upset her. Rather than do something different, she reverted to the old pattern of suffering.

Consulting Break

We were concerned that Mrs. Johns might give up because of this "relapse," particularly since she continued to believe that "talking to him" would work magic, but it had not. Therefore, we split between continuing the same intervention plan, which had been working, and suggesting that she continue with the same old pattern, which is exactly what she was doing. Essentially, we believe the choice of changing or not changing lies with the client, and that if Mrs. Johns chose not to change in the ways we suggested because it involved her "being mean," and she did not want to be mean, then we needed to change our approach to fit better with her way of wanting to do things.

Intervention Message

THERAPIST: Half the team thinks you're not mad enough—too nice to do things that will put you in charge of your situation. They have some doubts about whether you'll ever be mad enough, which will mean that you're going to just go on suffering and hurting and crying and so on.

The other half of the team thinks that if you get yourself mad enough at the situation, there are a couple of things you can do, instead of just expecting him to come around on his own. You have to do something, like going out on your own, like making it a mystery to him.

Since talking makes him think everything is fine, if he talks to you for two hours, then he thinks everything is smoothed over and good for two years or so. So he can do anything he wants to do after he lets you talk. Then everything is fine. He can go out like before. Obviously, talking to him is not going to do anything. You get his attention by doing something. Your being nice to him certainly doesn't—

MRS. JOHNS: —help it.

THERAPIST: He listens when you act, not when you talk. You asked about whether you should go out or not go out, when he does, or the night after, or whatever. Our suggestion is: The only way to decide is, if you are sure you *shouldn't* do it, then you shouldn't do it. But if you're not sure you shouldn't do it, then you should do it [phone call from behind the mirror]. I agree, you're such a nice person that most of the time, you'll decide you shouldn't do it.

MRS. JOHNS: All this is so foreign to me. My philosophy always has been "be nice" and "don't make a lot of waves."

THERAPIST: What you'd consider "mean," most people would not consider all that mean.

MRS. JOHNS: That's a good point.

The next session was set for 3 weeks later.

Session 5

Most of the interval went much better. The whole family went on a camping trip, and they went out together a couple of times. In the 3-week period Mr. Johns had gone out only once, in the first week, but it was too late for Mrs. Johns to get a sitter. She noticed the old symptoms starting to come back when she went to bed, so she set up a bed in the spare room. Not only did this eliminate the symptoms, but she slept soundly. Neither of them said anything about this.

Mrs. Johns was becoming more aware of her anger toward her husband. She thought that if things did not change, in a couple of years she would go after a divorce. But even if things did change, she would still have the resentment. Therefore, she started to make some plans for a career.

Consulting Break

We were pleased that things were once again on the track. She had figured out what to do when our suggestions were impossible to implement, and it had worked. This was a good indication that she was beginning to step outside the original frame of her situation. If she had not stepped outside, she would have continued to suffer in the same old way. He was going out less, and she was doing something different, and therefore, she was feeling and thinking differently.

Intervention Message

As part of the message, we suggested the following to Mrs. Johns:

> We think Hank [Mr. Johns] likes what you are doing about his going out and the changes you are making. He may be going out to force you to make the changes *he wants*. He may continue to go out until you've changed enough.

The rest of the message was much the same as before, complimenting her on the changes she made and the new behaviors she had developed and repeating more or less the same suggestions.

Since she asked, we also told her that we thought she would not think about getting sick again because she knew what to do.

The final session was set for 5 weeks later.

Session 6—Final Session

Mrs. Johns reported that everything was just fine. She had used our ideas and, as she said, they worked. In the first week after the previous session, Mr. Johns had gone out, and she had known about it far enough in advance to make plans. She hired a babysitter, went shopping, and rented a motel room. When she returned home at 5:00 a.m., he was there. He had returned at 2:00. He never asked her where she had been or what she had done, and she had not volunteered the information, even though she saw that he was quietly angry. He did not go out again, however.

Four weeks later, he asked her permission to go out. She answered, "You have to do what you feel you want to do." (He had never before asked.) He decided to go out, and he invited her to spend the evening with his friend's girlfriend. She said, "I decided that wouldn't work because then he'd know exactly where I was and what I was doing, so I said, 'No, I've already made plans to go out.'" Several hours later, he said, "Let's both cancel our plans and spend the evening together." This is what they did.

The change in his behavior is exactly what she wanted to have happen, and therefore the goal of therapy was met. She was pleased and optimistic about the future, and she felt that she knew what she needed to do if the problem ever came up again. Of course, we worried about her deciding to go back to feeling bad, or being too nice, but we also expressed our confidence in her ability to keep control. She was invited to return if things ever went out of control again.

Conclusion

The case we have just examined followed the somewhat typical pattern of early change, "relapse," and then a continuation and solidification of the early changes. Not only did Mrs. Johns continue the changes in her actions and reactions (begun between the first and second sessions) during the 8-week period between Session 4 and the last session, but these changes (following the systemic concept of wholism) led to some changes in Mr. Johns's behavior. First, she invented something to do on her own when our suggestions were impractical (rather than the old suffering pattern) by moving to the spare bedroom (a change in the context and the context marker), and she did not force him to listen to her talk about it. Second, when he did give her enough advance warning before going out, she made plans and carried through with them. Again, she continued not to talk about this. Third, when he asked permission to go out (a new behavior on his part), she did not say yes or no, but left it up to him. When he made plans *for* her, she refused; consequently, he changed his plans and invited her to go out with him. During and after the final session, we were convinced that the pattern had changed and that she would not revert to suffering silently if he were ever to go out alone again when it was not O.K. with her. She was no longer framing her situation as one in which she was helpless and had no choice but to suffer. Instead, she now framed the situation as one in which she had the ability to do something to make things better for herself.

Mr. Johns seemed to respond in a more positive and desirable fashion to Mrs. Johns's more confident, independent behavior.

Acknowledgments

With special thanks to the rest of the Brief Family Therapy Center team: Eve Lipchik, Alex Molnar, Elam Nunnally, and Marilyn La Court (formerly a member of the team).

References

de Shazer, S. (1982). *Patterns of brief family therapy*. New York: Guilford Press.
Gordan, D., & Meyers-Anderson, M. (1981). *Phoenix: Therapeutic patterns of Milton H. Erickson*. Cupertino, CA: Meta Publications.
Haley, J. (1963). *Strategies of psychotherapy*. New York: Grune & Stratton.
Watzlawick, P., Weakland, J., & Fisch, R. (1974). *Change*. New York: Norton.
Weakland, J., Fisch, R., Watzlawick, P., & Bodin, A. (1974). Brief therapy: Focused problem resolution. *Family Process, 13*, 141–168.

Chapter 5

Obstacles to Differentiation
of Self

Michael E. Kerr, MD

The development of a coherent systems theory about the human family was a major scientific step. An appreciation of what makes family systems theory such an important development is necessary for adequately understanding this new theory. Many mental health professionals who become interested in the family grasp a few points of family theory that distinguish it from other theories of human emotional functioning but fail to comprehend what this new theory represents in terms of progress toward a better understanding of the activity and behavior of all livings things. This broader relevance of systems theory results from the fact that *Homo sapiens* is a product of the same natural forces and laws that govern the evolution of all life on the planet. Now that a systems theory has significantly enhanced our understanding of one product of evolution, *Homo sapiens*, it seems likely that similar theories can be developed about the other products of evolution, namely, plants and nonhuman animals.

Such systems theories do not at present exist in the life sciences, and many biologists are rightfully skeptical of attempts to use systems thinking to explain a wide range of natural phenomena. These biologists view such attempts as simply drawing analogies between the living and nonliving world. While certain aspects of what occurs in families are indeed analogous to many physical systems, the biologists are certainly correct that analogy is an inadequate base on which to develop a theory. Bowen's theory of *family emotional systems*, however, did not

111

result from any transfer of concepts from the physical sciences or from *general systems theory* to the human family (Bowen, 1966). It is not based on analogy. The concepts of family systems theory were generated by extensive clinical study of the family. Each concept is an abstraction that is firmly rooted in clinical observations. Most of what composes family theory does not even exist in general systems theory.

The assertion that family systems theory is well supported by clinical observations is often challenged. Few people are convinced that sufficient data exist to prove this new theory. This is a challenge similar to that faced by Copernicus in 1543 when he published his proposition that the sun, not the earth, was at the center of the universe. It is important to remember that, for the most part, Copernicus saw the same movements in the night sky that everyone else saw. His remarkable achievement was the ability to think about these observations in a radically new way. His detractors wanted more proof for the validity of this new way of thinking, but it took nearly a hundred years to assemble "enough proof" to preclude retention of the pre-Copernican world view. A new way of thinking about old facts is rarely provable to a majority, especially in the beginning. Family systems theory is currently in a position similar to that of the Copernicus model in the mid-1500s.

Systems theory also largely originated from an ability to think about old facts in a new way. Mental health professionals had been making observations about families for years, but it was not until the 1950s that anyone could integrate the observations into the bold new conceptualization of the *family as an emotional unit*. It is likely that several generations will pass before this new way of thinking is regarded as an accepted theory.

Despite family theory being an important new way of thinking about living systems, the family movement in mental health tends to be viewed by people within and outside the profession as mostly promulgating a new treatment method called *family therapy*. This chapter, focusing on a clinical case presentation, could foster this skewed emphasis on family as a method of therapy. When people watch therapy sessions or read transcripts of them, the importance of theory can easily be overlooked in pursuit of trying to learn how therapy is done. The observer who bypasses theory is assuming that therapy is a product of what the therapist says and does in a session. This is a prevalent assumption, which is perhaps rooted in the strong tendency in all of us to believe that the way we *think* about ourselves and others is not a major source of human problems. On the contrary, we assume that problems usually stem from not being able to figure out *what to do, what to say, or how to act* in a given situation.

A corollary to this belief is that human problems will ameliorate if we or those close to us can be taught new ways to respond. Examples of this pervade therapy sessions. Mrs. Smith says, "My husband either needs to learn to be more responsive to me and my needs or I guess I will have to learn not to care what he does." She considers neither option particularly attractive. Past experience has shown her that attempts to change her husband inevitably end in frustration, but thoughts of giving up on his ever being different portend loneliness and a dull marriage. She has long assumed that if she works hard enough, her husband will eventually change and the marriage will improve. The passing years, however, have witnessed a growing anger in her about Mr. Smith's continued "nonresponsiveness." *There is no resolution of this dilemma within the constraints of Mrs. Smith's present thinking about the nature of the problem.* This irresolvability is a function of each spouse's subjectively based attitudes concerning what the relationship "needs" and what "should" happen. This subjectivity is reinforced by emotional reactivity and, in turn, is used to justify that reactivity. Mr. Smith says, "I would not be so critical of you if you did not place such unrealistic demands on me." He justifies his feeling reaction, in other words, on the basis of his attitude that his wife *should* be different. A therapist might tell Mrs. Smith that if she could set her fears of isolation "aside" and not pursue her husband so intensely, he would eventually be more available to her. Mrs. Smith does back off, and indeed the relationship "changes." She has implemented a technique. Mrs. Smith has likely tried doing this in the past, but the support and encouragement of the therapist probably helped her control her feelings better this time and sustain her efforts. *What has not changed is Mrs. Smith's basic thinking about herself, the marriage, and the nature of the human process in general.* She is no more emotionally detached or objective than she ever was. Emotional detachment depends on a change in the way people think about relationships and the sources of human problems. The implementation of techniques and observation of their effects can be a stimulus to thinking, but that is not necessarily the case. In this instance, while Mrs. Smith can cope with her marriage more effectively, she still harbors deep resentment about what she views as her husband's "nongiving" nature. This resentment and other unresolved feelings are fostered by the subjectivity that still heavily clouds the situation.

Mental health professionals seeking to learn "how to do" family therapy have Mr. and Mrs. Smith's problem. The extent to which a trainee assumes he can be taught "what to do" determines his proneness to learning family therapy as a set of techniques. When a trainee approaches it with this kind of attitude, his basic thinking about the nature of the human process will not be seriously challenged. He will view emotional detachment and control of emotional reactiveness as no more than techniques. The point is that emotional detachment is not a technique. Detachment is intricately tied to theoretical understanding. Achieving more detachment depends on changes in the way people *account* for what they observe. We are all heavily embedded in subjectively determined ways of accounting for the nature of the human process. We have numerous ways of explaining *why* people do the things they do, almost all of which are born of a hopelessly narrow perspective. New theory is an effort to broaden that perspective, if only by a fraction of an inch.

Knowledge of natural systems, the earth, the solar system, and the entire cosmos now increases exponentially each year. Our understanding of human nature must continually be adapted to these new scientific facts. The advent of systems thinking in reference to the human process has provided an incredibly significant key to integrating this new knowledge and placing humankind firmly in the context of all life. The roots of Mr. and Mrs. Smith's problems, in other words, can be seen to extend back over 3 billion years.

Theoretical Principles

Family systems theory posits that two basic variables, *differentiation of self* and *chronic anxiety*, significantly influence the origin and course of all clinical problems. The recognition that fluctuation in the level of these two variables can alter the thinking, feelings, and behavior of family members is what guides the conduct of family therapy. If the therapist is aware of the fact that these two underlying variables are regulating the details of the thinking, feelings, and behavior in the family, then the therapist is seeing *process*. If the therapist loses sight of these underlying variables and becomes preoccupied with details, he is focusing on *content*. The capacity to distinguish between content and process is essential for doing effective therapy.

Differentiation of Self

Differentiation of self is a complex and insufficiently developed concept. A broad overview of the concept is presented here, and later its details are outlined in the clinical presentation. There are differences between people in terms of level of differentiation of self, differences that can be characterized on a continuum ranging from high to low levels of differentiation. The higher the level of self or differentiation, the greater a person's capacity to be closely involved with others and still maintain his individuality. The lower the level of self, the more an individual's beliefs, attitudes, emotions, and actions are governed by the emotional aspects of close relationships and other emotional forces in the environment. The more poorly differentiated the person, the more his individuality is compromised in favor of satisfying togetherness needs for emotional closeness, acceptance, and approval. A low level of differentiation can be manifested not only in an automatic compliance with what the group believes but also in an automatic rebellion against group norms. Individuality, in other words, is not equivalent to being a rebel. Individuality is a thoughtful stance based on principle. It is important to keep in mind, however, that emotionality is a significant influence on the beliefs and actions of all people. This is not considered to be a "bad" thing. Differentiation merely describes the fact that emotionality is more influential in some people than others. While there are fairly obvious psychological and social factors that influence both a person's capacity to be an individual and his need for togetherness, these two life forces have even more important biological roots that are a product of evolution. One day we will be able to better define the operation of individuality and togetherness in nonhuman animals and perhaps even plants.

The concept of differentiation describes not only differences between individuals but also differences between family units. Families can be distinguished by the balance of individuality and togetherness that is characteristic for them over time. The lower the level of differentiation of the people who comprise a particular family system, the more that system is balanced toward togetherness. As the system's level of differentiation decreases, individuality becomes increasingly tenuous and fragile. It can reach a point where the functioning of family members is seriously affected by a sense of having too little *or* too much to-getherness. At the most extreme levels, serious physical, emotional, and social impairments become a permanent feature of the system. So much flexibility has been lost in the system that it is no longer possible for the system to adjust its balance to eliminate chronic clinical impairments.

In a given nuclear family system, the basic level of differentiation of each parent is the same, a result of the fact that people with similar basic levels of differentiation are attracted to each other. There is some variation possible in the basic levels of differentiation of the children depending on the degree to which a particular child is caught up in the family emotional problem. Certain children may emerge from their family with a slightly higher basic level, others with similar level, and others with a slightly lower level than their parents. Since each child will be attracted to someone with a similar basic level and will then produce their own children with some variation in level, the basic level of differentiation in family units can gradually increase or decrease as the generations pass.

BASIC VERSUS FUNCTIONAL DIFFERENTIATION

There is a distinction between the *basic* and *functional* level of differ-entiation. Basic differentiation is deeply wired into a person, a product of his multigenerational past. The assessment of basic level requires not only evaluation of a particular individual's total life course but also an evaluation of the lives of those people closely connected to that person. These connections to be evaluated include past, present, and future generations. The reason that basic differentiation requires such extensive evaluation is that it is masked by functional self. What the observer sees is functional self, and, as will be described momentarily, functional self is influenced by many more things than basic self. Basic self is revealed in the functioning of the person and in the functioning of those close to him only as it unfolds over the span of several gen-erations. People leave their original families with a level of basic self that is rarely altered by future life experiences. Therapy, however, is based on the observation that a directed long-term effort can produce some change in basic self. Functional level of differentiation is more "easily" defined. Basic and functional levels are interrelated in the following ways: The higher the basic level of self, the more likely a consistently high level of emotional functioning will be maintained by the person and those around him. High-level functioning is increasingly wired into the person as basic self increases through the generations. Consistent functioning becomes less and less dependent on factors in the environment. The lower the basic level, however, the more functioning does depend on environmental factors. As a consequence, as basic self decreases, there is a greater likelihood for inconsistent functioning by the individual and/or marked discrepancies in functioning between closely involved individuals. The discrepancies result from one person functioning at the expense of another, a phenomenon more likely to occur as the emotional interdependence, or "stuck-togetherness," of a system increases.

The level of functional self is affected by anxiety, emotional reactivity, and subjectivity. Since these things are strongly influenced by relationships, functional self must be understood in the context of relationships. The influential relationships may extend beyond emotionally significant people to include such things as emotionally significant beliefs and institutional affiliations. The main point is that the character of these relationships can "artificially" improve or undermine functional self. People who fall in love, join cults, or experience dramatic religious conversions often have similar improvements in their functioning and sense of well-being. This is an emotionally based borrowing process frequently described as "gaining strength" from a relationship or belief. All of us do a great deal of this emotional borrowing, but the lower the level of basic self, the more necessary the borrowing to maintain functioning. Changes in functional self extend deeper than the psychological and social levels. People may dramatically recover from serious physical illness after cutting off from *or* entering into an emotionally intense relationship. Such recoveries tap the biological substrates of functional self.

Chronic Anxiety

The second basic variable that influences the origin and course of all clinical problems is chronic anxiety. Anxiety can be defined as the response of an organism to a real or imagined threat. The response may be acute or chronic, the latter being more related to imagined or anticipated threats. The fact that chronic anxiety is a regular feature of *Homo sapiens* can be understood in the context of evolution. The fact that differences in the average level of chronic anxiety exist between members of the species and in the same member over time can be understood in several contexts. These contexts include the multi-generational family, the occurrence of real or anticipated life events, and the structure and balance of a person's relationship network. The average level of chronic anxiety that is characteristic of a given nuclear family unit parallels the basic level of differentiation of that unit. This is anxiety that is wired into the system irrespective of external events. It is a function of the emotional makeup of individual family members and the manner in which they interact. As in the case with basic level of differentiation of self, the average level of chronic anxiety in a nuclear family unit is the product of a multigenerational process. The chronic anxiety gradually increases in some branches and decreases in other branches of a family as the generations pass. An individual spawned at a particular point in the evolution of a branch is "imprinted" by his experience such that he develops a baseline level of chronic anxiety close to that which existed in his branch while he was growing up. As the person goes through adult life, he may experience chronic anxiety above or below this baseline depending on what he encounters. Real or anticipated events, such as deaths of close relatives, job pressures, and major geographical moves, can affect the anxiety level.

As described previously, level of differentiation is a major influence on the extent of the anxious reaction to these events. Perhaps a more important influence on chronic anxiety than particular events is the change in structure and balance of a person's relationship system that can follow those events. An individual's sense of well-being is intimately tied to his network of emotional attachments. Events such as births, deaths, and divorces can trigger important realignments in the balance of family relationships. If a man's father dies, for example, he may have to cope not only with the loss of that parent but also with the inherited responsibility for his surviving mother's emotional well-being. Another example of realignment can occur after the birth of a child. The mother's subsequent emotional overinvolvement with the baby may leave the father in an uncomfortable outside position. It is not so much the event but the shift in relationship balance after the event that increases the father's chronic anxiety. The functioning of each family member contributes to establishing the nature of the new balance. In this instance, the new balance may be associated with the development of a clinical symptom in the father. Again, the more differentiated the system, the more adaptive it is to such events and, therefore, the less the likelihood of symptoms.

Disturbances in the balance of an emotional system can increase chronic anxiety, *and* increased chronic anxiety can disturb the balance of a system. As anxiety increases, people experience a greater need for emotional distance *or* emotional closeness and become less tolerant of each other's actions in this regard. There is more felt need for emotionally significant others to think, feel, and behave in ways that will relieve one's own discomfort. As the process intensifies, people feel increasingly threatened and compromised by the situation. The most compromised ones feel painfully cut off or overwhelmed and overloaded. These compromised positions are an important emotional substrate on which physical, emotional, and social dysfunction can develop. Reduction in the level of chronic anxiety automatically changes the way people interact and the intensity of clinical symptoms subsides. Chronic anxiety is influenced by many things but is not "caused" by anything. It is a system of actions and reactions that can develop its own momentum. Preoccupation with its "causes" can obscure the fact that it is a problem in its own right.

One final point about anxiety is the distinction between chronic anxiety associated with attempts to change and anxiety associated with regression in a system. There exists a "natural resistance" to change both on the part of the person making an effort to change and on the part of those around him. Moving at variance to the emotional "flow" of a system automatically generates anxiety.

Therapeutic Principles

Family therapy based on family systems theory is guided by two general principles. The first principle concerns the value of achieving more objectivity about the nature of emotional systems and one's own participation in them. The second principle concerns the importance of working on oneself *in relationship to* emotionally significant others. *Basic* changes in differentiation are not achieved by cutting off relationships. The improved physical, emotional, or social functioning that may accompany ending a relationship is related to *functional* level of differentiation. The most emotionally significant relationships are usually with one's parents, spouse, and children. These are the relationships in which people are most prone to gain or lose functional self, and so these are the best places to learn about and work on that process. Remember that this lability of functional self is related to underlying basic self. The long-term goal of therapy, therefore, is to raise one's level of basic self. A person who is able to do this will be more capable of being in close contact with others and still being able to maintain functioning without impairing the functioning of those around him. This does not mean that a person trying to change his basic level is advised to focus only on his closest relationships. The emotional intensity of these very close relationships often precludes achieving much objectivity. Given this intensity of one's central relationships, it is always valuable to broaden one's scope of activity to include the larger extended family system. As a person begins to think about his family in broader multigenerational terms, his perspective on the nature of family relationships can change in a way that permits more objectivity about his closer and more active relationships. It is also important to remember that differentiation relates to areas beyond one's family. People encounter emotional reactivity and subjectivity in all aspects of their lives. The capacity to recognize the pervasive influence of emotional reactivity and subjectivity in society and its eroding effect on differentiation goes hand in hand with real progress in the family.

The factors influencing the effectiveness of a therapist are so complex that only broad principles can be discussed here. A therapist must make adequate emotional contact with people while retaining his objectivity. In others words, the therapist's effectiveness is strongly tied to his ability to function as a differentiated person in relationship to the family. The therapist is not teaching techniques for change, but operates in a way that helps family members distinguish objectivity from subjectivity, and thinking from emotional reactivity. A family member gains from getting a clearer picture of this within himself and how it operates in those around him. If a therapist has a broad understanding of human problems, or at least continually works toward such an understanding, he will not fall victim to simplistic explanations and solutions. When a therapist can do this, he is automatically a valuable resource for the family. People may want techniques for "change," but they are not necessarily best served by attempts to teach such things. Techniques can provide short-term relief in intense situations, but they contribute little to a long-range solution. People seem best served by regaining or acquiring objectivity about themselves and their life situations. Certainly they can also occasionally use some support in doing what is difficult. When the therapist can maintain his emotional detachment, he is free to express all manner of opinions and ideas to the family without being heard as critical, omnipotent, or as telling the family what to do. The therapist is effective simply by virtue of who he is and not by virtue of trying to change others.

Transference is one last area that requires some discussion before the clinical case presentation. This is a largely neglected issue in the family therapy field despite the fact that understanding transference is as important for family therapy as it is for psychoanalytic therapy. Systems theory conceptualizes transference and countertransference as the loss of differentiation, or the development of "fusion" between therapist and family. The forces promoting fusion in a clinical session are often very intense and operate on very subtle as well as on fairly obvious levels. The process is far more complex than obvious efforts by a family member to get the therapist on his side. Much of the lost differentiation between therapist and family can be triggered and maintained by cues such as tone of voice, facial expressions, and posture, among others. Words frequently just reinforce the process. Forces promoting fusion between therapist and family can operate as intensely in the therapist as in the family.

Transference and countertransference, or the loss of differentiation, in a clinical session are probably the most important factors influencing the course of therapy. When therapy becomes just another supportive relationship, or when the family terminates prematurely, a failure to recognize and manage transference is usually at the root of the problem. Even the most skillful of therapists cannot always negotiate through these transference "traps." But, if the therapist continually works at differentiation in his own life, he will recognize the problem more quickly and manage it more effectively in most instances. The therapist does not avoid transference. He functions in a way that automatically tones down the intensity and problems associated with transference.

The Costas

The Presenting Problems

Dr. and Mrs. Costa, both in their middle 30s and with two children, began family therapy in August 1976. Dr. Costa arranged the appointment for the two of them, but it was Mrs. Costa who most wanted them to have therapy at that particular time.

The presenting problems were in two areas: (*a*) growing tension and disharmony in the marriage; and (*b*) considerable discomfort within the wife about what she perceived to be a gradual decline in her sense of emotional well-being and ability to get things done. Both spouses regarded the presenting problems as much more chronic than acute. The situation in the family had been even worse 4 years previously, but things seemed again to be moving in that direction. The husband and wife each considered the particular nature of their relationship as the major component of the overall problems. Mrs. Costa said the following things about herself, her husband, and their relationship in the initial interview:

> I have sacrificed to make him a whole person . . . he plugged into me and wanted me there. . . . It has seemed like an either-or situation; either I am a wife to him or I am a whole person. . . . I am passive and he is aggressive. . . . He takes the lead and has expectations of me . . . I fear abandonment, fear losing him. . . . When he cuts me off with his denial of problems and withdrawal, I feel rejected and intolerably closed out. I fear being punished. . . . I feel blocked from change by him . . . things got so bad by the time we left Atlanta in 1972, I felt mentally ill.

The wife had been in individual psychotherapy for 6 months in 1972 related to what she described about that period in Atlanta. The situation improved for a time after the family moved to Washington in 1972, but in the last year or so pressures had begun to build again. Mrs. Costa began art school in the spring of 1976, and there were significant demands on her from that activity. She expressed concern about her ability to succeed in school and about the strain of her work on her husband and their two children.

Dr. Costa tended to fault himself for not being the kind of husband his wife seemed to need. It was clear from the first session that his thinking about the marriage was heavily colored by her opinions. It is an interesting paradox that while the emotional functioning of one spouse may be more compromised by the family situation than that of the other spouse, the values and attitudes of the seemingly more compromised one often still permeate the family atmosphere, defining what the problem is supposed to be about. The husband expressed the following about the problems:

I come from an unaffectionate family and need to learn to be more sensitive to my wife's needs. I need to be more aware of others. . . . When she gets so passive and pessimistic about things, I react emotionally, and it polarizes the situation.

Dr. Costa had had some very brief psychotherapy after his father died in 1973. He had been quite anxious for several months and had had numerous health concerns.

One feature of the early sessions with the family was that both conveyed a belief that, with some help, the situation could improve.

History of the Nuclear Family

Dr. and Mrs. Costa met in the late 1950s while both were attending the same high school in Springfield, Massachusetts. They became engaged in 1959, at which point he began college in Springfield and she began a clerical job. They were married in 1962 in Springfield and over the next 10 years lived in Durham, Knoxville, and Atlanta while he attended various graduate schools to complete his PhD in a field of engineering. The family moved to Washington, D.C., in 1972 when the husband obtained a high-level position in a small engineering corporation. A daughter, Alice, was born in June 1963; there was a miscarriage in July 1965; and a second daughter, Mary, was born in March 1968. It was in the years following Mary's birth that the first real strains emerged in the marriage and that Mrs. Costa began to feel increasingly overwhelmed and bogged down with her own life. The children were small, Dr. Costa was busily working to complete his PhD, Mrs. Costa was working part-time to augment her husband's income from teaching assistantships, and she was feeling particularly emotionally isolated in Atlanta. Toward the end of that period, she sought psychotherapy. The husband's father was also diagnosed as having lung cancer in 1972, while the family was still in Atlanta. During the 14 years of their marriage, other than periodic migraine headaches in Dr. Costa, both spouses had been in good physical health, and the two children seemed to have progressed fairly normally. A diagram of the Costa family history is shown in Figure 5-1.

HUSBAND'S EXTENDED FAMILY

Dr. Costa is 33 years old and the older brother of a sister in a family from Springfield, Massachusetts. His father, who died of lung cancer

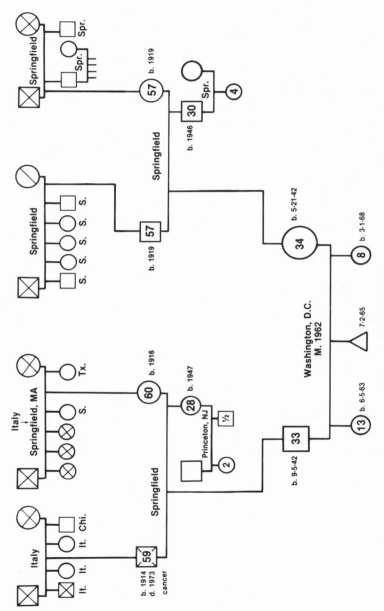

Figure 5-1. The family diagram.

124

in 1973, did not complete high school. He worked for the city in a road maintenance capacity for more than 30 years, attaining a fairly responsible supervisory position until ill health forced his retirement in 1972. Dr. Costa's father was born in Italy but left there at age 18 to come to the United States. He had limited contact with his family after leaving Italy, although occasionally he saw a younger brother who had immigrated to Chicago. Dr. Costa's father's parents died in Italy and his two sisters still live there. Dr. Costa described his father as a quiet, hardworking man but characterized the relationship he had had with him as "distant." Dr. Costa regarded his mother as an intrusive worrier. "I have spent most of my life fending her off," he said. She always seemed to want to be more involved in his life than Dr. Costa would permit. Dr. Costa's mother is 60 years old, is in good health, and lives alone in Springfield. Her family immigrated to Springfield from Italy 2 years before her birth. Dr. Costa's mother, in contrast to his father, remained closely tied to her family. The last three of the original six sisters in her family were still alive and in Springfield. Dr. Costa described his mother and her two surviving sisters as having "mental problems." His mother and aunts never saw psychiatrists, but he thought them neurotic to a paralyzing degree. Dr. Costa's younger sister is a college graduate, is married to an insurance company executive, and has two children. The couple lives in Princeton, New Jersey. Things seemed to be going reasonably well with his sister's family.

In general, Dr. Costa regarded his extended family as not of major importance to him at this point in his life. Visits home were infrequent and largely out of a sense of obligation. He had retained a little bit better contact with his sister. Dr. Costa never knew his father's family that well and thought that his mother and aunts had too many needs and problems to allow being around them to be an enjoyable experience. He had established a pattern of distancing from his family by mid-adolescence, and meeting his future wife accentuated that tendency. She quickly became his most important other.

WIFE'S EXTENDED FAMILY

Mrs. Costa is 34 years old and the older of two children in a family from Springfield, Massachusetts. Both of her parents are still living and working. Her father, who has been in good health, completed high school in Springfield and began working as a machinist in his father's shop. After Mrs. Costa's father's father died, her father inherited the business and still manages it. Mrs. Costa's mother is also a high school graduate and in recent years has been the bookkeeper for her husband's business. Mrs. Costa's mother also has artistic talents and in the early 1970s began a small ceramics business. Mrs. Costa's mother has had a moderately severe obesity problem and has experienced a series of non-life-threatening physical illnesses over the years. While both of Mrs. Costa's parents grew up in Springfield, all grandparents are now dead. All of Mrs. Costa's father's five older siblings are still living and in Springfield. Her father's family is of German descent. Mrs. Costa's mother's two younger brothers are also alive and in the Springfield area. Her mother's family is described as "poor," Mrs. Costa's maternal grandfather being an inconsistently employed house painter. The maternal grandmother was considered the family's stabilizing force. Mrs. Costa's younger brother is a high school graduate, currently a salesman, married and living in Springfield with his wife and one child. Her brother's wife is a registered nurse who works full-time.

Mrs. Costa considered her relationship with her mother to be quite problematic. "I frequently felt bad and unacceptable in her eyes," she said. The passing years and physical distance from her parents has led to some superficial improvements in her relationship with her mother, but Mrs. Costa did not delude herself that anything had really been resolved between them.

Initial Assessment

The basic or built-in emotional problem of any nuclear family unit will be played out in one or more of the following patterns: (*a*) emotional distance between the spouses; (*b*) marital conflict; (*c*) physical, emotional, or social dysfunction in a spouse; or (*d*) projection of the problems onto one or more children, which can be manifested in physical, emotional, or social dysfunction in the child. The lower the basic level of differentiation in a nuclear family system, the more intense any or all of these patterns will be. In addition, the higher the level of chronic anxiety at a given point in time, the more intense the predominant patterns will be. Each nuclear family has a kind of "fingerprint" that distinguishes it from other families, that fingerprint being determined by the predominant patterns that characterize the family.

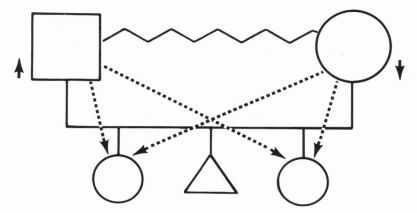

Figure. 5-2. The nuclear family process.

In the Costa family, the presenting problems are primarily expressed emotionally and are of moderate severity. The family problem is expressed in marital conflict and in some degree of impairment of the wife's emotional functioning. Based on the initial evaluation, projection of problems to the children is not a major feature of the family. The degree of emotional distance between the spouses is often difficult to assess on the basis of just a few interviews. The nuclear family process in the family can be diagramed. Figure 5-2 shows that the husband's *functional* level of differentiation has been somewhat enhanced by the family process (arrow pointing up) and the wife's level somewhat impaired (arrow pointing down). The jagged line betwen the spouses symbolizes the marital conflict. The dotted arrows to the children indicate that, while some degree of involvement of the children in the undifferentiation of the parents is unavoidable, it seems to be relatively mild in this case. This suggests that the two children are each developing a basic level of differentiation similar to, or perhaps slightly higher than, the parents. If one or more of the children were obviously a more intense focus for projection, a much heavier arrow would be drawn between the parents and that child. Such a diagram is a gross oversimplification of the emotional process in a nuclear family, but it is useful for quickly conveying overall patterns.

The specific emotional process between Dr. and Mrs. Costa can be diagramed. Figure 5-3 symbolizes that the emotional process between

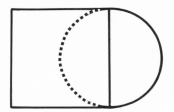

Figure. 5-3. The emotional process.

the two spouses has had more of a compromising effect on the wife's functioning than on the husband's. The diagram can be misleading, however, in not conveying the dynamic nature of the process and the fact that both spouses make many compromises to the emotionally determined togetherness. The wife has just made a few more compromises than the husband. It is important to remember that this is an *emotional* process. The husband of a chronically psychotic wife, for example, may say that he has given up nearly all of his individual interests to help his wife. He "must" drive her everywhere, make the decisions, pay the psychotherapy bills, and so forth. His whole life may be addressed to her dysfunction. He may even view her as a demanding self-absorbed person who "takes" and does not "give." She may very well view herself the same way. *But on an emotional level, he has gained self, and she has lost it.* The fact that the process is played out in a particular way in a relationship is a product of the way both spouses function. Neither person is the "cause" for the other's position in the relationship, although people typically assign blame to explain the situation.

Much of the confusion about the emotional nature of the process being described may stem from a failure to distinguish between emotions and feelings. Bowen intended the term *emotion* to represent something that existed throughout the phylogenetic tree. Ant colonies, baboon troops, and elephant families are all governed by an emotional system. The complexity and sophistication of emotional systems increased as the evolutionary process wound its way to *Homo sapiens*. The result is that the human is as regulated by an emotional system as all the other forms of life on earth. Humans, and perhaps a few other animals, can be distinguished by the recent evolutionary acquisition of a feeling system. This feeling system can be thought of as a capacity to be aware of the more superfical aspects of the human emotional system. While

Homo sapiens can clearly be motivated by feelings, human activity is rooted in a much older and deeper process.

Superficial assessment of the Costa family might suggest that the wife is a more needy and emotional person than the husband. She seems oriented to acceptance and approval, and he seems distant and "unemotional." In actuality, both spouses have the same togetherness requirements and are equally emotionally reactive. They do seem to manage feelings in a different way, but that difference is a fairly superficial aspect of the problem. When that difference gets defined as *the problem*, this subjectively based definition can acquire a high emotional valence and contribute to endless irresolvable struggles about what should change in a relationship. Irresolvable struggles can end in an impasse, or with a "winner" and a "loser." Differentiation can provide a path through these impasses and "victories." Reduction of chronic anxiety, while in itself not a resolution of an impasse, can take enough of an edge off the problem to allow a more thoughtful exploration of the nature of the problem.

The level of chronic anxiety in the Costa family has fluctuated over the years and has often been clearly related to events and circumstances. The level of chronic anxiety frequently builds after the birth of a particular child, and with the Costas it happened after the second child. If it had been only that event, the system might have adapted successfully. In this instance, however, the family was getting into an increasingly overloaded state. The husband was preoccupied with school, the wife was working part-time plus managing the house and children, they were geographically isolated from past support systems, and Dr. Costa's father had been diagnosed as having cancer. The factors influencing the more recent buildup of anxiety are less obvious. Mrs. Costa's being in art school was the one influence identified. Another influence may have been the simple fact that some old unresolved realtionship issues were sort of catching up to them. The survey of each extended family system revealed no recent occurrence that might be having an impact on the nuclear family.

Dr. and Mrs. Costa are both from relatively recently immigrated families in which, until this couple's generation when professional levels were attained, all the members had worked pretty successfully in blue-collar jobs. The overall level of problems in each extended system, which provides some indication of basic differentiation, appears moderate to moderately severe. There are a number of moderately severe neurotic-level problems, but nothing on a psychotic level. The death of Dr. Costa's father at a fairly young age may say something about the basic differentiation of his system, but one piece of data merits only tentative impressions. What is clear is that both the husband and wife regard their families as a problem and that they have maintained at least a moderate degree of emotional cutoff from each extended system. They have aspired to make a "better" life in their nuclear family than either felt they had experienced growing up. Recognizing emotional cutoff from the past generations is critically important. If people are managing one set of unresolved relationship problems by avoiding them, they are handicapped in working out what amounts to the same basic relationship problems in a marriage and with their children. As discussed earlier, objectivity and emotional detachment depend on a new understanding of the nature of the problem. People are so close to and so emotionally influenced by the situations in which they live that they find it difficult to focus only on the immediate situation and gain a different perspective. Understanding and becoming comfortable with the idea that the present is a product of the past can be a critically important step toward broadening one's perspective.

Therapeutic Planning

Based on the initial assessment, the therapeutic planning at this stage was to see the husband and wife in conjoint sessions and to focus primarily on their marital interaction. An important goal was to clarify the nature of the nuclear family emotional process that could impair the wife's functioning. This is not to say that the marriage was the "cause" of her problems. The marriage is a factor in her functioning and a valuable arena in which Mrs. Costa can work on herself. It is important to remember that family therapy is a project undertaken by individuals. Two people together do not improve a relationship. Each person works on himself or herself in relationship to the other, and if either person makes progress, the relationship will improve.

   Given the positive attitude each spouse had about the importance of therapy, it was anticipated that the heightened level of chronic anxiety would decrease fairly quickly and be associated with early *symptomatic* improvement. Symptoms can disappear without any change in basic differentiation. It was not planned to put much emphasis on either extended family in the beginning because people often fail to see its relevance when the immediate problems are intense. It did seem likely that later in the therapy, one or both spouses would be motivated to work on their unresolved emotional attachments to families of origin. Reduction of chronic anxiety usually does not depend on people getting involved with the extended family. When chronic anxiety is eventually reduced, people often find they have more energy to engage extended-family issues.

The frequent and logical question that arises is, How does a therapist lower chronic anxiety in a family? As described previously, the therapist's abililty to do this cannot be taught as a set of techniques. When a therapist is calm, emotionally neutral, and in good contact with an anxious family, the anxiety in that family will usually decrease. These are not things the therapist can pretend to do. If the therapist genuinely has the ability to wade into an intense emotional field, and to retain the capacity to see both sides and not become mired in subjective assessments of what is or should be happening, the family will recognize it and will automatically benefit. If the therapist is really not taking sides and passing subjective judgments, it will be reflected in the kinds of questions he asks, the tone of voice, facial expressions, and every other semblance of communication. Good emotional contact, objectivity, and toned-down reactivity in the therapist stimulates the same process in the family.

The principal technical question I had at the beginning of therapy was whether seeing the Costas conjointly would help to lower anxiety and increase differentiation or would undermine it. Treating people together can sometimes hamper one or both spouses' ability to think. They wanted to be seen together, and I had the impression it probably would work to the advantage of each person, at least in the early stages of therapy.

For reasons of convenience as much as anything, the appointments were initially scheduled on an every-other-week basis. There is an advantage to seeing people more frequently when the anxiety is very high, but that was not the case here. Two weeks between sessions often allows people more time to think and to come to the sessions with more of an agenda. I frequently start sessions by asking, "What has been your most objective thinking about the problem since we last met?" This kind of question sets an immediate tone for the session and permits people to talk thoughtfully and calmly about intense feelings and subjectivity. An intense expression of them in a clinical session accomplishes little of lasting value. This is not to suggest that the therapist makes rules against the expression of intense feelings in a clinical session. Rather, the therapist asks questions about the feeling process and the attitudes associated with those feelings. Aided by such questions, family members can literally teach themselves about the triggers for those feelings operating within them and within the relationship system.

The Process of Therapy

After reviewing the clinical course of the family for this chapter, it seemed useful to me to consider the therapy as having had four "phases." The designation of these particular phases is arbitrary, governed only by my retrospective thinking about the case. The presentation of the family's clinical course will be divided into these four phases or time periods, each of which had some unique characteristics. Therapy with the family was conducted over a 3-year, 3-month period and consisted of 124 1-hour sessions. Dr. and Mrs. Costa were seen individually and conjointly and were the only participants in the therapy.

AUGUST 1976 TO MARCH 1977

There were 17 appointments during the first 8 months of therapy. Each spouse was seen individually once, and the rest were conjoint sessions. The individual sessions resulted from circumstances, not therapeutic design. This period of therapy was characterized by (a) a significant reduction in the level of family anxiety; (b) some clarification of the nature of the emotional process in both nuclear and extended systems; and (c) an improvement in the wife's sense of emotional well-being and functioning. As described earlier, my main effort during this period was to ask questions that would help each person clarify his or her thinking, feelings, and behavior and at the same time monitor in myself the signs that I was losing a systems perspective. The particular signs of losing one's differentiation in a clinical session are things each therapist must learn about for himself. There are obvious signs, such as feeling angry at the husband for being "nonresponsive" or feeling sorry for the wife. A more subtle sign is pressure within oneself to somehow make the problem disappear. The pressure one feels usually results from reacting emotionally to the family's anxiety about the existence of the problem. The therapist does not need to feel with the family to be of value to them. There is nothing "wrong" with feeling with the family, however, as long as the therapist is aware of the influence of those feelings on what he says and does.

In the second session, Mrs. Costa described her central emotional dilemma in the following way:

> I need to find a core that is legitimately me. . . . I try to please, gain approval, and am so sensitive to other people's seeming disappointment in me. I hate this in me and wish I could change it, but I seem so in need of affection and acceptance. . . . I feel no loving connectedness to my husband . . . I actually feel inadequate around him. . . . He seems afraid of relating to me and I wonder if he cares. . . . He is so self-centered and I get angry at being used by him . . . I feel like I have been holding up too much of the relationship. It contributes to my being sexually turned off to him . . . I want to change all this, but at the same time I fear that what I might do will hurt him in some way.

The first part of her comments is a good description of her undifferentiation and tendency to lose self in a relationship. The need to please and be approved of and the relationship orientation are all aspects of the togetherness force. The degree to which these things dictate her thinking, feelings, and behavior is the degree to which it is difficult for her to be an individual. She accounts for her husband's behavior on the basis of his being "self-centered" and fearful of relationships. This diagnosis of him is strongly influenced by her own subjectivity. If this viewpoint is held as an explanation for *why* he acts the way he does, the fact that he is playing out one side of a system of interaction is largely obscured. Mrs. Costa's comments also demonstrate that there are factors within her *and* factors in the relationship that undermine her functional level of differentiation. It is also important to remember that her perception of a lack of connectedness between her and her husband is a product of the intense emotional impact that these two people have on each other. In other words, what feels like a lack of connection is actually a rather intense connection. Encouraging these two people to get together is equivalent to pushing two magnets together whose negative poles are facing each other.

Dr. Costa described his position in this way:

> I can experience her emotional needs as smothering and invading my privacy. I put up a wall against that the same way I did with my mother. . . .

> At the same time, when I do approach her, she withdraws—I don't know what to do. . . . Most of the time I feel frustrated and on eggshells. I'm trying to avoid triggering a reaction . . . I react to her hopelessness . . . I feel cut off from her too. . . . Sometimes I think I do too much and feel too responsible for making things right for her . . . I guess I can dominate her.

His comments show the relationship between the unresolved attachment to his mother and the nature of the fusion that exists with his wife. They also demonstrate the way his individuality also gets compromised by the togetherness. He orients many of his actions around her anxiety, a posture that buys a little peace but perpetuates a long-term problem. Although not stated at this point, he no doubt views her neediness as excessive, again a subjective assessment that fails to define his part in the system of interaction. Each person is responding from the threat they experience in response to the other's actions and inactions. Responding to a perceived threat is as natural as the sunrise. Viewing it that way allows a little detachment.

The wife later added the interesting comment that although she knew what her husband was like when she married him, she always felt he would learn "to love, to trust, to be open." Words like "love," "trust," and "openness" are all part of the togetherness and always hopelessly mired in subjective assessments of what should exist in a relationship. People wage long battles over whether there is enough of these things in a relationship. Whether there is "enough" is always a matter of opinion and not fact. Mrs. Costa went on to say that she had enough of a missionary streak to feel she could eventually change her husband. What is being described is obviously not peculiar to this family. It is part of all of us to some degree.

During the first 3 months of therapy, much of the problematic intensity of the family interaction diminished. Each spouse could talk a little more objectively about what transpired between them without blaming the other for it. The wife, partly stimulated by my questions about her family, became more interested in how her relationship with her mother influenced the marriage. She described her determination not to do things the way her mother did. She regarded her mother's "pushiness and neediness" as having "done in" her father and brother. She said the following:

I don't want to be like my mother, but I see myself doing many of the same things. . . . She dumped on us, hurt us, and could not see our side. . . . She was negative and hurtful and I felt disregarded . . . I still cannot be myself around my parents. I fall into trying to please them and trying to make things right for them. . . . In spite of all I dislike about my mother, I am acutely responsive to her unhappiness.

As was the case with some of the husband's earlier comments, the replay in the marriage of Mrs. Costa's unresolved attachment to her parents is striking. Regardless of wishes to the contrary, the process is built into her and when the emotional intensity mounts, she does and says many of the same things her mother did.

Mrs. Costa's brother and his family visited Washington in late November. This was the first face-to-face contact with either extended family since the initiation of therapy. During the first 3 months of therapy, I had talked about my view that the fusion or lack of differentiation in a marriage that can generate problems was related to the unresolved fusion of each spouse with his or her family of origin. The fusion with parents may become dormant after leaving home but is not resolved. The Costas had little difficulty accepting this idea, and so they were each primed for this first contact, particularly Mrs. Costa. It was a smooth encounter, but Mrs. Costa was able to observe how tension could be triggered in her just by being in physical contact with her family. Many more thoughts were triggered in the week after the visit. She said it was crystalizing for her how much of her identity was defined by being absorbed in someone else. She had a much better sense of the emotional reactions that fostered that absorption. "My goal has apparently been to restore and maintain harmony in all of my relationships," she said. In response to my questions to expand her thinking about it she added, "I guess I equate disharmony with rejection."

These observations by the wife did not result from any interpretation on my part. They were her ideas. I did talk about systems thinking as applied to relationships, the influence of emotional reactivity and anxiety, and the tendency of patterns to replicate down the generations. I talked about these things in a general sense, and she had the motivation and capacity to examine them in her own life. If she came into a session saying, "My parents won't let me grow up!" I would definitely respond in a way that indicated I thought there were two sides to that problem. If I was objective and neutral, I could just chuckle at her passionate indictment of her parents, and she would probably get the point. If I was reacting emotionally to her attitude, I could say there were two sides to the story, and she very well might not get my point. If I am reacting emotionally to her and that reaction dictates my response, then I am in the same position with her as her parents. An emotionally determined relationship in therapy impedes useful communication. My feeling reactions in a session, in other words, are an indication that I am getting caught up in the family problem. I use those reactions as a signal to work on me and rarely say much about them to the family.

It might also be useful to mention here that most of the therapy goes on outside the actual clinical sessions. If people leave my office a little calmer and a litle more objective than when they came in, and if the session has provided a stimulus for their thinking in the weeks ahead, I consider it a successful session. This is different from people leaving their anxiety in my office. When a therapist picks up the anxiety, that process is the result of transference or fusion.

There were two more extended family contacts in December. In early December the family went to Princeton over a weekend to visit Dr. Costa's sister's family. The visit stimulated thoughts in Mrs. Costa about her relationship to her husband's family. She said, "I have never felt acceptable to my husband, but I also have never felt acceptable to his whole family, especially his mother." She was not angry about this so much as her feeling reactions to her husband and his family were in better perspective. The problem was not all in her. In late December Mrs. Costa's parents visited Washington. The visit was less tense than past ones, and she later commented, "I could observe better. I never saw them this way before." It was difficult for her to comment on those obervations in much detail at that time, but something was different. A logical question would be why I am reporting all these observations by the wife and not by the husband. Well, she was making them, and he was not. I do not know how to account for that difference between them.

In March there was a session that seemed to be a culmination of all the thinking each person had been doing through the fall and winter. In an extremely thoughtful and relaxed way, they described the nature of the relationship cycle that occurred periodically between them, a cycle that might take weeks to months to run its course. The following were their comments about it:

MRS. COSTA: For whatever reasons, I start feeling depressed, needy, and passive.

DR. COSTA: I get anxious in response to that in her and become more withdrawn and dogmatic in my dealings with her.

MRS. COSTA: Over time, I feel drained and in need of support. I get increasingly fearful of being cut off. I can even see him as a powerful, punitive figure who is denying me needed absolution.

DR. COSTA: I do feel increasingly judgmental and harsh toward her as we continue deeper into these cycles.

MRS. COSTA: Finally, I begin to hit bottom and start feeling angry at him. I blame him and feel used. At this point I care less what he thinks.

DR. COSTA: I think I can deal with her anger more easily than her depression, neediness, and passivity.

The next stage in the cycle is a period of overt conflict between them, after which things settle down and a period of positive emotional closeness prevails. Inevitably, something that is usually inconsequential later sets yet another cycle in motion.

In that particular session, I just asked questions of each person that would help amplify the comments they were making. I went back and forth between them asking for the thinking of each that was generated by the remarks of the other. Over time in therapy, people tend to direct their comments to me rather than to the other spouse. I encourage this by the way I address my questions. I do this based on the observation that it is easier for each spouse to listen to the other when they are talking to and looking at the therapist. During the course of the discussion, both the husband and wife raised some questions about *why* this cycle kept recurring. Systems thinking focuses on defining *what* happens, *when* it happens, *how* it happens, and *where* it happens. *Why* something happens stretches the bounds of theoretical understanding. There are sociological, psychological, and biological factors that influence human activity, and one day a comprehensive systems theory will integrate all these various levels. At present all one can say is that this relates to that, which relates to that, which relates to that. Another safe statement within the bounds of present knowledge is that such cycles are a fact of natural systems. This does not "excuse" the participation of either spouse in the process, nor does it incriminate them. Considering it a phenomenon of natural systems does not preclude people's learning about it, and something about that learning fosters an ability to modify the process. Any change in basic differentiation depends on learning.

Toward the end of this phase of therapy, the subject of one of their children came up for the first time. Daughter Alice was having some academic problems, and this stimulated a lot of discussion about triangles. When I first mentioned the concept, something people usually have some sense of anyway, both were eager to do some reading about triangles and other aspects of family systems theory. I gave them a reprint of an article on the theory. The husband found particular use in the concept for seeing more clearly how he was getting tangled up in the relationship between Alice and one of her teachers. Both parents were able to pull back a bit, and the school problems improved. Alice worked them out.

APRIL 1977 TO DECEMBER 1977

There were 34 appointments during this 9-month period of therapy. The wife was seen individually for half those session, and the rest were done conjointly. The individual sessions were scheduled to alternate with conjoint sessions at Mrs. Costa's request. She thought she could work more productively on herself and on the relationship with her original family if she came alone periodically. While Dr. Costa continued to attend the conjoint sessions regularly and work on certain issues, his motivation was less than his wife's. As the marriage became calmer and more comfortable, he felt less pressure. In addition, unlike his wife, he had not been particularly concerned about his personal functioning, and so therapy was less important to him. Both spouses had become sufficiently interested in family systems theory to attend the Georgetown Symposium on Family Theory and Therapy in November 1977. By the end of 1977, the nuclear family seemed to have a pretty good adjustment in all areas.

Mrs. Costa initially used the individual sessions to focus on her inability to act on things that were important to her. She viewed herself as an odd mix of exquisite sensitivity to the obligations she felt toward others and a deep recalcitrance about meeting those obligations or expectations. The end result was often an action paralysis. She was unsure about what she wanted for herself, but also resented and fought what she perceived others wanted her to do. Obviously there is more to the wife's functioning than this, but this is the way some of her emotional reactiveness and subjectivity manifested itself.

Another aspect of her emotionality that she became more aware of was her strong tendency to focus on the problems of others and to get absorbed in that other person. In the triangle between her husband, her daughter, and herself, for example, she was aware of how they would drag her into their conflicts and became more aware of the strong urge in her to get involved and repair the disharmony between them. Mrs. Costa's overall comments are a good description of someone who tries to gain functional self through focus on and involvement with others. It is easy to see how this kind of emotional orientation can cross a line that leaves her feeling she has lost more than she has gained. How people around her seem to be responding to her "efforts in their behalf" becomes quite important, and it is easy to feel used and unappreciated. This is not to say that people do not take advantage of her. They do play out the opposite side of the process, and there is a lot of selfishness on all sides.

Again, the wife's thinking about all these things was not the result of my interpretations. Since what she says is consistent with my theoretical understanding of people, I do ask a lot of questions that tend to develop that way of thinking. I bias the situation in that way. I do that because I think my bias has a sound theoretical base, but it is clearly always important to recognize what I am imposing on the situation. It is also important to remember that a person can be saying what Mrs. Costa is saying with a strong emotional overtone that disproportionatley blames self or others. It can also be said as the reflection of an effort to increase one's perspective. When the latter is the case, the therapist has little work to do. On the other hand, if the emotional tone is high, the therapist has to have a way to relate to people that helps them recognize how the high emotional valence can be a major obstacle to change. The therapist's ability in this regard depends on his capacity to see the emotional charge, attach importance to its presence, and be genuinely uncritical of it. A therapist telling himself he "should not" feel critical is not an answer. Getting beyond emotionally based judgments depends on detachment, detachment depends on theoretical understanding, and sound theoretical understanding depends on many things, not the least of which is integrating theory into the way one lives one's own life.

During April, Mrs. Costa began a sustained effort to change the way she functioned in her nuclear family. The impact of her effort was felt mostly by her husband and older daughter. The wife described her change this way:

I am withdrawing more into my own head and not feeling so obligated
to respond to others. I still fear how what I am doing will affect them. . . .
What I am trying to do makes sense to me intellectually, but it definitely
does not feel right. It scares me.

Mrs. Costa described what is pretty typical of the experience someone
has when trying to change in relationship to others. There is a deeply
felt foreboding about how others will react and an intense uneasiness
born of trying to do something that runs counter to what has always
felt "right." The other obstacle to change is that other family members
will think, feel, and behave in ways that tend to undermine or neutralize
the efforts of the person trying to change. By the end of April, for
example, everyone in the family seemed to be having problems except
for the wife. Dr. Costa had an exacerbation of migraines, daughter
Mary was clinging to her mother more, and Alice was more inclined
to pick fights over minor issues. Mrs. Costa observed, "Now I feel good
and others feel bad. I *think* it's the right course, but I *feel* it's the wrong
one." Mrs. Costa was also having frightening dreams during this period
of trying to change. The content of the dreams was that she or someone
else was being hurt physically. She further remarked, "I've always had
trouble being competent. It is much easier to focus on others and to
take care of them." I responded to the wife during this period with
comments such as these: "Fascinating. . . . This all makes perfect sense
to me. . . . If you don't pull this off, maybe your husband's next wife
will. . . . I'll write you up in my next book."

The main purpose of my comments was to keep the sessions loose
and to communicate that what she and the family were experiencing
was predictable. I did not try to motivate Mrs. Costa, nor do I go out
on my lawn in the spring and encourage my grass to grow. When the
conditions are favorable, grass and differentiation will emerge. One
of Murray Bowen's favorite comments about motivating people is that
"you can't make a bean grow faster by pulling on it." A frequent
question I am asked is whether I attempt to "support" the husband
and kids through a period like this. Support might mean telling them
everything is going to work out for the best. I do not think that kind
of support is particularly necessary or productive. An important factor
blocking change in families is wanting to avoid the predictable reactions
associated with change. People react *instinctively* to preserve the existing
level of togetherness. The emotional reactions associated with an effort
to change are unavoidable and valuable for learning. It is important

for a therapist to know what this process is about and to keep an eye on it, but his role is pretty much limited to that. There are, of course, people who take "a bull in the china shop" approach to delicately balanced family situations, and the therapist does have a responsibility to recognize and squelch such approaches. But when somebody like Mrs. Costa is not acting on the basis of some technique picked up from her therapist but is acting on the basis of a gradual evolution of her thinking about herself and the family, the risks are minimal.

By the middle of May, the situation in the family was reequilibrating, and each person seemed to be functioning better. More of the time in therapy was devoted to their respective families of origin. Dr. Costa described his problems dealing with a mother he experienced as a "needy, anxious, overwhelming, talkative octopus." He found her exhausting to deal with. My suggestion that it would be profitable to increase his contact with and work on his vulnerability to his mother was greeted with a notable lack of enthusiasm. Again, I do not push these things. I often chuckle about the situation with people and respect the power of the emotional forces that promote cutoff. My main interest is in communicating that there are two sides to the story with extended family, and I wait for the person to be motivated to pursue the matter. During May, the news came that Dr. Costa's sister was pregnant and that her family was moving from Princeton to Cleveland, Ohio.

Through the spring Mrs. Costa continued to do a lot of thinking about a variety of issues in her nuclear and extended families. She made the observation that Alice would try to "plug into" her and her husband the same way she and her husband would do it with each other. A lot of Alice's testiness and procrastination served the function of involving her parents in her life. Viewed from this perspective, Mrs. Costa was able to respond to Alice in a more relaxed way. She observed the following about both Alice and herself: "The more you can rely on an outside party to step in, the more you have a license to be crazy."

The wife also began to focus on what she considered to be her own achievement blocks and the relationship of those blocks to her original family. She gave this example. She had been working on a painting prior to one of her parents' visits. When her parents viewed the unfinished painting and did not seem to respond very positively, she found that she could no longer work on the painting. Mrs. Costa liked the painting and wanted to finish it, but when she tried to work on it, nothing happened. She again emphasized, "I have been so oriented to doing things that are for someone else. I need an identity of my own and cannot seem to get it." She added that as much as she wanted to be free of the influence of her extended family, she was still dependent on her parents' approval. She remarked, "My contacts with my parents are almost ritualized now, but if I am with them very long, I can still get wiped out emotionally." Mrs. Costa, like all of us, obviously had a difficult time being objective. She could see the relationship between her parents more clearly on an intellectual level, but on a feeling level she still saw her father as the "victim" of her mother's neediness and pushiness. I made the comment that the more objective she could be about her mother, the more objective she could be about herself. I suggested that making contact with her mother's family would be a way to work toward more objectivity. "Try to think about your mother as your grandmother's daughter and get to know her that way," I said. Mrs. Costa went on to describe another aspect of the relationship with her mother in this way: "I really do feel the burden of my mother's neediness. My father runs from her and so I feel like her court of last resort. The more isolated she feels, the more she eats and I worry about that, too."

The unresolved attachment to one's parents is always complex and the wife's remarks certainly highlight that fact. "What would you be like if you were more of a self with your mother?" I asked. If Mrs. Costa became less dependent on her mother's approval and if she did not fall into the position of mothering her mother, certainly that would be part of the process of being more of a self. In therapy, however, one must always be cognizant of how easily this kind of thing can be picked up as a technique. Mrs. Costa could visit her parents with sort of a rule in her head that says she should not have to mother her mother or need the approval of her parents. Making such rules does not accomplish very much other than making it a little easier to cope with the visits. As described earlier, many unresolved feelings will remain, feelings that will influence her functioning in all other important relationships. Being more of a self in one's family depends on a new way of thinking about the family, and that is why an understanding of the multigenerational family is so important.

While things were generally better in the nuclear family, ups and downs continued. The wife concluded that the cycles seemed to revolve around her mental state, although she recognized her husband's equal partcipation in them. Both began to observe things that influenced the tension and cycles, such as problems with the kids. The husband made the comment that during these cycles, when his wife would get scattered and pessimistic, it put pressure on him to be the one that "always had it together." He began to see how much his functioning was addressed to his wife's functioning. The conjoint sessions provided a forum in which each person could listen to the other's views, and that seemed useful to them.

In July Dr. Costa was in Texas on a business trip and went to visit his mother's youngest sister. Dr. Costa's aunt and her family had moved from Massachusetts to Texas in the early 1960s, and it had been almost that many years since he had seen them. A particularly interesting observation came out of that visit, which he described as follows:

> Listening to my aunt did help put my mother in a different perspective. My mother apparently has been trying to hold the whole family together for years. It is easier when you begin to see what somebody is trying to accomplish rather than just reacting emotionally to what they do.

Meanwhile, Mrs. Costa was continuing to run into achievement blocks, incurring an *F* in English. She wondered if she could ever change. She further characterized her mother as someone who denied her own ability and competence and saw this as somehow related to her own achievement problems. "My mother is anxious about her ability to take care of herself and seems to have a lot of internal sanctions about going outside allowable behavior," she said. Allowable behavior was defined by the emotional aspects of the relationship system. For example, Mrs. Costa thought that both her husband and her father would get quite uncomfortable when their respective wives invested much energy outside the marriage. The obvious task for Mrs. Costa was to work toward being more emotionally separate from her mother, something that mere physical distance had not promoted. Emotional separation depends on more awareness of the reactiveness that cements a symbiosis, more ability to manage that reactiveness within self, and more objectivity. If there is not much contact, there is not much opportunity for learning these things.

In August 1977 the family went to Springfield. Mrs. Costa considered it one of her most useful visits home, although Dr. Costa still kept a distance from his family. Mrs. Costa made an effort to visit both of her mother's brothers, something she had made little effort to do since her marriage. "I find that I like my family now, and I thought I never could," she said. As she reflected on the visit a few weeks later, she said she had gotten a "high" from the experience, and that was followed by a letdown. During the letdown she felt more vulnerable to her husband's criticism of her and angry at him for seeming to have less motivation to work on things. The tension of that period subsided, but in the early fall the husband said he was losing interest in continuing therapy. His criticism of his wife heated up, saying that she was less romantic and caring. He was quite serious when he told her, "You're getting so healthy it's disgusting. It will ruin me!" As soon as he had said it, they both broke out laughing. Mrs. Costa had spent most of the year focusing on individuality, and it was altering the togetherness balance of the marriage.

While Dr. Costa was saying that the emotional part of him did not like that, they both agreed that they were actually talking to each more and listening better than at any time in their marriage. Both continued with therapy.

As the autumn progressed, both of them did more reading about systems theory. The reading stimulated their interest in attending the Annual Family Symposium, which they did, and it seemed to be a profitable experience. I encourage all the people in my practice who have some interest in theory to attend meetings and read articles. Such things can provide an opportunity for learning beyond what a therapist can provide.

A most interesting development occurred in the nuclear family soon after that meeting. Mrs. Costa started into one of her periodic funks about feeling blocked and hopeless. For the first time, neither Dr. Costa nor the kids got pulled into it. In the past, Dr. Costa would alternate between scrambling around trying to make things better for his wife and criticizing what he perceived as her childlike attitudes. Both approaches amounted to treating her like a child, as somebody who desperately "required" guidance. This time he could comfortably watch and not feel critical or that he was supposed to fix the problem. The kids seemed to take their cues from him. Mrs. Costa wallowed, and the rest of the family maintained a sense of humor. She criticized them for not taking her seriously, but that did not suck them into it either. It was beautiful! It was the most short-lived funk she had ever experienced. She began kidding about her family as three generations of procrastinators who, because of delays, inevitably produce a product below their capabilities. She added some other interesting things about her perception of the symbiosis with her mother:

> I always felt some level of expectation that I be competent and lead. How can I lead with all my problems? . . . Mother seemed to need me to shape up so she would feel better. That if I behaved properly, she would not be sick, seemed to be her attitude. . . . Dad reinforced that by insisting mother needed calm.

Again, the replay in the Costa marriage of what had occurred in her family was striking. Dr. Costa's vulnerability to participating in that process was related to his own unresolved attachment to his family.

The Costas' sexual relationship improved over the year of therapy without much actual discussion of it in therapy. The sexual relationship cycled along with the other aspects of their relationship, being just one facet of the fusion between them. It can be discussed in some detail or not, depending on people's interest. Sex is an obvious area where the less uptight people are about each other's behavior, the easier it is to discuss and work out problems. The husband commented, "Sex is like all the other areas of our relationship. We still both react emotionally to the presence of problems, but the recovery is faster. We both have a little more perspective." The wife drew a fascinating analogy that she thought relevant to many aspects of their relationship over the years. She remarked, "A flock of birds will peck to death the weak, sick bird. My submissive posture invited attack and more problems. It's a natural process." Maybe I brainwashed her into this way of thinking, but I do not think that I did.

At the end of December, a decision was made to stop all but occasional conjoint sessions and to see the Costas individually and alternately. The initiative for this came from Mrs. Costa, although Dr. Costa readily agreed to the change. While both people thought the marriage was on a much better footing, each wanted to continue to work on themselves.

JANUARY 1978 TO DECEMBER 1978

There were 42 sessions during 1978, all of which were individual sessions. There were 26 appointments with the wife and 16 with the husband. The year of therapy mostly centered on Mrs. Costa's continuing desire to resolve issues with her parents and on her continuing struggle to overcome achievement blocks. Dr. Costa was fairly comfortable during this period and seemed more interested in talking about issues than he was in undertaking new actions. An important area he still kept at arm's length was the relationship with his mother. The marriage remained fairly calm and harmonious, although there were points during the year when the wife talked about seemingly unchangeable patterns between them.

During early 1978, Mrs. Costa began taking more interest in learning about her multigenerational family. She felt sufficiently bogged down in trying to achieve more emotional separation from her parents that the value of gaining a broader multigenerational perspective on her family started to make more sense. As her research progressed, she became impressed with how little she had known about her father's family. "I really have no knowledge of the generations beyond my father's generation," was her comment. As she learned more about the lives of her father's siblings, she began to see many similarities between patterns in their nuclear families and her own. She also saw that the types of problems that developed were similar in the various families. There was something about this kind of exploration of her extended family that seemed to help Mrs. Costa place her immediate situation in more perspective. Gaining a new perspective on problems seems to help tone down emotional reactiveness to those problems.

It might be well to emphasize here that when people set out to learn more about their families, no one can hope to achieve more than a limited understanding of the family. The multigenerational family is too complex and information about it often too inaccessible to permit more than just partial learning. In spite of these built-in limitations, an important change in attitude can occur as a person explores his family of origin. This change is a gradual shift away from making a lot of assumptions and generalizations about the family toward an attitude of assuming less and trying to learn more. Subjectively based assumptions about our families are built into us; the lower the level of basic differentiation, the more this is the case. It is always easy to find support for these assumptions through agreement with other family members. When a person becomes more aware of the subjective nature of these assumptions and generalizations and attempts to get beyond that subjectivity, he quickly learns about the emotional forces in relationship systems that spawn and preserve subjectivity. Learning about the nature of these emotional forces and one's own participation in them is the principal value of focusing on one's family of origin. This is a far different process than simply doing a genealogical history of one's family.

A simple example of this process is a man who made contact with his father after years of no contact. The man's parents had divorced when he was 4 years old, and contact between father and son ceased at that time. While the man was interested in what his father might have to say about those early years, he had not anticipated the emotional impact his contact would have on his mother. She reacted as if he was a disloyal son who had no understanding of her feelings. She attacked him bitterly for his actions. The man was amazed at how devastated he was by her attack. He and his mother had always had a harmonious relationship, but he was beginning to see how many compromises he had made to retain her approval. When he saw that in relationship to his mother, he began to see how influential a force approval was in all aspects of his life. I tell stories such as this in therapy sessions to illustrate the principles that govern focus on family of origin.

In the spring and summer of 1978 the family made two trips to Springfield. The trips were especially productive for the wife. They went in April to attend Mrs. Costa's cousin's wedding and again in July. The following are some of Mrs. Costa's comments after those trips:

> I can see that my cutoff from Springfield began with my marriage . . . I can see that negative self-images permeate my whole family! . . . Things seemed to fall apart in my mother's family after her paternal grandfather died. My mother's father's drinking increased after that death. The family seemed never the same after he died. . . . I find myself wanting to be in more contact with home.

I think that Mrs. Costa's desire to be in more contact with Springfield was a function of her being a little more objective and a little less reactive to her family. Seeing the interrelationship of some of the events she described was probably an element in getting beyond blame and guilt and becoming more neutral about the family. One does not profitably march outside in the summer and scream at the grass for not growing under the shade trees. A complex of variables defeats most grass from growing under shade trees, and one easily accepts it. One's family can be understood the same way.

The wife's efforts with her family of origin again seemed to have an impact on the marriage following the April Springfield trip. Dr. Costa had another exacerbation of migraine headaches. The fact that this exacerbation occurred at a point when Mrs. Costa was functioning better than she had in years prompted her to say, "If I do what I want, will my husband and mother get sick?" I could not be certain that the migraines and some change in the togetherness balance in the marriage are related, but it was certainly a possibility. About a month after the second Springfield trip, Mrs. Costa described her perspective on the marriage in more detail:

> I notice that I am calmer and have more energy for outside interests when my husband is away on trips. When he's away, it frees me from conflicting demands and fear of disapproval. . . . There still is a lot that is not resolved between us and we still keep our distance from one another.

What Mrs. Costa describes is a pretty common phenomenon: the functioning of one being eclipsed simply by the physical presence of the other. Both people function in ways that promote the problem and often without much awareness of what they are doing. Again, it is the product of the fusion or undifferentiation that exits between people. Later on in the same session, the wife focused on her particular part in the problem:

> I am beginning to realize how little inner discipline I have, how I have depended on external structure to help me function. . . . As I strive now to be successful, it creates a lot of tension within me. I'm having a lot of minor accidents and stomach cramps. . . . It seems I almost need someone's permission to act . . . I seem to need structure, but I rebel against my husband trying to provide it.

Change is not easy. If the husband had been working a little more on himself at this point, it might have made it a little easier for Mrs. Costa. On the other hand, differentiation is a project for oneself, and nobody can really help with it.

As the fall semester of art school progressed, Mrs. Costa found that she was still unable to finish paintings. She began to doubt that she would ever get beyond "the blocks." It is important to mention that she was not looking to me to provide structure and direction for her, nor did I encourage that kind of relationship with her. If I had encouraged it, I would have been fostering a transference and moving toward a type of relationship therapy. I believed the issues Mrs. Costa was struggling with were tied to the unresolved symbiotic attachment to her family and they could best be resolved by working toward more emotional separateness from her family. I did not perceive her family to be the "cause" of her problems. Nothing is that simple. But I did believe that if she continued to try to work on herself in relationship to her original family, the achievement problems would ameliorate. A transference relationship would have shifted her energy out of the extended family and into her relationship with me.

In December Mrs. Costa decided to switch out of fine arts and into psychology. She remarked, "I walk around thinking images, but I still have fear and terror over success in art. Somehow I still think it is rooted in my fear that if I deny others, they will reject me." I do not know how to explain Mrs. Costa's change in career direction at that point, but it did seem emotionally based.

Some psychotherapists might argue that she had the kind of problem that would benefit from psychoanalysis. "Family therapy does not touch deeper problems," someone might say. I believe that even a small change toward resolving the attachment to family of origin can result in profound internal "psychic" changes. What is most important, however, may be the fact that Mrs. Costa had spent nearly 2 years trying to get past some of the emotional impasses in her extended family and was still shooting blanks.

The year ended with a Christmas visit from Mrs. Costa's parents and perhaps a portent of significant changes that were to occur in the coming months. While Mrs. Costa had been rather positive about recent family contacts, this one was a negative experience about which she expressed the following: "I experienced more need to get away from my mother. I felt so overwhelmed by her needs of me."

JANUARY 1979 TO DECEMBER 1979

There were 31 sessions during 1979: 18 with the wife and 13 with the husband. During the year, Mrs. Costa underwent major surgery, an event that probably contributed to her decision to seek a new type of psychotherapy in November. Dr. Costa terminated therapy completely in December.

The therapy during the early part of 1979 appeared to continue to be productive. The husband had another business trip to Texas, and it coincided with a reunion of his mother and her two sisters at the youngest sister's home in Texas. Dr. Costa spent 2 days with his mother and aunts and seemed to gain some perspective from the experience. Seeing that many of the same things that characterized his relationship with his mother also characterized his mother's interactions with her sisters was helpful. He commented, "Maybe I don't need to take the things she does quite so personally." A little later he added, "I guess I have been in a perpetual state of retreat from a clinging mother." In spite of all Dr. Costa's observations, however, he still regarded his mother as someone to be coped with rather than as someone with whom he really wanted a better relationship.

In early February, during a routine physical examination, Mrs. Costa was told there might be some kind of mass developing behind her uterus. A follow-up gynecological appointment was scheduled for late March. At her next psychotherapy appointment in February, she talked about the tendency of women in her family to get sick with serious, but not life-threatening, physical illnesses. This had been especially true of her mother and maternal grandmother. Mrs. Costa remarked, "When you are sick, you don't have to take responsibility." When the follow-up medical appointment occurred in late March, the "suspicious area" of late January had developed into a very definite and rather large mass. A malignant tumor had to be considered a possibility, although there were numerous other benign lesions possible. Surgery was recommended. The next few weeks were quite emotionally intense for the family. Much of the time was devoted to gathering other medical opinions. The seriousness of the situation semed to bring many of Mrs. Costa's thoughts into clearer focus. She said the following:

> What can eat me up is a struggle and no place where there is peace. The last few months have been like that and I don't want to fight anymore. . . . I just have always needed to be needed as a way of dealing with my own insecurity. . . . I have been trying so hard to reverse that.

The chronic feeling and emotional state of struggling against a seemingly insurmountable obstacle is often a feature of the period leading up to a physical illness (Kerr, 1981). The role of an emotional factor in the wife's illness can only be speculated about, but my impression is that it was a contributing factor.

The operation was in early May and was performed without complications. The tumor mass was benign. I saw Dr. Costa once while his wife was in the hospital and he remarked, "This whole experience has helped me to be aware of just how emotionally dependent I am on my wife." Mrs. Costa's next session was in mid-June, about 5 weeks following the surgery. She had been doing a lot of thinking about the past year or two and summarized her thoughts as follows:

> This sounds crazy, but at times I have *felt* like my mother and I were the same person. . . . I have been fighting not to be like what I saw in her . . . more and more I have felt like I wasn't getting anywhere.

One can review comments from the sessions in the summer of 1978 and be impressed that indeed Mrs. Costa was getting somewhere. She seemed more relaxed and comfortable around her family and more capable of being an individual in relationship to her husband and children.

In the fall and early winter, however, something seemed to change. She again felt blocked and without much confidence that she could find her way past the block. I could see this change in her but remain at a loss to explain it. The impact of the illness itself and the surgery seemed to complicate the situation further. On an emotional level, it was even more difficult for her after the surgery. Her parents visited in July, and Mrs. Costa again began to feel them as an emotional burden. In September she talked about needing some sort of "emotional calisthenics" before she could ever deal with her family again. As the fall progressed she reiterated the theme of not being strong enough to deal with her family, at least not right now. Finally, in October, she said she needed some kind of therapeutic relationship that would support her emotionally and help structure her life. She knew, and I knew, that my relationship with her had never been intended for that, and so we both discussed her options in a pretty thoughtful way. In early November Mrs. Costa began twice-a-week individual psychotherapy with a woman therapist who was a bit older than she. Dr. Costa came for two more sessions before terminating in December.

Final Assessment

There were clearly successful and unsuccessful aspects to the therapy
with this family. Based on reducing the level of chronic anxiety, there
was significant symptomatic improvement within the first few months
of therapy. Symptom relief based on reduction anxiety does not reflect
any increased adaptiveness in a system. The system, in other words,
remains as vulnerable to symptom development as it ever was. During
1977 and 1978, however, the Costa family did achieve some increase
in *basic* differentiation or adaptiveness. The changes in basic level were
the product of a gradual learning process and the capacity to convert
that learning into action. It is interesting that while a change in a
person's basic functioning may seem to occur rather abruptly, the
thinking and learning that fosters such a change in functioning has
usually been percolating for many months. In April 1977, for example,
Mrs. Costa "suddenly" changed the way she was responding to her
family, but she had spent 6 months trying to think more clearly about
her family before that "sudden" change emerged.

A therapist can never be sure of what is "possible" in terms of
change in basic differentiation. He cannot be sure of this for himself,
let alone for a clinical family. For this reason, there is no definite
"termination point" for working on differentiation. Some people are
motivated to work on improving basic differentiation for years and
years. They see it as a lifetime project. Other people would like to
accomplish more in terms of basic differentiation but keep encountering
internally and externally generated emotional impasses. Most people
fall into the category of losing their motivation for this kind of change
after varying lengths of time. The loss of motivation seems to relate
to becoming more comfortable, genuinely not seeing anything else to
be done, or both. Mrs. Costa falls into the category of someone who
wanted to keep working but who encountered major impasses. I wish
I could have been more helpful to her in navigating through the
obstacles with her family of origin. Had she been able to get through
some of them, the therapeutic result would have been better, and the
family would have had more of a "guarantee" for the future. If the
physical illness had not occurred, it is possible that Mrs. Costa would
have continued to focus on her family of origin and that progress
would have eventually occurred. Certainly by the summer of 1978,
there was good evidence that Mrs. Costa was more objective about

her family, and it is likely that that objectivity would have eventually translated into more ability to be a self when in contact with her parents and husband.

I saw the wife again in early 1981. She had brought Alice to our Center to undergo some brief biofeedback treatment for migraine headaches. Alice was the third generation of Dr. Costa's family with migraines. Mrs. Costa said that her individual therapy had worked out well and that things seemed to be going well for the whole family. She was more relaxed about school and was progressing on a master's degree in psychology. She again thanked me for the help I had given them over those 3 years and said that someday she would probably be back to talk more about her family.

References

Bowen, M. (1966). The use of family theory in clinical practice. *Comprehensive Psychotherapy*, 7, 345–374.

Kerr, M. (1981). Cancer and the family emotional system. In J. Goldberg (Ed.), *Psychotherapeutic treatment of cancer patients*. New York: Free Press.

Chapter 6
Learning Their Dance: Changing Some Steps

David C. Treadway, PhD

The man filled my office with his loud, intense voice. His wife seemed small and frail. Her manner was that of a scared rabbit, frozen and still, waiting. "What I'm saying is, young fellow," the man barked at me while pounding his fist for emphasis, "it's my problem and I've got to do something about it. Betsy here and I have a wonderful marriage except when I go and screw things up. I want to get to the bottom of this."[1] I watched the wife sigh and look away. He clenched his fists together and talked louder.

First meeting, first impressions. Couples show me their dance, their sequence of action–reaction–action that makes up their rhythm together and imperceptibly, perhaps inadvertently, I move with them. Do I sigh slightly and avert my eyes from him, or do I talk loudly and intensely? If I move my foot in a different pattern, am I stepping on toes or introducing a new step?

Couples Therapy

The problem of couples therapy is to learn the dance of the couple and change some of their steps; not so the couple dance the way that

1. The dialogue in this article is reconstructed from memory because I did not have tapes of my work with this couple.

155

I like to but the way that works best for them. What makes this couple work? What's blocking them now? How can I release them to go back to their own natural development? I know that I have to think simply about very complicated phenomena in order to make interventions that are salient and the results of which are observable. In this chapter I present how I think about couples, how I organize therapy, and what actually happens between a couple and me over time as I change them and they change me.

In order to appreciate the multifaceted nature of a couple system one has to look at it from a variety of perspectives. It is not unlike the naturalist photographer who goes into the field with several different lenses in order to capture a sense of both the macro and micro interaction between the elements that make up the whole environment.

The three lenses that I use to assess a couple system allow me to develop a comprehensive series of hypotheses about the relationship between the evolution of the couple and the particular set of problems that they want my help solving. I view the couple from the following perspectives:

1. *The Content Lens.* Each couple has to solve the problems of managing a joint economy, developing companionship, engaging in a comfortable degree of sexuality and intimacy, and providing a quality of reciprocal caretaking and nurturance. It is usually in one or more of these areas that the content of a couples problem develop. A couple may present around the issue of money or sex or how they spend time together. It is important for the therapist to help the couple apply their problem-solving skills in areas in which they do not have conflict to the particular problem at hand.

2. *The Process Lens.* How a couple manages their sequences of being close and then being apart is important because often the problem they are presenting for treatment helps regulate their pattern of closeness and distance. Also, the therapist examines the interactive sequence to assess how the presenting problem might represent a solution to the distribution of power and influence in the way this couple works together. For example, does he maintain a position of control by being the caretaker around her symptom? Does his having a symptom provide an "Achilles heel" for her to strike at?

3. *The Developmental Lens.* It is important to assess at what stage each member of a couple is developmentally. Each couple needs to be considered in relationship to the normative developmental issues

of age brackets, socioeconomic background, family of origin, and ethnic group.

As I develop a picture of a couple, I define them as either a Type A or Type B couple. Type A couples are organized around a symptom presented by one member of the couple. The marriage is not the focus of treatment, the individual is. Symptoms such as agoraphobia, alcoholism, depression, or psychosomatic complaints typify these couples. The organization of the relationship around one being strong and the other weak or one sick and the other well is often a solution for the problems of regulating distance and managing the hierarchy. Frequently the symptom allows the marital struggle to remain covert, unresolved, and stable.

Type B couples present the marriage or relationships as the symptom. In these couples the focus on the marriage is often an overt symmetrical struggle around the content and process issues. Frequently the focus on the marriage is a mechanism by which the couple protects one or both members from having to resolve their individual developmental issues.

In both types, A and B, the therapist has to deal with the question, How do I help a couple remove or accept the presenting problem without destroying the ecology of their system? We all know the dangers created by human intervention to "improve" the environment. The same risk of change is present for each couple that enters your office. Yet change is normative and necessary for all couples. Is there any question that we therapists must appear both naive and arrogant as we greet couples with the question, "What's the problem and how can I help you change?"

Treating Type A Couples

George and Betsy Hammerly came to me because of George's drinking. They described their marriage as basically good except for his periodic bouts of drinking, which were often accompanied by his disappearing from home for as long as a week at a time. In fact, the decision to come for therapy seemed to derive from George's just having returned from a binge, repentant and on his best behavior, and Betsy's need to extract some evidence that "this time things would be different." In that first interview I remember the sinking feeling of being a new actor entering in the middle of an ongoing play in which everyone knew the lines but me. There was a quality of resigned repetition to much that was said. Married for 25 years, with four grown children, and with a lifetime's worth of dance between them, the Hammerlys presented a problem that absolutely had to be solved, for which all previous solutions had failed, and which neither of them had the slightest bit of faith could be solved. Welcome to the dance, Dr. Treadway. Won't you lead us for a while?

Type A Treatment Model

I do not go sailing without a chart and an initial course. I need to know about the currents and shoals, the compass headings and distances. Then I can adapt to the vagaries of wind and wave. Montaigne once said that "a sailor without a destination cannot hope for a favorable breeze." A therapist without a treatment plan can easily become lost and not know how to judge a couple's responses or his response to them. However, the key to successful therapy is adapting the treatment plan to fit the unique needs of each couple.

The following is an outline of the treatment plan that I use for treating couples with an alcoholic member and, with some modification, most Type A cases:

Step 1: Disengagement. The initial stage is to shift the responsibility for change from the overfunctioning spouse to the underfunctioning symptom bearer. Generally this means having the alcoholic set up a treatment program or controlled drinking contract while having the wife disengage from monitoring his behavior (see Berenson, 1976).

Step 2: Differentiation. I focus the therapy on each individual, restrain him or her from working on improving the couple relationship, and work on each individual's development of his or her agenda for change in front of the other. This allows the husband and wife, who are predictably fused and highly reactive, to begin to allow each person a sense of autonomy and individual responsibility.

Step 3: Negotiation. When the couple have successfully learned to tolerate each person's working on his or her own issues, I then move the couple to begin to negotiate change between them. The work is focused on present and future issues, and the therapy is very directed toward helping the couple make compromises and agreements that they then can practice and carry out.

Step 4: Conflict Management. After the couple have learned to make agreements and keep them, I direct them to learn how to handle conflict. We enact disagreements, practice fights, and work on a set of rules for fair fighting. It remains critical throughout these steps that the couple not try to resolve past conflicts or attempt to attain closeness and intimacy.

Step 5: Resolution of the Past. Throughout the treatment, the couple are restrained from bringing up the past until this step. Now they are asked, in a ritualized, formal way, to address and resolve their history of having hurt, betrayed, and disappointed each other. The couple attempt to forgive each other and to create a boundary between where they are now in the present and where they were in the past.

Step 6: Closeness and Intimacy. The couple have been restrained from trying to be close throughout this process because it is almost always true in Type A cases that the process of becoming intimate is linked to the outbreak of the symptomatic behavior. At this stage the couple begin to work overtly and directly on the quality of their relationship. In essence they have become a Type B case.

Does actual therapy ever look like this precise treatment plan? No, no more than one's track over the water ever replicates the neat line drawn on your chart between point A and point B. However, the plan becomes the reference point that allows the therapist to asses the couple's progress, where the therapy is headed, and what the therapist is doing. Of course, the plan is arbitrary and does not apply to all couples. The therapist has to assess the uniqueness of each couple system and tailor the treatment plan to fit the couple.

In discussing the Hammerly case in detail, I attempt to demonstrate how I think about therapy, what I do in the room, how I identify and correct mistakes, and, finally, how I evaluate outcome. I would enjoy presenting a perfect case, but I know from my own teaching that it is often the probelms and mistakes of therapy that are most instructive. In this case, we may see the blending of the plan with the reality; the ways in which I shape and change couples, the ways in which couples shape and change me.

I once helped a good friend of mine build a small wooden boat. After considerable work on the plans, we set about building the frame. We worked hard on getting the frame just right. After the boat was built, the frame was used for firewood. The boat is still sailing, the frame is gone. I have not seen the Hammerlys for several years; I wonder how they remember the time we spent in therapy. I hope they are still sailing.

The Hammerlys

First Phase of Treatment

Entering a couple system is like being a visiting anthropologist to a foreign culture (see Bateson, 1971). The behavior of the unit is regulated by rules and norms that have evolved over time. It is the therapist's job to develop some hypotheses about the workings of this particular system and the relationship between how the system works and the presenting problem. Once I have some hypotheses, I define my goals and introduce interventions to accomplish them. I then have to pay close attention to the results of my intervention in order to refine my hypotheses further, evaluate my goals, and develop subsequent strategies.

The Hammerlys presented themselves in an unusual way. Unlike many alcoholic couples, it was George who sought treatment. Usually the wife is the primary motivating force. George had just had a serious binge and had called me for individual therapy to help with his drinking problem. Although my proposal for couples treatment surprised him, he readily accepted the offer. Clearly, my initial hypothesis was based on the notions that alcohol problems are embedded in a relationship system and that it is easier to treat alcoholism by working with either the couple or the family. My goal was both to assess the couple system and to set up the therapy in a way that I could be most effective. If I had started another way, the whole case would have been different. From the first 5-minute phone call, I am making interventions that will shape the therapy and shape my relationship to these people. Right or wrong, intervening is unavoidable. Who comes to the first session will influence a therapist's assessment tremendously.

First impressions: He is loud and domineering; she is timid and submissive. He wants to solve all the problems so that they can be close and have good communication. She wants him to stay sober. As I sit with them I begin to see their dance. He is the repentant little boy; she is the distant and disapproving mother. He needs her to respect him and build him up; she cannot respect him until he builds himself up. He drinks to engage her; she becomes engaged on the surface and more cold and withdrawn in her behavior. A sense of detachment and resignation comes from her recital of the number of times this binge cycle has been repeated. A sense of desperation and demand emanates from his discussion about how he wants it to be different this time. He implies that she does not appreciate him enough, and she implies that the only problem is his drinking.

I look for patterns in which the alcohol abuse is embedded (Bateson, 1971). I need to know how the symptom works between them. My questions are almost always what and how, when and where, rather than why: "What happens when you come back from one of these episodes?" "How does Betsy behave?" "How does your relationship change after you have been sober for a while?" "What is going on between you just before George breaks out?"

These questions elicit descriptions of interactional sequences from which I generate hypotheses about how this particular couple system works in relationship to the presenting problem.

At the same time, I attempt to join each member of the couple. I use *empathy* ([to him]: "Nobody else really knows what a struggle the alcoholic goes through"); *matching* (he pounds his fist for emphasis, and I slap my knee when making a point); *self-disclosure* ([to her]: "I'm not much of a fighter myself "); and *positive connotation*: ("It seems that in some ways these episodes allow the two of you to rediscover how important you are to each other and how committed you are").

In asking the questions about how the couple system works around the symptom and in working hard to join each member of the couple, I am trying to accomplish two goals: first, to develop working hypotheses that will allow me to develop strategies; and second, to create a workable therapeutic milieu in which the couple feel both understood and have some confidence in my ability to help change them.

My hypotheses by the end of the first interview were that the drinking episodes seemed to intensify their involvement with each other and at the same time put her in a one-up position and him in a one-down position. I also sensed that his drinking worked at the individual level for him in providing an escape from his feelings of insecurity and lack of self-confidence in his career. I found out that he had not been fully employed for 10 years. Drinking episodes and recovery from drinking episodes seemed to provide a considerable distraction for him from his career dilemma.

When I looked at the couple through each of the lenses mentioned earlier, I decided that it was best to focus on their process. The symptom seemed to regulate their degree of closeness and distance, although I did not fully understand this at the time. The episodic cyclical quality to the behavior was the primary clue. The symptom also seemed to provide a counterbalance to his being overbearing and her being submissive. Looked at from the content perspective, it was difficult to see which area of their lives was most the source of conflict. In fact, the attention they gave to the drinking and the struggle to overcome it by and large protected them from having to resolve the marital issues that might have existed. Developmentally, I assumed that the couple were relatively stable. They were in their late 50s. The situation had been going on for years. They were not in a marital crisis. I did guess that the reality of his unemployment history was catching up with them as he neared retirement age. There was some question as to whether I should see this couple as a symptom-based Type A case or a marital focused Type B. She clearly defined his drinking as the problem. He agreed but also made references to difficulties in their relationship around "communications issues." I chose to see and initially focus on the symptom and organized my thinking accordingly. They were not, however, a typical alcoholic couple. Betsy was not an overinvolved pursuer. In fact, it appeared that George was pursuing her. Interestingly enough, beginning with the disengagement stage seemed appropriate, regardless of who was the pursuer.

My first goals in the therapy were quite straightforward. I wanted to establish a facilitative therapeutic context, and I wanted to separate the actual drinking behavior from the recursive cycle in which it seemed to be embedded.

The initial strategies attempted were based on the assumption that George needed to get out of the repentant one-down position and that Betsy needed to move toward him when he was doing better, instead of subtly rejecting him. In the first several sessions, I urged him to go to Alcoholics Anonymous (A.A.), implicitly joined him against her by suggesting that her reluctance to go to Al-Anon was a big problem, and explicitly joined him by attending to his definition of the relationship problem; that is, Betsy did not want to communicate enough with him. I also unbalanced the system (Minuchin, 1974) through aligning with his rather aggressive, domineering personal style. I would tend to be loud myself and imply that Betsy's quiet withdrawal was as aggressive an act as his demanding pursuit.

The initial outcome of these early interventions seemed to be quite positive. I saw the couple every other week for about 2 months, during which time George went back to A.A., Betsy went to Al-Anon, and the couple spent more time together.

As we began to move into the differentiation phase of treatment, I found out considerably more about the Hammerly couple.

George, who was 58, was the eldest son of a very successful man who apparently had been both a wonderful man and an alcoholic. He had died 20 years earlier. George's mother was still alive and still a dominant matriarch over all his family. George clearly seemed to identify with his father and seemed unable to assert himself at all with his mother. George had a considerable independent income and had been relatively inconsistent and unsuccessful in his career. He had been engaged in business and seemed to antagonize and alienate people rather easily. He had been an alcoholic for at least 20 years, and beneath his loud bravado he seemed to be an intensely shy and insecure man.

It seems only natural that this insecure man would match up with a shy and timid wife whom he could easily dominate. Betsy had grown up in a family of all girls and had had very little experience with men prior to her marriage. She seemed to have had good relationships with both her parents, although she was somewhat intimidated by her father, who apparently was loud and brusque.

Betsy and George described themselves as having a relatively good relationship except for his drinking of 20 years and her reluctance to communicate. Three of their four children had completed the leaving-home process, but the youngest was still in a dependent position, although he lived away from home. George was unemployed and spent most of his time working around the house, running his mother's estate, talking about working, and trying to communicate more with Betsy. Betsy had a job as a secretary and was gone from 9:00 to 5:00 every day.

As I got to know George and Betsy I began to see more clearly how his symptom worked between them. As is often is the case, the symptomatic behavior had a variety of regulatory and balancing functions:

1. George's dominance of Betsy was balanced by his being the designated problem, i.e., alcoholic, and not being the victim.
2. Both of them explained and justified Betsy's distance on the grounds of George's alcoholism.
3. George engaged her through the drinking episodes more successfully than when he was not drinking.
4. George made the recovery from alcoholism his life's work and his explanation for his career problems; this necessitated that he periodically have a binge in order not to be fully recovered.
5. While a dutiful son to his domineering mother most of the time, George was able to reconnect to his irresponsible dead father through his binges.
6. When drinking, George experienced himself as completely self-confident and secure.

Clearly the couple had developed a ritualized pattern of behavior that included George's drinking. Although I had an initial success in joining the couple system and George was successful at not drinking, actually nothing had changed in the pattern, and I was simply joined with the couple in their "Now, George is doing much better" mode.

It was in Session 5 that I decided that George's underlying depression about his career issues and Betsy's quiet disrespect for him should be addressed in the therapy as part of the differentiation stage. He had been sober for 2 months and was making vague references to looking for work. Over two sessions, I moved in on George and began to pin him down on his work plans and how he was going to get started. I also pushed Betsy to be more supportive and more involved with George on these issues. I thought that I was going to be able to help George succeed at enhancing his self-esteem and feel more competent and that it would provide a vehicle for keeping Betsy in both a one-up and engaged position while changing the focus of therapy from George's alcoholism.

Within a week of my initiating these interventions, George took off on a week-long binge. The first phase of treatment was over, and I had guessed wrong. It seemed that I was pushing for too much closeness between Betsy and George and that George was not at all ready to find a career. Looking back, I now wonder if my sense that George should solve the job problem did not in part come from the assumption that people *should* work. I may have pushed George before he was ready because of my own implicit values. I also seemed to have missed some cues that indicated that Betsy was much too angry and frustrated with George to get very close to him.

Second Phase of Treatment

When George and Betsy came in after his drinking episode, they both looked despondent and dejected. Clearly they had had higher hopes for the therapy and had felt genuine progress had been made. They were not prepared for this type of slip. I also was taken by surprise because, quite frankly, I had thought the therapy was proceeding quite well. It is always hard to start over. I decided that my first goal was to help the couple recommit to the therapy and the effort to change. I chose to take the blame for the drinking episode. I said it was my fault because I had been pushing her to get too close too fast, and that had been hard on her because she could not trust or forgive George yet, and I had pushed George too hard on the career problem in a manner that demonstrated my youth and naiveté about the whole issue. I also positively connoted the outbreak of drinking as a mechanism for giving me necessary feedback about the course of therapy, and was understanding that it would have been hard for George to tell me directly that I was doing a bad job.

The results of this particular intervention were immediate. Both George and Betsy perked right up and rescued me from my self-abasement. They told me I was doing a fine job and that I should not get discouraged. George explained to me at length about how sometimes he got discouraged, but he knew one should never give up. He also pointed out that when I was older, I would learn that you could not always succeed at things easily or the first time around.

We successfully reestablished our therepeutic contract. George stayed sober and went back to A.A. I relearned a very powerful lesson: Never forget to assess the family's assessment of the therapist as part of understanding the system. Clearly, I had been off the mark in my interventions, in part because it was very difficult for George in his 50s and unemployed to be taking earnest advice from an employed 35-year-old. I had not even given it a thought. It was then that I ruefully remembered that he referred to me as "young fellow" in our first session.

Since George had regained sobriety, I decided that the next step should be to attempt to stabilize the sobriety while trying to maintain the rest of the system in the status quo (see Berenson, 1976a,1976b). Inadvertently, I had moved too far beyond the original treatment contract and had become invested in treating directly what appeared to be underlying causes, i.e., his depression and their couple relationship. According to the model of treatment that I use to treat alcoholic couples, I had broken two rules: (*a*) Don't push closeness; and (*b*) don't work on underlying individual issues during the early stages of recovery from active drinking. I never expect to conduct therapy precisely according to my treatment model; however, it is very helpful for me to have these preconceived ideas about treatment in order to have a framework within which I can assess what is taking place.

I decided that the therapy itself had become potentially threatening to the stability of his sobriety because it tended to focus on the need to change things. Therefore, I made the following suggestions:

1. A commitment to A.A. and Al-Anon was more important than therapy, and they should come in for therapy only once a month.
2. Therapy was creating an additional pressure for them, and we would concentrate only on the issue of how best they each could handle George's efforts to be sober.

These moves, coupled with my taking the blame for George's outbreak, seemed to help stabilize the couple, and 4 months went by rather easily. Our sessions were more in the nature of checkups than focused problem-solving therapy. I assumed that we were effectively maintaining a plateau while significantly increasing the length of time that George stayed sober. It was my assumption that I and A.A./Al-Anon had become the distance-regulating and power-balancing mechanism in their couple system.

As we continued to meet, I began to see the old pattern emerge. George began to seem depressed, needy, and more demanding. Betsy was becoming less involved and more withdrawn. Both of them were reporting that everything was fine, and the sessions seemed to drag a bit.

Put yourself in the role of the therapist for a moment. What would you do?

1. Confront directly what was going on and predict that George was going to drink again?

2. Shift the focus from sobriety to the dynamics of the marital relationship?
3. Begin to open up the family of origin issues?
4. Bring up termination as a means of inducing a crisis prior to the anticipated drinking episode?

There are many other possibilities. The problem for the therapist is almost always having too many options, not too few. I felt we were at an important choice point in the therapy. I was nervous because I sensed that if they slipped again, that might simply be the end of the therapy. Any number of options were possible, but I felt unsure of myself. According to my treatment plan, we should be ready to begin the negotiation and conflict-management stages of therapy. Still, I felt that they were likely to undermine that move and that they would protect the marital system by a renewed outbreak in George's drinking. In retrospect, it seems clear that I was being organized by my own anxiety that George would drink again. When I become overly invested in either changing people or preventing a regression, I become anxious and muddled. My responses were also being shaped by my experience with the couple. I had tried to work on George's depression and his needs for closeness with Betsy, and it had backfired.

I decided to move to Besty and attempt a major unbalancing of the couple system by working on shifting her position in the system. The following is a reconstruction of a part of Session 9 in which I attempted to block the cycle in a new way.

THERAPIST: Well, it seems that, uh, all is going well but, uh, I'm wondering if anything has changed or whether we are simply going through the same old cycle. Betsy, are you worried that George may be due for another episode?

BETSY: I don't know what to think. I try not to get my hopes up but it does seem that things are somewhat better. At least I—

GEORGE (*interrupting*): Of course things are better. You never give credit where it's due. I'm sick and tired of you always equivocating. You're being mealy-mouthed again and I don't—"

THERAPIST (*interrupting*): Wait a second, George. I'd like you to think about something. What does it say to you that Betsy always puts up with these episodes of yours? Here you go, you disappear for a few days or a week, no phone calls and no hint of your whereabouts, and Betsy just shrugs her shoulders and accepts you back like you were a wayward little boy. Is she really respecting you when she does that? It looks like she's really just sort of putting up with you. What do you think?

GEORGE: I always thought that she loved me and that's why she put up with it.

THERAPIST: Would you put up with it if the shoe was on the other foot?

GEORGE: You mean if Betsy was an alcoholic?

THERAPIST: No, I mean suppose Betsy just took off and went somewhere without telling you and left no word of where she could be reached or when she would be back.

GEORGE: Well, Betsy would never do that. Betsy's not like that.

THERAPIST: So you wouldn't like it?

GEORGE: Of course not. Anybody can see that.

THERAPIST (*to Betsy*): Have you ever thought that maybe you should give George a taste of his own medicine? Maybe George doesn't really believe that you love him, and maybe he doesn't respect that you stayed with him all these years. Perhaps he may feel that fear and insecurity rather than love was what caused you to put up with his episodes. Perhaps he will simply continue to do this as long as its clear that you'll put up with it. You know George doesn't respect weakness and—

GEORGE (*interrupting*): I think this is totally wrong. Betsy knows full well that I do the best I can. Alcoholism is a disease, and it's not the same as playing tit for tat, and besides (*turns to Betsy*), you would never do anything like that, would you?

THERAPIST (*before Betsy can answer*): Don't be so sure, George. Betsy really does love you and if not passively accepting your episodic drinking bouts would help, she might seriously consider a different response.

In the interview, the discussion continued. Clearly I had hit a nerve with George. Betsy was also quite anxious. A major rule of the couple system had been broken. Neither had ever openly considered the possibility of Betsy's having an alternative to her passive, long-suffering behavior or considered that her willingness to accept George back was anything but loving and benign.

In making this move, it was my thought that I might be able to interrupt the escalation of bullying behavior, demand for closeness, and underlying depression in George before he flipped into a drinking mode, by dramatically increasing the potential risk for him. The move was dependent on my being able to join and challenge Betsy successfully while still maintaining my alliance with George (by suggesting that her passivity was a lack of love for him).

The move had a rather immediate effect. Within a week of the meeting, George was off on another drinking episode. Betsy called to tell me. I realized that George was putting Betsy to the test and that perhaps he and I were locked in a power struggle over her. On the phone with Betsy, I was thinking I had made a terrible mistake. Then Betsy announced that she was not going to be home when George reappeared. She and her sister were going for a holiday to Florida, and she had asked people not to tell George where she was!

I was surprised. It was a powerful reminder of how little control we actually have over our clients. I had not been setting up this move. I had hoped that the suggestion of it would, in fact, function as a blocker so that it would not be put to the test. However, one of my strongest rules of therapy is never to suggest something that you are not prepared to have happen. Therefore I congratulated Betsy and told her that I considered her decision an act of love for George that might truly lead to an end to their merry-go-round way of life. I told her that George would likely be quite angry but might treat her with some new-found respect. I thought to myself, Betsy is not the only person George will be angry at when he finds out about this.

I did not see the couple for a while. Apparently George was reluctant to come back for more sessions. I chose not to pursue them. After a couple of months, they did come back. It seemed as though the old cycle had been broken. George treated Betsy with respect, and Betsy was clearly pleased with herself. The aura of self-effacing fragility was gone, and she was willing to engage with George in direct negotiation. The couple was closer with each other than I had ever seen them and seemingly more motivated to work on important issues. George handled his anger at me by calling me a "young troublemaker" and "women's libber," but he did so with some forgiving lightness. I acknowleged that I had been worried and thought that perhaps I had made a big mistake. George then told me that I should have the courage of my convictions and that it was not a mistake. At the end of the session, I suggested that perhaps they should consider separate vacations once a year. If George really wanted to have a binge occasionally, then perhaps Betsy could also plan further get-away-from-it-all trips. They united very quickly against that idea and told me in no uncertain terms that they did not need to go through this again.

Third Phase of Treatment

The therapy was at a new and critical stage. I wanted to solidify the gains made and restrain the couple from pushing for more and more closeness. I felt that the couple's new-found closeness was quite delicate. It had taken 10 sessions and 9 months to get through the disengagement and differentiation stages of treatment, but, finally, Betsy had stood up to George, and George was genuinely committed to sobriety. Would the old pattern reinstate itself?

I was undecided whether to recess the therapy at this point while prescribing more A.A. and Al-Anon or move onto the negotiation stage. The couple seemed to be experiencing a dangerous honeymoon mood. Perhaps I was being overprotective, but I chose to try to restrain them from getting closer and more intimate. I suggested we work on their learning how to negotiate with each other and manage conflict. I explained my position by talking about the risks of change, the dangers of rising expectations, and the profound sense of loss they might both feel over the painful history of their marriage as they became closer. The couple seemed relieved by my taking this position, and I also came in for some mild teasing from George on my new-found caution.

The next four sessions were spent with George and Betsy negotiating face-to-face, with me in a relatively inactive role. I frequently needed to encourage Betsy not to withdraw and demur to George as she used to do. George was my ally in this because he agreed that he wanted more than "phony agreements."

The couple successfully negotiated issues related to managing children, in-laws, money, and use of time. I did not get very involved in the content of these discussions. Whenever either one of them made reference to the other's past history or previous failings, however, I would block that and reemphasize the importance of their staying in the here and now. I would state that there would be a time and a place for dealing with the past and that they should be patient and self-disciplined. I felt like an enforcer of a weapons-ban treaty.

By the end of four bimonthly sessions, the couple had stabilized at a new plateau. George was much less demanding, and Betsy was more assertive and less withdrawn. They had also achieved an enhanced quality of closeness and harmony. I decided that it was time to begin to focus on the resolution of past issues. This stage is not always necessary for couples, but I felt that this couple needed to go through a conjoint mourning for their lost years together. They had had a lengthy and painful marital history, and I had frequently told them that we would address this before the end of therapy. I felt that bringing them together in a ritual that allowed them to forgive each other, their failings and inadequacies, would enhance their ability to truly start anew.

In a serious manner I asked them each to recapitulate in writing the specifics of all the resentments that they had held toward each other since the beginning of their marriage. I urged them to be unsparing in their blaming statements and as concrete and detached as possible. I tended to exaggerate the degree of repressed rage and bitterness they both must feel, in order to create a sense of acceptance for them to express their feelings openly. I also urged the couple not to show their lists to each other but to bring them to the next session.

In the fifteenth session, George and Betsy read their lists to each other, taking turns, item by item. They both cried. So did I. So many misunderstandings, false starts, conciliatory efforts, had gone into their years together. George mentioned that he always secretly thought she had wished she had married someone else who was much smarter than he was. She referred to how much she felt that his drinking was her fault because she was a failure as a wife. The lists went on. Having been enjoined to express their rage, they had each chosen to move toward focusing on their own hurts and feelings of failure instead. At the end of the hour I suggested that my presence might be in the way of their being as close as they might want to be. With that indirect suggestion, I stepped out of the room and left them alone for a few minutes.

The Last Phase of Treatment

Following the session that evoked the hurtful past, the couple seemed stable and subdued. There was no regression and yet there remained a pall of sadness about them, particularly with George. George began to talk about his family of origin, especially his relationship to his father. Many of George's complaints about what had been missing in the relationship with Betsy were expressed as regrets about his difficult and ambivalent relationship with his mother and his close but inconsistent relationship with his father, who had in esssence deserted the family.

I decided that these old wounds, which had been so aptly bandaged over by the years of alcoholism and the struggle with Betsy, could now be appropriately addressed directly. It was my assumption that George needed a new way of resolving these issues.

Over the next several sessions I worked primarily with George to get him involved in a major family-of-origin project. We constructed a genogram. He engaged in finding out information about his father from his father's side of the family. He began to communicate with his siblings about the management of his mother, for whom George had been taking sole responsibility and who was apparently quite a difficult old lady. George brought up the idea that perhaps he would write a biography of his father, and Betsy and I endorsed the idea and suggested that it would be a very important legacy for his children.

I included in this phase of the treatment two indirect suggestions that were important to keeping George and Betsy on track. First, I suggested to George that in order to do adequate justice to the biography, he should strongly consider not returning to any regular work for the near future. Second, I predicted that at times when this journey back through his past became too painful, he might find that Betsy would provoke him in the old way by appearing bored or withdrawn. Certainly her doing so would help him out of being too despondent. They both thought the idea that Betsy would purposefully do such a thing was rather dumb.

George launched into his project, and the couple were doing well. I began to discuss phasing out the treatment. The frequency of our meetings was changed to every 6 weeks, and I stopped being very active in directing the sessions or assigning tasks. It was barely noted when George hit the 6 months of sobriety mark that meant he had been sober longer than at any other time in the course of treatment. At this stage, as I became a less controlling and dominant force in the therapy, I think it is useful for clients to educate me. In this context I began to ask George questions about writing. He enjoyed being asked and clearly liked the notion of being my mentor. I responded to the drafts of his work about his father, not as a critic, but as an admiring junior.

In the meantime, Betsy was becoming more assertive and independent. She clearly was enjoying not being the entire focal point of George's life. She tended to have much more enthusiasm for him when he demanded less attention. She became more active at work and more involved in her own projects. She tended to follow my lead and show increased respect for George's activities. I felt that Betsy's changes in behavior represented a significant indication that the couple had made some definite and stable progress. Session 22 was the last session. I did not feel it would be helpful to highlight termination issues, so I suggested in the previous session that we might start scheduling therapy on a p.r.n. basis after the next scheduled meeting. In the last meeting we discussed their upcoming plans, what was happening with their children, and how things were going in general. I chose not to pay attention to opportunities to engage with them. We ended the session a little early. They thanked me, and I told them that in actuality I had not done much. The therapy had worked because of their motivation and commitment.

I have not seen George and Betsy in therapy since the last session. I did discover from a mutual friend about a year after the therapy was over that they were continuing to do well and that George was still sober.

I had three hypotheses in mind that had led me to end the therapy at the point I chose to.

1. The couple showed no need or interest in pushing further on issues involving the quality of their relationship. They seemed to have arrived at a comfortable balance of closeness and distance and distribution of power.
2. George seemed to be using successfully his new family-of-origin project and writing as a means of slipping gracefully from unemployment into retirement, and I thought it was important to allow him to do so without calling attention to it. It was also clear that Betsy was not interested in his being employed as long as he was not placing all his needs for positive reenforcement on her.
3. I felt that the couple needed to end therapy in a one-up relationship to me. I particularly felt it was important for George to be in a strong position vis-à-vis the therapist.

If I had tried to hold them in therapy at this point, I thought that I would be communicating a lack of confidence in them and indirectly suggesting that there was more that they *should* work on. In truth, I was not confident that they were completely through with their old pattern. However, I chose to keep my doubts to myself. The end of therapy is not the end of the dance. The dance goes on, for better or worse, without me.

Commentary

In evaluating this treatment, I look back with the wisdom of hindsight. Could the therapy have been more successful? Could it have been more efficient? Was the treatment model that I had in my head a help or a hindrance in my work with them? Should I have started with the family-of-origin work sooner or ended treatment sooner? There are many other questions we might ask.

The therapy took 22 sessions over a period of almost 2 years. I think the major errors were made in the beginning two phases of the therapy when I put pressure on George to solve his work problem and when I virtually precipitated a drinking espisode by so drastically unbalancing the system by prescribing Betsy's counterattack to George's drinking episode. At either point, I might have lost the case, and I considered myself fortunate that I did not. I think that the quality of my relationship with them and my willingess to accept responsibility for the setbacks kept them engaged in treatment. Clearly, it took me a long time to understand the importance of George's being empowered in the relationship with me. I do not know if direct attention to George's family-of-origin issues sooner would have been helpful or would have precipiated a protective regression on their part.

In terms of the use of the treatment model, I felt that the model stood me in good stead and that my deviations from it, particularly at the beginning, got me into trouble. Early on, I began to push at underlying issues, e.g. George's career, and tried to enhance closeness by engaging Betsy as a support to George. A week later, George was drunk. Why would I break the rules of the model when the model is my own? It is in the nature of the therapeutic relationship that one is led as much as one is leading. It is my job to have enough clarity about the treatment of the case so that I know when I have been led astray. It is unfortunate but true that since anything I do with a couple is by definition an intervention, I have to accept that therapy is inherently a trial-and-error process. The best that I can do is see errors as an opportunity to learn more about how a given couple works and how they will let me work with them.

Thinking about Therapy

It is late November, and I am alone in a borrowed house on a mountain in Vermont. Outside, a hard cold wind and thick clouds foretell the coming of winter. I am finishing this chapter. I have not seen or heard about the Hammerlys in 3 years.

I feel a bittersweet sense of sadness. I cared about George and Betsy. I even miss them. But they are neither family nor friends. I felt intensely engaged with the essence of their lives, and now they are gone. I hope they are doing well, but I do not know if they are. I lean on the "no news is good news" crutch.

I have written about their elegant dance. What about my own? What is this peculiar activity I am engaged in? I am paid to enter people's lives, engage them, struggle with them, and end with them. They go on. I fill the available hour. I am neither a savior nor simply the hired help. I used to liken my work to that of a surgeon cutting to the heart of the matter—solving the problem with precision and efficiency. I used to be younger, too.

I do not know ultimately what worked or did not work with George and Betsy. I accepted them, I enjoyed them, and I cared about them. I had a theory. I applied technique. I can organize my experience with them into a logical-sounding sequence of behaviors, actions, and reactions.

We all learn by doing. Today's dogma is tomorrow's foolishness. Yet we have to risk believing in ourselves and what we do because that is how we learn.

Each time a woodworker works with a piece of wood he learns more about the secret of unlocking the wood's potential for beauty and strength. He makes mistakes. He learns from them. He proceeds with care and attention to detail. The shape of the final form always transcends his ideas because the wood has worked him while he worked the wood.

References

Bateson, G. (1971). The cybernetics of self: A theory of alcoholism. *Psychiatry, 34*, 1–18.

Berenson, D. (1976a). Alcohol and the family system. In P. Guerin (Ed.), *Family therapy: Theory and practice*. New York: Gardner Press.

Berenson, D. (1976b). A family approach to alcoholism. *Psychiatric Opinion, 13*, 33–38.

Minuchin, S. (1974). *Families and family therapy*. Cambridge, MA: Harvard University Press.

Chapter 7

Marital Therapy in a Family Plagued with Physical Illness

W. Robert Beavers, MD

My approach to marital treatment is systemic. This means, for one thing, that I respect the many different systems levels on which we live and appreciate the powerful influence that each level has on the other (Beavers, 1983a).

A family is profoundly affected, for example, when a perfect child becomes permanently damaged by encephalitis. The biological event has its impact on the parental dyad. Genetic predisposition to manic illness, to schizophrenia, and to various temperaments has a profound effect on personality and family life. In turn, the family system impacts and influences the results of these biological contributions.

In the case discussed in this chapter there is an ever-present specter of death from serious illness that influences individual attitudes and behavior and family functioning. Though the family and therapist have little direct impact on these life threats, nevertheless, changes in family-system-level variables can assist in adaptation.

A further aspect of a systems orientation in marital work is that personality and psychopathology are not viewed as givens but as phenomena profoundly influenced and even defined by contextual issues. That is, one may identify a "compulsive" man or a "hysterical" woman at a given point in time, but the behavior patterns that these labels attempt to define may with lightning rapidity be reversed, the husband then busily personalizing and capriciously emotive and the wife distancing, objectifying, and hyperrational.

Individual symptoms can jump from person to person as well. Depression in one family member usually represents depression in other family members. Who openly expresses this depression depends on tacit bargains of which all participants may be unaware.

There are some common characteristics in almost all troubled couples who come for treatment, regardless of the presenting complaint or the individual symptomatology. These include (*a*) a doctrinaire mistrust of each other; (*b*) persistent attempts to coerce; (*c*) a breakdown in negotiating activity; (*d*) a pervasive sense of hopelessness or even despair; and (*e*) an effort on the part of each to "build a case," that is, to prove to anyone who will listen that the partner is impossible. Not all couples show these characteristics to the same degree, nor does each person show them equally; nevertheless, similar destructive beliefs and behavior patterns are part of the presenting problem.

There is characteristically a "spin-out pattern," a predictable, stereotyped interaction derived from both individual's neurotic styles. This spin-out pattern differs from couple to couple but is grimly consistent for a given pair.

The therapist may initially offer hope that is largely based on transference, but he works to convert this as quickly as possible to hope based on real improvement in each partner's ability to identify and satisfy deeply felt needs (Beavers, 1981a). These needs are always tied up with trust, sharing, feeling competent and significant.

I consider marital therapy to be a strategy in family therapy. In fact, I consider all forms of psychotherapy to be different ways of doing family therapy, whether one sees one person in a family or many (Beavers, 1982b). Therefore, many forms of treatment may be advised either in combination or sequentially. I routinely utilize individual treatment, whole-family work, group therapy for one or both spouses, and somatic treatments for symptomatic family members. (I have often thought of myself as a therapeutic "alley fighter," in contrast to a boxer, who follows a stylized code of rules. This is part of what I believe a systems orientation to be—calling on knowledge and interventive tools at many levels to achieve therapeutic goals.)

For severely ill people, whether they have schizophrenia, manic-depressive illness, or suicidal depression, it is dangerous and foolhardy not to utilize somatic treatments, and yet a sole reliance on such interventions is inadequate (Davenport, Ebert, Adland, & Goodwin, 1977; Goldstein, Rodnick, Evans, May, & Steinberg, 1977).

The G. Family

Both Mr. and Mrs. G. were under a sentence of death, he because of leukemia currently in remission with continuing medication, she because of a severe case of regional ileitis for which she also received regular medication. Of course, we are all under a similar death sentence; the distinction was that Mr. and Mrs. G. had knowledge that their lives would end sooner rather than later, and were reminded of the probable way of death with every day's medication.

Part 1: Individual Treatment

I encountered the G. family by agreeing to see Mrs. G. She was 56 years old, married, and the mother of Shawn, age 28, Jean, age 26, and John, age 18. Mrs. G. had made a serious suicide attempt; she had been hospitalized and then released. Her attempt at suicide had followed her being told that she might need yet another operation to prevent ever more painful bouts of intestinal obstruction. Mrs. G. had disliked her assigned psychiatrist because he was "too young" and "shallow." She was referred to me by her previous psychiatrist in Los Angeles (where the G. family had lived prior to coming to Dallas).

Mrs. G. was a bright, pleasant, emaciated, chain-smoking woman with a somewhat conspiratorial manner. She told of her anger about son John's "selfishness." He would take her car and leave her stranded at home; further exploration revealed that she had not spoken up for the car but had brooded silently. She expressed frustration with her husband, who was sick but so noble, so superior, that he never complained and never let her know his feeling state. Still another source of anger was her pastor, whom she believed had told some friends about her suicide attempt.

She had been placed on antidepressants while in the hospital, and these were continued.

I listened to her story with the mature, deep intensity guaranteed by my gray hair and suggested that since she was having many strong feelings about family relationships, we should invite family members in. She would have none of it. She and her husband had visited her old psychiatrist in Los Angeles and were doing quite well, sex was good, and she needed a doctor for herself. I subsided, accepting her wish for the moment. The next week, she came in feeling great, cheerful and crediting it all to me. I was able to understand her, and she was standing up for herself more. Just a little problem with her pastor, though—she still was most unhappy with his efforts to help by urging her friends to reach out to her. Those friends were not really friends anyway.

That Friday she overdosed again with alcohol and sleeping pills (not prescribed by me) along with her steroids. I saw her Saturday and put her in the psychiatric division, over her strong objections and her husband's rather frantic efforts to please and appease her. I then arranged to have family sessions in the hospital.

Comment: This treatment process got off on the wrong foot; I would not have let anyone I supervised do what I did. The patient did have many medical problems, she did have a psychiatric illness, it was an individual referral, and I did try to get the family or husband in. But she went down again before I accomplished the change in strategy from working with an individual to working with relationships. This occurred because I was lulled by her "flight into health" into thinking I had time. Mrs. G. told me that I was dumb—I should have seen through her cheerfulness and heard her worries about her minister and friends. Of course, I told her she should expect me to be dumb. But she was right.

Part 2: Family Work

The first family session was enlightening. The three adult children were more interested in Mr. G.'s illness than in their mother's depression! They were most frustrated that he had never revealed anything of his condition except the diagnosis. Dad defended his reticence from a religious standpoint. He had made a rather complicated bargain with God that boiled down to not complaining or burdening people about his illness in exchange for living longer.

Mother directed a great deal of anger at Jean and John, accusing Jean (who was married and pregnant) of being uncaring about Mother's feelings and of not acting like part of the family, and John of betraying her by calling for an ambulance and making her look bad. Mr. G. was composed and solicitous to Mrs. G., but he was not forthcoming as to any feelings about her intermittent bouts with obstruction, about her suicide attempts, or about the children's greater interest in his problems than in hers.

Shawn handled himself much like Mr. G.—cool and in charge of himself. He described his feelings of peace after becoming a "real Christian."

Subsequent family sessions were designed to (*a*) develop Mr. G.'s identity; (*b*) bring out and resolve some of the conflicts between Mother, Jean, and John; (*c*) find out who Shawn was and how he could help; and (*d*) take the spotlight from Mrs. G. and her conflicts with the children and focus on her relationship with Mr. G.

These therapeutic goals were reasonably well accomplished. Mr. G. became a bit more expressive, though any discussion of his response to his illness remained off-limits. He was shy and had always needed Mrs. G. to front for him socially. He tended to respond to her bouts of illness as he did to his own—by becoming more remote.

Mrs. G. had told Jean not to expect her to babysit when the baby was born. Jean was hurt and pulled away, drawing closer to her husband with ever greater intensity. After Mrs. G. vented her spleen at Jean and painted a rather unflattering portrait of Jean's husband, Jean in turn told her mother what she thought of being pulled toward the family and yet pushed away. Jean at one time had been her mother's favorite, but getting married and having a career (she was a commodities broker) produced independence that Mother experienced as a painful, unmourned loss. Mrs. G. realized that she was reacting to Jean much as her own mother had responded to her: Mrs. G.'s mother had always taken offense at Mrs. G.'s efforts at independent thought or action. Jean's pregnancy had heightened their unresolved mother–daughter conflicts. Understanding this with the background of previous generations softened and reduced the friction. Mother and Jean expressed some warmth toward each other.

Mother made some progress in recognizing her resentment toward John and doing something about it. John was able to express some of his mixed feeling toward Mother. He was frightened and angry at her illness but loved her and wanted to do something to help.

Shawn had been a hell-raiser in adolescence, making Jean look good and John look less bad. Shawn's religious conversion and personality change, all family members agreed, had produced a clone of Dad, and though Shawn was never in trouble in the family, he was a nebulous figure and remained so during the family work.

Mr. and Mrs. G. confronted the fact that she felt lonely and isolated from him; she resented his superior attitude, his strength in the face of illness and threatened death, while she was so weak. If he loved her, and she was feeling all of this, how could Mr. G. be so calm?

Comment: By this time, things were beginning to go right. It was easy to like these people, and the feeling was reciprocated. There was a great deal of "glue" in the family; they held together and tried to be responsible. Mother was nominated thus far to be the carrier and expressor of family pain. Her resentment and forays into outright paranoid thinking; for example, the alleged lack of caring on the part of Jean and John and church friends, was balanced or complemented by the bland and righteous equanimity of Shawn and Mr. G.

I began seeing Mr. and Mrs. G. as a couple during this period, alternating with family sessions. As Jean got into late pregnancy and John left for college, the stage was set for working with the couple alone. Though Mrs. G. had railed against the children's growing up and leaving, she and her husband had done a reasonably good job of allowing it. Left with each other as the remaining family unit, they now were willing to acknowledge long-standing unresolved conflicts between them that spoiled much of the value of the love that they possessed for one other.

Part 3: Couples Work—The Spin-Out Pattern

It had become apparent that this couple's spin-out pattern consisted of Mr. G.'s obliviousness (to his feelings, to hers, to interpersonal subtlety), on the one hand, and Mrs. G.'s descent into depression, severe mistrust, and helpless anger, on the other. Described another way, Mrs. G. would act in a helpless, angry manner, and Mr. G. would become stronger, more responsible. Mrs. G. would react poorly to this, feel more helpless. Mr. G. would try to carry more on his shoulders. And so on and on.

With Mrs. G.'s anger less often directed at one of her children, she became more forthright in her expressed dissatisfaction with her husband. She complained that he always got his way. In their last two moves, she had wanted to stay where she was, but he had made the decision for the family without consultation, and she had never been able to find new friends to equal the old. Mr. G. protested that he did not have any choice either; as an executive in a nationwide publishing company, he had to go where he was assigned. On closer examination, Mrs. G. was not quite as unreasonable as she sounded. She knew the family income had depended on those moves, but somehow his high-handed and self-righteous style of arranging things with no discussion had stuck in her throat. These moves were symbolic of her perception that she was small, incompetent, and poorly treated; while he was always strong, competent, and in control.

Though this shared view of their relative power had existed as far back as either could remember in their life together, the development of their illnesses had worsened the situation and increased the differences in apparent competence. Mr. G. had been quite ill but never complained, never questioned his doctors, and did as he was told. His remission was considered by his medical team to be most remarkable; as indicated earlier, he believed it to be from divine intervention. In contrast, Mrs. G.'s illness had made her feel openly frightened, more fearful of trusting anybody, including doctors, and still more helpless to control her destiny.

The most dramatic results of the spin-out pattern were the suicide attempts. At one and the same time, they were vivid evidence of her weakness and his strength, but they also turned the tables. He was frightened and helpless, and she was in control.

The job of communicating this pattern to the pair was made easier, of course, by the fact that they had taught it to me. I then set about to tease Mrs. G. about her power, pointing out that all she had to do was collapse into a heap and she had him by the short hair, and to invite Mr. G. to express his vulnerability, fears, and needs. To this day, I have never been able to get him to talk of any vulnerability in the area of his illness, but he did find it acceptable, even pleasant at times, to describe his doubts about his job, his fears for his wife, his shyness, and his needs for her leadership and support in dealing with people.

Mrs. G. had considerable difficulty in giving up the sick role. She would often rescue her spouse, when he was challenged or confronted, by reverting to her suicidal ruminations or threats. The gradual disappearance of this chosen sick role was (and is) complicated by the unpredictable occurrence of intestinal obstruction, which requires brief hospitalizations and intravenous steroids.

In about eight sessions, the couple accepted a systemic view of the disturbed part of their relationship: Each had a part in creating that which he or she did not want; neither was helpless in producing what he or she did want; both were able to influence but not control the other; and each was living out some feelings and wishes of the other. Mrs. G. would like to be seen as more effective and competent, and Mr. G. would like to cry and be comforted.

As this spin-out pattern became a part of the treatment mythology, an enduring belief providing the background for many other interactions, the threat of another possibly fatal attempt by Mrs. G. was lessened considerably. (There was one more suicidal episode, to be discussed later.) I began to relax a bit and to enjoy the sessions.

Discussion: We have now begun the couples work with identification of the primary pattern of disturbed interaction and development of a shared effort to reduce it.

The couple are imbedded in a family that would be described by the language of my assessment schema (Beavers, 1981b, 1982a; Beavers & Voeller, 1983) as a lower–midrange centripetal family. This means that the family members are quite concerned about *control*, of themselves and others. Indeed, a family rule is "Loving means controlling." There is a strong suspicion that people at their core are bad, which justifies efforts to control self and others. Personal satisfaction is suspect, and emotional deprivation is less disturbing than being out of control. Appearances are important, and dramatic evidences to outsiders of family conflict are embarrassing.

Such family members in treatment respond to being able to control better, to reframing helplessness as power, to a therapist sympathetic to the unspoken needs of the member with the most overt power.

The spin-out concept encompasses both family and individual reality. My short definition of neurosis is "stereotyped and repetitive attitudes and behavior that were once useful, even necessary, but are now maladaptive."

When couples come together, they can match these individual patterns into a dyadic form and produce a spin-out. When a therapist intervenes effectively, the couple can spin in: less A behavior, less B, therefore less A. Thus, there is less stereotyping in individual and couple behavior, which allows more energy available for adaptation.

Mr. and Mrs. G., under the impact of life-threatening illnesses, regressed from moderate marital friction to a blatant impotent–omnipotent way of relating. I consider the impotent–omnipotent interaction a hallmark of emotional pathology (Beavers, 1977). It is illustrated by the normal relationships between the caretaker and an infant. Each is helpless in the hands of the other. The infant cries, and the caretaker must respond to care for the infant, yet the infant is helpless and dependent on the caretaker for life itself.

As infants become children, this paradoxical impotent–omnipotent pattern gives way to defined boundaries, separateness, and the evolution of competence. In a competent mode, personal responsibility and personal esteem can evolve. Mr. and Mrs. G. had experienced competence, but under the impact of illness Mr. G. had developed omnipotent fantasies that he could control his disease and he therefore denied helplessness; whereas Mrs. G. developed a sense of impotence, and she therefore denied her nearly complete control over her husband whenever she thought or acted suicidally.

Part 4: Relating versus Coercing

The physical illnesses had coincided with other powerful stresses related to their family life cycle. Mr. G.'s position in his job had crested and was receding; Mrs. G.'s role as a mother was effectively ending. She was envious of Mr. G.'s definition of himself in his job; he was trying to avoid the specter of defining himself by a position that was deteriorating.

Mrs. G. had worked as a semitrained nursery school teacher in years past; she felt she could never function in that role again. She had taken up sculpting some 6 years previously; describing these efforts, she alternated between delightful enthusiasm and painful cynicism.

Both of these people were struggling with a sense of pointlessness and worthlessness if they were not *producing*. Both had more than an average share of perfectionism. Both had come from families in which achieving was emphasized and personal relationships were deemphasized. Neither had felt close to his or her own parents.

Fortunately, there were signs that both cared greatly about each other. Mrs. G.'s rage that Mr. G. never showed his pain could easily be reframed as love. Mr. G.'s tireless activity and uncomplaining stance when his wife was ill could easily be defined as evidence of tremendous need for her.

It seemed to me that the G's future together depended on discovering skills in relating and finding value in the emotional responses that each could evoke in the other. Then each could experience worth by existing, by playing.

Mrs. G. decided at about this time to stop smoking as a gift to herself. Twice before I had mentioned the importance of doing so, then let it drop for strategic reasons—not because of less concern, for she truly looked terminal, with skin on bones and a chronic productive cough. She enrolled in a copyrighted group method for stopping smoking, graduated, and has not touched cigarettes since. (Surprisingly, I stopped smoking soon after she did, and it is permanant so far.) We agreed that this represented a reduction in her suicidal wishes, a desire to feel good. Mrs. G. added that she expected it to improve her sex life.

Now the couple were exploring each other, holding hands more often in my office, reaching out sexually, talking of feelings at times other than with me. The principal roadblock to this pleasant movement was the intrusion of coercive efforts. He would preach to her of the necessity for accepting what the doctor had told her, of being reconciled to what her children were doing. She would flare up and withdraw. Sometimes she scolded him for not talking to her (forgetting to ask) and advised him how he should handle things at work. When they derailed, I would explore with them how they got off the track and how it felt. There was concentrated effort to provide emotional, "gut level" education in how it feels to be coerced, how it feels to be accepted. I pointed out that acceptance did not have to be agreement—it often is not. But as they learned to attend to each other, they were able to recognize the opposite, underside of feelings being expressed. Gradually the atmosphere became more pleasant and far more hopeful.

Comment: I have an enduring fantasy about Mister or Miss Everychild, age 2½. There is a thunderstorm, and Everychild turns to Caretaker. If Caretaker is receptive and holds Everychild for a minute or two, confidence is restored and an important lesson is learned and relearned: When frightened, reach out to a loved person and relate openly without coercion. In contrast, if Caretaker is feeling bereft, perhaps because of being isolated and distance or even abandoned by spouse, then instead of a receptive lap there may be a stiffening, or a nonempathic, "pro forma" gesture. In this scenario, Everychild learns something quite different: One cannot depend on relating when frightened. Rather, one must learn to coerce, to intimidate oneself by denying feelings, or to coerce others by tantrums, manipulation, or threat.

Much of what a good therapist does is related to reevaluating old lessons regarding the value of relating or coercing. I do not denounce control; all of us want to control people who are important to us. Many people have been encouraged by therapists to have needless guilt over their controlling tendencies. What I am contrasting with relating is coercion or attempts at *control without choice*.

Mr. and Mrs. G. had had a great deal of education in attempts to control oneself and/or others without attention to choice. With them, as with other patients, the needed emotional learning is about respecting feelings, ambivalence, and choice.

Part 5: Family of Origin

At this point, I describe the work with Mr. and Mrs. G.'s families of origin, though this work began on the first visit.

Blandness and distance would summarize Mr. G.'s description of his family memories. From good German stock on both sides, Mr. G. was bathed in an atmosphere of pragmatic, goal-directed industry. Most of his memories of parents popped out as he was pressured by his wife or me to explore some feeling or another. It was clear that he had never been rewarded for such self-indulgence. His church had been important to him all his life, as it was to his parents. His God was not a harsh one but a busy one who expected his charges to take care of their own problems, and of others' as well.

Mr. G.'s apparent self-sufficiency, relative silence, and desire to look after others was maddening to Mrs. G., frustrating to his children, and stunting to parts of himself; nevertheless, these behavior patterns were clearly valuable when he was growing up. He was thought to be a good boy, and his parents were proud of his success. He, in turn, was happy that they had lived to see him do well and be independent.

The discussion of his family helped Mr. G. to become more aware that the values found in this family were not universal ones. He had perceived in Mrs. G. different attitudes, different beliefs that were attractive to him; yet he had felt compelled to attempt to convert her to his way.

Mrs. G. had a quite different story to tell. She had always known open conflict as a regular accompaniment to living. She had grown up in a family with a secret: Her father had been convicted of securities fraud when she was small. This was both known and denied, told and yet not spoken of. Her father was relatively unsuccessful in business, forever struggling, always feeling poorly treated. Her mother had known wealth as a child and felt that she had married beneath her. She never criticized her husband openly, but tinges of marital dissatisfaction colored her discussions with Mrs. G. as a girl.

Mrs. G.'s mother was never satisfied with her daughter's performance either. She always could have done better or differently, and Mrs. G. had typically felt a mixture of guilt and resentment toward her mother.

Frustrated with her mother's lack of approval and in awe yet somewhat frightened of her frequently absent father, Mrs. G. learned early to find comfort in relationships outside the family. She developed social skills that brought her some self-esteem and were certainly part of her attractiveness to Mr. G.

With a minimum of therapeutic activity, Mrs. G. recognized that she was carrying over some expectations derived from the past into the present. She had never known her parents to get along well or resolve differences, nor had she experienced home as a place of intimacy. Blocked in their definitions of self through achievement, Mr. and Mrs. G. needed new learning about relationships to avoid despair.

Her relationship with her mother remained conflicted and painful. She believed that this had spilled over into her perception of Jean. Her criticism of Jean sounded like an echo of her mother's criticism ringing in her ears.

Mrs. G. had been an only child and had wished for a larger family. When she had the larger family, she believed she had not raised the children to care about her. As we explored the family-of-origin material she seriously considered that much, if not all, of her doubts about her children's love could be re-created from her own unresolved painful relationship with her mother.

As Mr. and Mrs. G. began to talk more, to share more feelings, and to become a bit more supportive to each other, Mr. G. was able to help his wife become less resentful and guilty. They visited her mother. Mrs. G. returned, saying, "I don't suppose I will ever please her. But it doesn't seem so important now."

Mrs. G. began to see that her husband's calmness and even his distancing, though maddening at times, were also reassuring. She had sought out a man who tried very hard to be at peace with the world. Conversely, Mr. G. acknowledged that Mrs. G.'s ready anger allowed her to express feeling for him as well as for herself.

Comment: Exploring family-of-origin material is a powerful tool in breaking up stubborn, stuck positions. Every troubled couple or family has problems with comprehending, much less accepting, the subjective nature of truth. There is a strong tendency to think of family-of-origin experiences as absolutely right or absolutely wrong.

Exploring family of origin is also valuable in helping people experience mixed feelings (Beavers, 1983c). "Mother was always critical of me, but she did make me try hard just to spite her." "I always adored Dad but he scared me." "My parents seemed so sure that their beliefs were right. I thought so, too, but somehow there was something missing."

People often marry to finesse their short suits, i.e., to find in their partners those attributes and capabilities that were not a part of their own growing-up experiences. Only after many years of trying to make do without a full deck do spouses begin to understand that marrying is not an adequate substitute for growing up.

Part 6: Negotiating

Mr. and Mrs. G. were less caught up in triangular struggles with grown children now. They accepted to some extent the idea that Mrs. G.'s episodes of excessive alcohol and drug abuse were related to conflicts within the family, particularly in the marital dyad. They had experienced some warmth for each other and had been able to express needs. But they were still apt to get into conflicts that were not resolved, with the beginnings of spin-out written all over the interaction.

Mrs. G. would characteristically take an extreme absolute position:

MRS. G.: John hates me; furthermore, he is a bum who comes back to our house and freeloads with no concern about my feelings.
MR. G. (*assuming a kindly, superior position*): Now, dear, John is just being eighteen.
MRS. G.: Easy for you to say since he's not shouting at you, and besides you get him off in a corner and talk with him and I'm left all alone.
MR. G.: Well, of course I get him alone to reason with him. It certainly wouldn't help to talk to him with you around. It would simply make matters worse, and John would leave for good.
MRS. G.: You see, he's not interested in my feelings, he's just interested in John.

This excerpt is a representative sample of the way that the G.'s become embroiled and frustrated with each other.

I do not believe that many therapeutic approaches to such fruitless, oppositional dialogue can be listed and then used well in some rote manner. In psychotherapy there is a similarity to the professional quarterback's speaking of the "feel of the game." One may have 70 offensive plays that could reasonably be used, but the history, remote and recent, of opponents and teammates are important in selecting well. In this instance, I chose to deal with the material directly and loosen up each person's stereotyped position by (*a*) asking each to experience the moment—the frustration, the tension, the general unpleasantness; (*b*) "cartooning" each position, that is, dramatically burlesquing the narrow and simplistic way each person is trying to get more comfortable; (*c*) reducing certainty and inducing some confusion; (*d*) forcefully pointing out the effects of each person's current approach; (*e*) observing how isolated both are; and (*f*) inviting a brainstorming session for ways to achieve the goals of both and how they could accomplish these goals together.

It was not hard to cartoon these positions. John was a useless, worthless clod who hated his mother despite her having nothing but loving feelings for him. Further, John wished to remain a child and never grow up or help anybody. Dad had no interests of his own in this struggle, he had no anger, no ugliness—just sweetness and light. Godly, you might say! Mother and John were totally unreasonable but should be placated at all times because open encounter would be disastrous. Mother would commit suicide or John would leave. Dad alone held the fate of the family in his hands and functioned selflessly and nobly.

Presenting in this fashion, that is, really listening and then feeding back the propaganda line without a twist, caused both to laugh a bit. When challenged, Mrs. G. did admit that she was angry at John and that he did have some good qualities. Mr. G. allowed that he was able to get angry, that he was angry right now, somewhat at me and somewhat at Mrs. G. and John; further, that he felt more scared than in control in the situation just described. Each had many more feelings and much more confusion than they had admitted in their first efforts at discussion.

I said, forcefully and intensely, "Mrs. G., I *promise* if you present such a one-way, damning viewpoint of anybody that you and a third person care about, you will force that third person to withdraw from you emotionally. Any third person, not just Mr. G." I then played out the triangle by pretending to browbeat Mr. G. as a malevolent, deceptive, insensitive incompetent and asked her if she wanted to reach toward me or toward her husband. (I find it useful to play-act such little dramas. They last only a minute or so, but often have a powerful emotional impact.)

To Mr. G., I said, "I *promise* that if you assume that superior, saintly, and godlike role [I already knew that his nickname in the family was "God"], you will alienate your audience, no matter who it is. By the way, in your experience, has it worked very often?" Mr. G. turned several facial colors but ruefully reflected that it did not seem to resolve anything; but it did stop some painful blow-ups.

Waiting a minute for the emotions to dissipate somewhat, I asked if they both felt isolated when they went through the routine they had just described and acted out. Mrs. G. readily spoke of her painful experience when her husband and her son were away in another room, leaving her alone; Mr. G., with some hesitation, stated that he did not feel close to either loved one as he went through his "sweet reason" performance.

Mrs. G. now spoke of feeling isolated, helpless, and enraged, with no place for the rage to go but inward. These are what I consider the three major aspects of depression, and I told her so. So, we all three had experienced an interaction that would lead her to being suicidal. Then we got down to brainstorming how they could get together on a few goals and accomplish them together. Mrs. G. thought she could limit her attacks on John to the very real problems of getting his room clean before he went off to college and being at least civil to her. The latter meant not using bad language about her in her presence. She, in turn, would lay off the character assassination. Mr. G. could support her in this—they would be on the same team—and he would try out the idea that blow-ups might be constructive if he did not move in and preach or get John off by himself.

The experiences in this session became a model, a benchmark to which we all referred at intervals. Subsequent sessions provided evidence that they were both wary of each other when John was an issue and that they felt a new sense of sharing.

Discussion: One of the classical bits that troubled couples play out is what I call "the unholy bargain." It goes like this: "You have mixed feelings that are unresolved, and I have unresolved mixed feelings, too. Resolving these mixed feelings in ourselves requires growing up, declaring ourselves and this is painful and possibly dangerous. So, let's make this unholy bargain—you take one half of my feelings and I'll take the other half of yours. Then neither of us has to resolve our internal conflict, but we'll fight like hell for the next forty years."

This is just what the G's had done in reference to John. Mrs. G.'s attacks were clear and absolute; she appeared to have no mixed feelings. Her husband expressed all the loving and caring for them both. He, in turn, could be saintly as she dutifully carried out her task of being the carrier of the rage for both.

The above illustrates why it is necessary to arrange to have people confused or "off balance" during the course of treatment. One does not kill or wound when one is confused; one is more apt to be destructive when the issues are thought simple and single-sided.

Some implicit shared beliefs make the unholy bargain attractive or inevitable. These include (a) At bottom, people have only one feeling about loved ones, not mixed feelings; (b) if I possess truth, it is pure and objective; (c) therefore, in a conflict, one person is right and the other wrong.

The G's had all three. The exercise in negotiation was designed to challenge these beliefs and refocus their energy on the pragmatic. This pragmatism can be expressed in two questions: "What do I want?" "How do I go about getting it?" Many times, in the midst of a session that consists of blame and attack, I will ask these two questions of the most vociferous partner. "What do you want?" usually stops the noisiest and most fruitless bickering.

I make every effort to have people leave treatment with a keen awareness of human ambivalence. If one absolute feeling is expressed, its powerful opposite is lurking somewhere. Moreover, the view that "my eye is God's eye" will negate any efforts at closeness. We will never know truth but only snatches of it, and people who disagree with us are valuable as teachers.

Part 7: Medication and Relationships

Mrs. G. had been on the antidepressant medication for a year. There were certain problems with her taking antidepressants. All of these medications have some degree of anticholinergic effect (like atropine or belladona) that inhibits bowel smooth-muscle activity, and her bowel was always on the verge of going on strike. So there was a continued effort to reduce the dosage, to find a drug with as little effect on the gut as possible, and to stop all antidepressant drugs.

We had two frightening times in this respect, one when she began to gain weight as a consequence of stopping smoking, getting less depressed, less isolated, and taking an antidepressant, which often induces weight gain. She was switched to another drug, one that was less apt to increase appetite, but unfortunately had more anticholinergic activity and had to be hospitalized with intestinal obstruction.

It became clear that she needed to be off the antidepressants if at all possible. She stopped taking them; the second scare followed 2 weeks later. She took excessive alcohol, overdosed on sleeping pills (prescribed by the bowel doctor), and spent a bleary, frustrating time in the emergency room. Mr. G., at his best in a crisis, accompanied her, stayed with her and got her home with my authorization for leaving the ER and not going back into the psychiatric unit. I believed the G.'s to be far enough along in getting a working relationship that hospitalization at that time would have set back our work. After another 3 months of couples treatment, the antidepressant was stopped again. This time, Mrs. G. remained relatively undepressed.

Comment: For a long time, I have observed an inverse ratio between the need for drugs and the availability of close relationships, i.e., less intimacy, more drugs, and vice versa. This correlation is evident with alcohol and illicit drugs as well as drugs prescribed for psychosis and depression. Probably no more clinically important effect of one system on another could be cited. I had guessed wrong the first time when discontinuing the medication; Mrs. G. still felt too isolated, too helpless, too angry. The second time, she had more hope and would reach out to her husband, to her therapist, or to friends before she would spiral downward.

Part 8: Meaning and Purpose

Mrs. G. was the voice for the family pain. As a result of the impact of severe illness, there was plenty of it. Initially the children were the focus of frustration; the hopelessness, bitterness, and despair were expressed about them. As this displacement was dealt with, hopelessness about the couple's relationship emerged. Finally, when they began to talk with each other and work better together, the despair became focused on, "What's the point? Why should we have to struggle to stay alive, to swallow steroids and antimetabolites? Why should we work to get together when I don't do anything meaningful; my children are grown, my husband is self-sufficient, self-contained and doesn't need me, my sculpting is second-rate and my chances of going back to a useful fulltime job are almost nil?" The foregoing is a paraphrased summary of Mrs. G.'s questions. Though Mr. G.'s religious faith was unshakable, it was not helpful in relating to his wife. Indeed, since it encouraged his quiet stoicism and saintliness, at least initially it was detrimental to their relationship.

Moreover, Mr. and Mrs. G. are people caught up in cultural transition. Though she had been raised to be a conventional housewife and mother, her own mother's background of culture and wealth had been superior to that of her father, and there was some idea from childhood that she should be more than she was, more like a man perhaps, with visible business success. The family was progressive and even could be considered avant-garde in this area. Jean became a commodities broker *and* had a family. Mr. G. was certainly raised to think of men as responsible and women as weaker and needing protection, but he had encouraged his wife in a career and in a vocation. The pessimistic side of Mrs. G. would not allow her to see the mother who has raised three capable children as being anything significant; she judged her value by what she considered male standards and believed herself to be nothing.

My judgment was that I could alter Mr. G.'s belief system to the extent of acknowledging his need for his wife and understanding that such a need could be considered virtuous and not weak. I could persuade Mrs. G. to reexamine her contempt for her mediocrity in sculpting. Was it a worthwhile endeavor? Could only a genius find satisfaction in creativity? I could challenge both of them to help each other with their harsh belief that people are only as valuable as their accomplishments.

Presenting these issues to the G.'s as clearly and as evenhandedly as I could, with the honest humility of one who struggles with the same uncertainties, allowed the couple to explore what was meaningful to them, how their religion could help, other sources of human value in addition to productivity. In time, they spoke of caring for each other as important, that being alive was important regardless of productivity. It encouraged Mrs. G. to return to her sculpting and create for herself and no one else.

Comment: I have repeatedly observed patients becoming interested in the point of it all as the neurotic struggles are transcended. To believe in something larger than oneself and one's family is a usual and expected part of health and healthy families (Beavers, 1983b). For these reasons, I do not believe that people who are trying to find some personal meaning for themselves are always resisting or displacing, as the old analytic theorists would have it (Freud, 1933). Rather, the neurotic interaction directs attention from intense and genuine human concerns. The circular, frustrating interpersonal games reduce the awesome mysteries of the universe down to the size of a phone booth. Mr. and Mrs. G., partly because of their illnesses, partly because of Mrs. G.'s suicidal bent, wanted to talk of purpose. As Samuel Johnson said, "A sentence to be hanged in a fortnight wonderfully concentrates the mind." The most powerful and tension-filled issues for people to talk about are sex, money, and religion. It seems that most therapists are trained to be helpful in only one of these and often are phobic about the other two.

Part 9: Relative Trust

By this time in treatment, the G.'s and I had gone through a lot together and had a good working alliance and some healthy respect for each other. The G.'s had learned about circularity of cause and effect, and the ubiquitous quality of ambivalence and conflict. They had learned about triangulation and displacement. We all had learned a little more about people's limited knowledge, and agreed that we would jump on whichever one of us made absolute, godlike pronouncements.

Mrs. G. was not taking any drugs for her mental state and was reasonably accepting of the unpredictable times she would have to return to the hopsital because of obstruction. Mr. G. had remained in medical remission throughout the psychotherapy interval.

Coming to see me once a week had become a habit, approached with a mixture of anticipation and mild apprehension (sometimes more one, sometimes more the other). We worked on no new issues but whetted and honed the G.'s capabilities of dealing with those already covered.

As we were no longer so often in desperate difficulty, I began to focus more specifically on boundary issues, that is, the many ways people who live together can blur and confuse individual problems, wishes, and actions to the detriment of working as a team, and the many ways these same people can stop a moment, take stock, and speak for themselves.

It was hard for Mr. G. to come off his mountain top and join us sweaty, brawling, emotive peasants. As he tried, he enjoyed "cutting loose" and getting mad, reaching for help, admitting uncertainty. But it was also painful.

And, of course, Mrs. G. would conspire with him to put him back on his pedestal by crying death. When Mr. G. was floundering, it was predictable that Mrs. G. would begin to swan-dive into depression and despair.

She was, of course, congratulated on her devotion to Mr. G., and on her desire to protect him at any cost. But I also wondered if she might risk a little and see whether he could take care of himself. The continual reframing of the family myth from him as powerful, herself as weak, to him as needful, often helpless, and herself as powerful, was effective in restructuring their interaction to include a much greater appreciation of separate identities, of clearer boundaries.

The G.'s planned a month-long vacation, driving together to visit family and old friends in places where they had previously lived. We all three knew this was a shakedown cruise for leaving treatment. Could they get along together? Would their physical state hold up? The trip exceeded all our hopes; they stayed close, had a fight or two, and came back together quite nicely. They seemed to develop a relative trust in each other. She knew now that he needed her; he knew that she would not do herself in. Soon after returning to home and treatment, they decided to try it on their own. With that mixture of sadness, wistfulness, pride, and delight that I always have after intense and gratifying treatment relationships, I said good-bye.

Comment: The most important process of which healthy families are capable is that of *negotiating* (Beavers, 1977). People always have different viewpoints and yet cannot live well alone, so ability to resolve conflict is a most important skill. Ambivalence at the individual system level corresponds to conflict at the dyadic and family levels, and they are related. As individuals identify and resolve mixed feelings, they can have clear boundaries of the self that help to resolve conflicts with each other. In this way, people become more trustable, and caring can overcome fear. Caring or loving is the only antidote to death and the fear of death that I know.

A few aspects of treatment techique might be emphasized. I believe it important to know many different ways of intervening, and to use them all with a clear idea of why any technique is used at a particular time. For example, Bowen (1978) has advocated channeling the couple's dialogue through the therapist, while Ables and Brandsma (1977) have insisted that couples speak to each other. Sometimes, when I ask a spouse to speak directly to the partner, it feels right. Other times, this maneuver seems to encourage a stagy, pretend quality with the therapist as audience, so I stop it. Each interactive style can be useful or ineffective.

When couples are in treatment more than 10 sessions, I try to establish a relatively small overt power difference between me and them. A significant power edge is useful only in short-term treatment; even then, one has to use more indirect and "paradoxical" methods in order not to be controlled by that power edge. With a good relationship and patients as partners, i.e., little overt power difference, I use paradoxical approaches less frequently. And when I do, I believe it works because it is not paradoxical. For example, I really did see Mrs. G.'s protecting her husband by threatening suicide as a caring gesture, and my congratulating her on it had a strong element of genuineness.

Patterns in different levels of systems reverberate and influence one another. If I wish to help a couple have clear boundaries, make choices, get close, and negotiate, then these very experiences must be a part of the treatment experience.

References

Ables, B. S., & Brandsma, J. (1977). *Therapy for couples*. San Francisco: Jossey-Bass.

Beavers, W. R. (1977). *Psychotherapy and growth: A family systems perspective*. New York: Brunner/Mazel.

Beavers, W. R. (1981). A systems model of family for family therapists. *Journal of Marital and Family Therapy, 1*, 299–307.

Beavers, W. R. (1982a). Healthy, midrange and severely dysfunctional families. In F. Walsh (Ed.), *Normal family processes*. New York. Guilford Press.

Beavers, W. R. (1982b). Indications and contraindications for couples therapy. *Psychiatric Clinics of North America, 5*(3), 469–478.

Beavers, W. R. (1983a). Hierarchical issues in a systems approach to illness and health. *Family Systems Medicine, 1*, 47–55.

Beavers, W. R. (1983b). Learning a systems orientation from parents. In H. Liddle (Ed.), *Clinical implications of the family life cycle*. Rockville, MD: Aspen Publications.

Beavers, W. R. (1984). Healthy couple interaction patterns. In R. Stahmann and W. Hiebert (Eds.), *Counseling in marital and sexual problems: A clinician's handbook* (3rd ed.). Lexington, MA: Heath.

Beavers, W. R., & Kaslow, F. W. (1981). The anatomy of hope. *Journal of Marital and Family Therapy, 7,* 119–126.

Beavers, W. R., & Voeller, M. N. (1983). Family models: Comparing the Olson Circumplex Model with the Beavers Systems Model. *Family Process, 22,* 85–98.

Bowen, M. (1978). *Family therapy in clinical practice.* New York: Jason Aronson.

Davenport, Y. B., Ebert, M. H., Adland, M. L., & Goodwin, F. K. (1977). Couples group therapy as an adjunct to lithium maintenance of manic patient. *American Journal of Orthopsychiatry, 47,* 495–502.

Freud, S. (1933). *New introductory lectures on psychoanalysis.* New York: Norton.

Goldstein, M. S., Rodnick, E. H., Evans, J. R., May, P. R. A., & Steinberg, M. R. (1978). Drug and family therapy in the aftercare of acute schizophrenics. *Archives of General Psychiatry, 35,* 1169–1177.

Chapter 8
A Differentiating Couple: Some Transgenerational Issues in Marital Therapy

William C. Nichols, EdD

The most important theoretical and clinical principles, prejudices, and beliefs that guide my way of working with couples can be described simply and straightforwardly. My theoretical approach is best characterized as an attempted integration of systems theory and psychodynamics, with attention to experiential elements. The word "attempted" is used because an integration in which all parts fit smoothly with no gaps or discrepancies in the theoretical explanation is not possible at this stage in human understanding, and it is doubtful if it ever will be possible. Hence, in dealing with the complexities of marital and family processes, I work with a series of guiding assumptions and principles, as I suspect most therapists do, rather than with a totally integrated theoretical system. Similarly, my clinical work is to a significant degree guided by pragmatic considerations. Not only politics but also therapy are in many respects the "art of the possible."

Describing my typical way of working with couples would not be easy because there is a considerable amount of flexibility and adaptation from case to case. Although there are some stereotypical ways in which I start an initial interview and some patterned ways in which things are done, the treatment basically is fitted to the couple, not the couple to the therapy. Simply put, I use what I know about family systems and personality to assess the relationship, current functioning, and difficulties of the couple presenting themselves for help. From my initial and continuing assessment of the couple and the context in

199

which they live, I try to make interventions that are sensible and seem to offer the most reasonable prospects for success. The needs and conditions of the individuals, the system, and the context, including relevant historical elements, play important roles in the determination of strategies and interventions. There are times at which something "feels right," and while it is important to pay attention to intuition, it is equally consequential to examine one's inspirations before acting on them.

There are common features that I cover in all couples assessment work, including how the partners are attached, emotionally and practically; their patterns of expectations at various levels (Sager, 1976); their respective levels of differentiation from their families of origin; the most important transgenerational factors operative in their lives; their difficulties in both personal and relationship terms, as they understand them and as I can comprehend them; the models of relationship (Skynner, 1976) to which they have been exposed in their families of origin and upbringing; their respective individual levels of functioning and interaction in their marital life cycle and family life cycle (Berman & Lief, 1975), including strengths as well as pathology; and the very practical question of why they have come to see me and what they would like to achieve through their contact with me. Assessment is combined with intervention, as it seems to be with most marital and family therapists today.

An underlying assumption or bias is that the client–patients themselves have the responsibility for change. Couples and individuals generally have a better opportunity to take responsibility for their own actions when they have a reasonable understanding of significant factors in their behaviors and the options they have to exercise. For these and other reasons, a considerable amount of the therapist's work, in my judgment, is that of an educator as well as participant observer in the process (Sullivan, 1954).

Typically, I see both partners together for the initial session(s), separating them only if it is evident that either or both cannot talk adequately in the presence of the partner. Most treatment also is conducted in conjoint meetings, separation again being made only when indications are that individual interviewing for a limited time can break a barrier and get the treatment process flowing more fluidly and smoothly. The techniques that I use are many and varied. They include interpretation, suggestion, role playing, side taking, questioning, humor, self-disclosure, didactic work, modeling, and other forms of teaching, and other techniques tailored to the needs of the case and situation. My degree of "directiveness" and amount of activity vary considerably according to the situation, ranging from "reactor" to "conductor" modes of functioning.

My work is conducted with careful attention to phases and inevitably involves short-term process goals that change with the course of therapy, as well as long-term outcome goals. At times the needs of the case call for concentration on one part while other parts are put "on hold" temporarily. Again, for me this works best when such moves are made in an essentially overt manner with the "informed consent" and cooperation of the clients to whatever degree possible, rather than with a more concealed manipulation or coercion of the system.

Exposure to clinical anthropology and cross-cultural and social-class materials has made me acutely aware of factors associated with different ethnic groups and differences stemming from sociocultural and educational backgrounds. Currently I work as a solo practitioner in an independent practice setting, dealing essentially with a middle-class and upper-class professional and business clientele. These circumstances and the absence of institutional subsidy that would permit the luxury of the massing of multiple therapists and resources for therapeutic intervention shape the treatment that I conduct.

The case that I have chosen for this chapter is both typical and atypical.

It is typical of my cases in that: it deals with some of the trans-generational issues that appear as important features in all marital therapy; it involves the flexible use of various modalities of interviewing—conjoint, individual, and family-of-origin sessions—in varying combinations, depending on the needs and circumstances of the case—and the flexible use of roles and tactics, including teaching, uncovering, and others; and it features a concern with systems and dynamics.

It is atypical in that it is longer than most cases of marital therapy—it lasted more than 2 years—and the difficulties of one spouse receive more time and attention than is usual in a marital therapy case.

This was not a star case in which everything went well so that the therapist can demonstrate clearly and easily how brilliant interpretations or interventions were made and immediate changes occurred. It was a difficult case. Change came slowly. The young couple—they were both in their late 20s—who were differentiating from their families of origin demonstrated both some common emancipation–maturation issues and difficulties and some unusual transgenerational enmeshment.

The Browns

"Can you take another case right now?"

"Probably, if we can get together on scheduling. Tell me about it."

The caller was a clergyman I had known for more than a decade, since he had taken a couple of courses I had taught. His periodic referrals generally were appropriate and adequately prepared for therapy.

Proceeding to describe succinctly his own brief contacts with a young couple, he ended by saying:

> They were with a therapist for approximately a year. He seems to have gone as far as he could with them. He's rather sociologically oriented and seems to have worked most of the time on communication. She [the wife] has some real problems, particularly with male fantasies. She may have some individual agendas that need attention. He's a typical engineer. He's committed to the marriage. He'll learn as fast as he can learn, he's very trainable.

After a few more questions and pleasantries, I requested that he suggest that the couple call me when they wished to make an appointment. Within 2 weeks of the referral, Paul and Carol Brown (pseudonyms) were in my office for an initial appointment.

Assessment

An attractive, neatly dressed pair, the Browns manifested little that would distinguish them from many other white middle-class couples. Paul, age 28, was dark-haired, bearded, slim in build, and average in height. Carol, a year younger, was a tall, slender blonde. In contrast to Paul's pleasant, rather bland demeanor, she obviously was tense, occasionally flashing a stricken look that was one of her characteristic responses whenever she felt pressure. According to the background information forms that they had completed just prior to the appointment, they were in excellent health, were not taking any medication, and had received a year's psychotherapeutic help with their marital problems. Each was the second of three children, having an opposite-sex older and a same-sex younger sibling. Paul was a graduate engineer. Currently a homemaker, Carol had taught school briefly before the birth of their first child. Married nearly 6 years, they had two daughters, ages 4 years and 18 months.

Carol took the lead in responding to my opening question, "What brings you in?" That was typical of the couple. She usually spoke first and more frequently than Paul. Although obviously anxious, she was quite articulate at some points. At other times she was unable to speak or to elucidate her meaning, instead manifesting her pain and tension. Paul's reticence, it soon became clear, stemmed from his fear of committing himself and risking discomfort. Their different modes of dealing with their fears and anxieties were complementary.

The presenting problems were both individual and marital. The Browns agreed that there were marital difficulties and on the major features of most of them. They experienced trouble in "relating," and communication was still a problem, despite working on it for nearly a year in their previous therapy. Carol was troubled by fantasies about males whenver she became emotionally close to a member of the opposite sex. This, combined with her acknowledged dependency needs, had caused her a considerable amount of internal and relationship conflict and problems over the past few years, leading her to questions whether she could ever relate satisfactorily to males. Neither of them pinpointed Carol's fears and fearfulness as a significant source of concern, although this turned out to be among the more important issues of treatment.

"Tell me about yourselves and your relationship. How did you meet? What attracted you to the other person? How did your dating go? How did you decide to get married? How have things changed since you got married?" Posed in a clump, these and related queries typically engender a large amount of reaction and information. The Browns were very articulate. They provided me with a number of facts, impressions, hypotheses, and tentative conclusions about the nature of their relationship, how they were attached, and how they were coping with the task of leaving their respective families of origin and beginning to form a marital dyad and family of their own.

Paul and Carol met at college and became emotionally involved almost immediately. Within a month they were actively engaging in heavy petting, a new experience for both of them. Carol initially found him to be a source of comfort at a time at which she was experiencing strong fears about being on a large university campus and about new academic and social experiences and expectations. As she explained it, by the time she began to have some doubts about whether Paul could meet her needs, she was too deeply involved to feel that she could get out of the relationship. When she resolved to do so on a couple of occasions, Paul became so depressed that she became frightened and relented. They dated for 4 years before marrying.

As best Carol could articulate them, her hopes had been essentially that Paul would meet her needs for a relationship that would release her from the enervating tensions that long had gripped her. It seemed evident that her expectations of what the relationship with Paul should do for her had been unrealistic and doomed to more than the usual disillusionment that follows the breakdown of the early idealization of a prospective mate. Given her personality makeup, even as it came through in the first appointment, her reaction to the disillusionment could be expected to be more that of raw fear than that of masked fear or anger.

Carol's ambivalence and confusion about Paul and his appropriate role in her life thus began early in their relationship. As she described what she thought had happened, a paramount factor in her rapid attachment had been the fact that her mother had always told her that a female needed a man to make her complete, to fulfill and liberate her. To use Stierlin's (1977) term, Carol had been sent on a kind of "mission" by her mother. Eventually in treatment it became clear to all of us that her mother's mission instructions had not been intended to lead Carol to attach to a male and detach from her family of origin but to secure a male and bring him into the family.

Paul's choice process had been less complex. Carol was physically attractive to him. She was bright and thoughtful, kind. Their values were similar. Her obvious integrity and loyalty were attractive also. Her desire to have children and conduct an essentially traditional family life was evident to him. Carol's strong dependency on him at the outset was pleasing, even though it seemed somewhat overwhelming at times. She was something of an enigma to him in that she seemed to need affection very strongly but was guarded and wary about accepting emotional closeness.

That Paul was committed to the marriage seemed clear from the beginning of my contacts with the couple. He wished to be married to Carol, although he acknowledged that her negative reactions and expectations of him were bewildering. Feeling hurt when faced with her ambivalence and expressions of dissatisfaction, he would withdraw. The cycle had begun during their dating but had intensified following their marriage. Under some probing, Paul indicated that Carol's fearfulness also confused him and made him feel powerless.

Pointing out that she frequently was doubtful that Paul would ever have the capacity to meet her emotional needs, Carol said that he related to her as if she were his parent. According to her, Paul wished to come and go very much as a teenager, expecting the home and household to be there when he returned. She complained that it was as if she had three children, since he basically watched television when he was home. He would go to church with her and the youngsters, but that was the major thing that he did with them. During much of the year he would spend his spare time running, preparing for marathon races. Otherwise, according to Carol, he essentially went to work and came home and watched television. Under prodding from Paul, she did add that, reluctantly and awkwardly, he would help her with child rearing on occasion, when asked, and that he took responsibility for some outside chores, such as lawn maintenance. Paul added that he also took care of their automobile. This was a source of friction, however. Carol said that she felt that the car was "his" and that she and the children had to be very careful when they were in it. They must not create clutter and dared not eat anything inside it. "I know it's a little thing, but it gets to me, his wanting it all dusted clean and wrapped in a ribbon almost," she added.

From his perspective, Paul was doing everything that a decent and responsible man was supposed to do, yet Carol was not satisfied. The indications were that he did his job effectively and was appropriately rewarded by his employer. His behavior, it quickly became apparent, was modeled after that of his father, who worked hard outside the home but did almost nothing at home and provided very little companionship for either wife or children. At the same time that Carol complained, Paul noted, she did not respect his wishes about such things as the automobile and thus was being unreasonable. At another level, he seemed to feel that she was not fulfilling her end of the marital bargain by asking him to give more time and help with the children and by not providing the kind of general acceptance and affection that he desired. Carol similarly felt very keenly Paul's disapproval and rejection of her when she did not meet his expectations. It was evident that there was some substance to the feelings of both of them. Some brief examination and explanation concerning expectations was conducted at the time of assessment and returned to subsequently.

The difficulty Carol was having in differentiating from her family of origin came through in several ways. For example, in a brief discussion of her pregnancies, the following picture emerged: Both children had been wanted, and both pregnancies had gone well, being essentially uneventful. She had used natural childbirth and had nursed both infants. Her major difficulties had come from her mother's constant "helpful suggestions," which Carol had experienced as criticism and interference. Paul confirmed that his wife's mother did tend to be intrusive and provide Carol with reasons for being upset.

The strength of Paul's ties with his family of origin did not come through so clearly. That there was need to work on differentiation was evident, but the extent to which he had to struggle in order to become more appropriately individuated emerged only later in treatment. His family of origin would permit him to marry and have a family of his own in a much more free fashion than would his wife's family. Unlike Carol's family, which did not wish her to go away at all, his would let him separate but would call him back periodically to exercise (what emerged as) his role as parentified offspring. For example, his mother called him once in the early morning hours because his father had not returned from a trip as expected, even though Paul's grown younger brother was at home and had made the only telephone calls to the state highway police that were indicated under the circumstances.

Satisfactory answers and impressions concerning several other factors were obtained in the initial assessment. For instance, it appeared that slight differences in the socioeconomic backgrounds of Paul and Carol had been minimized by his upward mobility through education. Differential diagnostic work produced adequate understandings of the two individuals. Both were free of gross abnormalities, of strong psychopathology or behavior pathology, although they manifested indications of appreciable amounts of unconsciously determined behavior.

Carol's expressed needs were to feel some relief and improvement in both her personal and marital situations, which had created a state of desperation for her by the time we met. Paul, obviously threatened by his wife's complaints and demands, was a somewhat reluctant participant in the assessment process. His immediate needs, in brief, included a desire to avoid feeling blamed for what was going wrong in the marriage. There was a voiced need for both of them to feel that things were going to go differently than they had in their previous therapeutic effort.

(Although one may or may not agree with Bernard Greene's idea that hope needs to be experienced as early as the first 10 minutes of an initial marital interview [Greene, 1970], it is important in my judgment for clients to leave sessions, including the first, with some realistic feeling that benefit has been derived [Sullivan, 1954].)

Treatment Planning

The immediate needs in this case, including the fact that the Browns were wary of securing improvement through conjoint sessions, contributed to my decision to recommend a combined approach involving both individual and conjoint interviews. As Wynne (1983) has put it:

> The relevance of the systems hierarchy is this: At which system level is it most strategic to intervene? Where is the most salient presenting problem about which people will feel something useful is happening, and where will the therapist gain the leverage through generating hopefulness as quickly as possible, preferably in the first meeting? (p. 263)

The plan, arranged with the couple at the time of the first interview, was for the wife to be seen once weekly in individual interviews. Conjoint appointments were to be used every 3 or 4 weeks in lieu of an individual session. It was explained that this approach did not signify that either of them had more problems than the other but that Carol was experiencing more personal tension and pressure at the time, that she obviously was "hurting more right now." Currently, the focus would be on her needs and those of the marriage. When an appropriate time came, it was explained, we would give more attention and time to working with Paul, and would work more extensively on the marriage. The approach worked well in that it gave some immediate relief to both partners. Paul was relieved that the difficulties manifested by his wife were being given serious attention, that he was not being called on to make any immediate changes, and that he was not being targeted as the source of the problems.

This "phase-centered approach to treatment," so succinctly described by Wynne (1983), has been a part of my approach to marital and family treatment for the past quarter-century. It involves dealing with the problem or problems that are most pressing at the time while keeping in mind other difficulties that must be addressed subsequently. Treatment foci and interventions are altered as therapy progresses.

Goals were established for both Carol and the marriage. The immediate goals for working with her were reduction of her fear and anxiety, moderation of her depression, and expansion of her coping abilities. Outcome goals included helping her to become essentially fantasy-free so that she no longer had to use sexual fantasies as coping devices or defenses, appropriately dependency-free so that she no longer needed to latch on to others in the ways that she now did, and reasonably fear-free. All these goals were seen as necessary achievements in order to help her separate from her family of origin in a fitting manner and function adequately as a married adult.

The immediate goals with regard to the marriage were to stabilize the marital interaction and to discover whether there were qualities within the relationship that could be developed so as to sustain both Carol and Paul and provide adequate satisfactions for them. Once the commitment of both partners to being married to the other was clearly established—and this happened for Carol only after a clarification of her distortions and confusions surrounding the relationship, and a recognition of the fact that Paul really was committed to her—setting an outcome goal for the marriage was possible. In the broadest sense, the outcome goal finally set was an improved marriage that would provide room and opportunity for fulfillment of the classic "two irreducible functions of the nuclear family," stabilization of adult personalities and primary socialization of the young (Parsons & Bales, 1955).

Individual Sessions with Occasional Conjoint Meetings

Two themes predominated in Carol's early individual sessions, her fearfulness and her sexual fantasizing. She struggled with a number of daily reality problems that also required attention. We worked carefully on those situations, detail by detail. On one occasion, for example, Carol became upset with a woman with whom she was involved in a neighborhood social group. It was apparent that the neighbor was browbeating Carol and unfairly holding her responsible for differences between them. We examined what was happening and dissected the lack of logic and validity of the woman's claims against her. With support and encouragement, Carol became less afraid and began to manifest some ability and willingness to stand up to the neighbor. Subsequently, she was able to cease permitting another neighborhood woman to hold the older Brown child responsible for the playmate spats that periodically erupted between Carol's daughter and the neighbor's child.

My intention was to help Carol learn how to reality-test different sets of circumstances while providing her with support for trying to take steps that would enable her to cope more adequately with the situations that she was encountering. Such a stance was very different from what she had always experienced from her family of origin. Even the basic idea that one could examine what was happening and being said and take a proactive, rather than a reactive, defensive position was new to Carol. From her mother she typically met denial that there was any difficulty in any situation that she faced. The mother glossed over problematic situations in such a way that Carol ended up feeling either guilty for internally disagreeing with her or demeaned and helpless because she had given in to someone else or feeling both ways.

There was a movement back and forth in the sessions between the present and the past and between a focus on Carol as an individual and on the marital and family systems in which she was located. Attention was given to loyalty–conflict possibilities when she was being encouraged to follow a different route than her mother would choose, for example. Also, the neighborhood reality situations were dealt with in the conjoint sessions, and Paul's help was enlisted where possible.

This work and the building of a common universe of understanding and discourse enabled us to move fairly quickly into Carol's sexual fantasizing in the individual interviews. It was apparent that the fantasies were related to a complex of factors, including specifically her need to be touched and, more important, to be accepted. Consequently, I pointed out that her fantasies were not sexual per se but that they were related to needs for basic human acceptance. They seemed to be associated with sex essentially through her childhood incorporation of a family myth set forth by mother about how great sex was, how holy, etc. At the same time, the mother had indoctrinated Carol with traditional gender role values that made females dependent on males. Carol had been conditioned very early to turn to males rather than to her mother for emotional acceptance and support. Carol had not seen very much touching or emotional interchange in her family or experienced much emotional closeness or physical affection. Evidently, there had been a growing idea on Carol's part that males were the source of acceptance, touching, and love in general.

The interpretation of the adaptational nature of the fantasies, combined with Carol's increasing ability to discriminate and cope more adequately in social situations, led to a temporary diminishing of the sexual fantasies and fears. Concurrently, this began to bring more pressure on the marital relationship. Carol was able to make more appropriate and direct requests of Paul for emotional support and closeness. Predictably, this was accompanied by an increase in some of her negative attitudes toward him when he did not respond. For a brief time she considered separation and divorce.

(Carol's questioning whether she wished to remain in the marriage or get out of it was not brought into the conjoint sessions. If it had been something other than part of her struggle to clear up the distortions between her feelings about her husband and those about her family of origin and an essentially transitory defensive reaction, it would have been brought into the conjoint meetings. Certainly Paul was aware during the period in which Carol was having that struggle that she was putting distance between them, but his denial and willingness to trust the treatment process in the hope that things would get better contributed to my decision to keep this "secret" until Carol had clarified her feelings adequately. This was the only significant item in the individual sessions that was not made available in conjoint meetings.)

Obtaining relief from the fear that long had gripped her and spread throughout her life was a major key to Carol's improvement as an individual, marital partner, and parent. Her earliest memories were recollections of being afraid. All memories before approximately age 8, except for her recall of being afraid when entering kindergarten, were blocked out at the beginning of therapy. Understanding her fearfulness and uncovering the sources was a focus from the time of the individual interviews.

Explaining that they could be helpful to us in understanding her earlier life, I asked Carol fairly early in treatment if she could bring in some family photographs. We spent an exceedingly productive hour with a superb collection of her family's 35-mm color slides that covered the period from her infancy until she was approximately 12 years of age.

Among the more significant observations were the following: the lack of touching by the parents as the children got out of infancy; the differential treatment of the children, particularly with regard to Carol and the more favorable treatment of her more assertive older brother; the affective frozenness and postural stiffness of Carol's father. Each of these became part of our working material for subsequent sessions.

As Carol struggled with a cluster of difficulties in relation to her parents, the transgenerational nature of her problems in relating to her older daughter was becoming somewhat evident to her. She was in pain about her ambivalent feelings toward the child, particularly as she became aware of how she got angry with the youngster and yelled at her so often. What brought things into focus most starkly was the recognition that her daughter was yelling back at her in an angry, defiant, and nasty way. Carol became more upset as she realized how the interaction was part of her conflict with her own mother. The youngster was responding to her as she had wished to respond to her mother but had been—and still was—afraid to react. Vicariously Carol expressed her rebellion against her mother's controlling, rejecting behavior. The cycle became clear: Carol would induce the behavior and then punish the child. Punishing the youngster enabled her to identify with her mother—as a "good" mother who did not allow "bad" behavior—by carrying out her mother's patterns of child rearing and being loyal to Mother and, at the same time, to struggle with and punish a mother substitute with some degree of impunity.

Conjoint Sessions with Occasional Individual Meetings

After approximately 5 months of individual sessions with Carol, combined with periodic conjoint appointments, we moved to a pattern using primarily conjoint meetings. As we succeeded in providing sufficient support and assistance to Carol to help her elevate her mood, decreasing both depression and fears, it became possible to deal more totally with the marital problems. By that time Paul had gained a fairly high degree of confidence in the therapeutic process as a result of witnessing improvements and settling down by his wife and establishing a workable relationship with me in the conjoint sessions.

Paul's limited involvement in marital and family life came in for some attention early in the conjoint meetings. He was a "structural" type of person, literally a structural engineer, so I entered the discussion in rather logical, "structural" terms, even using a few diagrams for illustration in talking about his "family career" and sharing with his wife the "executive" leadership and responsibilities at home. In facilitating communication and understanding, I emphasized that it was not merely a matter of "I'll do whatever she asked me to do"; rather, what Carol was asking was for him to share the responsibility for planning, executing, and "worrying" about the functions and tasks of home and family life. He was able to begin "seeing" what was involved in this aspect of being a family man, although change was slow and uneven. The concepts that we used here served as a baseline for intermittent work in this area over the next several months.

For a short time after we started having regular conjoint meetings, there was a pattern reversal. Paul, rather than Carol, was seen individually on occasion in lieu of a conjoint meeting. Ordinarily I prefer to construct genograms and explore a client's family of origin in the company of his or her spouse. In this instance, having done a considerable amount of family-of-origin exploration with Carol in her individual appointments, I chose to do similar work with Paul in individual sessions. With both of them, however, I encouraged the sharing of their findings and understandings with their spouse. We also used such material freely in the conjoint meetings. Working with Paul in this way essentially completed establishment of a relationship of trust with him.

Helping both Paul and Carol to rework their family-of-origin relationships and to differentiate themselves more appropriately was made an explicit therapy goal with them at this juncture. The major principle followed in this regard was that of exploring those areas that seemed to require opening up in order to permit and facilitate the ongoing flow of adaptation processes and growth.

Paul obviously was more deeply enmeshed in his family of origin than it had appeared at the beginning. He was more individuated than Carol, but still not adequately separated out and established as an adult. Both came from midrange families (Beavers & Voeller, 1983), that is, families that tended to hold on to their children and produce neurotic offspring. Comparatively, the "centripetal" dimension (Beavers & Voeller, 1983) was more pronounced in Carol's family. Paul's family could be located more closely to the mixed stylistic dimension and a little more closely to the healthy family range of the scale than could Carol's family. Paul basically tried to stand outside his family of origin and protect himself by ignoring his parents and tacitly freezing them out, although the ties were still strong. Carol was continuing to strive desperately to get outside her family of origin and was terribly frightened of leaving or offending her parents or siblings.

It seemed possible to accomplish the necessary tasks that Paul had to perform with his family of origin by helping him to deal with his family on his own outside of the therapy sessions. He had good recall for most of his life, and there did not appear to be any family secrets or other issues that were not reasonably accessible. This was unlike the situation with Carol in which I had begun to suggest to her early in treatment that meeting with her family of origin would be highly desirable and potentially beneficial.

As part of an ongoing effort to aid their differentiation, foster sharing, and increase the range and quality of understanding between the Browns, I deliberately focused on some relevant aspects of family-of-origin concerns of each of them in conjoint sessions. A significant part of this endeavor involved encouraging each spouse to support the differentiation efforts of the other. Just as Paul was enlisted to help Carol in restructuring relations with her parents, so her assistance was sought in several of his endeavors with his family.

The primary issue with Paul was establishing a workable relationship with his parents, keeping some contact while avoiding their triangling efforts. Over the years he had gradually pulled away, starting with his elementary and junior high school years when he had spent large amounts of time with a neighborhood family. Having incurred expressions of disapproval from his parents because he had been "away from home so much" and had "preferred being with the neighbor's family," he subsequently had used a variety of more "acceptable reasons" for avoiding contact, including college, work, marriage, and running.

With Carol's support, Paul began to reestablish a structured relationship with his family. For example, they scheduled some contacts with his family of origin on a family-to-family basis in which he and

Carol and their children would visit on an occasional Sunday or have his family over for a meal. Paul did not go to his parents' home alone to "solve their problems." Also, feeling that he had succeeded in breaking his father's assumptions that he "owned" him on Saturdays through a lengthy period of avoiding contact with his father prior to entering treatment, Paul arranged to spend part of a Saturday with his father and brother in recreational or work pursuits every couple of months.

At a middle treatment stage we worked on helping the Browns take some additional symbolic and practical stands in favor of their own marriage and family unit. I coached them, for example, on ways to deal with the need of Carol's mother to get everybody in the larger family's orbit to conform to whatever norm the mother deemed necessary or appropriate to the occasion. When the couple faced an essentially "mandatory" 2-week vacation to help Carol's parents and siblings build a vacation cottage, we discussed how they could maintain the separateness of their own family unit to a reasonable extent while relating to her parents on an adult basis. They decided to rent a separate cottage across the lake and to withdraw with their children for meals and nap times and for some personal marital and family time.

Use of humor, with an explicit awareness of the possible family loyalty conflicts and attention to respect for the Browns' feelings toward their parents, enabled us to eradicate some of the "heavy" atmosphere surrounding their dealing with their respective families.

We explored the "models of relationships" (Skynner, 1976) from their families of origin that were influencing the couple's current marital and family action. There were similarities among the differences in the models. The husband–father had not been actively involved in either family. Paul's parents had openly engaged in verbal battles and tugs-of-war and had sought to triangulate him into their relationship at least since his middle childhood. Carol's parents had shown very little overt emotion between them, but high tension had been felt in the family. When Paul related that "my folks never hugged us or touched us much at all in an affectionate way, and we never saw them being affectionate with each other," he could have been describing Carol's childhood as well as his own.

At one juncture, I spent a large part of a tender but confrontive session working with Paul on how he might deal with "decompression" needs after work, as well as spending more time with his wife in a better balance of "private" and "shared-interactive" time. As we looked at what kept him from doing the things that he said he wished to do and that Carol asked of him, some of the reasons why he was remaining "a child" at home began to emerge for him. Exploration of his feelings about having been pulled into a spousal surrogate role in the past, and about being made to feel disloyal to his father because of loyalty to his mother in triangled situations, helped him to see how he was currently being loyal to his father by repeating essential elements of his father's patterns. Consciously, he had not wished to model after either the parental marriage or his father's role.

Another step in Paul's movement away from behaving as "a third child" came when we returned to the automobile matter raised at the beginning. Exploration disclosed that his actions there were consistent with how he had always acted with regard to "his" possessions. He recalled that as a child he had always carefully reboxed and often rewrapped his toys and put them away when he was through playing with them. Seeing that his behavior in both the childhood and adulthood settings was similar helped Paul to become more aware that he was functioning currently much as he had in his family of origin and that there was substance to Carol's complaints that he was not behaving as an adult at home. He began to be able to kid himself about his "wrapping and boxing" of the car.

One of the major problems acknowledged by Paul was an inability to make decisions, whether at home or at work. He was reluctant to take a stand in any situation because he admittedly feared that others would not like him or would disapprove of his answer or decision. "Only if I get angry enough can I make a decision," he said. Typically, Paul related, he used humor to mask his reluctance to make decisions. Only during therapy had he become aware of his avoidance tendencies. Much of the time now, he said, he would become aware of being reactive, waiting on others to take their stands and hoping that he would be able to remain inactive and uncommitted.

Relating the indecisive tendencies to the triangled position that his parents had continually attempted to draw him into over the years was an easy matter. His life had involved a continual need to "walk the line" between his parents and not take sides in this disagreements. Placed very much in the middle, he had felt that there was no way that he could win. Currently, Paul was not caught in a bind between his wife and some other person, as he had been trapped between his parents. Rather, he was entangled in fears that if he did what his wife wished him to do, either as a husband or as a father he would be disliked or disapproved of by "some vague force." Similarly, in the work world and in social situations he was vaguely uneasy. He caught on rather quickly that it was "the ghosts looking over his shoulder," the internalized perceptions of how others would react and the unaltered patterns of relationships that he had carried into adulthood from his past, that were hampering him.

We tackled the task of helping Paul to move out of his indecisive proclivities by focusing on three fronts—his work, his current family, and his family of origin. Taking the course of dealing first with the easier and less threatening areas, we examined a number of work and social situations very carefully, going over in detail what had happened or could be expected to occur. Occasionally we role-played some work, social, or family circumstance. As with Carol earlier in her dealings with difficult neighbors, we worked on "building up behavioral muscles." Once Paul became able to be proactive and reasonably successful in the easier situations, he was ready to try working on the more sensitive relationships in his family of origin and current family life.

Having taken these steps made it feasible for us to begin dealing with residual problems and unresolved issues from earlier in the Browns' marriage. One involved a situation in which Carol's emotional vulnerabilities had placed her in a painful position and left its scars. The male member of a couple whom they had seen socially had expressed interest in her in a variety of flirtatious ways over many months some 2 years earlier. This had fed her needs for approval and her fantasies at a time in which the marriage was going badly and providing her with minimal support and satisfaction. When she finally responded in a mild way, the young man acted as if he had not given her any indication that he was interested in her, as if she were initiating something on her own. At the same time, he called the situation to the attention of his wife and Paul. Carol was blamed by all for creating a bad social situation. When she brought this matter up for reworking in therapy, Paul was able to be understanding and helpful. Reviewing what had happened and recognizing that his wife had been "scapegoated," Paul then apologized for his lack of sensitivity when the incident had occurred. Subsequently, when the other man attempted to renew acquaintance with Paul on terms that would have placed a wedge between the Browns, Paul firmly rejected the overture and took a stand supporting his wife.

Building up the Browns' shared experiences and achievements took several forms, including dealing with their parental roles. They had "spiraled" each other's concerns about their older child. Slight progress made with Carol in connection with separating from the child for kindergarten attendance was easily undermined by Paul's apprehensions about letting the youngster go out on her own. Both feared that the youngster was becoming seriously disturbed because of her difficulties in separating from them on various occasions. I referred them to a child psychologist who also had a strong background in family work. She found the child essentially normal and free of psychopathology. Several sessions were used by the consultant in calming the Browns' fears (and thereby reinforcing work I had attempted to do earlier) and feeding what she aptly described as their "starvation for information and help around normal child rearing." In conjoint sessions we worked for a brief time on the transgenerational aspects of child rearing from both their backgrounds and tried to reinforce their efforts to put into practice what they were learning.

Discussing fatherhood in a conjoint session led us to one of therapy's major breakthroughs. Continuing to be haunted by the fact that in many of the family's slides Carol's father had looked as if he had witnessed something horrible, I finally responded to something in the discussion by sharing with them an anecdote describing some of the effects of learning about a family secret. Carol was hit strongly by the explanation of how secrets may be transmitted nonverbally, but said little and worked with it on her own for a few weeks. Then the door swung open for her, and she related the following story:

She had been a teenager when she learned that she had a paternal grandmother who had been in a nearby mental institution for the past 40 years. Until then, the extent of her knowledge has been that her father and his siblings had been reared by relatives. He continued to tell even close friends that his mother had died when he was a young child. Carol did not learn the entire story, the remainder of the family secret, until after she became an adult. The grandmother's difficulties began when Carol's father was 4 years of age. His mother had accidentally caused the death of one of her older children. When the distraught

woman suffered a collapse, a "nervous breakdown," her husband placed
her in a mental hospital, put the surviving children with relatives,
secured a divorce, and departed for several years. The family still
would not talk about the events. Carol had secured her information
from her mother.

Paul and Carol talked about the effect that they thought this had
had, not only on her father, but also on his siblings and their offspring.
Their tensions and inability to relax had long been apparent to the
Browns. Paul described the other members of that family as being
similar to Carol's father, emotionally frozen and wary of touching and
relating warmly, adding, "It's as if the thing were spread through the
whole family." The unresolved mourning had kept the issues alive.

The family secret had traversed four generations. It began to
appear that Carol had long been exposed, at whatever level of consciousness, to the family secret that mothers not only can harm their
children but also that one mother in the family had killed her child,
though accidentally. Carol struggled with questions about how the
family secret and its effects had been transmitted to herself and her
daughter. Specifically, she was concerned about how the fears that she
had about the older daughter—although not about the younger
daughter—had been derived and transmitted. The concepts of "non-
genetic transmission" and "nonverbal transmission" had particular significance for her in comprehending how feelings and attitudes had
been passed through the generations. She was helped to some extent
in recognizing how she had zeroed in on one child and not the other.
A more complete understanding and diminishing of fearfulness relative
to the child came later.

(When all of this emerged, I began to spectulate to myself about
Carol's fear of her father, which she had essentially denied in favor
of being fearful of her mother. Carol by this time had been able to
recall being uncomfortable around her father when she and her brother
had been left with him when their mother had been in the hospital
for the birth of the family's third child, but she could not even guess
what had made her fearful.)

Family-of-Origin Sessions

Finally, after a year and a half of treatment, Carol indicated that she
was ready for family-of-origin meetings in which she and I would get

together with her parents and siblings. When the idea had been suggested originally, she had been extremely threatened at the prospect and would not consider it. We scheduled a 2-hour Friday night meeting and a follow-up on Saturday morning, modeled after Framo's (1981) pattern. Two preparatory sessions were spent with Carol. Along with examining her fears and dealing supportively with apprehensions about meeting with her total family, we specifically addressed the questions: What did she wish to learn? What did she wish to accomplish in the meetings? Essentially, she wished to obtain information and understanding about certain times and events that she could not remember. Also, she wished to change her relationship with her parents and brother.

The two meetings were eventful and painful. She did manage to alter her relationship with her brother to a significant degree. Confirmation of the extreme difficulty all the children had experienced in attempting to separate was abundantly clear. It was evident in the fright and conflict all reported experiencing when they went to college. At the time of the meetings, the youngest was the most tightly wound into the family. The oldest, who had suffered strong feelings of loneliness and depression when he entered college, also was still bonded very firmly to the family, much to the frustration of his wife. He had had trouble deciding to marry originally. The girls had married the first males with whom they had become deeply involved emotionally, but after lengthy dating periods. In the sessions the parents, especially the father, made it clear that it was very painful for the children even to talk about separating from the family. He cried as he said, "I don't want to lose you. I don't want you to move away and not be close." The tenacles of guilt induction reached almost visibly toward all three children.

My interpretation of what was going on with the parents ran as follows: They protected themselves from a repeat of earlier losses by trying to make certain that their own children did not separate from the family. At the same time, they appeared to be trying to re-create the family that the husband–father had lost, getting their children to serve as parents for them. (Not only had the father lost his family at an early age, but also the mother had lost three brothers by death during her childhood and had gone through several years in her early teens in which her father was hospitalized with a series of disabling physical and emotional problems.)

A startling discovery for Carol was the fact that it was not her mother that she feared so much as her father. Her mother did come through in the meetings as an intrusive and controlling person but as less aggressive and more accepting than Carol had perceived to be the case. The fears of her father obviously were complex. Immediately following the family sessions Carol was flooded with the recall of fearing his angry outbursts, his sharply critical tongue, and, most of all, his emotional cutoffs when she was a child. A deep feeling of sadness and aching pain followed her acknowledgment that "my dad did a lousy job of being a father."

The recognition of the paramount role played by her mother's use of denial also was surprising to Carol. Earlier, she had talked about such matters as her mother's need to be right, saying, "You don't criticize my mom or infer that she is wrong. She'll argue it out until she is back on top." From the family sessions it became clear that a wider meaning was present. Mother had established a family rule for the children: "Don't criticize. Don't talk about anything in the family in negative terms."

Both Paul and Carol had recognized to some degree—as had Carol's siblings—that her mother was communicating behaviorally, "Don't leave me alone with this man. I can't supply all his emotional demands or meet all his dependency needs." Consciously the mother was saying quite different things, extolling the virtues of family-of-origin life, although putting her own energies into the family she had formed at marriage. Much of the behavior appeared to be motivated by the dual desire to ensure retention of her husband so that she would not lose another significant male and to keep the children and their male spouses in particular around so that they could serve as a support system and buffer between herself and her needy and increasingly critical, bitter husband.

"Don't leave me alone with this man" was a plea easily identified with by Carol. Her own discomfort at being alone with her father continued to be strong. A major source of the lack of ease seemed to be the bad-mother object relations role that she evidently fulfilled for him, manifested in his anger and emotional cutoffs after setting her up for such reactions (Dicks, 1967; Fairbairn, 1954). (His object relations splits seemed to put his wife primarily into a good-mother role, although there was some ambivalence in his dealing with her when she did not supply his needs adequately, and his son into a good-father role.)

A second part of Carol's discomfort—her apprehension that her father might unload his massive dependency needs on her—became apparent a few weeks later. Originally, her recognition of how she was fearful of her father and his emotional needs began with the comprehension that her increasing uneasiness at being around her mother stemmed from her concern that her mother's denial might break down and that she would be overwhelmed by her mother's dependency needs. At approximately the same time, Carol realized the lengths to which her mother went in protecting herself from being alone with the care of her husband, assuming the role of protecting him and trying to make the children responsible for him. If Mother caved in, Carol feared, she would inherit the responsibility for protecting Father emotionally, of providing the family life that he had lost as a child.

Several factors and experiences had reinforced Carol's apprehensions that responsibility for Father could fall on her if Mother's denial ever collapsed. These included her identification with Mother by extended-family members and family acquaintances, Mother's preparation of her for such a caretaking role, an experience in her early teens in which Father jokingly introduced her as his wife at a social function, and her role as "the family star" (the child who always performed well and who, in the words of her father, "was running the school when she was in the sixth grade").

Over the years the family had not been aware of Carol's fearfulness. Prior to the family sessions, the parents evidently had not comprehended that she had been fearful at each step of the way toward adulthood. Fears of separation had dogged her from the time of entering kindergarten. The pattern had been repeated when she became fearful when her older daughter reached the same point. As a result of the family sessions, Carol's fear of being separated, of going out, took on new meaning. She recognized how she already had taken some responsibility emotionally for her father and had been carrying his fears of being separated and abandoned. As this became evident, Carol's fears of going to kindergarten, of being left outside on the first-grade playground after recess and lunch, of college—where she had become physically ill to the point of vomiting at the start of each term—and other fears become more explicable and, eventually, more expendable. She began to realize that there had been no realistic danger to her welfare in the past, thus releasing some sizable amounts of tension.

Part of the releasing process involved breaking current reinforcers of her fears. For example, she noted that she had "kind of peaked in high school and gone downward after that." I pointed out that she had literally left home after high school and that she had received a double message—as had her siblings—about going to college: Get a college education, but don't go away and separate from the family. She will still getting the same kind of message: Be married and have children, but don't go away and separate from the family.

Conjoint Sessions Continued

All of the findings and subsequent reactions to the family sessions were shared by Carol with Paul, and were dealt with in the conjoint interviews.

Several interrelated observations and interpretations provided the impetus for a significant surge forward for Carol out of the deeper shadows of fear. We had discovered that her fearfulness had first appeared when she was approximately 4 years of age. That was when she was finally able to recall her first experience of her "body feeling like steel." This coincided roughly with the birth of her younger sibling. My interpretation of Carol's reactions to her father during that time was that she seemed to have been reacting to his fears of her mother's being away from him and not returning. (Supporting this interpretation were a number of things that Carol had reported, the observations made of her mother and father's interaction in the family sessions, the circumstantial–dynamic factors of ordinal position, and the possibilities of transgenerational identification. Carol, incidentally, by this juncture in therapy had become aware that she had long regarded her father as if he were 4 years of age, the age at which his mother had left him.)

Additional support for the interpretation concerning Carol's fears about separation and her assumption of her father's fears and apprehensions concerning the absence of his wife, and specifically for the beginning of Carol's fearfulness around age 4, came from one more source. Near the end of the therapy she was referred at her request to a psychologist colleague for hypnosis because she wished to be absolutely certain about the sources of her fears and fearfulness, that there was not something else that she was not recalling. The session was confirmatory of our earlier findings. It provided memories in which she was not tense and tight before age 4 and of a graphic incident soon after age 4 when the fearfulness had been present with concerns about separation and feelings of emptiness and vacantness.

A number of things helped Carol to begin moving out of the orbit of her centripetal family. One of the more striking was her recognition that she had been *passing through her family* rather than being destined to be a permanent resident in it, controlled continually by her mother and, indirectly, by her father's needs for protection. The image, which came to her in an "Aha" experience at home, was that instead of being made up inside only of the confusing parts that were present in the functioning of her family of origin, she had an integrity of her own and that she was passing through the family. It was possible to point out to her not only the correctness of her observation in terms of life cycle and family life-cycle perspectives but also in terms of the relation of this process to the feeling of being like steel and having armor. Her steel-like feeling was related to defending herself primarily from invasive actions, attitudes, and feelings that threatened her from *outside herself but inside the family*, threats that came after her basic personality strengths had been established. Recalling the slides also was helpful in this regard. She had been given early nurturance by her mother and her maternal grandmother.

A significant corollary of Carol's "Aha" experience was the simultaneous release from certain attitudes toward her own children. She was able to perceive the youngsters as similarly passing through their own family of origin. This lessened her fears for them and helped her feel accountable for them in a different way than previously. As she put it, "I could see myself as responsible for teaching them the best that I could and for launching them. I didn't have to take care of them all their lives. It was all right for them to leave me eventually. Somehow, it was all right for them to leave me temporarily, going to school, going to play. That was training for leaving me totally to be on their own eventually."

A major shift occurred in the marriage at approximately the same time that Carol became more free in dealing with the children. She recognized that many of the problems she was experiencing came from "my negative views or percepts. When I realized that it was the way I was looking at things (i.e., in marriage), rather than things being wrong, this spread to other things. I realized that I had projected my feelings on to Paul. I realized that I didn't know him. This lifted the blame off of him and our relationship."

As Carol's fearfulness receded, it became possible to deal with her fantasizing again and in a more definitive way than previously. Her eventual recall was that the use of fantasy first began in elementary school when she fantasized leaving her own family and living with the family of a male teacher. As we traced them, the fantasies had been altered as she moved through the life cycle, eventually culminating as she reached adulthood in fantasies about being loved sexually. That was the route to getting the approval and acceptance that she felt had not been forthcoming for her. The crux of this part was her mother's often repeated dictum that "you've got to fall in love and get married." Carol's use of fantasy had begun as a way of trying to escape from the tensions and lack of love in her own home and had continued as an effort not only to escape tension but also to find acceptance and approval. Her later work on this in treatment focused on new attempts to cease using fantasy as a substitute for dealing with real life and to live more completely in the real world.

These transitions created greater expectations for Paul but also made it easier for him to relate to Carol without invoking the old feelings that he had to "walk the line" and not take stands and make choices. Paul was able to talk about how he also had used fantasy to avoid risking discomfort and in efforts to piece together some guidelines for behavior by imagining how others would act. We spent some time working explicitly on the factors involved in risking for both of them and in tenderly encouraging stances and actions in which they would try to "live as yourself." Basic communication about what they were feeling, fearing, and desiring was given attention as I tried to serve as a "midwife" to the development of a relationship at a much more deep and personal level than the Browns previously had experienced.

A confirmation of the changes in the marriage and in Carol came near the end of therapy. Carol's mother called three times in a couple of days, offering unsolicitated child-rearing advice in each call. The "final straw" was thus heaped on an overburdened relationship between Carol and her family of origin. She recognized that she could not continue to carry her family of origin emotionally and that it was not her responsibility to do so. At that time she became ready to move to another state, something Paul had been urging for both personal and career reasons for several years. He saw the decision as a firm opting for himself and the marriage on Carol's part, as did she.

Termination

As we moved toward termination I conducted an inventory session in which I asked the Browns to look at "what brought you in originally, and where you are now."

For once, Paul responded first. "I didn't know what marriage was, although I didn't always know it. I wasn't a good husband or father." He went on to explain that it was Carol's fantasies that actually brought them in, but that he soon saw that their difficulties were more complex than that.

"Now I see the relationship with my parents differently. I recognize the influence my family and my family's family has on me. I have thought about sitting down with my family and totally hashing it out with them, but have decided that it would be better not to confront them any more directly than I have. I think it's best to *live my life myself*. My personal growth over the last year has freed me up a lot. I think that knowing about my parents and recognizing the influence that they have had on me has freed me up from having to dominate things."

At that point Carol interjected, "Thank goodness!" with a laugh. We all laughed.

Speaking directly to Carol, Paul continued, "I have learned to respect you a great deal, for what you want for us and our children. Things are out of the way so that I can love you as a person now."

Carol chimed in to agree that the marriage was "one hundred percent better." Jointly they noted that they communicated better, were less defensive, and were "better at forgiving each other."

I asked about the tender areas that still remained. Paul mentioned "the whole financial situation and the way we deal with finances," an area that we subsequently examined. Carol talked about "family relationships," noting that Paul had come a long way in the assumption of responsibility for the children. She added, "We function more as an independent family unit than ever before in our history. We take the initiative to do that and are not reluctant to do it, even if it means stepping on fingers."

Paul confirmed with a statement ending, "We had a heated discussion last night, but I feel O.K. today. I'm not fearful that [Carol] will leave tomorrow" (indicating that formerly he would have been constrained from expressing his opinion in the situation at home and fearful that if he disagreed that Carol might leave him).

As Carol summarized her individual responses to the questions, she expressed a continuing concern about how Paul "perceives our kids and where they're going. There's no pattern in your family or in mine for you to grow up and leave. It seems like you [Paul] are kind of panicky about the kids growing up."

"Yes, to some extent I still am, but I think that I feel better than ever about this," Paul responded.

Carol agreed, signifying that she did feel more supported than formerly by Paul. "Things in our marriage have come a long way. When I came in originally, I was confused as to what our problems were, I mean what was me and what was the marriage. We have come a long way. I feel a hundred percent better about our marriage now. That's since Christmas. There has been much progress in how I feel about the marriage. I still have pain, but much of that was me. The first year and a half I can hardly remember what we talked about in therapy. It was layer and layer and layer that had to be dealt with."

Speaking directly to Paul, she echoed some of the old feelings at the same time that she gave him credit. "Once a problem was identified, you could handle it. I feel that it's so much easier for you. I feel that you don't understand that it's much harder for me to make the same kind of progress that you do. I fall back."

The latter statement was another indication of the difficulty to be experienced in helping Carol to diminish her dependency on therapy and in assisting her to believe more in herself and to rely more on herself and the relationship with Paul.

Subsequently, she was able to report a number of incidents and situations in which she functioned without bothersome fear. For example, she noted with some degree of astonishment that she was no longer afraid of crowds, citing some incidents in which she had realized at the time or afterward that she was not fearful. Also, she was beginning to make major purchases on her own, instead of leaving such matters entirely to Paul. Moreover, she reported that she had managed to teach music lessons successfully for several months, preparing several advanced students for paid musical positions.

Final Note

Not everything was completely wrapped up and totally under control at the time of termination, if indeed that is ever the case. I wish that it had been possible to help each of them establish more open and productive bilateral relationships with their families of origin. Working with the Browns was a curious mixture of pleasure and pain. They worked hard, but progress often was slow. Could I have moved things any faster with them? I think that I could if I had been the original therapist, but that has to remain a matter of conjecture.

Carol will have to continue to work on accepting Paul's love and support as the Browns persist in working to differentiate themselves from their families of origin and to build an adult marital relationship and family system in their 30s. She was able prior to termination to sort out their dating and marital relationship from the haze of confusion in which it had existed so that she could accept the fact that "Paul has always been for me and not against me." Paul, on the other hand, continues to have to push himself to risk being disapproved and to refrain from withdrawing and living in a safe world in which he takes no stands and expresses no opinions that may offend others. The Browns do make their individual and collaborative efforts without much of the emotional baggage and relationship enmeshment that formerly hampered them.

References

Beavers, W. R., & Voeller, M. N. (1983). Family models: Comparing the Olson Circumplex Model with the Beavers Systems Model. *Family Process, 22,* 85–98.

Berman, E. M., & Lief, H. I. (1975). Marital therapy from a psychiatric perspective: An overview. *American Journal of Psychiatry, 132,* 583–592.

Dicks, H. V. (1967). *Marital tensions.* London: Routledge & Kegan Paul.

Fairbairn, W. R. D. (1954). *An object relations theory of the personality.* New York: Basic Books.

Framo, J. (1981). The integration of marital therapy with sessions with family of origin. In A. S. Gurman & D. P. Kniskern (Eds.), *Handbook of family therapy.* New York: Brunner/Mazel.

Greene, B. L. (1970). *A clinical approach to marital problems.* Springfield, IL: Charles C. Thomas.

Parsons, T., & Bales, R. F. (1955). *Family, socialization and interaction process.* Glencoe, IL: Free Press.

Sager, C. J. (1976). *Marriage contracts and couple therapy.* New York: Brunner/Mazel.

Skynner, A. C. R. (1976). *Systems of family and marital psychotherapy.* New York: Brunner/
    Mazel.
Stierlin, H. (1976). *Psychoanalysis and family therapy.* New York: Jason Aronson.
Sullivan, H. S. (1954). *The psychiatric interview.* New York: Norton.
Wynne, L. C. (1983). A phase-oriented approach to treatment with schizophrenics and
    their families. In W. R. McFarlane (Ed.), *Family therapy in schizophrenia.* New York:
    Guilford Press.

Chapter 9
Alone Together

David J. Moultrup, MSW, LICSW

Loneliness is a feeling of isolation. Intrinsic in it is an emotional insulation that precludes any awareness of a connection with the world.

This is a story of two people who felt alone. As it happens, these two people, who are here called Dick and Jane, were husband and wife. Since they lived together and did the usual kinds of activities together, they certainly were not living a solitary life. But each *felt* alone. They were alone together.

This is an opportunity to get to know Dick and Jane and to begin to understand, as they did, the meaning of feeling alone together. It is important to know from the start, however, that the answers are complex and incomplete. There is no simple, facile answer that explains the enigmatic puzzles posed by individual feelings and their interaction with a family emotional system.

The story goes beyond Dick and Jane as a couple. They are involved in marital therapy, which obviously includes the therapist. My part of the story includes my conceptualization of family dynamics and how Dick and Jane fit into the model. A therapist, however, is more than a conduit for the implementation of theory. The person of the therapist is a major ingredient. Therefore, I include some ideas about who I think I am, and how I used myself in the most creative and useful way I could with Dick and Jane.

The core of my theoretical model for working with couples is the same as my thinking about families. I begin with an integrated model of family therapy (Moultrup, 1981). The model is a distillation of many complex ideas. I present here a distillation of that distillation, making this presentation somewhat similar to dehydrated hiking food. The model is now divided into three main sections: Self and the Family, Time and the Family, and Social Context. Under the heading Self and the Family, there are four subdimensions: differentiation, structure, communication, and behavior. Under the heading Time and the Family are two subdimensions: the nuclear family life cycle and genealogy.

The heading Self and the Family speaks to a fundamental fact about families: They are made up of individuals. For a marriage and family therapist to forget that there are individuals in a family is the opposite mistake that individual therapists make when they forget that there are families in the lives of their individual clients. Both mistakes are equally limiting, but both are equally understandable. It is much easier to attend to only one level at a time, either the individual or the family. The subsections under the heading Self and the Family acknowledge the complexity and organize the difficult, sometimes conflicting, issues encountered when reconciling the life of one individual and his or her connection to the family.

Differentiation as a concept never was defined very clearly, and the ambiguity in definition, particularly the ambiguity in an operational definition, has lead to the development of almost as many idiosyncratic definitions of the term as there are people using it. My own working definition of the term is that it addresses two broad issues, one being separateness and connectedness, the other being the question of overall level of functioning. Regarding connectedness, a differentiated person is one who is able to be involved in a warm, loving relationship yet able to retain the ability to live an independent life. In other words, differentiation involves the freedom to be connected and the freedom to be autonomous.

The issue of level of functioning is more difficult in that it is ambiguous, value laden, and controversial. Essentially, the ability to establish and maintain a healthy, productive life course implies a higher level of functioning, thus a higher level of differentiation. The concept of differentiation, complete with problems, ambiguities, and pervasive implications, acts in many ways as a foundation for most of the other concepts in the model.

The second dimension, that of structure, has been articulated extensively by Minuchin (1974). In broad terms, it refers to the ever-present subgroups in a family. This dimension asks questions regarding the functioning of these subgroups. Are they functioning in a way that promotes healthy individual and family functioning, or they in some way sabotaging this process?

Communication, the third dimension, is seen as a reflection of the dynamic issues delineated elsewhere in the model, as is the level of behavior. Both areas, however, can be seen as avenues of access to the family system and can be treated systematically, using the full range of treatment strategies found in the literature.

The elusive issue of time begins with the life cycle. The development of a perfect conceptualization of the nuclear family life cycle has yet to happen. Despite the conceptual problems, there is a glaring need to include family developmental issues in both conceptual and clinical work with families. Duvall's (1977) family life-cycle model, with its acknowledged limitations, is the model that seems to offer one of the broadest ranges of information and most useful conceptual frameworks for looking at family development. Its limitations are in the normative and, at times, value-laden life style it describes. It does, nonetheless, offer a useful set of probable developmental tasks that families may be struggling with currently, and it anticipates future unfolding.

Genealogy, the second dimension, refers to the multigenerational patterns passed down through families. Concepts such as the multi-generational transmission process and the family projection process (Bowen, 1978), and intergenerational loyalties, indebtedness, merits, and obligations (Boszormenyi-Nagy & Spark, 1973), can all be thought of as ways to understand the multigenerational pressures influencing the current functioning of a family.

Social context is a new addition to the model. It adds an element to the model not strictly within the standard boundaries of "family," but it cannot be ignored. Socioeconomic factors, geopolitical factors, and ethnic and cultural factors can be included in this dimension of the model. A thorough discussion of this dimension is outside the scope of this presentation, so I therefore simply add a word of caution.

There is, clearly, an interaction between the family system and systems larger than the family. For example, ethnicity has been high-lighted by McGoldrick, Pearce, and Giordano (1982), and social–po-litical–family issues have been masterfully explored by Yankelovich (1981). However, conceptualization of the mutual interaction is still extremely rudimentary. A cautious sensitivity to the interaction, and an avoidance of overly simplistic cause-and-effect thinking, will permit the dimension of social context to augment rather than diminish the overall conceptualization of the family.

Dick and Jane

Dick and Jane were referred to me by their family doctor. They lived in a wealthy suburb and came across from the start as bright, educated, perhaps overly motivated people. Dick was a successful business professional, and Jane was invested in activities in the home. My initial agenda, as usual, was to elicit from each person his or her particular view of the reason for coming to therapy.

Dick saw the problem as one of a self-perpetuating pattern in which they had become progressively more distant from each other. He had tried over the years to change the pattern but had been unsuccessful. Jane saw the problem as an inability to feel totally comfortable with one another, which led to feelings of emptiness and a lack of fulfillment. Both reported that the problems included decreased satisfaction with their sexual relationship. Both agreed that divorce was not an option that they were considering.

After this initial description of the problem, which took approximately half of the first session, I asked Dick and Jane if they had any questions for me. They had many of the usual questions people have when they begin treatment. They wanted to know how to address me and what my qualifications and credentials were. I told them that my preference was to be on a first-name basis with them, and I told them the major points of my training and work experience.

The next question, again from both of them, was, "How does this [the therapy] work?" I responded by explaining that I saw the therapy as a process in which the three of us together would become more familiar with their family and how it worked. My overall agenda was to make them experts on their own family so that they would eventually be able to make decisions about what changes needed to be made and how to make them. I went on to explain that I believed that the family operated as a system in much the same way as the environment was a system, and made a comparison to the environment.

Dick and Jane both indicated an appreciation for the systems metaphor, and Dick followed up with the next, and last, question. The question was wrapped in a businesslike demeanor that belied the "bottom-line, fast track, no-nonsense" business behavior that had contributed to his successful career. Dick simply and concisely wanted to know how long the therapy would take and what he could do to accelerate the process.

I told them that the length of therapy depended on how much they wanted to accomplish. Some people were satisfied with the changes they saw after a relatively short time; others, though seeing some change early in the therapy, stayed longer to work on other issues. As far as what he could do to accelerate the process, I explained to him that the most important thing he could do at this stage of the process was to begin to observe even more carefully the patterns that evolved and repeated between him and Jane. I elaborated by suggesting that he might even consider watching events around the house as if he were a camera simply recording and not evaluating events. I encouraged Jane to do the same, and both agreed to the task.

At that point in the session, after I had an initial idea about them, and they an initial idea about me, I told them that I would like to get a more thorough understanding of their home life, problems, and some ideas about the time leading up to the present. I proceeded to pick up a pad of paper and a pen, and listened to the two of them describe their history. I recorded the information on the genogram and time chart under the genogram, using a shorthand that made it easy to get and keep the important information, and still stay connected with them.

The information on the genogram was collected over the entire course of the therapy. Although the bulk of it was amassed in the first several sessions, I added to both the genogram and the time chart throughout the treatment, whenever pertinent information emerged. My usual style, which I followed with Dick and Jane, is to write the genogram on a paper to which I can refer (see Figure 9-1). Later, if useful, I put a larger version on the blackboard in my office if I want to use it to highlight patterns or an issue being discussed.

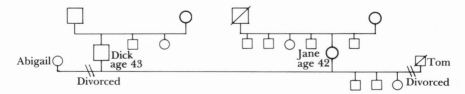

Figure 9.1 Dick's and Jane's family genograms.

Family History

Collecting family history is part of the very fabric of therapy. It is *not*, as some have suggested, a boring chore to be done before beginning therapy. *No one* can do family therapy without some family history. So the question becomes not whether to collect family history, but how much history, and when to collect it in the therapy? The information is then used to understand family dynamics, to get a sense of the evolution of the family over the years, and to begin to develop a treatment plan.

Jane and Dick described a family history that was simultaneously familiar and unfamiliar. Please note that I have changed some of the factual information and blurred some of the other information to protect the confidentiality of the couple. In fact, when I collect information, I ask for specific dates, places, etc. Because the presenting problem was marital conflict, I initially collected just enough information to give me an overall sense of the family system but avoided getting involved in "early unresolved issues" to a degree that would have left the couple impatient to "get to the problem" and threatened by opening old wounds.

I accomplished this by returning to the presenting problem and having both Dick and Jane talk about the escalating tension between them from their different perspectives. Moving backward in time from there, I listened in the history for a point in the story at which the conflict might have become markedly worse. Both told a story of a chronic, slow deterioration with no major point of significant decline.

As can be seen from the genogram, Dick and Jane are both married for the second time. The early years of their marriage had been spent raising Jane's three children from her first marriage. Dick offered that he had never felt accepted by Jane and the children as "the man of the house." Jane agreed with him and offered her own reasons for that situation. However, all the children were living away from home when treatment began. Therefore, the issue of conflicting loyalties and animosity created by the exclusion of Dick from the family was an old wound. Though not exactly alive currently, it probably was contributing to their overall sense of alienation from each other.

A second theme that emerged as a long-standing issue in the marriage was that of Dick's work. His work career was punctuated by periods of total absorption in new projects he would begin and periods of depression resulting from a lack of enjoyment of his job. This vacillation contributed to an overall lack of availability on Dick's part. As they began therapy Dick was looking forward to leaving his current position because he was displeased with the company and his role in it. The anticipation of great amounts of time together after Dick left his job was one of the motivating forces pushing them into therapy at the time they came.

Several other pressure points emerged while discussing Dick and Jane's families of origin and their first marriages. The details of their first marriages and their subsequent marriage to each other were the first to emerge in our discussions together. In our initial discussions of that time, I heard just the basic facts and did not probe unresolved feelings about the events.

Dick was married to Abigail, and Jane was married to Tom. Tom and Abigail, as the story goes, began seeing more of each other than they did of their spouses, and eventually, after a relatively short time, decided to make it a legal, permanent shift in partners. Dick and Jane, meanwhile, having been friends anyway, banded together for emotional support and eventually married, also after not too long a time.

In her marriage to Tom, Abigail had three children, something she had not done in her marriage to Dick. Dick, however, described her as remaining "as crazy as ever." Jane related that she remained very close to Tom, in fact being somewhat of a clandestine confidante for him. Tom died in an accident several years after Dick and Jane got married. Jane became very depressed when Tom died, and both she and Dick described her as never quite having recovered from that depression.

The family's story moved from that time to the period around the death of Jane's father, who died soon thereafter. Again, Jane and Dick painted a picture of strong feelings that never subsided. Jane's father had been a dentist, and she became visibly uncomfortable when beginning to talk about him. Since time ended in the first session in which her father was discussed, we stopped without any clear indication from Jane about the reasons for her feelings.

Jane began the next session almost before she and Dick sat down, with an explanation that she needed to describe something about her relationship with her father that probably had a lot to do with many of her current feelings. She also mentioned that Dick was familiar with what she was going to say.

Jane then blurted out a story that was obviously painful and confusing for her. She avoided eye contact with both me and her husband and squirmed, looking at the floor and out the window while telling her story. Jane is the fifth of six children, and the second daughter. While growing up with all the material comforts she could hope for, she described her home as being an emotional wasteland. Her father was overinvolved in his work, and Jane's recollection of the relationship between her parents was one of a distant, unfulfilling relationship.

Jane's story, however, continued past the description of an uninvolved, distant family. In a deceptively flat, analytical voice, Jane proceeded to report that she had been the victim of incest for a period of several years while she was growing up. Rather than elaborate at all on her initial statement, she immediately switched to the present and related her experiences with her father with her current sexual difficulties with Dick. She reported experiencing many of the same uncomfortable feelings in both situations.

Dick and Jane, despite their mutual awareness of the situation, became noticeably disturbed as Jane related the story. Dick expressed his aggravation that anyone could do such a thing and that he was stuck living with the aftermath of this inappropriate behavior. Jane, meanwhile, basically agreed with Dick, although emphasizing that they both were living with the aftermath.

Rather than pursue the sexual difficulties between the two of them, I gently asked Jane if she could elaborate a bit on the situation with her father so that I could have a clearer idea of what she was dealing with. Although uncomfortable with the idea, she agreed, saying that she would tell me whatever she could remember. I said that it would be helpful if she could remember how old she was when this happened, if it was an isolated incident, and just what she meant by incest.

Jane's memory of the time was blurry. She thought it happened when she was in the sixth, seventh, and eighth grades. It happened more times than she could remember over that period, and her father did not have intercourse with her but did fondle her and touch her. She recalled the horror she felt when he invited her to go along with him to his office by herself. She knew "it" would happen when they were alone at his office.

Despite the overwhelming impact of this experience on her life, and the obviously unresolved nature of the situation, Jane was unable to proceed any further with the topic at that time. Simply relating the story had left her spent. Dick reiterated his animosity toward her father, and the session was over.

In the next session, Jane indicated that she was still not ready to talk about the issue more than she had done, so I respected her feelings and asked Dick to tell me about the family in which he had grown up. Although Dick's story was not as powerful as Jane's, his, too, was a story of strong feelings. His, however, had been handled to a certain extent in his adult life by a geographical relocation that had kept him out of the immediate emotional whirlwind of his family.

Dick is the eldest of three children, born and raised in Australia. His mother was a domineering woman who controlled not only the children but her husband as well. Dick acknowledged that one of his primary reasons for moving to America was to distance himself from his mother's aggravating, controlling manner. He described involved, difficult fights between his first wife, Abigail, and his mother. He went on to say that Jane had done much better than Abigail in handling his mother. Dick returned to his experiences growing up and told a story of himself as a bright, unathletic, scientifically minded boy who was unpopular with his more athletically oriented peers in an all-boys school.

He had memories of being shunned and mocked as a child by his peers and expressed his belief that his experiences with his peers were probably more meaningful to him than his experiences with his family. He became reclusive and developed a dislike for sports that later became one of the bones of contention between him and Jane. Jane had been very involved with her son's athletic activities, including an exhausting and consuming baseball schedule.

The Course of Therapy

Most of the historical data described above was discussed in the first four sessions. I did not push to "resolve the issues." It was apparent to me that the business left unresolved was substantial and that if there was to be any resolution of those feelings, it would happen later. My intuitive judgment about that was fueled partly by the obvious emotional tension generated by discussing the topics, as well as requests from both Dick and Jane that we also look at the current situation and work on concrete, specific ways to begin to change the uncomfortable patterns at home.

With a richer developmental history to act as a backdrop, the discussions began to center more on day-to-day patterns and problems related to them. Two patterns that were obvious in the first session were reviewed with slightly different content issues and slightly different emphasis. The two patterns can be seen as relating to Bowen's (1978) concept of differentiation of self. Regarding Dick, his overly intellectual analysis of the problems between him and Jane continued in the following sessions, demonstrating a basic inability on his part to identify feelings, distinguish feelings from thoughts, and articulate the feelings. Regarding Jane, she continued to be overly focused on feelings, not only her own feelings, but what she perceived Dick's feelings to be. She coupled this with a lack of awareness of how her feelings might be different from what she might think, and she was unable to articulate any personal opinions, any "I statements," about her life situation. (Note the basic complementarity in the cognitive–affective styles of Dick and Jane.)

My interventions addressing these issues were suited to the circumstances, but a certain few ingredients emerged continuously. These ingredients included an educational component, a humorous component, a confrontive component, an empathic, joining component, a paradoxical component, and a questioning, exploring component. All these components fit together in a personal way that culminates in a definition of myself as a professional that is consistent with who I am as a person, and my beliefs as to what the situation demands.

For example, as mentioned, Dick would soon be quitting work. Relatively early in the therapy, a typical exchange between Dick and myself would be as follows:

THERAPIST: Dick, how are you feeling about your upcoming termination at work?
DICK: I think it's a great idea. It will really give me the time and flexibility to develop some of my other ideas, and give me time to be with Jane and get this darned thing straightened out with her.
THERAPIST: O.K., so that's what you think about it. But I'm interested in a different track. I want to distinguish between two different tracks, the thinking track and the feeling track. What you just told me about was your thinking track. There's another one entirely. Most people experience that other track as coming from below their necks. It's in their guts, it's

a feeling. [My brief remark here was a combination of being educational, empathic, and because of a tone of voice that does not come across a printed page, even a bit humorous.]

DICK: But I just don't know what it is that you want! [Dick's response begins to elucidate his own inability to identify feelings.]

THERAPIST: Well, feelings. Feeling words are like *anxious, angry, happy, sad, frustrated.* . . . [My remark here was meant to give a little direction without telling him how I thought he was feeling about the upcoming transition. I wanted him to "do the work."]

DICK: I guess I'm feeling good about it. I'm excited. [Dick's initial identification is one of a positive feeling that would be consistent with the opinion he expressed earlier about this being a good thing for him to do.]

THERAPIST: Thank you.

I chose not to pursue any ambivalent feelings about the transition at that time, figuring that he had just begun to be able to identify positive feelings and that ambivalent ones could wait for some later time. Instead, I turned to Jane. I realized that she operates on the opposite track from Dick, so I phrased the question to her in the opposite fashion. A predictable exchange would have been as follows:

THERAPIST: What do you think about Dick's idea of quitting work, Jane?

JANE: I've been feeling very worried about it. Financially, even though he says we'll be all set, I still get a little concerned, and I'm very worried about what will happen when we spend all of that time together.

THERAPIST: You're pretty good at identifying your feelings, aren't you? Getting back to that distinction that I was just making with Dick, could you distinguish between any feelings you may have about Dick leaving work, and what kind of thoughts you have about it? How about some type of opinion?

JANE: I guess I think it's a good idea in the long run, despite the complications. When I look at the figures on paper, I know we will be able to handle it financially, and I'm pleased that Dick will be able to have an opportunity to get into a work situation that suits him more.

This type of dialogue was reenacted on any number of issues until both Dick and Jane became more able to distinguish for themselves thoughts and feelings. It is not an easy distinction to make, and there would be times in the therapy when I would ignore a confusion of thoughts for feelings, or vice versa, because the content was sufficiently important, and the ideas clear enough, that to force a distinction would have disrupted a more productive line of conversation.

Another major issue woven into the work with Dick and Jane was that of sexuality. The complications were on several levels. To begin with, Jane acknowledged a general discomfort with physical closeness, and both she and Dick related a large part of that feeling back to Jane's experiences with her father. Second, Jane accused Dick of being unable to express physcial affection in a way that was casual and tender. She felt as though every expression of physical affection from Dick was an attempt to initiate lovemaking

Obviously, Jane and Dick were both distressed by the status of their sexual relationship. Although they were willing to discuss it as candidly as was necessary, their anxiety about the topic revealed itself in an overly intellectualized style of discussion. Dick, for example, initially opened the topic with a brief exposition of his particular views on the subject. Then, in a perplexed, but business-flavored style, he asked to be told exactly what they should do about this problem.

With an idea of the kinds of exercises Kaplan (1974) and Masters and Johnson (1970) might propose in this situation, along with relevant individually oriented dynamic formulations, I made a conscious decision to explore the issue from a family systems point of view and to resist the temptation to offer a solution that would put me in the role of expert. Instead, I put myself in the role of researcher, remembering Bowen's (1978, p 246) observation that his "research" families did better than his "clinical" families.

Thinking in this vein, the answer to Dick's question about how to fix this problem became very clear. I told him that I did not know for sure, and I suggested that we talk about it more so that we could all understand the problem. Although not brilliantly successful, this tack did yield some rather interesting results.

On a dynamic level, Jane began to articulate the almost overpowering feelings of being too connected to Dick that she experienced during sexual intercourse. Pursuing the transparent issue of differentiation and fusion, I asked Jane whether she perhaps felt like part of a two-headed animal, with no clear boundary line between the two animals. She replied that she did not exactly feel like that, but that when she thought of the feelings, she imagined a beach scene. She imagined that she felt like the sand, with Dick being the ocean. Every time the ocean washed up on the sand, and then backed out, it took part of the beach with it.

She also described the difficulty of "getting in the mood for sex." She talked about feeling so distant from Dick on a day-to-day basis that she felt alienated from him and not at all inclined to make love. She was able to acknowledge an awareness of the two extremes of connection she was describing, and to admit her frustration with not knowing what to do about it.

Dick, the eternal pragmatist, had a different, and quite predictable, angle on this particular problem. He admitted to the general alienation between Jane and himself but asserted that part of the feeling was caused by *not* making love, and that if they would make love more frequently, that feeling would go away. Reluctantly, Jane agreed that there was some logic to what Dick was saying, but she, nonetheless, was not ready to barge ahead in the same way that Dick was.

I challenged the couple to reconcile the feeling–emotional issues with the practical issues, at least to the extent that they come up with some practical plan for exploring this issue after the session. My intervention was not profound or erudite. It was something like, "So what are you going to do about all this stuff when you leave here?"

Dick and Jane, interestingly, devised a plan in which they would carry out what amounted to the "sensate focus" exercises described by Kaplan (1974). This would last until the next scheduled session, at which time the results would be assessed and decisions made for future strategies. I had not told them anything about the exercises, and they had not had any previous awareness of it. For Dick and Jane, it was simply a way of getting to know each other physically and emotionally without the emotional intensity of sexual intercourse.

They were so pleased with the results of the experiment that they decided to continue the project for a second week. However, they reported that in the middle of the second week, they defected from their plan and had intercourse. Dick told me that it was a very good experience for him, and Jane echoed his opinion. Dick then went on to say that he wondered whether I had intended for that to happen all along. I did not respond.

Despite the relatively satisfactory experience with the sensate focus excercises, Jane was unwilling to follow up on the issue of emotional closeness in a physical relationship in a direct way at this time. Since there had been a general decrease in tension regarding sexuality, Dick was equally willing to defocus that topic.

Instead, they began looking at a wide variety of other stresses in their relationship, including Dick's exclusion in years past from the alliance between Jane and her children, Jane's relationship with her sister and mother, the value of discussing with her sister Jane's relationship with her father, Dick's relationship with his parents, strategies for addressing old business between them, and thoughts and feelings about Dick's upcoming job change. Laced in with these discussions were ongoing discussions regarding daily life events between Jane and Dick, looking at feelings involved, the implications of the events for both of them individually as well as for the relationship, and possibilities for alternative strategies in future similar situations.

Dick finally left his job several months after they had begun therapy. Despite claims from both of them that they were ready and willing for Dick to be at home, the first session after Dick's "retirement," after missing only 2 days of work, found the couple in a serious state of tension and aggravation. They were angry with each other, and neither was able to define the problem.

I listened to each of the stories chronicling the events over the few days since Dick's last day of work. I heard a rather continuous series of unfulfilled expectations, and I saw two people who were extremely agitated, sufficiently so as to be unable to "hear" anything the other person was saying. I made a decision to use my own subjective experience, my own biased perceptions, as an intervention in the session.

My formulation was based on the obvious disturbance created by Dick's leaving work. I surmised that the anxiety had to do with the sudden shift in emotional distance between Dick and Jane, most probably in the direction of too much closeness. As I listened, however, I heard a decided shift in emphasis compared to earlier discussions. Before the actual job change, Jane had been the one to express all the reluctance about the change, and Dick had been the one to voice all the enthusiasm and optimism. In this discussion, however, Jane was the one to express the positive feelings about Dick's being home, and Dick was articulating his concerns.

My operational formulation during the session was that the change had to do with Dick's feelings about separating from his support system at work, Jane's initial enthusiasm about having some help around the house from Dick, Dick's reluctance to take on the household responsibilities, and the underlying fusion regarding emotional closeness and distance in the relationship.

I encouraged Dick to express some of his feelings about leaving his job. The work we had done earlier regarding expression of feelings obviously had helped Dick develop the ability to be aware of appropriately sad feelings and be able to express them. He went on to say that simply expressing those feelings made him feel better. There was, though, the more complex issue of emotional distance between them, and neither of them was able to identify any of the components of that process.

Since Dick and Jane were unable to see the shift themselves, I opted to facilitate their understanding of the process at work by offering my own systemic interpretation of the situation, in the form of a metaphor. I raised the issue of emotional distance, which they were familiar with from earlier sessions. I told them that I saw them as having switched roles. Jane had been the distancer earlier, and Dick had been the pursuer. They had apparently reversed roles since Dick left work. I said that I felt like I was watching two speed skaters who just switched lanes in a race, with the one on the inside going to the outside, and the one on the outside going to the inside.

Since time was up in the session, they had time only for a brief acknowledgment of the fact that the metaphorical interpretation made sense to both of them. However, their anger with each other was still substantial and very alive, and Dick wanted to know, as usual, what to do about it. I reviewed the options in my own mind, including telling them that time was up and that I was sure that they would figure something out until our next scheduled session, or offering the possibility of a follow-up session on the following day. I chose the second option, and they eagerly accepted the opportunity. I also suggested that they make an effort not to discuss these matters for the remainder of the day, and to wait until tomorrow to resume discussion of the problems. They agreed readily.

The next day found Dick and Jane greatly relaxed, sensitive to the nuances of the shift in emotional distance between them, appreciative of the metaphor of the skaters, grateful for a night off from bickering, and ready to begin looking ahead and making longer-term plans for Dick's time off. They did want to make those plans in what they described as the safer atmosphere of my office rather than at home. They began planning for a trip, looking at ways to resolve differences in expectations, and reviewing the trauma of what they had just gone through.

In the next several sessions, we continued to focus on these issues and, more specifically, anticipated the upcoming trip. The planning of the trip stimulated the discussion of power issues between them, such as who makes what decisions, how it is done, and what possibilities there were for renegotiating the power balance between them. They left on their trip with confidence that things would go well between them, and indicated that they would call me when they returned in 6 weeks.

Six weeks came and went, and as it stretched into 9 weeks, I began to wonder what had happened, so I called them. Dick answered the phone and reported that they had returned on schedule, the trip had gone well, that they were very busy at present, and that they would call me in about a month. Again, the month passed with no word from them, and again, after several weeks more than a month, I called them. I spoke with Dick again, who said that Jane was still very busy. She was out of town visting friends, and he, meanwhile, had begun seeing a spiritually oriented therapist for himself. He reported that this was helping him individually but that his relationship with Jane still was not as good as he would like. Again, I encouraged him to call after Jane returned.

Some 4 months after their last session, I again called them. This time I had a more extended conversation with Dick, who said that he and Jane had finally reached the point of realizing that things were again deteriorating between them and that something needed to be done. However, they were not sure that I was the right person, for two main reasons. First, I was a man, and Jane was not sure that I was going to be able to support her and confront her in the most useful way, especially concerning her feelings about her father. Second, from Dick's perspective, he was unsure about whether I would be able to help them get better enough, fast enough. I responded briefly, to each concern, saying that I believed very strongly that the sex of the therapist matters very little in the long run, but if that was important, I would respect Jane's feelings and would help them find a female therapist. Regarding Dick's concerns about getting the most for his time, I said that that was a very complex issue and suggested that we have an evaluation meeting to assess generally the status of our work together. Dick agreed to the meeting, and we set up a time.

The first session after their 4-month hiatus was a contracting session. Jane came in feeling resolved regarding the issue of sex of the therapist. Dick had reported my opinion to her, and she had heard the same opinion from a friend who was a therapist. She felt no need to have a female therapist just to have a female therapist. Most of the discussion, then, focused on expectations of me and the treatment. My working formulation was that the progress made during our initial work together had been satisfactory to me. The layoff was a combination of a healthy attempt to do things independently, an annoyance with me for not fixing their relationship by saying or doing just the right thing, and a basic resistance to change. I made use of that formulation during the session by accepting their suggestion to work with a different therapist as a legitimate concern, and to help them define what they might want out of someone else.

I gently suggested that the time away from therapy may indicate some ambivalence about change and that they would have to be fairly specific about what they wanted to get out of therapy in order to choose just the right therapist. I expressed confidence in my own ability to work with them but did not overtly interpret their consideration of seeing a different therapist as a form of resistance. They made the decision to renew our work together, with Dick highlighting his need to be able to define the progress more clearly in his own mind.

With a renewed commitment to looking at specific things that were going wrong between them, Dick and Jane began in the next session to talk about a pattern of negativity between them, in which Dick would be unreceptive to Jane and what she was talking about, and Jane would negate anything that Dick would talk about. They felt hopelessly caught up in the pattern and were unable to generate any ideas for breaking the cycle. After exploring different possibilities for devising a type of contract between the therapist and the couple as described by Stuart (1971), I decided instead to give them a homework assignment addressing the issue of control of the negative talking itself.

The homework was to use dinner time as a "controlled" time each day. While they were eating, they were quite consciously to speak only positively to each other. At the end of the meal they were to adjourn to another room and spend another 10 minutes with each other. At this time, however, they were to be as negative as possible. I referred to their earlier descriptions of how they were negative with each other, and admitted that although the definitions of positive and negative discussion were not as clear as I would like, I wanted them to do their best.

I received a call from Dick later that evening. He said that they had had their best dinner in years but that they still needed some help with the part about being negative with each other. Was I really serious? Smiling to myself, I told him that I was entirely serious. I wanted them to do the best they could to be negative with each other. Perhaps on this first night they may have some trouble with it, but I wanted them to keep trying. I wanted them to keep mental notes of how they are negative with each other through the course of the week, and to use those strategies during their negative time at night. Dick responded that it sounded like they were both developing a war chest.

In the session that followed the "paradoxical" homework assignment, Jane began by relating her experience of the positive talk eventually becoming superficial, and that the assignment had not helped establish a deeper level of intimacy between them. I initially asked her what she was getting out of remaining distant from Dick. In response to Jane's quizzical look, I explained that the distance between them was so persistent and intransigent that it must be fulfilling some need. She was unable to identify anything positive in maintaining the distance between them, so I asked her to tell me about what the closeness was like between them over the course of their relationship.

This precipitated a long and detailed conversation about the issue of closeness and intimacy, and how they have experienced it over the course of their relationship. They essentially described a relationship born under adversity and in a time of crisis. They experienced closeness and intimacy initially because of the shared experience of being rejected, abandoned, and vulnerable. From shortly after that time, the closeness between them began to deteriorate. We explored the implications for those times and for the present. Jane expressed satisfaction and a good feeling that we had reviewed the past. Dick expressed enthusiasm that we had been able to identify so accurately the flow of intimacy, and lack of intimacy, between them.

Our work together continued on for five more sessions. During that time, we continued to examine critical incidents during the week, and to develop ideas as to their overall meaning within their emotional system. We returned to the idea that there was some need for them to maintain the status quo as tenaciously as they were, with equally uninspired results. The old and unsolved issue of Jane's feelings of anxiety related to physical closeness was aired, and Jane confessed to strong ambivalent feelings about the situation. She wanted to discuss them, and be rid of them, but was unble to force herself to do any work on them. One final theme was that of Dick's mood. He had been feeling increasingly depressed over his prospects for business opportunities. His depression was influencing his emotional availability to Jane.

We agreed to suspend meeting temporarily because Dick was working feverishly on his new business. We talked about the fact that the hiatus would be a recapitulation of one of their long-standing patterns. Nonetheless, both Jane and Dick were willing to carry out the plan. Within a month of our last session, Dick's work efforts had blossomed, his mood had improved in turn, and the situation between Dick and Jane was very comfortable. Jane reported over the phone that her anxieties about physical closeness were still troublesome and that she still was interested in alleviating them. She thought she might at some point in the future seek out a group of women with similar experiences as an avenue for exploring her feelings. Meanwhile, since she and Dick were doing well overall, they saw no need for further sessions, but would call if the need arose.

Theoretical Foundations

The interventions I have described in working with Dick and Jane are related to my theoretical and philosophical beliefs about family systems, individuals, and change. Although I briefly presented my integrated model at the start of the chapter, a more thorough discussion may highlight the interaction between theory and practice. The important triangle in this discussion is that of therapist, theory, and family, for it is in the interplay of these three factors that the differences between one therapist and another become manifest.

Beginning with the therapist, I have searched almost continuously for some concept or metaphor that would capture the essence of what I believed, and felt like, I was doing with a family during therapy. Bowen shunned the title of therapist, and instead preferred the metaphor of a coach, a person who stays outside of a competitive, win-or-lose situation and offers strategies and support to the people who are playing the game. Although I, too, felt uncomfortable with the ambiguities of the title of therapist, the coach idea did not work for me. I have never been able to presume that I knew the exact right way that a play should be made; moreover, I wanted people to be their own player–coaches.

Whitaker (1981) uses the metaphor of parenting to refer to his experience in psychotherapy. Although many clients would communicate to me a desire to be parented, and their wish to have me do the parenting, I consciously resisted assuming a parenting posture. Aside from the personal fatigue involved in having so many children, I preferred to work toward establishing and maintaining an adult to adult relationship with my clients.

It was in looking at the overall evolution of change that I was able to arrive at a metaphor that described my experience with my clients. It seemed to me that a new couple, family, or individual came to me with the explicit request to help them change their life circumstances to such a degree that they were more satisfied with them. That request precipitated a process of varying lengths but with distinct similarities in process. Change, then, seemed to have a certain consistency in form from one situation to another. To me it felt like a journey. It felt like I was accompanying my clients on a difficult, at times intimidating, and at times exhilarating, journey through difficult terrain so that they could begin a new life "in a new place."

After I had taken the journey a number of times, I began to recognize more and more about the territory over which we were traveling. I began to be able to talk about others who had traversed the same terrain, and how they had done it. I began to be able to anticipate difficult spots in the journey, coming just over the next hill, where my client had not yet been. I began to be able to provoke people when that would facilitate the journey. I began to see myself as an escort, or a guide, that people would engage to accompany them through the territory of change.

This, obviously, is highly metaphorical. But, for me, it works. I think of myself as a combination escort, tour guide, and at times, pathfinder, pointing to paths that have been fairly reliable in past similar situations. It is built on the idea that different people will take journeys of different lengths; that not every path is right for every client; and that the client, ultimately, can and must maintain control of his or her own life. At the same time, however, I have a responsibility for bringing every bit of my experience and expertise to bear on the situation in order to ensure the best possible trip for the client.

The pragmatic implications for the metaphor of escort are profound. Not every path (i.e., theory or intervention) is right for every client or every circumstance. Therefore, a sound integrated model is truly the most viable foundation for practice. Second, we do have refined theories and strategies, but to assume that we "know the entire territory" can unnecessarily limit creativity and the need for ongoing exploration. Finally, the issue of responsibility for change gets framed in such a way that neither the client nor the therapist is responsible for doing "all the work." Each person has to assume and maintain individual responsibility.

The second corner of our triangle, theory, has been equally difficult to describe either conceptually or metaphorically. The most useful metaphor for an integrated model has been described by the Duhls (1981), who use the metaphor of a gazetteer. A gazetteer is a map of a given territory, with a series of transparencies that can be placed over the map to highlight and describe different characteristics of the territory. My use of this idea implies that each dimension of the model can be seen as a transparency over the broad map of the family. Each dimension refers to one aspect of family life. In typical fashion, all the dimensions in the model interact systemically. My job, as a family therapist, is to assess any given family coming to treatment, decide which area of the family is problematic, and make a treatment decision as to which theoretical model and type of intervention will be the most useful at any given point with any particular family.

Although those familiar with Bowen's ideas will recognize his influence in my work with Dick and Jane, I obviously have translated his thinking in a personal way, and I have not limited myself to his theory. The integrated model represents a synthesis of my personal and professional influences in such a way as to be part of a process of a personal definition of a professional self. The personal style that evolves from the definition of a professional self, in conjunction with basic clinical judgment, are the variables that ultimately govern treatment decisions.

The last corner of the therapist–theory–family triangle is, of course, the family. Dick and Jane present a challenge. Their overall level of functioning is quite high. They have been successful economically and socially, and are generally intact as a family unit. This very strength in the family poses a formidable obstacle to discerning the problem area and strategies for improvement. Can the therapist come up with any ideas about new ways to see the situation, or do things, beyond what the family already knows or has done?

A corollary to that problem is that the family itself is more likely to challenge the therapist overtly. How can the therapist explain and define his belief system, competence, and general usefulness to the family in such a way that the expenditure of time, money, and energy by the family is seen as being worthwhile? This is accountability in its most basic form. The therapist is indeed accountable to the family in all these ways. An intelligent, articulate couple such as Dick and Jane demand a level of interpersonal accountability between therapist and clients that greatly transcends the bureaucratic utilization review standards.

This couple also expressed an interest in having the treatment be as rapid, efficient, and thorough as possible. Although Dick was the one to express this desire most frequently, the view was shared by Jane. I see this attitude as being an expression, in a rather transparent form, of the positive side of every family's ambivalence toward change in therapy. For the therapist to be seduced by these kinds of feelings is just as dangerous as to be overly discouraged by equally intense expressions of resistance to change.

Homework in Marital Therapy

The paradoxical homework assignment described near the end of the case operated like most of the paradoxical interventions I have used. It served to control the symptomatic behavior by keeping it at a conscious level in the minds of Dick and Jane. It provided some relief from the symptomatic behavior by limiting its frequency of occurrence, and it generally served to decrease the level of tension between Dick and Jane regarding the problematic area.

On the other hand, it was insufficient in its impact on more abstract, dynamic issues such as intimacy. The primary importance of the paradoxical intervention was that it stimulated Dick and Jane and seemed to facilitate a readiness in them to discuss the issue of closeness and intimacy. The session that followed the paradoxical homework assignment was a particularly rich discussion of the oscillations of closeness and distance between them.

The use of homework assignments in general, either paradoxical or "straight," then, takes on an importance as a part of an overall process more than as an end in itself. Although homework usually stimulates some change, it is impossible to predict the exact nature of the change, and usually quite possible to predict that whatever the change, it rarely will be sufficient to qualify as being a miracle cure. My job as escort–tour guide–pathfinder is to be able to understand where the homework assignment has taken the couple and be able to keep the process moving from there.

The work with Dick and Jane, although it is not finished, is done temporarily, at least. I am pleased that their relationship is operating more smoothly, despite the obvious continuation of long-standing patterns. I am also pleased that our relationship is strong enough that they will call if the need arises in the future. A careful analysis of the couple, in terms of my integrative model, could serve as an outline for developing future treatment issues. This, however, would be cumbersome and redundant. Nevertheless, some specific bits of unfinished business could be mentioned here.

Both Dick and Jane have relationships with their families of origin that create ongoing pressure for the couple. These relationships relate to the present as well as the past. Jane could benefit from further exploration of her relationship with her dead father, and acquiring some insight into the difficult issue of his inappropriate sexual relationship with her as a child. Perhaps a support group such as she mentioned *would* be a way for her to feel mutual understanding and support. Dick, meanwhile, could benefit from a more thorough understanding of intimacy patterns in his family, as well as an understanding of what his mother's domination meant to him and to the whole family.

As you will remember, Dick and Jane came to treatment with a concern for the emotional distance between them. Although they are no longer alone together to the degree that they were initially, the issues of intimacy, and the related sexual distance, are not thoroughly resolved. Further therapeutic explorations of these issues will undoubtedly relate to the question of differentiation and fusion between Dick and Jane and the behavioral patterns that reflect these dynamics.

Creativity, Orthodoxy, and Therapy

Therapy is an interpersonal experience demanding every bit of creativity and improvisational energy I have to give to it. I find that I do my best work when I do not have any rigidly established agenda that I impose on the family. This creativity is disciplined by theory, structured by the client couple, and enriched by an intense absorption in the therapeutic process.

The story of Dick and Jane should not be seen as a comment on "the right way to do marital therapy," since my own views are ever in flux. It was the right way for me at that time. The creativity necessary in therapy is very much the same as the creativity needed in artistic improvisation, such as music or other art forms. This case example is simply one recording by an improvising artist.

There is, of course, a viewpoint on therapy that provides stark contrast. The idea of an orthodox, technically precise, fail-safe protocol for psychotherapy remains like a siren wailing in the distance. The actual probability of developing such a method is slim. For, ultimately, the most consistently meaningful behavior by the therapist in the interpersonal encounter called psychotherapy is tempered by creativity and responsiveness to the situation.

References

Boszormenyi-Nagy, I., & Spark, G. M. (1973). *Invisible loyalties: Reciprocity in intergenerational family therapy.* New York: Harper & Row.

Bowen, M. (1978). *Family therapy in clinical practice.* New York: Jason Aronson.

Duhl, S., & Duhl, F. J. (1981). Integrative family therapy. In A. S. Gurman & D. P. Kniskern (Eds.), *Handbook of family therapy.* New York: Brunner/Mazel.

Duvall, E. M. (1977). *Marriage and family development* (5th ed.). Philadelphia: Lippincott.

Kaplan, H. (1974). *The new sex therapy.* New York: Brunner/Mazel.

Masters, W. H., & Johnson, V. E. (1970). *Human sexual inadequacy.* Boston: Little, Brown.

McGoldrick, M., Pearce, J. K., & Giordano, J. (1982). *Ethnicity and Family Therapy.* New York: Guilford.

Minuchin, S. (1974). *Families and family therapy.* Cambridge, MA: Harvard University Press.

Moultrup, D. (1981). Towards an integrated model of family therapy. *Clinical Social Work Journal, 9,* 111–125.

Stuart, R. B. (1971). Behavioral contracting within the families of delinquents. *Journal of Behavior Therapy and Experimental Psychiatry, 2,* 1–11.

Whitaker, C. A., & Keith, D. V., (1981). Symbolic–experiential family therapy. In A. S. Gurman, & D. P. Kniskern (Eds.), *Handbook of family therapy.* New York: Brunner/Mazel.

Yankelovich, D. (1981). *New rules.* New York: Random House.

Chapter 10
The Marriage Contract as Wolfbane, or The Way We Were

M. Duncan Stanton, PhD

The first question that pops into my mind on being referred a couple for therapy is, Why now? Why didn't they come in 6 months ago, or 2 years hence? What is different about them and their context that has prompted them to seek help at this time? What has changed?

Such questions obviously relate to issues pertaining to family life-cycle events. They speak to changes in the way the couple and family must operate in the here and now—alterations in the structure of their relationship that require new rules that they have been unable to define or assimilate. Knowledge of such changes is of more than academic interest. Indeed, it can, as Haley (1973) notes, set the direction for the whole treatment effort, or at least dictate who is to be involved in therapy and what issues are to be dealt with.

The therapeutic approach that I have found to be most effective generally combines features of the structural (Minuchin, 1974) and strategic (see Stanton, 1981c) modes. Since this paradigm has been described elsewhere (Stanton, 1981a, 1981b), space is not given here to its details. However, some of the basic ideas and methods follow.

View of the Couple or Family

1. People are seen as interacting within a context, both affecting it and being affected by it.

253

2. As stated, the family life cycle and developmental stage are important in both diagnosing and defining therapeutic strategy.
3. Symptoms are both system maintained and system maintaining.
4. The couple or family can change, allowing new behaviors to emerge, if the overall context is changed. Moreover, in order for individual change to occur, the interpersonal system itself must change. This would permit different aspects of such family members' (potential) "character" to come to the fore.

Therapy and the Therapist

1. Treatment is viewed pragmatically, with an eye toward what "works."
2. Emphasis is on the present rather than the past.
3. Repetitive behavioral sequences are to be changed.
4. While the structural approach may not be as symptom focused as the strategic, both are much more symptom or problem oriented than psychodynamic approaches.
5. Process is emphasized much more than content. This includes interventions that are nonverbal and noncognitive, in a sense, "doing away with words." Such interventions derive from viewing the system from a meta level and recognizing that verbalizations, per se, by therapist or family are often not necessary for change.
6. The therapist should be active.
7. Diagnosis is obtained through intervention.
8. Therapeutic contracts are negotiated with clients revolving around the problem and the goals of change.
9. Interpretation is usually employed to "relabel" rather than produce "insight."
10. Behavioral tasks are assigned.
11. Considerable effort may go into "joining" the couple positively and reducing apparent "guilt" or defensiveness. This is more than simply "establishing rapport" as it is often done selectively and with regard to what the therapist deems necessary for system change.
12. Therapy usually cannot progress from the initial dysfunctional stage to a "cure" stage without one or more intermediate stages,

which, on the surface, may also appear dysfunctional. For instance, a therapist may have to take sides with a spouse (thereby "unbalancing" the couple in an opposite way from which it entered treatment) in order to restabilize at a point of parity.

13. Therapy tends to be brief and often does not exceed 6 months.

It may be apparent that some of the above points are shared by other, more active marital therapies, such as the behavioral and "communications training" approaches. However, many of them are distinctive of structural and strategic therapy.

In addition, I have identified several general rules for the concomitant and/or contrapuntal use of structural and strategic techniques.

1. Initially deal with a couple through a primarily structural approach—joining, accommodating, testing boundaries, restructuring, unbalancing, increasing intensity, etc.
2. Switch to a predominantly strategic approach when structural techniques are either not succeeding or are unlikely to succeed. This might include the use of positive interpretation, the introduction of paradoxical instructions, or the use of "strategic disengagement" (Stanton, 1981a).
3. Following success with strategic methods, and given that a case is to continue in therapy, revert once again to a structural approach.

The above guidelines are not meant to be limiting. On occasion I find it necessary to draw on a broader therapeutic repertoire, such as including the couple's parents and network, dealing with deathbed instructions, and entering into grief work. In other words, the rules provide an outline, a sketch, not necessarily a completed canvas.

The Case

This was a "premarital" case in which life-cycle and countertransference issues were salient. The case illustrates a number of the "traps" that can occur in this work. It is hoped that the reader might profit both from the mistakes made and the interventions that did prove effective.

This couple was seen 7 years ago, in early 1978. Both partners, Jean, age 33, and Bernie, age 40, had been divorced from their spouses for over 8 years. They had been dating steadily for 3 years and working in the same office during that period. Jean had two children and Bernie four by their former marriages.

I had previously seen Jean and her ex-husband for 10 sessions over 5 months around problems they had been having with visitation and behavior of their 13-year-old son and 11-year-old daughter. The therapy had gone well and had terminated 8 months before the present contact.

I had not had occasion to meet Bernie during that therapy as, despite his lengthy relationship with Jean, she had scarcely mentioned him and had not included him in a parenting role with her children. It was evident that she would not be capable of doing so until her unfinished business with her ex-husband was resolved. Thus, at the start of this premarital therapy, I essentially had no relationship with Bernie and a positive relationship with Jean. Indeed, I was pleased to learn that she appeared to have progressed beyond her former marriage to the point where she was ready to deal with a more solid relationship.

Jean, one of nine siblings, was an attractive, bright, thoughtful person. Both her parents were reported to be alcoholics. As a teenager she had run away with a man in his 50s who also had a drinking problem. Subsequently, at age 18 she became pregnant by, and had married, her ex-husband, apparently as a means of getting out of the home.

Bernie presented as handsome, intelligent, engaging, and shrewd. His style might be described as effetely energetic. He was also a gourmet cook. He was raised at a boys' home following his father's death when he was 10 years old. His younger sister was placed in a girls' home (his mother continued to live with her parents and to hold a job). When he first got married, his mother was opposed to it. She then married his wife's father within a year of Bernie's marriage. He had continued to see his mother, usually weekly, up to the present. He sometimes wondered whether his mother wanted to have sex with him. Jean complained that in recent years Bernie drank too much and too often.

Jean contacted me this time because in the past few months she and Bernie had gotten into a vicious, draining, repetitive pattern of fights and infidelities. During the years of their steady dating, Bernie had pushed Jean to get married. She had resisted this. Then, 2 months earlier, she had consented, and that was when the trouble began. He took up with another woman, Jean grew increasingly paranoid, and they began battling. Jean recognized a pattern, in that in the past (before she dated him) Bernie had severed relations with three or four other women when things had begun to get serious. In her phone call to me she expressed concern that she might be merely the latest in this parade of lovers. She said that Bernie had agreed to attend one session with her, and an appointment was made.

Session 1

This was a long meeting. We talked for 30 minutes about how their relationship had developed and about the present situation. I then met with each of them separately. (I frequently do this with couples to allow each person to state honestly whether he or she wishes to remain in the relationship.) Bernie told me that he had always been the one who wanted to marry, not Jean. He also said that many of Jean's suspicions were not justified, in that the "other woman" was an old friend who had called him because her husband had just died (she was also in a financial and vocational crisis) and that he had not been intimate with her. Jean essentially repeated what she had told me over the phone, adding new bits of information here and there.

We then reconvened, and I had them work extensively on their expectations, discussing what had and had not changed in the last couple of months, etc. Jean noted that since she had gotten her relationship with her children in order, and had resolved many of the problems with her ex-husband, she had eventually, albeit recently, reached the point where she could commit herself to a more stable relationship with Bernie, probably including marriage. This was the change that had made a difference. Although she had heretofore apparently been the more "standoffish" partner in the relationship, during this phase of the session she became considerably more open than Bernie. She laid herself bare and told Bernie she would meet whatever conditions he wanted because she desired that the marriage be successful.

Although it was a rather moving display of vulnerability, Bernie remained implacable. He could not respond to her pain. Finally, I asked him if he could put his arm around her. He hesitated at first, then said "sure" and flamboyantly swung it around, hanging it woodenly in place. This was not the kind of display of fond support I had in mind. Since I was not able, even after what I viewed as a considerable effort at joining, to connect the couple in a positive way, I decided to change tack. I backed off, while noting that the two of them seemed to be on a roller-coaster of ups and downs. I wondered whether they needed a brief respite in which to "mark time." They nodded slightly.

I then asked, for the sake of changing the pattern and at least temporarily preventing the situation from becoming more complicated, if Bernie would agree not to go to bed with the other woman for the next week; could he hold off for a short period because, if he slept with her, this might markedly complicate his relationship with Jean. He said he could not agree to such an arrangement, even for a week.

This brought me up short. I was both astonished and somewhat irritated. I felt conned. I had been working in what was essentially a structural mode for over 2 hours—joining, defining turf and needs, having them interact, trying to effect compromise, etc. I fully expected, based on the nonverbal signals I had been getting, that he might hesitate initially but would agree to refrain for a week. When he did not, I reacted firmly to his response, stating to him outright, "You don't want this marriage." Since I had been soft-spoken and rather gentle up to that point, my abruptness startled them both. I continued, "You have been straight with Jean so far [noting to her in an aside that he could have agreed not to sleep with the other woman and gone ahead and done it anyway] but, for whatever reason, you don't want this marriage. This is a situation where one person pursues another relentlessly, but when the pursued person suddenly turns around with open arms, the pursuer quickly backs off. You don't want to get married and you are making it clear by not consenting to even a little request for the sake of this relationship."

Bernie sat and said nothing, looking not angry but confused. After a minute, Jean looked at him and asked, "Is that it?" and, following a brief pause, said, "We don't have to get married." Bernie gazed back and asked, "Really?" She said, "No. I don't have to be married to you. I just don't want to lose you. Just love me—that's enough." For the first time, Bernie warmed up to Jean. He touched her and they hugged. His relief was apparent. Jean wept a little. I then told them I was going to leave them alone, and they could stay in the room as long as they wanted—until they were ready to leave. I told them to decide together whether to get back to me about another appointment.

There were several reasons for this last intervention. First, it respected their privacy as a couple, giving them space to say or demonstrate any intimacies they might choose. Second, it removed me as a distraction from their relationship—they couldn't look to me as a detouring object. Third, it took me out of competition with Bernie for Jean. Fourth, it was an affirmation of them as adults who were able to make decisions on their own.

Sessions 2 and 3

The next day Jean called and asked for an appointment alone. I agreed to it because I felt that she was ready to work conscientiously and I did not trust Bernie. This was probably a mistake because it compromised my joining adequately with Bernie and thereby dictated the later stages of therapy. When we met, she told me they had talked a great deal on the way home. Bernie had said he needed a "time out" and asked that they not date or meet for 10 days. (They could not avoid seeing each other completely since they worked together.) He had told her he needed a breather to get his head together. Jean had agreed to this.

Jean and I also met briefly a week later (the third session) as a support for the time out. At that session Jean mentioned that Bernie wanted to see me alone and would call.

Session 4

Bernie reached me soon after, and we set up an appointment. When he came in, we discussed whether we would want to meet any more and for what reason. Jean had told him he did not know himself well if he was going through these patterns repetitively, implying that he needed treatment. He admitted feeling somewhat guilty about the recent goings-on, and about the pain he was causing the other woman. He seemed to want to find out from me what his "diagnosis" was and whether he was blind to something I might see in his behavior. I felt as though he was trying to trap me into making a statement that he could then disprove. In fact, I felt I had been drawn into a very subtle and skillfully orchestrated sparring match. I was interested, however, in determining whether Bernie felt there were any problems on which he was motivated to work, either individually or with Jean. We discussed several directions that we might take: meeting with Jean together; exploring some of what was going on in his life at present and working to change this; meeting with his mother and perhaps his stepfather to see if they could help (this was one of my own secret agendas). He denied interest in any of these ideas, and we parted amicably with my saying, in essence, "If you don't see a problem, it either isn't there or it isn't bothering you enough to make you want to work on it." Although his inclination seemed to be not to attend additional sessions at the time, I did not want to make that an explicit agreement. I preferred to keep the door open. By not reaching closure, it would be easier for him to agree to come in later—he still had a face-saver, since he had not been put in a position of having to refuse to return.

Session 5

Jean called me the next week and came in for an appointment by herself. She said that Bernie was not interested in continuing therapy and that on the previous Saturday he had called off their relationship. However, they had had tickets for a double date on Monday with his mother and stepfather and had decided to keep this date. After parting with his parents that night, Bernie had asked Jean if he could talk with her at her house. He had cried while there, and ended up staying the night. Jean was confused. She wondered (but did not ask him) whether he did or did not want to stay involved with her. She was pleased that he had come back to her, but was not sure where to go from there. She added that she had canceled plans to go skiing with another man on Thursday so that she could see Bernie off on a plane to Florida. He was going away to spend a few days with the other woman. Jean and Bernie had sex in the afternoon before his flight and then he left to join the woman. Jean seemed to have gotten devilish pleasure at this little escapade, as if she had "soiled" Bernie before she handed him over to her competitor.

Three other features of this session with Jean deserve mention. First, she expressed a fear that she was somehow getting stuck with men who drank too much, perhaps because one or both of her parents were alcoholic. I pointed out to her that neither of the two men with whom she had previously had the best relationships—her ex-husband and an earlier boyfriend—were heavy drinkers. I then took a more strategic tack and noted that even if such a pattern did exist, it might not be too bad a thing because she had a sort of family tradition that might need to be upheld; it would be difficult to break this tradition, and maybe it should not be done. As I had hoped, she strongly resisted this idea; the desired reaction had been achieved.

The second aspect of the session dealt with the future of her relationship with Bernie and her job. After some discussion, I told her that whether or not she and Bernie stayed together, she should realize that she would eventually have to find work elsewhere. First, if they broke up completely, Bernie might make her work situation intolerable, since he was her supervisor. Second, if they stayed together, she would have to leave because their employer had strict rules against dating or marriage between employees (up to that point their relationships had been *sub rosa*). She seemed to accept this eventuality without much difficulty.

The third facet of the session dealt with boundaries between Jean and Bernie. She was, as stated earlier, confused, and not sure she wanted to get back into a seesaw relationship with him. I wondered whether *she* could set up a time out by postponing their dating for a month. She thought it was not a bad idea and that she could. I then cautioned her that this would not be easy to do—especially during the latter 2 weeks—and that Bernie would probably pressure her to take up with him again. She agreed to try it nonetheless.

Session 6

During the next week, Jean told Bernie of her decision, and he began to put tremendous pressure on her, placing his hand on her knee, calling her, cajoling, etc. She was very ambivalent about this, and it became clear that they would soon lapse into their previous up-and-down pattern.

This meeting also clarified for me that I had some work of my own to do. I was getting into a countertransference problem, having thoughts about rescuing Jean from this miserable relationship—as if I could do for her what her boyfriend could not. Mixed with this were several sexual fantasies, and I found myself sneaking peeks at her breasts when she was not looking. While these diversions were eminently pleasurable, they certainly were not going to help the therapy. I determined either to stop the fantasies or at least keep them out of the way of the work that needed to be done. In addition, I had to wrestle with the issues of (*a*) whether I was seeing Jean alone for my own reasons or because Bernie would not come in; and (*b*) whether I could conduct successful therapy without including him directly.

In the end I decided to take a chance. I concluded first that, for the reasons mentioned previously, Bernie and I were insufficiently joined, and I had inadequate leverage with him to effect change. In addition, he appeared too confused and ambivalent to be reengaged at that time. Second, Jean had shown enough motivation and concern for me to be able to work with her alone toward changing the relationship to something more mutually satisfying to them both. I was also aware of the risk that their relationship might not withstand the change, as I was unsure of Bernie's readiness, or even his ability, to form a tighter bond with Jean, considering the number of triangulated relationships within which he was embedded. However, I also believed that if things became too strained, and if Jean was determined to hang on, I would get adequate forewarning to be able to shift direction if need be.

Session 7

This meeting started off with Jean's lamenting the bind in which she felt caught, what with her attempt to distance in the face of Bernie's onslaught of overtures. After discussing this at some length, I got an idea. I presented Jean with the following proposal: She should draw up a contract for Bernie to sign in which he agreed to marry her at the end of the time-out period (in 3 weeks). It also specified that he would agree not to call her, date her, or engage in any physical congress with her during the 3 weeks. A statement was included acknowledging that he was aware that this contract was legally binding. It was to be signed only by Bernie and a witness, but *not* by Jean. She was to place a copy in his mailbox at work every day for 3 weeks and to carry a copy on her person at all times. If he approached her and tried to make affectionate advances, she was to pull out the contract and ward him off with it. (The analogy to using a crucifix against Dracula, or wolfbane to ward off a werewolf, was not wholly unintentional.) She laughed at the idea and thought it was worth trying.

Session 8

Jean related the events of the past week. Two days after our previous session, she had put a copy of the contract in Bernie's mailbox. As one might expect, his initial response was one of confusion. He was caught off guard. Soon, however, he regained his composure and made an amorous advance toward her. She quickly pulled a copy of the contract from her purse and parried him by sticking it in his face. He cringed and retreated.

The next day, when he found another copy in his mailbox, he got angry. He told Jean he was going to consult a lawyer. As the week went on, each day being greeted by a new copy of the contract, Bernie tried a series of ploys: He called her "unfair" for not signing it herself; he questioned whether it could be legally binding; at times he became solicitous, at other times antagonistic. In contrast, Jean remained relatively unflappable during this period, apparently deciding that she needed her space and that, whatever the upshot might be, it had to be better than the present situation.

Toward the end of that week (i.e., following the eighth session), Jean broke ranks. She called Bernie. She had dated an old boyfriend a couple of times and decided that this other man was not for her. She decided she "missed" Bernie. That Saturday, Bernie signed the contract, using as a "witness" his 5-year-old daughter, and mailed it to her. He did think that the marriage date on it was unrealistic because it gave them no time to plan a wedding and set up house; she agreed with him. She rewrote the contract on Sunday, stating that the marriage should occur within 1 year, but she "forgot" to include the clause about needing a time out for the remaining 2 weeks of her respite. This kicked off a series of events as follows:

1. On Monday a friend accompanied Bernie to Jean's house and witnessed his signature. Bernie and the friend then went out to dinner, Bernie returning later with a bottle of wine and the intention of staying overnight. Jean said she still needed her 2 weeks of space; he persisted; they fought; and he left.
2. The next day she went to his house for a prearranged dinner with him and his daughter; while there, the other woman called. Jean got angry; they fought again; and Jean eventually left.

3. On Wednesday Bernie was angry; he met with Jean at work and told her he was not sure what he wanted. He said he did not want to see her over the upcoming weekend.

Session 9 (telephone)

The next day Jean called me, sounding distraught. She said she wanted Bernie back and asked me what she should do. We discussed the sequence of events and how it compared to their past pattern. I noted that the fact that she broke ranks indicated that she was not ready to terminate the relationship. I told her she seemed to have no control over the pattern, following it like a script, and then suggested (paradoxically) that maybe she should go through the experience three or four times more so that she could get a handle on it. I said that she was still hoping Bernie would change, but that that might not be possible. If she went through the sequence again, she might be better able either to make a decision to end it or to decide that it was not so bad and was, indeed, what she needed at that point in her life. I likened the relationship to a TV mystery or horror show—it might be unpredictable, scary, and wrenching, but it was nonetheless exciting. I reminded her of the roller-coaster metaphor, noting that while she and Bernie might encounter many twists, turns, and surprises, at least their relationship was not *dull*. I asked if it was common for her to call Bernie over the weekend. She said that it was, and I recommended that she be sure to call him this weekend also. (Note that the structural idea of her keeping Bernie away for another week or two was avoided, mainly because it had so far not been fully carried out, and I was dubious that she would follow through if I prescribed it.) She asked whether, instead of trying to make a change, the cycle might eventually dissipate if she just waited long enough. I said, "Yes, you probably won't have to go through this more than ten or fifteen times and it should all be over in two or three years"—an example of strategic "overestimation" (Stanton, 1981c) or "positioning" (Rohrbaugh *et al.*, 1981). This scared her into bravery, and she said she thought maybe she should try *something* different—to take a chance on change. I said that was up to her, and we made an appointment for the following Monday.

Session 10

At the next session Jean told me she had talked to Bernie by telephone on Friday. She had told him he had to decide about her and their relationship one way or the other; she was tired of the "neither fish nor fowl" approach. He had then asked her to spend Saturday night at his place, and she had agreed. However, she had had a prior engagement with a female friend and did not arrive until 3:45 a.m. Bernie was furious. They did not make love, slept apart, then got up in the morning and had a fight. Eventually they began talking. They both decided that neither wanted to get married or to live together. They drew up and signed an agreement that encompassed the following conditions:

1. For the next 3 months they would date other people if they wanted, plus each other. (Jean did not particularly like Bernie dating other women, but finally agreed to this because she felt she was "smothering" him.)
2. If either went out with someone else, they were not obligated to tell who the other person was.
3. No queries were allowed as to how a date with another person "went," what happened, whether it was enjoyable or not, etc.
4. They were not to utter any binding or endearing phrases, such as "I love you," for 3 months.
5. They would cease discussing their personal relationship while at the office, since it was getting in the way of their work.
6. Jean would start actively looking for another job.

In essence, then, the original marriage (wolfbane) contract had helped to break the dysfunctional pattern of waxing and waning that had typified Jean and Bernie's relationship up to that point. It was a way of saying, "I want you, but under different conditions." It allowed her protection, giving her space, without rejecting Bernie out of hand. It pulled him in with a message of marriage, thus demanding a commitment, while deterring partial commitments such as simple sexual liaisons. It also helped Jean to avoid getting sucked into the cycle long enough to open up other options. It allowed the rules to change so that new rules (namely, their conjoint contract), more consonant with their developmental stage, could be adopted (Haley, 1973).

Sessions 11–13

I met with Jean three more times during the next 8 weeks. She noted that Bernie had tried to set up one or two weekends in advance for them to go away together. She thought she might take him up on one of these but was not sure she could, or wanted to, make them both. Later, when she told Bernie her decision about the weekends, she reported that he was much less pushy than he had been. She also mentioned that some friends wanted her to attend an Est program and asked my opinion. I did not want to be put in a position of advising her on this, or of giving her direction, because if it was a bust I would be blamed, and if successful, she could take the credit. Consequently, I stated that some people whom I knew and respected had found Est to be of value, but it may not be appropriate for everyone; there was no guarantee one way or the other, and she would have to make up her own mind.

Before the next-to-last session she attended an Est weekend and was quite enamored of it. Her relationship with Bernie had stabilized, and she was satisfied with it.

In the final (thirteenth) session our discussion was rather superficial. She felt no more need for therapy, being pleased with her life at the moment. She had no major complaints about Bernie, even concerning his occasional drinking—apparently this had ceased to be a problem. We terminated the treatment. It had extended over a period of 3 ½ months.

Follow-Up

Two months after termination I received a note from Jean. She said her life was going "great" and that she had never felt better. She thanked me for helping her not to need help.

Nine months following termination, I received an invitation to Jean and Bernie's wedding. It was set for exactly 1 year and 1 week from the date designating when they *should* be married that Jean had included in the revised contract she had written between the seventh and eighth sessions. (I figured the extra week was tacked on in deference to Bernie's pride.) They got married on schedule, and a few weeks later they contacted me about undertaking a status report on one of Bernie's daughters, as he was attempting to obtain custody of this 8-

year-old from his ex-wife. I referred them to a colleague who specialized in such evaluations. They also informed me that Jean had become president of her own business firm and that things were going very well in general. To the best of my knowledge they have not sought psychotherapeutic help in the subsequent 6 years.

Discussion

This case demonstrates the kind of "rejection–intrusion" (Napier, 1978) or "alternating distancing" (Karpel, 1976) between individuation and fusion that couples go through as each traverses his or her *interpersonal orbit* among significant others (Stanton, 1984). Jean and Bernie were caught in a pattern of repeatedly coming together and drawing apart, much as if they were involved in an all-encompassing barn dance or Virginia reel of closeness and distance, love and hate. The marriage contract helped to break this cyclic sequence by drawing them together— "compressing" them—and holding them there at a kind of set distance. It stopped the dance between the partners, even though the music from the larger system may have continued. It allowed them to waltz, fox-trot, and even try new steps. They were able to get beyond an impasse regarding their relationship and come to grips with the decision facing them and the commitment that this entailed.

One reason that I chose this case for inclusion in this book was to illustrate the options a therapist has for recovery—for redesigning therapeutic strategy—when he or she makes a mistake. The beauty of a systemic approach is that one's alternatives keep unfolding. My decision to continue the therapy by primarily seeing Jean alone stemmed from my overidentification with her, Bernie's ambivalence and slipperiness, and my failure to join him. It subsequently became clear to me that change was possible within such an arrangement. Essentially I had (*a*) taken a structural tack by joining her and attaching or hooking her to me as a means of unbalancing the system—a strategy that might have paid off even if Bernie had been present in the sessions; (*b*) worked strategically with them around the marriage contract; (*c*) helped Jean resolve her ambivalence about a steady relationship; and (*d*) toward the end of therapy, empowered them to continue as a couple without therapy. Sometimes, as in this case, one must go with the point or person with whom there is leverage, working with the system through one member as Bowen (1978), the Brief Therapy Group at the Mental Research Institute (Weakland *et al.*, 1974), Landau (1981), myself (Stanton, 1985), and others have done over the years.

One might wonder whether this couple were truly in need of more therapy. However, they had not asked for it, even at the point of subsequent contact nearly a year later. It should be remembered that throughout treatment I continually attempted to convey a message of competence—that they had the wherewithal and resources eventually to manage their own relationship. If, on the other hand, they had requested additional treatment, I very possibly would have wanted to include Bernie's mother and stepfather. From what I could determine, this woman was pulling many of the strings for her son, and some restructuring vis-à-vis their relationship would have been in order. Alternatively, and depending on the strength of the "resistance," a strategic approach to this issue might have been taken. This could have included the mother and might have involved, as my colleague, Thomas Todd (1979) subsequently suggested, the drawing up of a contract for Bernie *not* to get married—this contract to be signed both by him and by his mother. Thus, their subtle coalition, if it had remained a problem, would have been precipitated into the open and dealt with forthrightly, where it could be either confirmed or consciously repudiated. However, the extent to which the couple pulled their lives together and eschewed further therapy may indicate that they had found ways to deal satisfactorily with these issues on their own. If therapy is successful, clients often do not feel the need to return. They find ways to manage their lives without constructing the kind of artificial support system that is psychotherapy.

Acknowledgment

Appreciation is extended to Judith Landau, MD, for helpful comments on the manuscript of this chapter.

References

Bowen, M. (1978). *Family therapy in clinical practice*. New York: Jason Aronson.
Haley, J. (1973). *Uncommon therapy*. New York: Norton.

Karpel, M. (1976). Individuation: From fusion to dialogue. *Family Process*, *15*, 65–82.

Landau, J. (1981). Link therapy as a family therapy technique for transitional extended families. *Psychotherapeia*, *7*, 382–390.

Minuchin, S. (1974). *Families and family therapy*. Cambridge, MA: Harvard University Press.

Napier, A. Y. (1978). The rejection-intrusion pattern: A central family dynamic. *Journal of Marriage and Family Therapy*, *4*, 5–12.

Rohrbaugh, M., Tennen, H., Press, S., & White, L. (1981). Compliance, defiance and therapeutic paradox: Guidelines for strategic use of paradoxical interventions. *American Journal of Orthopsychiatry*, *51*, 454–467.

Stanton, M. D. (1981a). An integrated structural/strategic approach to family therapy. *Journal of Marital and Family Therapy*, *7*, 427–439.

Stanton, M. D. (1981b). Marital therapy from a structural/strategic viewpoint. In G. P. Sholevar (Ed.), *Handbook of marriage and marital therapy*. Jamaica, NY: S. P. Medical and Scientific Books.

Stanton, M. D. (1981c). Strategic approaches to family therapy. In A. S. Gurman & D. P. Kniskern (Eds.), *Handbook of family therapy*. New York: Brunner/Mazel.

Stanton, M. D. (1984). Fusion, compression, diversion and the workings of paradox: A theory of therapeutic/systemic change. *Family Process*, *23*, 135–167.

Stanton, M. D. (1985). Breaking away: Using strategic and Bowenian techniques in treating an alcoholic family through one member. In E. Kaufman (Ed.), *The power to change: Family case studies in the treatment of alcoholism*. New York: Gardner Press.

Todd, T. C. (1979, February). Personal communication.

Weakland, J., Fisch, R., Watzlawick, P., & Bodin, A. M. (1974). Brief therapy: Focused problem resolution. *Family Process*, *13*, 141–168.

Chapter 11
Building Marital Trust and Treating Sexual Problems

Gayla Margolin, PhD

Although sexual problems were the presenting complaint in the case that follows, the most important issues were jealousy and trust. The treatment to be described reflects an amalgamation of principles from cognitive–behavioral and systems perspectives. A brief description of the conceptual framework that guided this intervention is presented. The case illustrates that framework but is only one example of a model that can assume a number of specific formats.

Defining Characteristics of the Model

1. *Change is to occur at the relationship or interactional level.* For change to occur at the relationship level, the problem first must be understood as a relationship or systems problem. Problems are not defined as one person's jealousy or the other's withdrawal, but are conceptualized instead as a cycle in which the partner's actions elicit and also maintain the one person's jealousy or the other's withdrawal. The problem overall is maintained by repetitive interactional sequences that involve both partners and can be altered only through change on the part of both spouses.

2. *Dysfunctional interactional sequences can be disrupted in a variety of ways*, for example, by changing behaviors, cognitions, discriminative or reinforcing stimuli, or by changing a combination of these com-

271

ponents. In changing behavior, the goal typically is for the spouses to engage in behaviors that are antithetical to how they currently respond to the problematic situation. The spouse who generally retreats from relationship stress would be encouraged to acknowledge directly when he or she feels upset. The other spouse, who may complain about the withdrawal but still sabotage the spouse's attempts to be direct, would be taught to acknowledge rather than ignore or criticize the partner's efforts to avoid withdrawing.

Since cognitions often are as much a part of the problem as behaviors, they also serve as important targets in the solution. Reframing is a treatment commonly used to alter spouses' perceptions of specific problems. The mutual labeling of one spouse's interpersonal style as withdrawing may, for example, reflect healthy differences between the two partners in their need for distance. Similarly, using distance to reestablish relationship equilibrium or avoid a rapid escalation of anger can be interpreted as a sign of strength rather than weakness in the individual. Alternatively, spouses may simply have distorted images of one another based on misperceptions of the other's character. A distressed spouse may insist, for example, that his or her partner shows no signs of caring when, in fact, signs of caring are quite evident, even during the therapy session. In such cases, the therapist may need to identify and label behavioral examples that are contradictory to the spouse's preconceived image or may need to identify unrealistic expectations that contribute to the negative evaluations.

Another rather powerful intervention comes from altering the stimulus situation that sets the scene for repetitive sequences. For instance, with couples who become alienated as soon as they greet each other after their separate workdays, the focus must be on rearranging this all-important daily reunion. What is it that each partner anticipates finding on his or her return home, and what, in reality, awaits that spouse? Although spouses generally want this to be a time when they are relaxed and cared for, what they typically encounter is a myriad of demands surrounding dinner preparations, caring for children, and household problems. Behavioral and attitudinal changes are partial solutions to this problem, but there are environmental changes to consider as well: staggering the spouses' work schedules so that one arrives home an hour earlier; preparing large quantities of food ahead of time or relying more on carry-out dinners to minimize dinner preparations; or clearly designating one spouse's responsibility as taking care of the children while the other prepares dinner so that the overall level of chaos subsides.

3. *Because patterns are disrupted does not mean that the disturbed pattern will not reemerge.* The difficult task in marital therapy is not disrupting the pattern once but maintaining the desired change. In most instances, this cannot be left to chance. For example, therapy can focus on the establishment of rituals that serve as cues for the new, preferred behavioral sequences, for example, weekly "dates" to assess how the marriage is doing. Second, the development of new skills, particularly communication skills, often helps to circumvent the old patterns. Third, the acute awareness on the part of each spouse as to what she or he does to foster the dysfunctional pattern and what is likely to provoke the undesired response from him or her often helps to avoid repeated occurrences of this sequence. In general, the more spouses know about how their own problems escalate, the more capable they are in handling them. All it takes is for one spouse to refrain from engaging in his or her prescribed role, and the cycle cannot proceed. Finally, the therapist can predict that, at times, the couple will backslide and will reexperience their old patterns. The important ingredient is that they recognize the cycle and terminate it as soon as possible.

4. *Disrupting relationship patterns also may involve or lead to individual change.* Although the focus is on interactional events, this is not done to the exclusion of individual characteristics. As already stated, individual changes, for example, increased behavioral skills, altered expectations, may be part and parcel of changing the transactional patterns.

When individual targets for change are identified, it is helpful to consider how they fit within systems considerations. If individual changes occur bilaterally, for example, the emphasis on spouses' mutual responsibility for problems is maintained. Individual change also may occur as an outcome of the relationship change. A spouse may begin to view the partner or the relationship in a more positive and realistic fashion. Or a spouse may begin to feel better about himself or herself, for example, less depressed, less anxious, or more competent.

5. *Dysfunctional patterns in relationships occur at many different levels.* The assessment of dysfunctional patterns must include moment-to-moment patterns: the rapid escalation of anger, spouses' collusion in switching away from a conflictual topic, faulty assumptions on the basis of previous discussions, and so on. Assessment must also be directed to other patterns that occur less frequently and unfold less

rapidly but that still occur at relatively regular time intervals. Examples include the mutual alienation after work, disappointment every weekend about how recreational time is spent, or arguments every payday about how the money is doled out. Finally, there are patterns that occur at infrequent intervals, maybe one or twice a year or even less often, but that have high impact on the relationship. Issues of trust typically fall into this category. The repetitive cycles surrounding these high-impact, low-frequency issues tend to be self-maintaining. The first blow dealt to trust in the relationship, for example, discovering that the partner has had an affair or has gambled away the family's savings, often is followed by overly solicitous attempts to correct the situation: showing extra concern, being overly compliant with the jealous spouse's demands. This reaction often leads to an immediate improvement in the relationship, but the long-range response is increased resentment and further disappointment when the demands no longer are met. The low frequency of these events coupled with their tremendous emotional impact and the tendency for immediate self-corrective reactions present a particular challenge in therapy. This type of repetitive pattern is discussed in the case presentation.

Alice and Albert A.

This case example covers 62 therapy sessions that occurred over 3½ years. Therapy sessions took place approximately once a week or alternating weeks for the first 18 months. After that, therapy occurred on an "as needed" basis, with sessions scheduled at 1- to 2-month intervals.

Alice and Albert A. were referred to me after seeking therapy at a program that specializes in sex therapy. Their presenting complaint was that they had had no sexual contact for 4 years, and Albert reported problems maintaining an erection. However, because of the severity of their marital problems, the A.'s were referred for marital therapy before receiving sexual therapy. The A.'s had been married 28 years at the time of referral. They had raised one son, age 25, who lived with his wife and two sons in a town several hundred miles from the A.'s.

Alice A. was a slender, attractive, 52-year-old woman who dressed in a highly becoming, well-groomed fashion. She gave the impression of a soft-spoken yet gutsy woman. Certainly not overdemanding and rather conventional in her view of marriage, she knew her limits and would articulate them when encouraged. Five years ago, Alice had contracted multiple sclerosis, which had forced her to slow down her physical activity and give up favorite activities, such as dancing and tennis. She was mobile but walked hesitantly and with a limp. Physical and emotional stress exacerbated her condition. She discussed the disease only when asked and then conveyed a picture of a realist but a fighter. Alice had earned a college degree and had enjoyed a successful 30-year career as a nurse. She left nursing only 2 years ago when she felt that she no longer was physically strong enough to meet the demands of her job. She described herself as a moderately active Presbyterian who enjoyed church services but did not attend regularly.

Albert A., age 56, put forth a somewhat gruff front but underneath was a sensitive man concerned with his wife's welfare. In contrast to the restraint in activities forced on Alice, Albert was an extremely energetic and vital man whose life was becoming increasingly active. Albert had always been an entrepreneur who worked hard to maintain his small business. The business currently was expanding, however, and showed financial growth that almost was inconceivable to him. Albert's work schedule of 12- to 14-hour days, 6 days a week, showed no signs of easing. If anything, the pressures on him were expanding, and he had an increasingly active travel schedule. Despite his articulated desire eventually to slow down, Albert thrived on the challenge of his business. A highly competitive tennis game, which also was a source of pleasure for Albert, was about the only thing that removed business concerns from his thoughts, at least for the 1 hour of playing time.

Albert was raised in a small midwestern farming community. He had had two years of college. Orphaned as a young child, he prided himself on self-sufficiency and made it clear that he had no idea of "pouring out his inner self to anyone." He had agreed to attend the sex-therapy program only because that was being run at the same hospital where Alice had received help from a pain-control clinic. It was with considerable skepticism and caution that he followed the recommendation concerning a marital-therapy referral.

First Contact

The picture presented by Alice and Albert in the initial conjoint session was that of a devitalized relationship. Albert derived his excitement from work, and, in return, that was where his energy was divested.

While Alice occasionally helped out in Albert's business decisions and was available to him as a sounding board, her energy was directed primarily to running their home and caring for her ailing mother and an elderly aunt. They described their lives as "comfortable" but felt that something was "wrong" in that they did not have a sexual relationship. Although their activities as a couple were greatly limited by Alice's illness, they maintained a network of close mutual friends with whom they socialized frequently.

The history of Albert's affairs was briefly acknowledged and discussed during this initial session. Alice first learned of his affairs 10 years ago on a Christmas eve. She recalled feeling like her "world was falling apart." Despite her protests, Albert had been involved in a series of affairs over the intervening years with the most recent one ending 6 months before this meeting. When asked whether either of them currently was involved in an affair, both reported that they were not. Alice acted surprised that the question even would be addressed to her. She indicated, however, that she currently had doubts about Albert's fidelity.

The A.'s had had sex only once in the past 4 years. The one time was when they jointly perused a sex manual. Before their cessation of sexual intercourse, Albert had been having difficulties maintaining an erection. Albert estimated the difficulties as occurring less than 50% of the time, while Alice estimated it was over 90% of the time. What particularly upset Alice was her understanding that Albert's erectile problems were specific to their marriage and did not occur during Albert's affairs. It was surprising that no connection was made between the onset of Alice's illness and cessation of sex. Moreover, the topic was quickly diverted when I brought up this possibility.

Several features of their interaction, as observed in that first session, are noteworthy. First, it seemed as though the A.'s had an understanding between them that therapy really was Alice's domain; she had made the initial call, she was to do most of the talking, and she was to take charge of all continuing arrangements. Albert would go along in whatever fashion was required but would not take any initiative. These roles were representative of the way the A.'s handled most domestic, as opposed to business, endeavors. Second, this couple was remarkably nonconflictual. To the contrary, they were genuinely complimentary of one another and showed considerable respect and appreciation for one another's good qualities. There was tremendous poignancy in the paradox of their situation: Their disappointment in the marriage was ever so much more painful in view of their basic liking and esteem for each other.

My goal in this first session was to establish some equilibrium in the therapy relationship. It would have been easy to accept their modus operandi in this situation and focus primarily on Alice. It was obvious from the start, however, that I needed to involve Albert. Addressing questions specifically to him or asking him to respond first to a question meant for both of them was one strategy. The other was showing interest in his business and relying on my familiarity with small, self-owned business to establish a common ground.

Another goal in this first session was to begin to refocus attention from sex as an isolated component to the relationship more generally. After spending a brief time on the sexual history, the majority of our discussion explored the details of the A.'s lives together, for example, what it was like when they got together at the end of the day, how they spent their weekends. To focus further on their marriage in its entirety and to relieve some anxiety about what was "wrong" sexually, I summarized the session by attributing the sexual problems to the overall relationship malaise: How would it even be possible to generate sexual excitement in view of the overall lack of excitement in their lives? This formulation then become the rationale for conducting a wide-ranging assessment of the marriage.

Formal Assessment

In addition to continued interviewing, the formal assessment included a variety of self-report questionnaires concerning the marriage, an MMPI for each partner, and several sexual inventories requested from the referring sex-therapy program.

Their scores on the Marital Adjustment Test (MAT; Locke & Wallace, 1959), a general inventory of sexual satisfaction, were 49 and 92 respectively for Albert and Alice. Since scores lower than 100 generally are considered in the maritally distressed range, it is obvious that Albert experienced (or at least expressed) more dissatisfaction than Alice. On the general satisfaction rating, both spouses rated themselves as halfway between "very unhappy" and "happy." They also indicated that sex relations and philosophy of life were two important sources of disagreement. Albert additionally indicated that he "occasionally" wished he had not married and would marry a different person if he had his life to live over. Contrary to this picture of moderate to severe distress on the MAT, the A.s' scores on the Areas of Change Questionnaire (AC; Weiss & Birchler, 1975) seemed more satisfactory (total score = 8 when 14 or higher usually indicates distress). In other words, despite their dissatisfaction, the A's expressed relatively few complaints or desired changes. Albert wanted nothing more from Alice than increased sexual frequency. Alice also wanted sexual changes; in addition, she wanted Albert to drink somewhat less, to stop engaging in extramarital affairs, to spend more time with her, and to express his emotions clearly.

This picture of few complaints was further borne out by the Spouse Observation Checklist (SOC; Weiss & Perry, 1979), a 400-item listing of pleasing and displeasing events. The A.'s had relatively high mean levels of daily pleases (22.9 for Alice and 37.7 for Albert). Albert presented an unrealistic picture of zero displeases for the entire week. (Did he not care enough even to be troubled by Alice's behavior? Did he not take the time even to monitor the basis of his feelings?) Alice marked 1 or 2 displeases a day, with consistent dissatisfaction across the week for the item "Spouse did not share his feelings with me." She spontaneously wrote in the following comment on the SOC: "Albert doesn't share his feelings—especially when he has many business problems—or any other problem for that matter. He just doesn't want to share—and doesn't like being asked how things are going. So it's a challenge to show I care and am interested without displeasing him." While Alice's daily satisfaction rating ranged from 4 to 8 (1 = low; 9 = high), Albert's rating ranged only from 7 to 9.

Discussion of the SOC during the next therapy session centered on the question, "What makes a difference or seems to alter your satisfaction ratings?" Although satisfaction increased for Alice the more time they spent together, the opposite pattern held for Albert. His highest satisfaction occurred on days when they saw each other 1 or 2 hours a day. What emerged from this discussion was the limitations they experienced in the light of Alice's illness. They never really had discussed what would be desirable substitutes for the times they previously had spent playing tennis or taking nature hikes. Their unstated belief was that Alice simply could not partake in activities that Albert still enjoyed.

As an indication of individual functioning, the A.s' MMPI profiles showed no signs of individual psychopathology. Albert's profile, which revealed a relatively open and candid test-taking attitude, indicated a tendency toward excitability, overproductivity, and expansiveness. Alice's profile, in comparison, reflected somewhat less candor, greater concern with social desirability, and more emotional control. Her public role appeared to be one of cooperativeness and sociability. Her tendency toward somatic complaints followed logically from her chronic disability.

Finally, the assessment data from the referral agency indicated tremendous dissatisfaction on both spouses' parts regarding their sexual relationship. Albert claimed that he accepted Alice's advances reluctantly but would like to accept them more readily. He further reported having very little control over his ejaculations and thus anticipated intercourse with fear, anxiety, and resentment. His personal goals for sexual activities included a greater frequency of intercourse, more lengthy intercourse, and a quicker, more definitive arousal. Changes he would like for Alice included developing some way to stimulate his interest, loosening up, and "having her physical condition be such that I do not fear hurting her."

Alice concurred that the length of sexual foreplay and the length of intercourse were unsatisfactorily brief. In addition, her questionnaires indicated that their range of activities during foreplay was extremely limited, excluding, for example, having genitals caressed. Goals that Alice set for herself included (a) "knowing what I can do to improve the relationship as a whole including ways to cope with past behavior of mate and his apparent guilt feelings"; (b) "achieving behavior that will attract my mate sexually"; (c) "learning ways not only to initiate intercourse again, but ways to help us continue to grow in satisfaction in the years ahead"; and (d) "knowing ways to help mate want to be true to me." What she most wanted to change in Albert's behavior was his "need to find someone else to satisfy his sexual needs instead of me, his impotence with me—but not others—and his reluctance to get past a kiss, caress, or other show of affection." While Albert and Alice both tended to focus on Albert as the primary source of the problem, each of their concerns communicated helplessness, frustration, and lack of control over what was happening sexually.

Session 2

Therapy began along the lines of a behaviorally oriented treatment with an emphasis on increasing the positive exchange of this couple (Jacobson & Margolin, 1979). The goals were for these spouses to become aware of ways that they could please one another and to develop a repertoire of activities that they could mutually enjoy. The SOC, which previously was used as an assessment device, now was employed as a treatment procedure. During the first day following their second treatment session, each spouse was to read through the entire SOC and indicate, with a check mark, which pleasing items they would like for the other spouse to continue doing or increase in frequency. These check marks then would provide guidance to the other person about what indeed would be pleasing. Albert and Alice also were to examine and discuss SOC items during the week, identifying which companionship and affectionate items they both would enjoy. Mutually agreed-upon ideas in the companionship category included listening to music, reading or watching television together, working on decorating their home, playing board games, going for rides, going out for something to eat, going to movies or plays or concerts, and watching the sunset or sunrise. In the category of affection, separate from sex, both partners wanted to hold each other, warm each other in bed, hug and kiss, cuddle, and greet affectionately.

In addition to their work with the SOC to develop new ideas, it was suggested to the A.'s that they give free rein to their imaginations and generate some "zany ideas" of what they could do together. Albert initially chuckled at the suggestion of a "zany idea" but then suggested that he could leave for work a bit later on Wednesday morning so that he and Alice could go out to breakfast together. Alice quickly accepted the invitation, and I complimented Albert on his flexibility in this regard.

Session 3

The therapeutic focus initiated during Session 2 was abruptly interrupted by the following letter, which I received from Alice prior to the third session:

> I find it more difficult to work on the assignment this week. . . . This is due to the fact that I've again (or still) been holding in my feelings that Albert has had some contact with another woman. Timewise they have to be "quickies"—specifically, last week on a travel day, that his schedule appeared to be quite full. I did not dispute his answers to your question during our first meeting that he was not at present seeing anyone. I, of course, could be wrong this time, but it would be the first time I was

wrong! This has gone on and off for so many years that long ago I was able to note certain mannerisms and I guess intuition helps. . . . It's a moral issue for me—I can't accept, tolerate, or have understanding of adultery in our marriage. I'm eager to work, compromise, or whatever to help our relationship, except in that area. . . . I'm tired of living under a cloud of doubt and distrust.

On receiving this letter, I debated whether to telephone Alice before our next meeting, but decided against it for fear of developing an unbalanced alliance with her. Fortunately, she arrived for the next session a few minutes before Albert, and I took this opportunity to speak privately with her. I mentioned that I had received her letter and saw it as essential to discuss her doubts in Albert's presence. Alice concurred and agreed to voice these doubts during the session.

Once Albert arrived, the first order of business was to debrief how they had done with their assignments from the previous session. This topic, although less momentous than the "bomb" that Alice held, was addressed early on to emphasize the importance of homework assignments and guarantee that any positive happenings of the week would not be overlooked in the light of negative information. According to both their reports, the Wednesday breakfast had gone well. Albert found it relaxing, while Alice indicated that it had a positive effect on her mood all day. They agreed to repeat this activity one morning the following week.

Discussion then turned to the SOC, at which point Alice mentioned that she could not do certain of Albert's preferred items because she was aware of "his activities." Albert, asked to paraphrase what he had just heard from Alice, skirted the topic altogether and brought up his own complaint about the SOC—that he believed it was not founded in reality. Albert's point was acknowledged, but he was asked again to respond directly to Alice's comment. Despite the vagueness of her statement, Albert knew exactly what Alice was implying and responded by becoming resentful at her distrust, particularly when, in his view, there was "no basis" for the accusation. Nonetheless, Alice maintained that there was a basis and that there were "certain mannerisms" Albert displayed when he was being unfaithful.

Here was one of those common instances in marital therapy when there would be no getting to the truth of the issue. Albert was adamant in stating that currently he was not involved in an affair; Alice was equally convinced that Albert was having an affair. I pointed out that, in the short run, this issue would impede our work together. While indicating that he understood this, Albert still expressed his exasperation: "I don't think anything I could say would create this trust. I can say it, I can mean it, but there are certain things that get in the way." Alice claimed that fidelity was one area in which she could not compromise, while Albert argued that this was an unrealistic expectation for any marriage. Clearly, there was an important clash of principles here.

In discussing the 10-year history of jealousy and affairs, it turned out that Alice's distrust tended to rise and fall over time. When her distrust increased, she would start making accusations. Albert at first denied that he had been unfaithful. After several weeks of repeated accusations, however, Albert typically conceded that he had been un-faithful. This admission then would be followed by an intense but brief argument, which reduced the tension and smoothed out the relationship. On hearing this pattern, I half facetiously but half seriously suggested that they go home to blow up and that Albert confess to an affair, whether or not it had occurred. Albert vehemently negated this suggestion on the grounds that he did not want to admit to something he had not done. Moreover, he hinted that in such a situation he would be tempted to collect on the confession. In view of his persistence, I proposed the temporary solution that Albert commit himself to no affairs while in therapy, but cautioned against more long-range com-mitments that, in his own words, would be "unrealistic." This stopgap measure was agreed upon as a way to continue working in therapy.

Before ending this session, I returned to the goal of improving the relationship. For the upcoming week, the A's again were to use the SOC to identify items that they currently were not doing but that would please the partner. For this week Alice presented the "zany idea" of meeting in some faraway place for lunch; since both were frequently on the road, this was easily arranged.

Comment: After this session, I was feeling as stuck as the couple with their painfully discrepant values regarding marital fidelity. The stuck feeling was compounded by the fact that, despite their profound differences, separation was out of the question for this couple largely because of Alice's illness. Thus the leverage that typically stimulates movement in one direction or another (e.g., threats to the effect of, "I'm leaving the next time this happens") was absent here. I learned from this session that the A.'s were accustomed to getting back on an even keel after a crisis—how incredible that Alice possessed the motivation to conjure up and propose her luncheon rendezvous even when she was at wit's end regarding the fidelity issue. Despite the temporary closure we obtained on fidelity, I was left with a sense of uneasiness. This agreement was essentially no different from the one reached during our initial session, except that its importance was further highlighted. It certainly would not solve the problem but might buy some time to explore other issues.

Sessions 4–7

Over the next month and a half, there were two predominant themes to the sessions: increasing mutually enjoyable activities and communication skills training. For the focus on increasing positive activities, a modification of the Weiss *et al.* (1973) "love days" was used. During one "love evening," Albert would be in charge of planning something that would please Alice; the roles would be reversed on another evening. Reports the following week indicated that these evenings were "very pleasant." Alice prepared a special dinner, bought several small presents for Albert, and pulled out family pictures to mull over. Albert's plans included dinner at a favorite Italian restaurant and a drive along the beach, but because of fatigue, the drive never occurred.

The question we struggled with in that session was how to get beyond "pleasantness." This relationship truly "suffered" from being too comfortable and too secure. In efforts to disrupt this serenity, I assigned them the task of doing something surprising for one another, something that was out of the ordinary and humorous.

Predictably, Albert did not do his surprise because "there just didn't seem to be any time to think it up, or plan it, or come up with anything special." Alice, however, dressed up as a flapper for Halloween, carting her costume with her out of town to a motel where she and Albert made plans to meet during his travels. Albert, asked about his reaction, said, "I had a pretty heavy, tiring day. Something must have been on my mind when she was in the bathroom so long. My reaction was not as spontaneous as it should have been. She did surprise me. I was appreciative of what she had done and how she worked to carry it off." I then questioned Albert as to when he might carry out his agreed-upon plan, but Alice immediate defended him by pulling out a copy of Albert's work schedule for the week and indicating how pleased she was that he even had been able to get away for Sunday brunch. When I questioned Alice directly about her feelings in regard to Albert's not doing his surprise for her, she responded with the following mixed message: "I had a lot of understanding and empathy for him because I didn't know what I would have done. I thought there may be time for some little spontaneous thing. I understood why he didn't do it." While commending Alice for her understanding, I also suggested that there was room for expressing disappointment and for definitively stating her preference that he actually do the "some little something." Albert agreed to take the lead for the following week.

The concurrent therapeutic intervention was communication skills training so that the A.'s could communicate more directly and openly about what was troubling them. Initially, they were given a copy of the problem-solving manual from Jacobson and Margolin (1979), which they decided to outline together. As it turned out, basic listening skills, such as paraphrasing one another's statements, were really a problem for this couple. To practice listening skills in the therapy session, the A.'s took turns expressing their ideas on a topic, after which the other paraphrased those ideas. Albert tended to capsulize information into one predominant outcome while losing many of the details along the way. His listening skills improved, however, with an emphasis on strictly "feeding back" information and feelings.

Following this practice in the therapy session, the couple agreed to discuss and audiotape one problematic topic at home during which time they were simply to paraphrase, but not respond to, each other's position. On a strictly content basis, the A's did relatively well. Their next assignment, to be completed before the eighth session, was to brainstorm solutions to the problem.

At the end of the seventh session, Albert queried, "Where are we going with all this? What is going to happen?" Essentially he was interested in knowing how the therapeutic efforts thus far related to his primary goal of an improved sexual relationship. When asked what he saw happening, his reply was, "Not much." While Albert joked about being too goal oriented, he made it clear that he was not seeing enough progress in terms of his personal yardstick of success. Taking the opposite viewpoint, Alice indicated that she was feeling very good about what was occurring. She speculated that "maybe it is because I'm trying to work and really make these things part of my life, I feel progress. I feel I'm capturing some of the things I might have been aware of, but now I'm making them part of my life." I reflected on the fact that it appeared Alice had put more time into the therapy. Furthermore, thus far therapy was directed toward her goals more than toward Albert's. Since we were out of time, I indicated that I very much appreciated their feedback, wanted to think this through before we met again, and would like to address the issue again in our next session.

Comment: Albert's concern about therapeutic progress was not particularly surprising. Despite my rationale of an improved overall relationship and my repeated efforts to describe this rationale to the A's, I still had lost sight of exactly how singleminded Albert's goal actually was. My evaluation of therapeutic progress was somewhat less extreme than either of theirs. I felt that they were becoming more attentive to one another's needs. This was aided in part by the fact that they were less restricted about expressing their own needs. On the other hand, it was obvious that their affective experience in the relationship remained unchanged. Each intervention led to an "O.K." reaction rather than an unmitigated strong reaction, be it joy, relief, apprehension, anger, or disappointment.

Although I was not really concerned that Albert would stop coming for therapy, I did see the risk in his viewing it as his obligation to Alice instead of something from which he himself would benefit. Enough groundwork had been done that we could begin to work on the sexual goals. Since it still was important not to lose sight of the more general relationship goals, we could continue the communication training around issues of sex.

Sessions 8–11

The primary focus during the next four sessions was establishing greater physical intimacy between the A.'s. The first order of business, however, was looking into the problem-solving task they had done at home as an extension of their communication training. This task went very well in that they had actually resolved the problematic issue of how to arrange their office. Albert, in particular, was pleased by the *tangible outcome* that had occurred.

The rest of the eighth session was devoted to obtaining a detailed history of their sexual relationship and instructing them in the sensate focus "pleasuring" exercises of Masters and Johnson (1970), with the stipulation that, for the upcoming week, they avoid pleasuring genital areas. The more general ground rule for this stage of the sexual assignments was that they restrain from sexual intercourse. Having not had sex for years, the A.'s found this assignment humorous. Their mutual relief, however, was unmistakable.

Over the next three sessions, the intensity of the pleasuring sessions was increased, with the gradual introduction of the genitals. They also were to engage in individual pleasuring exercises (LoPiccolo & Lobitz, 1972), since neither was very aware of their own arousal reactions. Since Albert had no difficulty achieving an erection through masturbation, he was instructed in the squeeze technique (Masters & Johnson, 1970) so that he could begin to have control over his own erections. The message throughout these assignments was that each spouse was responsible for his or her own arousal.

Over time, the mutual pleasuring sessions showed improvement. Albert was able to obtain erections in response to Alice's manual stimulation of his genitals. Caressing of other body parts did not arouse him. Alice also was becoming highly aroused but tended to "hold back." She was learning a great deal about her own responsiveness, however, from her individual pleasuring sessions. Albert, for the most part, did not follow through on the individual pleasuring sessions.

Comment: The sexual enhancement exercises were progressing relatively well, although we still had not approached the major hurdle— Albert's maintaining an erection upon intromission. The overall affect during these sessions was more intense. Anticipating the assignments and actually doing the assignments evoked a combination of positive anticipation and anxiety. Therapy was moving at a relatively rapid pace with increasing demands for greater intimacy. These demands may have helped provoke the crisis that emerged before session 12.

Sessions 12–15

Mid-afternoon prior to our twelfth session, Alice called to inform me that Albert had not been faithful. She agreed to discuss this in our session that evening. The problems, as it turned out, had been multifold that past week, including a very tight financial situation, a particularly heavy work schedule for Albert, plus the question of mistrust. Alice and Albert had not communicated about any of these issues until they reached crisis proportions, thereby exacerbating the tensions overall. Albert's intentions in remaining silent, particularly on the financial question, had been to protect Alice. Her reaction, predictably, was to feel shut out and ignored.

Alice timidly brought up the issue of trust, 'For the first time since we started in therapy, I need to be reminded about not doubting any of Albert's activities. I've tried to block these thoughts out, but. . . .' Albert indicated that he had sensed Alice's lack of trust and was irritated by it but had not addressed this issue directly. In hearing each of their perspectives, I expressed my confusion about where to go with this issue. "There's nowhere to go" was Alice's hopeless reply, while Albert echoed the frustration with dry humor: "I thought of putting Alice in my shirt pocket so that she knows exactly what I do."

Interestingly, the A.'s spontaneously suggested that they wanted to apply the problem-solving model we had discussed to this issue. Without any closure on this issue, Albert unexpectedly switched topics and suggested an additional problem that concerned him and that he wanted to brainstorm. "How am I going to cover two spots simultaneously, to be home and be aware of emergency situations that might come up as well as cover other work bases?" Asked to clarify "emergency situations," Albert discussed his concern about Alice's falls, which sometimes occur when he is not home. Since the session was ending, it was agreed that the A.'s would have two separate problem-solving discussions, one on Albert's concern about Alice's falls and one on Alice's problem of "not feeling secure in the relationship."

Problem solving on the topic of Alice's physical safety went extremely well and led to a variety of agreed-upon solutions: regular times for Albert to call-in, leaving a key with the neighbor, and calling the neighbor if Albert cannot reach Alice at the prespecified time. Not surprisingly, problem solving on the trust issue was much more difficult. While the A.'s came up with 15 potential solutions, these ideas tended to be too vague, to avoid the central issue, or simply to reiterate what they currently found problematic (e.g., make sure there are times for sharing with each other, start to build trust on a positive basis, encourage social situations which involve the two of us, don't make verbal put-downs that put the other party in an unfavorable light). Extensive discussion of these 15 ideas led to two conclusions: First, it became obvious that a problem-solving format, with solutions generated by the couple, was not going to work for this particular problem. The couple correctly identified fragments of the problem but did not have a perspective on the overall pattern. Second, the withholding of information, which currently represented this couple's attempted solution to the problem, actually was responsible for perpetuating the problem. According to Alice, the worst time was when Albert attempted to protect her by denying the affairs. Similarly, Albert's irritation was fed more by Alice's hints than by her actual confrontations.

Considering all this information, it was clear that I needed to devise a plan that disrupted the entire jealousy cycle. My mistake thus far, in attempting to stop Albert's affairs temporarily, was pursuing too narrow a focus. That objective obviously was unacceptable to Albert and had the unfortunate consequence of relieving Alice of her responsibility in the overall pattern. My new plan for breaking out of this devastating cycle involved reframing, cognitive restructuring, and behavioral sequencing.

Session 14 began with an announcement that the time had come to deal wholeheartedly with the core issue of jealousy and trust. First, trust rather than Albert's fidelity was identified as the issue of paramount importance. Alice's lack of trust in Albert was what caused her the most unhappiness and caused him the most frustration. Thus the reformulated goal was that affairs would be handled in such a way that trust was not dissolved. Second, to work on the issue of trust, each spouse was instructed to examine one basic assumption.

THERAPIST: Each of you has to put aside one basic assumption. This is not going to be easy, but you absolutely have to do this. Alice, in the interest of building trust, you have to put aside the assumption that your relationship will always be monogamous. This is not denying that monogamy is a value for you or an ideal, but you have to put it aside as the most important thing. Albert, you have to put aside the idea that, in order to protect Alice, you have to withhold information. The only way to get Alice's trust is not to withhold information.

Third, the behavioral sequencing took the following form:

THERAPIST: You need to build in a step to reassess trust in your relationship very frequently, at least once a week, maybe even on a more frequent basis. . . . Alice made the comment earlier about putting aside the past, and that's what needs to be worked on. Both of you have been hurt by this, a lot; I don't even know if one has been hurt more than the other. . . . In order to put aside the past and build up trust in the present, you need to regularly deal with the issue of trust. . . . Each week you have to put aside a certain time that the two of you sit down and have a brief discussion about whether or not you feel trust. It seems one-sided because, Albert, you've never expressed concern about Alice's faithfulness—

ALBERT: I never let her know.

ALICE: He's said that to me too—as long as he doesn't know, it's all right.

THERAPIST: O.K., well, if we are going to build trust in both directions we've got to do it right. What that means is each of you says to the other, "I've been faithful this week," or, "I haven't." The other person responds, "I know you've been faithful," or, "I know you haven't." Each of you makes two types of statements. If one says, "I haven't been faithful," and the other says, "I know you haven't," all that takes place is what would occur anyway, but it would happen weeks in the future after many accusations, recriminations, and hurt feelings. The most destructive situation is for one to say, "I've been faithful," and for the other to think, "No, you haven't," but not to say that. It is just as hard to say, "I don't think you've been faithful," as to say, "I haven't been faithful." Either one is a shattering statement. But the only way to devolop trust is to be very straightforward on both sides. Can you see yourself doing this?

ALBERT: I don't know. . . .

THERAPIST: What does it depend on?

ALBERT: Just doing it—set the time, set the circumstance, just doing it.

THERAPIST: Let's just see what it would be like. For the sake of practice, let's take the worst situation. Albert, you say, "I haven't been faithful," and Alice, you reply, "I know."

ALBERT: I haven't been faithful this week. I had sexual relationships with another woman.

ALICE: I know you haven't been faithful.

ALBERT: Do you want a cup of coffee?

(*They all laugh.*)

THERAPIST: That was very hard to say. Where would the discussion need to go now?

ALICE: I don't know it has to go further.

ALBERT: I'm sure it would go further—that's my belief.

ALICE: All I'm thinking about right now—and I hate to bring up the past— but once that initial acknowledgment is out, all the rest is easier.

THERAPIST: That's so essential—what you're saying. If the acknowledgment is the point that finally eases the tension, then the best thing is to get to that point as soon as possible. . . . In addition to the hurt of finding out, there's also the hurt that comes from covering things up. In addition to the hurt that comes from the unfaithfulness, there's the hurt from ac- cusations and dragging things out. The other problem that exists right now is that no one gets any credit for being faithful. Probably weeks go by when affairs are not an issue but the trust is not reaffirmed. Each week that you can say, "I've been faithful," and, "I know you've been faithful," there is a reaffirmation of trust.

It additionally was recommended that in cases of disagreement, when Alice says Albert has not been faithful and he claims that he has, Albert is to ask for the cues on which Alice drew her conclusion. This step was to relieve the mystery of Alice's intuition and make Albert more aware of ways that he communicates or fails to communicate to Alice.

When asked if they were willing to try this strategy, Albert asked, "What alternate courses are there?" In evaluating the alternatives, they once again discounted divorce as an option. "In our age bracket, financial situation, physical conditions, and so on, splitting up would be harmful to both of us." What Albert saw as the other extreme, that is, promising never again to have an affair, was equally disastrous in that both would suffer if the promise were broken. The third option, that of continuing in the current pattern, simply was untenable.

Although the A.'s were to take a week to decide whether to adopt this plan, they put it into effect immediately. During the first trial, Albert began with the least threatening alternative by asking Alice whether or not she had been faithful; the answer obviously was yes. Alice expressed doubts about Albert's faithfulness, but he claimed that he had been faithful. They then discussed Alice's "mysterious" cues, which it turned out were rather indirect signs: Alice claimed that Albert's sleeping patterns changed, that he drank more, and that he was not sexually attentive to her.

In debriefing this interaction in the session, Albert indicated that the "confrontation" was useful because it brought out the issue. I concurred but relabeled the process as "confirmation" or "disconfirmation." Albert also suggested that this procedure might stop him from having affairs. I indicated that this was unlikely, given his past, and emphasized that was not the intention of the procedure. With that out of the way, a decision was made for the A.'s to return to pleasuring sessions and to schedule a dinner date for the upcoming Friday evening.

Comment: Finally, in Session 14, we dealt with the couple's core issue. The message given was both encouraging (i.e., I felt something could be done) and cautious (i.e., it would take a major upheaval of their basic assumptions and patterns). As it turned out, the A's were ready, if not eager, to approach this particular issue with the intensity it demanded. Soon after our discussion of these procedures began,

Alice relived for Albert and me the trauma of "stumbling across" evidence on a telephone bill of one of his early affairs. The vividness in her account of this event had a visible effect on Albert. Shortly thereafter, in describing his hopelessness about this problem, Albert described himself as reacting "down deep." The high affective level that accompanied this session reinforced the strength of the intervention.

The intervention itself had several purposes. First, it was designed to make both spouses, not just Albert, responsible for trust. Second, having the meeting at regular and frequent intervals would speed up the cycle that was occurring anyway and relieve the tensions that built up whenever Alice had suspicions. Third, if trust was not there, the couple had a structured format for handling the situation. Fourth, since each meeting applied only to the previous week, there would be many instances in which Alice would affirm Albert's faithfulness, thereby building a basis of trust. Finally, although not articulated to the couple, this plan also was likely to cut short the affairs, since Albert ended them anyway as soon as they were discovered by Alice.

As Tiesmann (1979) suggests, the plan was presented as something very different, novel, and risky to capture the attention and interest of the couple. As the therapist, I was quite directive—there was no negotiation about how this task was to be implemented. The only decision left to the couple was whether or not to adopt the plan.

With little direction on my part after that one session, the A.'s weekly discussion, which they referred to as "Monday night meetings," continued uninterrupted. By the second week, Alice confirmed Albert's faithfulness but phrased it quite negatively: "He didn't show his usual signs plus he was more attentive." Much to Albert's satisfaction, Alice was encouraged to state this in a more positive way. The next several Monday meetings were reported as "uneventful." Approximately a month later, Albert reported that "there is a positive feeling after I know the week is behind, particularly if there have been any issues hanging loose. Right now, we are limited to the one issue of faithfulness, but perhaps we'll deal with other issues as well. I have a feeling that she's going to clear her mind, and I'm going to clear mine." Alice concurred and added, "The checking is good. It brings us together to face a problem that's been with us for a long time. We have a responsibility to each other." I shared their enthusiasm but cautioned that the meetings might not always go as smoothly in the future as they had these past several weeks.

Sessions 16–30

The next 14 sessions spanned approximately 11 months, primarily because of Albert's travel schedule. The main focus was on improving the A.s' sexual relationship. Their Monday night meetings continued religiously throughout that time and even occurred by telephone when Albert was out of town. As a result of the continued hectic nature of their hours, particularly with Albert on the road several days during the week, there periodically was a need to enhance the nonsexual aspects of the marriage. This was accomplished through "dates" and occasional out-of-town weekends. One of the biggest breakthroughs occurred when Albert taught Alice some card games, which revived the sense of gamesmanship and competition that they sorely missed. In general, there was an increasing closeness between these spouses, which they freely acknowledged to each other. Albert included Alice in more business decisions and began to invite her on short business excursions rather than assume she could not handle these activities physically.

Sex therapy was resumed at the point it had been interrupted the month previously. The goals were mutual pleasuring with a focus on the genitals plus an emphasis on individual exploration of their own bodies. Albert had the additional task of learning that all was not hopeless if he lost his erection. Through the squeeze technique, he was to practice getting an erection, losing it, getting another erection, losing it, and so on. The ban on intercourse remained in effect.

The major stumbling block in sex thereapy was Albert's anxiety over losing his erection, his depression when he did lose it, and his difficulty in freeing his mind from the hassles of his workday to focus his attention on a sexual experience. Although Alice was experiencing orgasms in the pleasuring sessions, she was frustrated that she was not better able to arouse Albert.

Cognitive restructuring, stimulus alteration, and paradoxical instruction proved to be the important components in reducing Albert's erectile problems. First, in Session 22, I presented a strong message that the mind was the most erotic organ. The thoughtful, planful approach this couple took toward life in general, while contributing to success in many aspects of life, actually interfered with sex. I said, "What we have to focus on is turning off what you are so good at doing—the planning, thinking through, evaluating—all of that has to be left behind when the two of you are together sexually. You have to use your mind in a different way. . . . I want to challenge you to become the most sensual people you can become." Several strategies were followed to help them develop their sexual imaginations. They explored erotic readings, first reading alone and then reading aloud to one another and discussing the readings at the beginning of pleasuring sessions. Although the readings per se did not prove to be particularly arousing, they served as a stimulus that disrupted the A.s' normal thought processes and took their minds off the performance side of sex. As Albert summarized, the reading "has provided a conversation piece, it all becomes part of the whole process. . . . it starts the mental process, sets the mood." Along the same lines, the A.'s went to their first pornographic film together, after which they had a wonderful pleasuring session.

The second major intervention concerned stimulus variables surrounding sex. Careful observation over a number of weeks revealed that sex was more enjoyable when there was time for a clean break from work. One pleasuring session scheduled at 4:30 a.m. before Albert dashed off to work was a complete fiasco. Friday nights, when Albert's thoughts still were engrossed in work, usually were not good times for sex either. Saturday mornings, in contrast, tended to be much more satisfying, particularly if there were no early morning telephone calls. The strategy that the A.'s adopted was to define Friday evenings as "warmups" for Saturday morning. More generally, they came to realize that something had to intervene between work and sex, whether it was a good night's sleep, a tennis game, getting out of town, or a good movie.

With the cognitive and situational interventions, Albert was attaining and maintaining erections more regularly through mutual manual and oral stimulation. His erections were stronger and sometimes he even came to orgasm. More important, Albert finally was beginning to say that "losing an erection is not the end of the world; I wasn't accepting that before. . . . Failure is failure and another failure adds up, and after a while, why try? I think that idea has been reversed somewhat."

Although their sexual contact was enjoyable, the A.'s, understandably, still want to move ahead to intercourse. The series of assignments proceeding toward this goal always were designed so that the sexual contact was terminated at the point that the A.'s still wanted to go one step further. Since Albert's history was that he tended to lose his erection soon after intromission, the demands for intromission and for thrusting after intromission were minimized. The steps were assigned over a course of approximately 3 months with each step lasting until the couple convinced me that they barely could restrain themselves from going further, or they "accidentally" went further than my assignment. Each step followed a full-body pleasuring exercise. First, Albert was to move his penis all around Alice's body and, alternatively, Alice was to move her vagina around Albert's body. Second, Albert was to rest his penis at the entry to Alice's vagina and to keep it there regardless of whether he had an erection. Alice, likewise, was to have her genitals rest on Albert's penis. The next step was partial intromission, that is, Albert was to stop before full intromission and there was to be absolutely no thrusting. They were to engage in partial intromission regardless of whether Albert had an erection. This step was continued for several weeks until much of the anxiety about intromission was reduced. When they finally requested it, thrusting was introduced, but still there was to be no ejaculation. Eventually Albert sheepishly reported that he had ejaculated intravaginally; I then permitted them to go on to this step, but only if they felt it was inevitable. Otherwise, Albert still was to pull back prior to ejaculation. As is obvious with this assignment, I simply recommended that they continue what they already were doing. The A.'s finally reached their goal of sexual intercourse around our thirtieth meeting, which occurred 10 months after beginning therapy.

Comment: It was a major accomplishment for this couple to discover that, after 4 years, they still were capable of having sexual intercourse. The most important change was overcoming their feelings of hopelessness and despair so that they were willing to experience each other sexually. Their involvement in therapy and with each other was very intense during this period. They mutually responded to the challenge of therapy, opening themselves up to substantial risk. It should be noted that while some of these same steps were attempted during the earlier therapy sessions, they did not take hold prior to the jealousy intervention.

Their progress still was very fragile. For every satisfying sexual experience, there still occurred a disappointing one. The most important change, however, was that they would persist and allow themselves another opportunity.

Sessions 31–39

After attaining their sexual goals, there was somewhat of a setback in therapy, with the surfacing of several new problems and the reemerging of the trust problem. Because of Albert's summer schedule, there was a 1-month hiatus from therapy prior to our thirty-first meeting. Alice was discouraged by their lack of time together and was acting suspiciously. When our session finally occurred, Albert expressed anger at Alice for emitting cues of suspiciousness and yet not stating her concerns directly in their Monday meetings. Alice claimed that she was unaware she was giving off cues, although she was feeling less trusting. In the session we examined how this had been blown out of proportion by their not fully confronting the issue in their Monday night meetings. With this airing of feelings, problems with trust again receded.

During this time, Albert also went into a personal slump lasting several weeks; it was unrelated to the relationship but took its toll on the marriage, particularly on sex. Alice was concerned about Albert's drinking and the fact that he had given up tennis. In Albert's words, at the beginning of Session 33, "I think we are back to square one." Albert agreed to cut back on the drinking, but this was only a Band-Aid effort. What was needed at this stage was a return to earlier stages of therapy, for example, pleasuring without intercourse and nonsexual dates. Albert also was taking a careful look at his life in general and wondering when there was time to relax. Together they concluded that they needed at least a day a week to unwind in order to have positive sexual experiences. They also started to plan "warmup" sessions followed by a more intense sexual experience on the following day.

Albert's mood lifted over the next couple of weeks, but his desire to reevaluate his life and set long-range goals persisted. His business was changing dramatically, and he faced the potential of selling it for a very large profit. Both spouses, but Albert in particular, seemed rather confused about where they were heading. Since we were not going to be able to meet in therapy for the next month, I recommended that the A's expand their Monday night meetings to include a discussion of long-range goals. This seemed like an important step toward phasing out of therapy as well. The following summarizes the goals they presented when we next met.

For Albert: (*a*) Keep time schedule flexible to permit me to be close to Alice; (*b*) arrange more leisure time; (*c*) fulfill some financial planning; (*d*) finalize some realistic and viable plans for withdrawing from the daily work schedule; and (*e*) yearly fishing trip and learn to ski.

For Alice: (*a*) Be as mobile as I can be and maintain good physical health; (*b*) make home even more physically comfortable; and (*c*) do at least one outside-the-home activity on a regular basis.

For both of them: (*a*) Continue Monday night meetings; (*b*) feel even freer to experiment and talk about sex; (*c*) continue close and good relationship with son and his family; and (*d*) have balanced friendships and regular social contact with long-time friends.

Therapy continued with semiweekly meetings over the next 2 months to discuss these goals and continue to assess how sex was going. They both concluded that things went well as long as they had time together. In the thirty-ninth session we all came to the conclusion that the relationship basically had stabilized. Despite the sexual ups and downs, they were feeling closer. In Albert's words, "We are very close all the time now." They were learning how to optimize their sexual relationship by spreading out contact over two consecutive days. In view of this consolidation of progress and the fact that the sessions were becoming more "chatty," it seemed like a good time to reassess the marriage and possibly phase out therapy.

A readministration of some of the original assessment measures revealed considerably more overall satisfaction than 14 months previously when therapy began. Albert's MAS score had doubled to 98, while Alice's was now at 135. Both spouses' mean daily rates of pleases on the SOC were quite high, 54.7 and 63.0, respectively, for Alice and Albert. Both reported no displeases at posttreatment. Although the AC score of 11 at posttest showed a slight deterioration, it still was well within the range of nondistressed couples.

Comment: This stage of therapy provided a realistic portrayal of what the A's might experience in the future. There were certainly going to be periods of frustration and irritation, but it was heartening to see that they could rebound in relatively short order. Even through the most difficult phases, they continued their Monday night discussions. Thus at least one channel of communication remained open, even though they periodically retreated from each other sexually. There were signs that they could creatively solve some problems on their own; it was their idea, for example, to turn unsuccessful sexual experiences on one day into "warmup" sessions for the next day. While the A.'s readily recognized their progress, they still were reluctant to discontinue therapy sessions. Perhaps being overly protective, I too worried about their potential for relapse. Thus, a three-way decision was made to continue meeting on a periodic basis.

Sessions 40–62

All told, there have been 23 more therapy sessions with the A.'s spanning a 2½-year time frame. The meetings typically occurred at 1- or 2-month intervals, although at times we scheduled several meetings in succession and then followed with a 4- or 5-month lapse. For the most part, these sessions reviewed what was covered during the previous sessions. A repeated focus, for example, has been their frequency of sexual contact. Despite their desire for an active sexual relationship, they allowed other priorities, namely work and family commitments, to interfere. Periodic erectile problems for Albert also were associated with a reduced frequency of sexual contact. Returning to sexual pleasuring without intercourse usually helped the A.'s surmount these trouble spots. At one point, Albert's erectile problems became more persistent because he was taking a new medicine for high blood pressure. Despite the potential for external attributions, Albert's conclusions in our final session about his periodic erectile difficulties were as follows: "I think it's a matter of detaching myself. If I can detach myself from some of the responsibilities I have, that seems to help a lot."

Jealousy issues surfaced once during this time. Alice had trouble announcing her concerns in the Monday night meeting; instead, she wrote about them in a note to Albert. (Finally, she was writing to Albert instead of to me!) Since the tension between them quickly was aired and dealt with, the note served the same purpose as bringing up the issue in a discussion. Several months later, during one of our therapy sessions, Albert spontaneously announced, "I don't feel doubted anymore."

In addition to the recurrent problems there were several developments external to the marriage that the A.'s wanted to discuss in therapy. A repeated theme surrounded changes in Albert's business. After a lifetime of struggling, his business continued to expand beyond all expectations. The magnitude of the financial decisions that confronted them was, at first, overwhelming. Although several successive therapy sessions were used to lay out the issues, the A.'s own resources for rational decision making proved sufficient.

A second and more devastating crisis occurred when their only son announced that he and his wife were separating. The A.'s immediate response was to try to help out in any way possible. This resulted in a tremendous work load for each of them. Since the son recently had joined Albert's business, any hours he was absent from work fell on Albert. Alice, meanwhile, was saddled with an inordinate amount of babysitting for their two young grandchildren. This experience proved to be extremely draining, both physically and emotionally. Therapy served the purpose of allowing them to see that they could set limits on their time and commitments. They also wanted feedback on their perceptions of how the grandchildren were adjusting and requested therapy referrals for one grandchild.

The third crisis revolved around the same theme of overextension. Alice's mother, who was in a nursing home, suddenly became quite ill. Previously, Alice's pattern had been to make the 180-mile journey to visit her mother once a week. During this illness, she was visiting four or five times a week. Although Albert was tremendously worried about Alice's health, he did not express this concern overtly to Alice or apply his otherwise good problem-solving skills to help Alice consider alternatives. The focus in therapy during this time was to encourage the A.'s to speak directly about Alice's illness. Albert needed reassurance that he could express concern without appearing oversolicitous. Alice required a forum to evaluate her own physical needs against the importance she placed on spending time with her mother.

The A.'s repeated concern during each of these difficult situations was that they had little time for one another. They reported feeling emotionally close to each other but were unhappy when outside circumstances interfered with their opportunities for time together. Thus, a consistent part of our work during this phase of therapy was devising creative solutions to the perpetual problem of finding time to be together.

During our final (or at least most recent) meeting, the A.'s indicated that they probably had reached the goals they initially set out for themselves. When asked to review what those goals were and what had changed, Albert summarized: "I remember the lack of confidence Alice had in me. My faithfulness was the big item, I think, at the time. It was an obstacle in the way of any kind of intimacy. We were going along, each of us pursuing our own paths. I think my work activities at the time also were a problem. My activities were such that they kept us apart. We've changed that pattern considerably. At that time, of course, we were in a rocky spot, and I don't think that exists now." Alice added: "Our Monday nights are an example. We have serious decisions to make, and we have a way of attacking them. For example, on the way home on Saturday (from a weekend trip) we found a shady spot, had a bite to eat, and just sat for an hour, and we wrote, brainstormed, so to speak, got something down on paper. We never would have thought of that."

Comment: The greatest change I observed in the A.'s over the last 2½ years, compared to the previous 14 months, was their commitment to the marriage and their genuine desire to protect and extend their emotional closeness. Rather than battle each other, they now were battling external circumstances. With this mutual support and and cooperation, this couple no longer presented the struggles and challenges characteristic of marital therapy. Instead, our work together had become a supportive therapy for coping with changing life circumstances.

Was there a reason to continue seeing the A.'s periodically over this 2½-year period, or was I fostering an unnecessary dependency? This is a question I have struggled with, particularly since this length of therapy is not typical of my clinical practice. Had the A.'s not already been in therapy, none of the "crisis" situations of the past 2½ years would have brought them to a therapist. Moreover, I imagine that eventually they would have coped successfully with each incident on their own accord. Although I frequently questioned whether we should continue our work together, the A.'s always opted for some further contact, be it a follow-up telephone call or a regularly scheduled session.

Why have the A.'s continued to request therapy sessions? My impression is that the infrequent therapy sessions buttressed the weekly Monday night meetings as a reaffirmation of their marriage. Since their marriage continued to compete with other priorities in their lives, they benefited from periodic nudges to get back on track. Furthermore, it is likely that the act of coming to therapy serves as a mutually symbolic communication that, through their willingness to work on the relationship, the relationship continues as a high priority.

Summary

This presentation of marital therapy involved two emotionally healthy individuals who, in their own ways, wanted their marriage to work. The increasing tension and discontent over the previous 10 years could be traced to two main precipitants. First, the A.'s held vastly different values about sexual fidelity. Albert felt that affairs were inevitable; if kept private, they would not hurt the spouse and not be disruptive to the marriage. For Alice, on the other hand, affairs were totally contradictory to her basic moral fiber; moreover, they signaled Albert's rejection of her. Second, the A.'s tended to react to problems by withdrawing from one another and holding back their feelings. This problem really took its toll with the onset of Alice's illness, which was surrounded in a shroud of silence.

The sexual dysfunction, which the A.'s presented as their major complaint, can be construed as a sympton of the values clash and the communication difficulties. While certainly a problem deserving attention in its own right, the sexual dysfunction was exacerbated by the mistrust and resentment surrounding the affairs. Similarly, their communication problems, particular their hesitancy to make direct requests and give feedback, stymied the potential for any spontaneous solutions to the sexual problems.

The interventions for these three focal problems—trust, withdrawal, and sexual difficulties—built on each other. Increased trust was necessary before the A.'s could allow themselves to show their vulnerability, as well as provide each other with support and encouragement, regarding sex and also regarding Alice's illness. Once trust, rather than Albert's affairs, was defined as the problem, the Monday night meetings proved to be the key component in the trust intervention and, in fact, the turning point for the entire therapy. First and foremost, these meetings provided a new context for interactions surrounding jealousy. Over time, the meetings became a uniquely personal tradition for renewing contact on a weekly basis and solving whatever problems may have arisen, from redecorating their home to scheduling pleasuring sessions. As such, the Monday night tradition inadvertently offset the A.'s tendency to withdraw.

One of the overriding messages to the A.'s was that they could not afford to take their relationship for granted. It needed to be nurtured and savored. For a "workaholic" couple like the A.'s, this could have been a risky message. The "nurture" part, which they translated into "working at the relationship," was one they could readily accept. One time their hard work even included setting the alarm clock at 4:30 a.m. so that they could complete their relationship assignment. However, the idea that they could relax and take delight in their relationship and in life more generally is a message that they enjoyed contemplating and a goal that they continue to promise themselves for the future. Whether or not they reach that particular goal remains to be seen.

Acknowledgments

Preparation of this chapter was partially supported by NIMH Grant 32616. The author wishes to express appreciation to Anna G. Heinrich and Beth E. Meyerowitz, who consulted on the sex-therapy portion of the treatment.

References

Jacobson, N. S., & Margolin, G. (1979). *Marital therapy: Strategies based on social learning and behavior exchange principles.* New York: Brunner/Mazel.

Locke, H. J., & Wallace, K. M. (1959). Short-term marital adjustment and prediction tests: Their reliability and validity. *Journal of Marriage and Family Living, 21,* 251–255.

LoPiccolo, J., & Lobitz, W. C. (1972). The role of masturbation in the treatment of orgasmic dysfunction. *Archives of Sexual Behavior, 22,* 163–171.

Masters, W., & Johnson, V. (1970). *Human sexual inadequacy.* Boston: Little, Brown.

Tiesmann, M. W. (1979). Jealousy: Systematic problem-solving therapy with couples. *Family Process, 18,* 151-160.

Weiss, R. L., & Birchler, G. R. (1975). *Areas of change.* Unpublished manuscript, University of Oregon.

Weiss, R. L., Hops, H., & Patterson, G. R. (1973). A framework for conceptualizing marital conflict, a technology for altering it, some data for evaluating it. In L. A. Hamerlynck, L. C. Handy, & E. J. Mash (Eds.), *Behavior change: Methodology, concepts, and practice.* Champaign, IL: Research Press.

Weiss, R. L., & Perry, B. A. (1979). *Assessment and treatment of marital dysfunction.* Eugene, OR: Oregon Marital Studies Program.

Chapter 12
Tradition and Transition:
A Rural Marriage in Crisis

Alan S. Gurman, PhD

It was 5:30 in the afternoon on a raw October day, a long one; the end of a day that had begun for me at 8:00 a.m., a day taken up, like most of my workdays, with a bit of everything—a morning seminar, a couple of hours of supervision, a department committee meeting, three other families, and some pencil pushing administrivia. I was about to meet the Olsons. It was an unusual time for me to be seeing them, since I rarely schedule patients for appointments that end after 5:00 p.m. It was even more unusual for me to be having a first session so late, since I usually prefer to spend an hour and a half in a first interview. My infrequent late sessions are generally for "emergency" meetings, and this was not an emergency, in the usual psychiatric sense. I had spoken to Gwen Olson on the phone a few days earlier to schedule our first appointment, and agreed to meet at 5:30 the following Tuesday, but had pointed out that if we continued to meet after that, we would have to arrange an earlier time. Soon enough I would come to appreciate the significance of Don Olson's telling his wife to schedule the meeting as late as possible. In fact, meeting at this time was, for Don, a compromise. Before Gwen phoned me, he had insisted that he could not come to a meeting unless it was at night or, preferably, on Saturday. "Sorry," I had said to Gwen, "I just don't see patients at those hours."

I walked out of my office to go to greet the Olsons in the waiting area a few doors down the hallway. But rather than waiting there, they had taken up a position right outside my door. Was that a sign of how desperate they were to see me? Did one or both of them not want to be easily identified as "patients" by sitting in the waiting area? The answer to both of these questions that flashed through my mind in the few seconds it took to walk over to them and introduce myself turned out to be, "yes."

"Hi, I'm Al Gurman," I said as I reached out to shake Don's hand first, not quite consciously remembering that he had not seemed very eager to meet at all. Before we had ever seen each other, I had inferred from my brief phone contact with Gwen that forming a therapeutic alliance with Don would probably not be easy, and certainly would not be swift.

I gestured to the Olsons to direct them toward my office door. Walking alongside Don, I said impulsively to him, "You look terrible!" "Hardly a way to make a reluctant new patient feel right at home off the bat," I thought. But Don looked so disheveled, I could not resist. His hair was tussled, he had what appeared to be about a week's growth of beard, and his eyes were reddened and swollen. Had he been crying? Yes. Had he been sleeping poorly? Yes. Was he strung out on drugs? No, not then, not ever. He was, as Gwen once said, "as straight as they come."

The Olsons had been referred to me by a family practice physician from a small farming town that bordered Madison. Since most of my patients are physicians, attorneys, professors, teachers, business people, and other professionals in the very educated city of Madison, I was frankly a bit intrigued about the possibility of working with a farm couple. No doubt, that had had something to do with my scheduling such a late first interview. I was also intrigued about the notion of seeing whether the way I do marital therapy would "fit" with people who were so different from most of the hundreds of couples over the last decade with whom I had been evolving what, for definite lack of a better appellation, I had come to call "Integrative Marital Therapy."

*   *   *

Integrative Marital Therapy (IMT) (Gurman, 1978, 1980, 1981, 1982a, 1982b, 1982c, 1984) is committed to three basic premises:

1. The practice of marital therapy (indeed, of any psychotheapy) requires a broad explanatory basis of human behavior.

2. A singular focus on intrapersonal "versus" interpersonal aspects of psychological experience is arbitrary.
3. Systemic thinking applied to clinical practice requires awareness by the therapist of all levels and dimensions of human experience, from biochemical and psychophysiological to cognitive, affective, and behavioral, to cultural and social.

Given these premises and an acknowledgment that even when therapists intervene at a single level of experience change inevitably occurs on multiple levels (of both the organization of social behavior and of consciousness) and dimensions, the integrative therapist remains sensitive to the idea that different methods of family therapy seem to be particularly helpful for different sorts of problems. For example, structural (Minuchin, 1974) interventions are especially well suited to problems involving issues of inclusion/exclusion; behavioral interventions (Jacobson & Margolin, 1979) may be called upon for issues involving control and decision-making, and psychodynamic approaches (Sager, 1981) are well suited for problems of intimacy (Doherty & Colangelo, 1984).

In order to understand the multiple levels of experience that *are* a marriage (or other intimate relationship), IMT borrows systematically from a variety of schools of thought about human behavior that appear to have particular explanatory power in regard to particular levels of intimate relating, specifically, object relations theory, social learning theory, and General Systems Theory.

This approach offers an integrative framework for the understanding of marital attraction, conflict, and satisfaction; and this framework provides the basis for the actual conduct of couples therapy. As a particular organization of self-regulated social behavior, marriage is seen as best understood, for clinical purposes, in terms of the implicit "rules" of what behavior is allowed and what is disallowed. Conflict arises, then, and continues when "rules" are violated which are central to each partner's sense of self. These relational rules begin with both the conscious and unconscious expectations of, and anxieties about, intimate relating that are brought to the relationship by each partner. The patterned regularities of marriage, then, do not evolve randomly or only from repetitive interactions but also from a subtle interplay of the implicit relationship rules of each individual (Sager, 1981).

The mutual regulation of marital behavior is a function of the needs and efforts of each partner to shape the other to stay within,

or get within, the limits of behavior allowed by that person's "rules."
In this vein, Bagarozzi and Giddings (1984) clearly articulate what
they call "mutual shaping toward the ideal," or what I have called
"implicit behavior modification" (Gurman, 1982c). That is, people unwittingly (and wittingly as well) reinforce and extinguish behavior in
their mates that is allowed and disallowed, respectively, according to
their own internal expectations of a marital partner, and do likewise
in response to the behavior of their mates that is allowed and disallowed
according to the internal "rules" of how one needs to "see" one's self.
Defenses, then, operate in order to avoid "seeing" behavior that is
inconsistent with one's internalized image of one's ideal mate and/or
with one's requirements for maintaining a consistent view of one's self.
It is the utopian and anxiety-based expectations that people bring to
marriage that sensitize them to slight deviations from these relational
"rules" which, when they occur, increase the amplitude and frequency
of counter-control maneuvers.

Now, this discussion might seem to suggest that marriage is a state
of existence worthy of being avoided by any sensible person. Quite to
the contrary. The processes described above, often referred to as "collusion" (Willi, 1981, 1984), in fact represent, in part, attempted solutions
of individual difficulties. That is, not only is it true that marriage is
potentially healing of past wounds, but also that people who stay in
(even many of the most conflicted) marriage(s), do so for just such
reasons.

This having been said, two essential principles of IMT become
understandable:

1. Since people shape each other's personalities, marital therapy
   can lead to "individual" change.
2. Behavior change can change the inner schemata both of one's
   self and of one's partner.

The aims, in general, of IMT, then, are: (1) to interrupt and
modify the couple's self- and other- protective collusive processes so
that each partner may be "exposed," in the safety of the therapeutic
experience, to anxiety-arousing aspects of self and of the partner; (2)
to identify and clarify the links between individual experience (conscious
thoughts, preconscious "automatic thoughts," conditioned affective responses, etc.) and the marital interaction; (3) to create therapeutic
tasks which both challenge the couple's reflexive, rule-governed prob-

lematic behavior and allow in new information about each partner, in order to restructure both self-perceptions and perceptions of the partner; and (4) to teach interpersonal relationship skills (e.g., problem solving, conflict resolution, and communication skills), as needed, if they are missing from each partner's repertoire. Or, when these essential skills are in each partner's repertoire (i.e., they can be seen in each person's interactions with people other than their spouse), but are not "used" in the marriage, the goal is to remove the blocks to their appearance in the marriage.

To these ends, the integrative therapist calls upon specific interventions from a variety of therapeutic traditions, e.g., interpretation to enhance both intrapersonal and interpersonal insight (psychodynamic); training in communication and problem-solving skills, behavior rehearsal, and modeling (behavioral); cognitive restructuring and self-control methods (cognitive); enactment and task assignment (structural/strategic); and paradoxical techniques such as prescribing symptoms and reframing (systemic). These varied techniques are called upon not from the eclectic therapist's stance of "doing whatever works," but from the integrative perspective in which each of these particular operations, and others, is seen to be fully consistent with the integrative conceptualization of marital conflict and distress, and to foster the integrative goals of more accurate self-perception and perception of one's partner and the adoption of alternative styles of intimate relating that are both personally more adaptive and relationship-enhancing (Gurman, 1981, 1982a, 1982b, 1982c).

* * *

First Session, Continued

My comment, "You look terrible," seemed to linger in the air for the half a minute or so it took for three of us to enter my office and sit down. Perhaps what was so striking about Don's appearance was not just that he looked depressed, but that, in referring the Olsons to me, Gwen's family doctor had said he thought that *she* was depressed and might require antidepressant medication.

"Where should we begin?" I asked. "Dr. Johnson really didn't tell me a lot about your situation," I continued, looking first at Don, then at Gwen. Silence. Gwen was turned to the side, staring out the window with tears in her eyes. Don kept on looking at Gwen, his posture silently saying, "You go first." Slowly, with a lot of probing on my part, their story began to be revealed. Don, age 27, and Gwen, age 24, the parents of a 2-year-old boy and a 5-year-old boy, had been married for 6 years. They met in their local small town of about 4000 people when Gwen was 17, at the beginning of her senior year in high school. Don had graduated from the same high school 3 years earlier. They'd been "fixed up" on a blind date by an older female friend of Gwen's, who had known Don for some time and thought Don would be "just right" for Gwen. "What did she have in mind?" I asked. Gwen said that Carol had described Don to her as "quiet, gentle and reliable," and thought that that was the kind of man Gwen needed. Even without really knowing Gwen's personal history very much, Carol had intuitively tuned in to Gwen in a remarkably perceptive way.

Gwen, the oldest of four children spaced about 2½ years apart, had been a "junior mother," as she described herself, virtually all of her adolescence. Her father was an alcoholic who rarely got involved with his children except to discipline and punish them and regularly raged against Gwen's mother, abusing her verbally "all the time," accusing her of infidelity, and pushing and hitting her on numerous occasions, sometimes in full view of the children. He was "a womanizer and a liar" Gwen said. "Was?" He had died of uncertain causes when Gwen was 16 years old. Her father had overdosed on a mixture of alcohol and other drugs, and suicide was suspected, but never proven. Though Gwen had "despised" her father, she pitied him, and apparently had mourned his death relatively well. "I could always tell there was a little boy inside him," she added empathically. As a junior mother, Gwen had had nearly total responsibility for running the family household and caring for her younger sibs. Gwen's mother had to work at two, sometimes three, part-time jobs to keep her family afloat financially. Gwen felt sorry for her mother's lot, but just as sorry for her own. With all her parent-like responsibilities, she had had almost no social life and rarely dated, though high school boys had often asked her out. She was a warm, demure, very attractive young woman, with sad blue eyes.

When she met Don, there was, indeed, a strong initial attraction to the very qualities her friend Carol had predicted. Don "put her up on a pedestal" from the first, and proposed marriage to her within a couple of months. Gwen felt "very comfortable" with Don, and saw him as "someone who would always listen to me, even if he had things of his own on his mind."

Don's family was, in many ways, the antithesis of Gwen's. They had had a very "stable" life together. In fact, it was so stable that it was very difficult to leave the family or to "think for ourselves." Don's father was an autocrat who had taken over the running of the family dairy farm from his father, who had taken it over from his father. For Mr. Olson, life *was* the farm, and everyone and everything else was a distant second. Don was the middle child of three. His younger sister was married and lived a few hours away. His older brother, who "never really took to the farming life," had struggled with his father for years about maintaining the tradition of the family farm. Unable to emancipate himself in the way he preferred, he had found it necessary several years earlier to move to Europe (specifically, Norway, from which his great-grandfather had emigrated around the turn of the century!) in order to "have a life of his own." As a matter of unquestioned course, it then fell to Don to assume the job of running the farm. Actually, Don had all the responsibilities of the farm, but little power. His father, who was "semi-retired," still owned the farm and paid Don a salary. Don, it seemed, had the farm life "in his blood," though he was indeed bitter at his father, who had rejected several (halfhearted, according to Gwen) offers from Don to buy a controlling interest in the family operation. According to Gwen, Don "did the work of three men" on the farm, but was rarely praised by his father for his efforts or shown any signs of appreciation. "Someday," Don often mused, "it'll be mine and I'll run it the way I see fit." Though Don was always angry at his father for all this, he would rarely challenge Mr. Olson. It was as Carol had said. Don was quiet and reliable.

Don's interpersonally passive style and his no-nonsense, shoulder to the grindstone life style felt very safe to Gwen. Moreover, she hesitantly acknowledged, marrying Don was an acceptable way to get away from the constricted and burdensome life she had known in her own family. For a long time, all she could see about the Olson clan was its reassuring predictability and deceptive sense of unity. This "unity" required that Don and Gwen at first take up residence in the Olson house, where they lived for several months after their wedding. Given their limited financial resources, this at first made sense to them. Then, with their first child on the way, they moved into a mobile home on the family land. Gradually, Gwen began to appreciate the grip Mr.

Olson had on Don's life, and found his control too stifling of both her and her marriage. For example, Mr. Olson demanded advance notice any time Don and Gwen would be away from the farm for more than a few hours. In what Gwen felt to be a major breakthrough, she had finally persuaded Don to buy a small house of their own, a couple of miles down the road from the farm. But, because of Mr. Olson's disapproval of this move, Gwen had to promise her husband that she would continue to work on the farm. Mr. Olson, it seemed, was threatened by Gwen's increasing desire for her and Don to quit the farm life altogether. Don was readily intimidated by his father's anger, and, in a coerced symbolic spirit of seeming detente, let his father know that the family tradition was not in great danger because both he and Gwen would continue to work the farm. Don felt controlled by his father, and Gwen was feeling increasingly controlled by Don.

But Gwen's self-confidence and urgent need for a feeling of independence had grown in the last couple of years, and she had taken up a part-time waitressing job about a year ago. That sent shock waves through the Olson family, Mr. Olson especially (Mrs. Olson remained nearly mute on the subject), and Gwen and her father-in-law rapidly grew even more angrily distant. Don, the "gentle, reliable" one, was pushed into the position of intermediary and peacemaker, alternately defending both his father's position and his wife's. Gwen grew increasingly angry at Don as well, and attacked his family loyalty. "When you get married, your wife is supposed to come first," she stated unambiguously. At one point in the first session, she turned to Don and challengingly asked, "Are you married to me or to the farm?" Don sat in frozen, paralyzed silence.

Very recently, Gwen "went too far," according to Don. She announced that she was not going to be a farm wife ("like Don's mother") with no life of her own, and refused to continue helping Don with his daily farming tasks. Instead, she was going to use that time to try to find a full-time job. Since there were few jobs available in their small town or nearby for someone with limited previous paid work experience and few marketable skills, she began to investigate possibilities in Madison. For her job-hunting ventures, she would doff her blue jeans and work shirt, don a more feminine blouse or sweater and skirt, and put on makeup, which she rarely used except for special occasions. Though Don had grown up only 15 miles from "the city," he had rarely ventured into Madison, and when he did, he felt very awkward and out of place. Gwen, who had somehow developed very good social skills despite her relatively isolated adolescence, was pleasingly surprised by the ease with which she began to meet new people, and had even struck up a couple of new friendships with young women she met in her job-hunting. After years of being cut off from peer contact, Gwen was starting to move out into the world. All of this infuriated and terrified Don. How could he "explain" it to his father? What if Gwen "met some guy"?

On the occasion of Gwen's going into "the city" about 2 weeks before our first session, the usually controlled, cautious Don had become enraged upon her late return home, and they had "the worst fight of our marriage". Though Gwen continued to have some positive feelings for Don, she increasingly saw him as unlikely ever to "ever act like a man while his father is still alive," and started talking about divorce, even though she was very frightened by her own images of again living in a "broken up" family, and become depressed, imagining herself "having to live like my mother." She also feared that her own children would have to "go through what I went through." Don was at least as depressed about the possibility of divorce. Earlier the day of our first session he had literally begged Gwen to give up "this stuff about getting a job in Madison," but she would not relent. Don had been crying most of the afternoon. He also had been sleeping very poorly for several days.

"How can I help?" I asked. Gwen said she really did not want to divorce Don, but could no longer stand "the way we live." Ideally, she wanted Don either to quit the farm altogether or "at least stand up to your father" about his own relationship to Mr. Olson and about Gwen's moving out into the world which, in principle, Don could acknowledge "made sense for her." At the very least, she wanted "to feel like we're really a couple." That meant Don should spend more time away from the farm, and with Gwen. They should "find some new couple friends" (they had essentially none); they should "go out socially" (Don was very uncomfortable and anxious at parties, restaurants, etc.); Don should "get more involved with the boys" (whom he usually saw only at breakfast and for a short while at dinner, before returning to his farm chores); and Don should "talk to me once in awhile so we know what's going on in each other's life." For Don's part, he wished Gwen would "drop her new life style crusade," though he knew she would not. Basically, he wanted things to be "the way they used to be," though he knew they could not. Since the "leaver" in a marriage always has more power (control of resources) than the "leavee," Don did not feel there was much he could ask for. Indeed, all he seemed to want was for Gwen to stop rocking the boat. The despair in his face expressed his feelings without words. "Please just don't leave," it said poignantly and silently. As it would later emerge, Don also feared a divorce because it might mean that his sons would not ever get involved in the Olsons' farm, and continuation of the family farming tradition would be threatened seriously.

The sense of despair and futility in the marriage was overwhelming. In an effort to help to foster some degree of a working alliance between Gwen and Don, I did several things during the first session which were aimed at evoking some mutual empathy and providing a new cognitive understanding of their difficulties. I pointed out that even though their families of origin appeared to have been quite different, the *experiences* for each of them in growing up in their families were not so far apart: Both of them had been unable to get close to their fathers; both of them had felt taken advantage of and had grown up believing that their mission in life was to serve others at the expense of rarely meeting their own needs; each of them, in their own way, was struggling to establish a life of their own apart from family, etc. To this I added that, in light of the turmoil they had experienced almost throughout their marriage, there must be something very powerful and important that had kept them together. I offered some new (to them) ideas about the behavior of each that the other found unacceptable: Don was not uncaring of Gwen or uncommitted to her; he was frightened, terrified, that a serious rift between him and his father could mean that everything he had hoped for and worked so hard at for so long could evaporate. Working long hours on the farm was not an expression of disinterest in her and their children, it was the best way he had learned *to express* his interest and concern for his wife and children. Gwen was not failing to live up to her end of their bargain (to continue to work the farm), she was finally being honest and forthright about what she needed in marriage, and in life in general. Gwen was not attacking what Don stood for, but was intuitively and sensitively supporting Don's quest for independence by showing him, through her own self-help efforts, that people should not give up pursuing what is really important to them.

Given the Olsons' rapidly waning sense of hope about the future of their relationship, and their apparently "irreconcilable differences," something had to happen in the first session to increase the chances of their finding enough common ground to begin to collaborate on their problems. While the views I offered them of their situation could be seen as mere strategems to this end, it is more fundamentally true that I offered them because I really believed what I was saying.

By the end of our first session, some of the Olsons' tension seemed to have been relieved. To *my* relief, they both seemed to accept my ideas about their dilemma. I felt I had managed to establish a good alliance with each of them, mostly by showing interest in what each of them felt and wanted to say. Perhaps I was becoming a "good enough father" to each of them.

Though Don "didn't really believe in counseling—people should be able to work out their own problems," he took up my offer of seeing them together again, and in accordance with my usual work hours. Gwen also accepted. We seemed to reach a consensus that the aims of our work together would be to help them find mutually acceptable ways of "being more of a couple," and, at the same time, to help each of them achieve some of their individual life goals, while remaining sensitive to the impact on the other person of such efforts.

Second Session

The second session with a couple is often the one I anticipate with the most mixed feelings. For me, it is most often the session in which the couple begins to appreciate how much of the initiative for our work must come from them. Since my first session with a couple is always longer than subsequent sessions (90 minutes vs. 60 minutes), and since I want to cover a lot of territory in the first session, I am extremely active and regularly take the lead in exploring a wide range of issues (the presenting problem, previous attempts to solve the problem, the role of various "third parties" in the problem, the couple's history together, their individual developmental and family histories, how they are getting on as parents, the nature and degree of their motivation to change, their commitment to the marriage, etc.). If I am not especially clear about their problem and do not have at least some tentative plans for how to intervene, the second session is likely to be a continuation of the first in format. But usually this is not a problem, and the flow then shifts from one of establishing the basic structure of our work to one of communicating that the therapy is the couple's, not mine (not unlike Whitaker's [Whitaker & Keith, 1981] "battle for structure" and "battle for initiative," but without a sense of being embattled). My ambivalence about second sessions, then, reflects, on one hand, my belief that since the aims of therapy must be the couple's, they must begin to "own" their therapy, and, on the other hand, my belief (Gurman, 1981) that the therapist must do something very early in therapy that not only continues to challenge the couple's initial problem definition, but that also begins to generate new behavioral alternatives for the couple's problem solving and coping. The second session, then, is more like subsequent sessions than is the first, and is, one hopes, a prototype of the collaborative problem solving relationship that I will continue to evolve with the couple. Problem solving efforts may begin in the first session as well, but in that session, there is greater conscious emphasis on my part three other areas:

1. Understanding both the two individual histories and the couple's relationship history, and how these have set the stage for, and are reflected in, the couple's current difficulties.
2. Creating an atmosphere in which it is "safe" for the couple to begin to take risks with each other, particularly in terms of self-disclosure.
3. Fostering a climate, of collaboration within the couple that increases their optimism about joint problem solving.

Typically, then (and with the Olsons), I begin the second session by expressing curiosity about several things which simultaneously tell me about the couple's readiness for change and how likely they are to respond to my efforts to help: What were their reactions to our first meeting? Did they find it at all helpful? If so, in what ways? If not, what got in the way? Did they learn anything new about themselves and their mate? Do they now have any different ideas about their problem than before our first session? Did they talk to each other about the session in the intervening week? If not, did each of them think about the session at all? How did they each feel with me and about me?

Don still did not think he needed to see a therapist for the couple's problems, but he was relieved that I seemed to be a "pretty regular guy, even though you have all those degrees on your wall." (Predictably, he usually felt intimidated by doctors and other professional people, and he did not have much in common with "city people.") Gwen had felt comfortable with me, but she was most concerned about whether Don would continue to come for therapy. Though she did not say it, I suspected she thought that if she backed down at all from her demands of Don, he would quickly back out of therapy, or that if he somehow were to develop more personal resources and feel "stronger," he would return to his earlier adamance about their lifestyle, etc.

They had not talked about our first session, and what they had thought about independently mostly had to do with *being in* therapy. Don was there reluctantly, and Gwen was aware of Don's reluctance. These reactions to me personally, to the idea of being in therapy per se (i.e., dealing with someone outside the family), and to each other-in-the-context-of-seeking help, suggested the direction and focus of the second session: I would need to join further with Don, and I would need to do so in such a way that Gwen not feel I was taking her husband's side (Gwen had had a lifetime of men's needs coming first). I would need to respect Don's inclination to be a "doer" by proposing some kind of out-of-session task for him to "carry out on your own," and I would need to push both of them to interact more with each other than they had (or, than I had asked of them) in the first session. Because Gwen seemed much more immediately committed to therapy (or to changing, at least) than Don, I felt less need, early in the session, to do anything very overt to engage her, preferring to direct her to engage more actively with Don, from whom she had withdrawn so much.

Hearing how they had reacted to and processed our first session, I turned to Don, expressing my (genuine, though slightly overstated) ignorance about running a farm. What was a typical day for him on the farm? How were new federal farm policies affecting his work? What did he like most about farming? Least? Etc., etc. This was all an area in which Don felt quite competent and knowledgeable. And, showing obvious pride in his achievements and skills, Don was much more expressive and articulate about these matters than about the more elusive domain of feelings, relationships, and the like. This discussion of farm life led quite naturally, as I had hoped, into other dimensions of Don's farm life, that is, "life with father." Don and I talked for about 20 minutes about his own farm activities and his respect for his father's farming expertise. Gradually, we got to his feeling of being "alone" in his own family. As we talked on, what became clearer to me was that Don did not defend the family tradition simply out of fear of being disenfranchised by Mr. Olson (though this was a real worry), or out of any kind of blind addiction to tradition. Continuing his loyalty to "the farm" was the only way Don could conceive of ever getting close to his father; indeed, even as a boy, doing farm chores with Mr. Olson were the only times he ever felt that the two of them shared anything in common, and so they became rather special times, their being coerced notwithstanding. Don had hoped that as he entered adulthood and assumed major responsibility for the farm, his father would feel less need to relate to him "as though I was just one of the hired help that he needs to teach things to," and that they could find other grounds for being together.

After several minutes of this part of our conversation, I turned to Gwen, who had been listening attentively. "What's your reaction to what Don's been saying?" I asked. "I've never heard him talk so much about him and his Dad." "Why not?" I asked Gwen. "I think I've told her most of this before," Don interjected, starting to seem irritated at Gwen. "But you never tell me how you feel about your father, except that you're as mad at him as I am," Gwen countered. "I've tried to, I think," Don said. "O.K., but when you've tried to, what's happened?" I asked. "She tells me he's a lost cause, and I should give up on him. You kinda get started saying what you feel and . . . . And she cuts me off." I pushed further, "She won't this time" (thinking to myself, "If she starts to, I won't let her"). "You told *me* a few minutes ago what keeps you so hooked into the farm, to your Dad, that is, now tell Gwen." "She heard me," he snapped, growing annoyed with me (for not allowing their usual collusion with each other, with me). "I'm not so sure; say it again. Look at her and say it again." "Because I want him to approve of me. I want him to like me," he finally mumbled, with tears coming to his eyes. "Right. I think Gwen can understand that, but, at the same time, it's not easy for her," I added, glancing at Gwen. "And, do you know why?" I asked Gwen. "No, not really," she answered, appearing curious about my idea as to why, but apprehensive about asking what I had in mind. I answered the unasked question anyway, "I think it's hard for you for a couple of reasons. First, you care about Don a lot, so it's hard for you to see him upset about this, so you try to get him off the hot seat by cutting him off. And second, *you*'ve given up on *your* Dad. You've had to, he's not here anymore."

In this middle part of the session, I had tried to (1) begin to unblock some of Don's feelings about his relationship with his father, not for cathartic reasons, but so that they could be brought back into the marital sphere; (2) block the couple's usual "collusive" manner of short-circuiting how they dealt with Don's feelings about his father; and (3) interrupt Gwen's reflexive habit of projectively identifying with Don by simply labeling it, and by so doing, bringing *it* out into the open, just as I had tried to bring Don's feeling into the open. What I also thought at this point, but kept to myself was that, as much as Gwen wanted Don to be more self-revealing to her, she was, at the same time, quite uncomfortable about that happening: The only man she had ever known at close range was her father, whose explosive rage and unpredictability were the antithesis of Don, the "quite, reliable" one. She had needed such a rock earlier in their marriage, even if it meant that intimacy had to be sacrificed for safety. She felt distant from Don, but out of danger. Were Don to let out his feelings more fully, I conjectured, not only might Gwen become anxious, but also she might feel compelled to be his caretaker, a role she had learned so well growing up, and which she was now trying to get away from somewhat, lest her own needs be ignored, as they had been so regularly in the past.

I thought that we had broken important ground in these 20 or so minutes, and that to introduce any of these ideas at that point might arouse more anxiety than Gwen could tolerate at that moment. Considering Don's reluctance even to enter therapy, I judged that he, too, had taken enough of a risk for that session. I let my comment about Gwen's projection simply speak for itself, and in an effort both to relieve their anxiety and to help them start to translate this brief experience into what it meant for "real life," I switched the focus to life outside the session. After half a minute, I broke the silence: "What's this like for you two, what's it like to talk this way to each other, and with a third person?" "It's like this at home, but it's different," said Don. "I mean, it started out the same way, but it didn't end the same way." "Sure didn't," added Gwen, giving me a look that seemed to say, "You sure call 'em like you see 'em, don't you?" I let the nonverbal message pass without comment, but smiled at Gwen as I nodded and said, "Sorry about that." She returned the smile, apparently getting my drift.

After a pause, I continued. "I think there's something we can *do* with this outside of here. After all, talk is cheap." Don chuckled. I suggested that they try "an experiment" for the next week (the way I usually introduce an out-of-session task). Were they interested? "Maybe, it depends what you have in mind," Gwen offered. I suggested to Gwen that she might find it interesting, and that it would certainly provide useful information for me (so I put it, thinking "useful for you"), if every time in the next week she found herself starting to become irritated with Don for any reason that had anything to do with the farm or with Don's father, she would try to say nothing to Don, and instead ask herself, "What's he (Don) feeling right now? Besides being angry, what else am *I* feeling?" She would try it. To Don, I said (with an implicit parallel reference to him and his father), "I obviously can't do all of this myself, Don. You're as much your own therapist here as I am" (validating his penchant for self-reliance), "so I'll need your help. After what just went on here, I suspect you might feel inclined to try to talk more openly about things than you usually do, maybe also because I know you're a guy who likes to get things done when they need to be done. But don't, because Gwen isn't quite used to you yet that way. Instead, there's something that only you can do, and you'll have to carry it out on your own. I'd like you to watch Gwen as closely as you can, and see if you can tell when she's doing what I just asked her to do. It won't be easy, of course, because she isn't to say anything to you about it. And I don't want you to ask her what's going on with her, just kinda do it quietly and under cover, you might say." Don smiled. "See you next week."

These "experiments" had several purposes: (1) to interrupt Gwen's showing her reflexive anger at Don with a concrete self-control technique in order to break into part of that cycle and, in so doing, to get Gwen to coach herself to be more empathic to Don, but without having to lose face by showing just yet that she was doing that; (2) to get Gwen to take back her projection; and (3) to give Don a task in which he would have to be curious about Gwen ("We should know what's going on in each other's life"), but in a way that was comfortable for him, that is, silently ("do it quietly and under cover"). All of this was also intended to shift the focus from what usually got Don's and Gwen's attention, and to introduce new information into the relationship, in an indirect manner that did not require, and in fact in a limited way, restrained, overt change.

Third Session

Gwen seemed less depressed, and Don was looking better, as well. I asked about the "experiments." Gwen said she hadn't felt as angry at Don as she usually did, but that when she did, she had been able to stop herself and remind herself that Don was scared about his relationship to his father. Could she identify any other feelings at those times? Yes, she felt "kind of alone." I suggested to her that she and Don had gotten into "such a habit about this that, as lousy as it feels to try to fight with Don, at least then you are still trying to make some contact with him, so when you stop yourself from showing your irritation, you feel more alone. Maybe there are some other ways you can make contact with him without having to feel so rotten. Let's get back to that in awhile."

For his part, Don had tried to "read her under cover", but he didn't think he had succeeded. "Maybe there was just less to 'read' this week," I wondered aloud. Don had a different idea, "Maybe but I'm just not real good at that kind of thing." Privately, I agreed with him and thought I had made an error in what I'd asked him to do. Here was a man who had kept to himself most of his life, and kept most of his feelings to himself; he had not had much experience with the nuances of feelings and relationships, and I had, I thought, asked him to do something that was just too unfamiliar to him. Though I thought I had erred, I didn't want Don to feel that *he* had failed, so I reminded him that this was "an experiment," "O.K., like I said last week, this was just an experiment, and I think you've helped me understand you better, anyway. I think it's easier for you to 'read' Gwen when you don't have to read between the lines so much." He agreed. "So, can you try to 'read' her now? Can you think of some ways she's already mentioned that *she* thinks she might be able to make contact with you without having to get angry at you, like we were talking about a little while ago?" Don offered a few ideas, but was offering them to me. "No, please tell Gwen. I'll just listen in."

The idea that attracted Gwen most involved the Olsons' sons, whom we had hardly talked about in the first two sessions, except for my inquiring in a general way about whether they were having any difficulties. Though Don and Gwen had said they were not, in fact, they were. That is, Gwen had been having a rough time almost every night getting Jonathan, their 5-year-old, to stay in his room at bed-time. Don guessed, accurately, that Gwen would appreciate some help with Jonathan, since she always put the boys to bed by herself.

I knew from the first session that the reason Gwen handled the bedtime ritual alone was that Don returned to his chores after dinner almost every night. I left that unsaid, thinking it would only cue Gwen to get annoyed with Don if I mentioned it. Instead, I would just go for direct behavior change. I also liked the idea because, in addition to Don's sharing the task with Gwen having the potential of her feeling cared about, it would also put Don in contact with the boys. Maybe they could start to reverse a multigenerational tradition of fathers and sons being distant, a "tradition" as powerful as the farming tradition. I also assumed that Jonathan might be feeling anxious at bedtime out of fear that his parents would be fighting again, so that their sharing this parental task might be reassuring to him.

I asked what the usual bedtime "scene" was. Gwen would bathe the boys, read them a story, hug them "goodnight," and go downstairs. In about 5 minutes, Jonathan would appear on the first floor, com-plaining that he could not fall asleep. Gwen would walk him upstairs, irritated, and read him another story. This would happen three or four times each night, until Gwen would "explode" at Jonathan, he would cry, she would comfort him for a couple of minutes, and he would finally stay in his room and fall asleep. "A miniature version of the marriage," I thought, "except that Gwen has quit comforting Don."

"Besides just deciding to put them to bed together, what else might need to be different for it to work?", I asked. "Nothing much", Gwen answered, "I think if we do it together, it'll work." "O.K.," I replied, "but may I suggest a few new wrinkles in the routine?" I suggested that for the first three nights in the next week, Don just accompany Gwen and back her up on whatever she said; mostly, he should just "watch" to see what Gwen does. I said I thought he would catch on by three nights, and that for the next four nights, there should be some "minor" changes: First, *Don* should announce bedtime to the boys; second, *Don* should read the story to them; and third, if Jonathan came downstairs, Don and Gwen should "escort" him upstairs, get him in bed, without another story, and leave his room at once, with Don saying to his son, "You've got to go to sleep now. Mom and I want some time to be together, and we don't want you to bother us." Gwen smiled approvingly. "By the way," I asked as an apparent afterthought, "what'll you two do with all that free time?" Don shrugged his shoulders. "Well," I said, standing to signal the end of the session, "I guess that'll be another interesting experiment!"

Walking to my car to go home, I thought about the session. I thought I had salvaged the "failed" experiment from the previous session well enough, and I was pleased with how the rest of the session had gone, the bedtime prescription, and so on. With my closing comment, I had even managed to slip in a perhaps not-so-subtle reference to sex which, in the despairing air of the first session, and the intensity of the second, I realized just then, hadn't even been alluded to. Still, something did not "feel right" to me. Don was expressing his feelings, in the sessions at least, more readily than I had predicted at the outset he would, but somehow it seemed to be happening a bit too easily. Maybe I had "underestimated" him—bought into Gwen's characterization of him too much. I tend to do that at times with women married to "unexpressive" men and, especially with women married to controlling men who fear their wives' independence, having grown up with that in my own family. But that seemed too intellectual to me—I hadn't *felt* particularly pulled to her side. It also seemed out of character for him to agree to the bedtime arrangement, not only given his history with that, but also given that he must have been aware, while we were discussing it, that he would have to cut short his postdinner farm chores to pull it off, yet he did not even mention that. My "worst case scenarios" about Don were that he was following my directives out of a kind of transferential "cooperativeness" (a real possibility, given his reluctance to start therapy), or that he was simply so desperate about the idea of losing Gwen that he would do just about anything to show good faith, even if his heart was not in it.

I sensed something "funny" going on with Gwen, too. Even though she seemed more "psychologically minded" and open at first, I had the uncomfortable feeling that I had really gotten closer to Don in the first three sessions, and understood him better. I was concerned that, in my efforts to engage Don, Gwen might have felt unattended to. But even though I had been talking more to Don than to Gwen, we did seem to "click" nonverbally several times. And as pleased as I'd been that Gwen had been able to short-circuit her unproductive anger at Don in the past week, that, too, seemed like an extraordinary change in such a short period. I'd had the thought earlier that I was becoming a "good enough father" to her, but maybe I was just becoming *a* father to her, one she had to tiptoe around for fear of reprisal.

I got home and ate dinner, did the usual early evening things with my family, went through *our* typical bedtime rituals with the kids, and forgot about the Olsons for the while.

Fourth Session

The bedtime prescription had gone well, and the Olsons had played their parts in the new script just about as we had written them. Jonathan, not surprisingly, had tried to stick to his old role, and had challenged the new ("minor") arrangements. He wanted Mom, not Dad, to read the boys' story, and he had come downstairs more than once most nights in the past week. Fortunately, though, Don persisted with his story reading responsibility, and worked cooperatively with Gwen, as we had planned. Predictably, Gwen was pleased with these changes. Don, understandably, had felt "kind of awkward" at the kids' bedtime, but conceded that even though putting the boys to bed was "kind of a pain," he could see that "it could get to be fun sometimes." In fact, Don was even thinking that he might *want* (not just be willing) to give the boys their bath by himself "once in a while".

Clearly, this bedtime task was a more helpful strategy than the one I had had the Olsons experiment with between the second and third sessions. For Don, it involved his *doing* something concrete, and in collaboration with Gwen, rather than in his usual solo style. As a result, Gwen felt more "like we were on the same team," and was actually rather moved by seeing that both Don and the boys seemed to enjoy having some time together. My error with the earlier assignment was that I had been pushing for change with Don in a way that asked for too much (implicit) intimacy with Gwen (albeit under cover) before Don was even behaving as though he was a part of *this* family. Reconnecting him with the boys, at least in this beginning way, was safer for him and, thus, more easily accomplished.

What had they done with all their "free time?" I inquired. "We just sort of sat around," answered Gwen. She had returned to some sewing (significantly, of clothes for herself) she had not had time for

for quite a while, in the room in which Don watched television. So, they had not really been "together" in the way they had implied to Jonathan, but at least they were in the same place at the same time more than usual, and without fighting. Don discovered some new television shows that he enjoyed. "But what about your chores?" I teased. "Screw'em, they'll get done," he laughed. "T.V. can get to be addicting, you know, you'd better be careful," I continued. Either I was being too subtle in my indirect reference to how Don would deal with his father if "this T.V. stuff got out of hand," or he got the message, but just was not biting. I decided I needed to be explicit. "Seriously, Don, I happen to think that putting kids to bed can be fun—my wife and I do it together almost every night—and taking out some time that's just for yourself is important, too. But, if you really get into this stuff, you're just not going to be doing quite as much around the farm. You *know* your father will notice, he watches you like a hawk. What are you going to tell him?" He started getting visibly anxious and looked at Gwen. I persisted, "What does that look mean, Don? *'You* got me into all this'? or, 'Help me out'?" "Both, I guess," he said. I pushed a little more, "You're starting to see some of the payoff for being on the same team with Gwen, but there are no free lunches, eh?"

This was the right moment to get Gwen more involved. Though I'd surmised that it would be uncomfortable for Gwen to reinforce Don's being more expressive of his feelings, I sensed that this would not be very likely if she felt she was allying herself with Don about an issue that mattered as much to her as it did to him. There would not be the danger of his feelings being directed at her. Perhaps she could be Don's peer instead of his caretaker.

I asked the Olsons to imagine that Mr. Olson had just started catching on to Don's "wasting time" at night, and had "come down pretty heavy on Don." What could they do? I asked them to brainstorm all the possibilities they could think of, without evaluating them at first, then they would "go back and look at each idea one at a time and decide together how well it would work." I would serve as the "recording secretary" while they did this, writing down all their ideas. Don seemed to like this more action-oriented approach, and clearly was pleased that Gwen was working with him on the problem, which she was doing rather energetically. Apparently, it *was* easier for her to not "cut him off" when he was taking on the loaded father issue by trying to formulate a plan of action than when he was focusing on his internal feelings about his father.

Several possibilities were proposed. A couple involved Don and Gwen confronting Mr. Olson together, and some involved Don dealing with his father by himself. The Olsons considered the pros and cons of both approaches, and I offered a couple of reactions of my own. Finally, and not surprisingly, Don said he favored the latter approach. I agreed with Don's choice, "It's important for you to know that Gwen's on your side in this, but, in the end, it's *your* father, Don, not Gwen's. And she wants to be helpful, but if she's *too* helpful, like you do it together, you'll probably have a nagging doubt about whether you could have done it yourself. Besides, if Gwen does it with you, your Dad will probably think she just put you up to it, like it's not really your own idea, and so he might not take you very seriously in whatever you say." The next few minutes were spent doing some behavior rehearsal, with me alternately role playing Mr. Olson and "coaching" Don by giving him feedback on what he said, and how he said it. Don decided he would take basically the same position with his father as he had taken with his son: "We need some time together," and would amplify it with, "and I want more time with the kids, too." Playing it cautiously, Don decided he was not going to bring up the matter with Mr. Olson, but would "wait until *he* brings it up, and he will," he added with a nervous laugh.

As we were all getting up to end the session, I reminded Gwen and Don that it was important to continue the new bedtime arrangement they had been working on together.

What impressed me most after this session was that dealing directly with the Olsons' mutual projections, by talking explicitly at length about their fears of intimacy and the like, was not going to work. Rather, what I had been realizing more and more was that I would need to keep our talking about these areas brief, as I had thus far, so that they could each continue to be exposed to their intimacy anxiety (Don, anxiety about fusion, Gwen, about abandonment) and, I hoped, become gradually "desensitized." But, just as important, these internal excursions would help me to be sensitive about where it was therapeutically safe to push for change, when it was safe to do so, and how best to create tasks, both in and outside our sessions, that might help the Olsons keep moving forward, without challenging them so much that they would either resist my interventions or bolt from therapy.

Fifth Session

All our rehearsal for the potential "showdown" between Don and Mr. Olson had been just that, a rehearsal. Somehow, Mr. Olson had not yet noticed Don's absence from evening chores. I suspected that Don had not been doing less work, but had been getting as much done as ever before before the boys' bedtime. I was right. I found this very interesting and informative, in that it suggested that, were the conditions right, Don could find (make?) time to be with his family. The new "condition" was that Don was not picking up so many ambivalent, contradictory messages from Gwen about his dealing with his father. He was feeling more support from Gwen, at least at this point, about his *intent* to affirm the primacy of *their* family life. Gwen said that she could "just feel" Don's anxious anticipation about the eventual "showdown," even though Don did not bring it up this week. And, when she sensed Don's tension about this, she did not feel quite as angry at him as she had in the past. Interestingly, she had not found it necessary consciously to monitor her negative feelings toward Don, as I had asked her to do in the second session. She seemed to be more silently empathic toward Don more automatically. This more empathic stance was probably aided to some degree by Don's continuing to carry out his part in the new bedtime arrangement.

In fact, her anger had subsided enough in the past week that she wanted to make an attempt to "do something as a husband and wife." Her idea, it turned out, was for them to go out together for dinner at a local restaurant/bar. Though Don was hesitant about going, he felt that this was not a demand on Gwen's part, but a genuine expression of her wanting to spend time with him, so they went. Unfortunately, in small towns such as the one the Olsons lived in, "everybody knows everybody," and, despite their having chosen a table "in the back, so we wouldn't see anyone we knew," they saw several people they knew. Two of the couples, out for the evening together, "sat down at our table with us even though we didn't exactly invite them to," as Gwen put it. The next hour or so was very unpleasant for Don, who did not do well in such social situations. The more anxious he felt, the angrier he felt toward Gwen. By the time they returned home, he was "really pissed off."

As we discussed what had made him so upset, it was readily apparent that Don's discomfort in most social situations centered on his acute awareness of other people's judgments of him (evaluation anxiety). I told him I thought that, just as he had had trouble "reading" Gwen a few weeks earlier, he "over-read" what people thought of him. We worked for a while on identifying his reflexive and unquestioned assumptions that he had to get the approval of others, that if someone did not like him, that proved there was something wrong with him, etc. I suggested we might pick up on these individual issues again, and encouraged him to read a trade book (Burns, 1981) based on cognitive therapy that many of my patients find helpful for problems like this.

I was also aware that Don's social anxiety did not result simply from his "self-talk," but that his self-talk reflected his (accurate) awareness of his limited social skills. Without identifying this dimension of his difficulty explicitly, I suggested to him that his rather cloistered experience growing up made it seem understandable that he would feel awkward in some situations like the one the previous night. Social skills training was beyond the scope of our work together, and, furthermore, it seemed that for Don it would call for more intensive individual work than could be taken on now, or for referral later to a specialized social skills training group.

I reminded Don that how he and Gwen dealt with each other about this problem was just as important as his doing some work on his own (reading the book I had mentioned) about it, and asked them to talk to each other about that aspect of the issue. For about 15 minutes, and with prompts and feedback from me, they addressed the matter of how they might go about spending "an evening together as a couple" in a way that each of them would find reasonably comfortable and enjoyable. I advised them of the value of defining the problem they were dealing with as concretely and succinctly as possible, dealing with only that problem for the moment, "brainstorming" potential solutions (as they had done vis-á-vis Don and his father's as yet nonexistent confrontation), then taking turns expressing their thoughts and feelings about each possible solution, etc. I welcomed this opportunity to help them with some problem-solving training. And, given how unfamiliar they were with tackling their problems in this fashion, it progressed quite well until they got to the point at which they needed to choose among their various alternatives. They weren't bickering about which alternative to try out. Rather, Gwen seemed suddenly blocked and more uptight than usual. I switched gears. "There's something going on in you right now that you're really bothered about, isn't there?" I encouraged her. "Do you know what it is?" "I'm not sure," she said haltingly. I wondered aloud whether she might be concerned that if she and Don made a decision they were working toward, and if they carried it out and it went well, then they might start to feel "cozy enough" that sex would become a possibility. "Something like that," was all she could offer. Since the time for our session was nearing an end, I suggested that if Gwen and Don could agree on a plan for being together in the next week, they should act on it, but that having sex should be left aside until we could have a chance, in the next session, to talk more about Gwen's (and, I assumed, Don's) anxiety about that part of their life.

Sixth Session

Sex became the focus of the next session, to be sure, but not quite as I had anticipated it would. Gwen arrived alone for the session. Something of an apparent emergency nature had happened at the farm, and it required Don's immediate attention. It had something to do with the cows. Even after Gwen explained it to me, I still didn't quite understand it, or maybe the details just didn't seem important to me. "It's just as well," she said, "I really wanted to come by myself today, anyway." Gwen was tearful and distraught.

She went on to say that she felt terribly guilty because "I lied to you the first time we met. Remember you asked Don and me if we had been involved with anyone outside our marriage? I said I hadn't, but that's not true." The story unfolded. While waitressing a few months ago, she had met Steve, a customer. Steve was a 40-year-old, divorced man whom she began talking to "as a friend." They talked a bit about his divorce, and mostly about Gwen's marital problems. Steve was warm, caring, and "a good listener." Their friendship took on a sexual dimension after a few weeks. That relationship, she insisted, was over, and she and Steve had "called it off" quite amicably. The "big thing" about the relationship for Gwen was not that it had happened, she said, but that she had gotten pregnant and had had an abortion. In fact, the time when she and Don had had their major blowup about two weeks before our first session, and just before she had seen Dr. Johnson (her family physician), was the day of the abortion. *That* was why she had seemed so depressed to Dr. Johnson, she said. "And," I thought to myself, *"that's* why you've seemed to be holding back in here; *that's* why your anger at Don waned so quickly; *that's* why I've been feeling I wasn't getting to know you very well; *that's* why you got blocked last week when you and Don were at the point of choosing a plan for being together."

The affair with Steve really was over, and he had been very "kind and considerate" at the time of Gwen's abortion. Not only had he paid for the cost of the abortion, but had gone with her for it, and had stayed with her all afternoon after the abortion "to help me get through it." Though they were no longer getting together, he called "at least a couple of times a week, to see how I'm doing." Gwen had no ill feeling toward Steve, she said.

She had told literally no one about the abortion (or the affair), but had desperately wanted to "get it off my chest" to someone. She had not brought it up in our three-way sessions "for obvious reasons." She was terrified about what Don (or maybe even Don's father) would do, either to her or to himself if he found out. He must never find out, she said, seemingly reminding herself to be extremely careful about revealing it, as much as implicitly asking me if I would keep her secret. Gwen felt that she had trusted me enough to talk about the affair and the abortion, but had just never had the opportunity to do so. After about half the session, she said she was already starting to feel "a lot better, just being able to say it out loud to *someone.*"

I told Gwen that I appreciated her telling me about what had gone on, and that it was not just her sense of despair about the whole thing that got her to tell me, but that it took a lot of courage, as well. The worst thing that could happen for Gwen at that moment, I thought, was for her to see me as another critical, disapproving father.

Typically, when one partner of a couple I am seeing reveals an ongoing affair to me, I make it clear that I will never take the responsibility for telling that person's husband or wife what has happened. If, in my judgment, however, the nonrevelation of an ongoing affair clearly seems to become a major impediment to the progress of my work with the couple, I will arrange for a brief individual session, and will certainly press the spouse to reveal his or her secret. Failing that, I will terminate my work with the couple, leaving it to the patient to deal with his or her spouse about the termination. If the affair is no longer continuing, I usually feel less of an ethical and practical obligation to press the secret-holder toward revelation. Moreover, in both circumstances (current versus past affairs), it is essential, I believe, that the therapist use his or her most carefully considered professional judgment about the likelihood of genuinely destructive, and possibly irreparable, consequences (e.g., homicide, suicide, physical abuse) that might ensue, were the affair to be revealed. Gwen's affair had ended, and I thought that she was not exaggerating at all the possibility of irreversible consequences were she to reveal her secret. Moreover, I felt doubly concerned about such a revelation because of the abortion on top of the affair. Therefore, I took the position that I agreed with Gwen that while she would always have the option of revealing her secret to Don in the future, I, too, thought it unwise, and unnecessary, to do so now. At the time of that session, that was the only time in my years of practice that I had ever taken such a position, and have done it only one other time since then. I felt simultaneously very uncomfortable about my stance with Gwen, but also confident that I had taken the most appropriate position, given my judgment of the circumstances and context of her secret.

The rest of the session was basically a lot of empathic listening on my part, and catharsis, on hers. I had no doubt that Gwen had profited immeasurably from simply having had the experience of "someone" listening to her pain without judgment or criticism, especially under these unusual circumstances, and especially that the "someone" was a male. The major concern that this session raised for me was my increased sense of uncertainty about the extent to which Gwen's understanding behavior toward Don in the last few weeks, and her recent efforts at conciliation, had been a mere defensive, guilt-generated "cover." I kept these musings to myself.

Seventh Session

Don apologized for having missed our last session. The emergency with the cows the previous week had turned out to be more than just a technical problem. Though Don denied any contribution to the situation, Mr. Olson blamed him for the difficulty, and barraged him with criticism for several days, threatening to dock his salary for the expenses they incurred, etc. After 3 days of this "harassment," Don "lost my cool and let him have it!" By his own account, Don unleashed all the anger he had felt toward his father for so long, told his father that he never felt Mr. Olson loved him, or even appreciated his contribution to the farm. Don certainly must have been acting out of character, because his mother, who rarely got involved in Don's relationship with his father, took Don aside a couple of days later and pleaded with him to apologize to Mr. Olson who, she said, felt "devastated" by what Don had said to him. But Don would not relent. "Let him stew with it for awhile, maybe he'll get the point," he said to me. "Besides," he added, "he'll probably just write the whole thing off as there being something wrong with me in a few days." "But even if he does, at least you finally told him how you feel," Gwen inserted, to which I added, "And that's something *you* won't forget, even if he does 'write it off'."

I was very impressed by Gwen's unprompted, clear and soothing support toward Don, and I began to feel less suspicious about the genuineness of the changes she had been showing since therapy began. While I still wondered whether Don's changes were transitory, produced merely out of his immediate fear about losing Gwen, I began to feel more believing of his changes, as well. After all, he could as easily have stood before his father, staring vacantly under the attack, as he usually did. And we certainly had not rehearsed for *this* kind of showdown. But perhaps Don had *prepared* for it.

Eighth Session

It had gone as Don had predicted. Within a few days, Mr. Olson was acting "like nothing ever happened." Don, resolute though he remained in "not taking back anything I said," nonetheless felt he had better "watch his step" with Mr. Olson. Though Mr. Olson still had not become aware of Don's having stopped doing many chores after dinner, Don had decided that "one confrontation like that is enough for a while, thank you," and had cut back some on putting the boys to bed with Gwen, though most nights, he still participated. Jonathan's behavior had changed moderately. "I think he's really getting the message from you, actually two messages: that you can be firm with him, *and* that you *are* his father," I said. "Yeah," Don replied, "a father can be a tough guy and still be fun to be with." His eyes teared just a bit. Obviously, he was lamenting never having had the chance to see the fun, playful, tender side of his own father. After a minute of silence, I said, "You know, Don, it may take a long time for you and *your* Dad to get together like you're doing with your own kids, but I think maybe it's still possible. I think your mother was telling the truth when she told you that your Dad was 'devastated' by what you said to him a couple weeks ago. I don't think he would have let your mother know that he felt devastated unless he figured she'd pass it on to you. Maybe that's his indirect way of letting you know that you *do* matter to him, as a son, not just as a sort of glorified hired hand." "I wish I could believe that," he responded; to which I said, "You're still so mad at him that, maybe for now, you won't *let* yourself believe it; maybe you'd be afraid you'd back off from what you said to him. You know, you *could* do both: you could stick by everything you said, and *still* believe it."

In a gentle way that seemed aimed not to get Don off the hook from the intensity of what he was feeling, but seemed to be more of an empathic appreciation of Don's pain at the moment, Gwen switched the subject. This time, I did not interrupt her as I usually did when I thought she was "cutting him off." Gwen had a "real job possibility" lined up, and was very excited about it. She was being considered for a half-time position as a salesperson at a local women's clothing store. She would have to be trained for it, but felt that "maybe there's somewhere up to go from there, if I do O.K." I congratulated her, and wished her luck on getting the job. Don's reaction to the news, earlier that week, was, "at least it's not in Madison." He wasn't trying to be "cute" or humorous; he meant it just the way he said it.

Without thinking, I reached out to shake Don's hand as we got up to end the session. "Take it easy," I said, "See you next week."

Ninth Session

Gwen got the job. And even though it was not in Madison, Don felt threatened, no doubt by Gwen's competence, because he knew she would do well at it and eventually move on to a better position. It was as if he felt that she might not only quickly outgrow the new job, but might outgrow him, as well.

Don had a new "ally." When he had gone to the University Bookstore a few weeks earlier to buy a copy of the book I had recommended he read, he started flipping through several other books in the "self-help" section. The book that attracted him, written by some male psychologist (the author and title of which were familiar to me then, but I've since forgotten), was about "men's liberation," emphasizing the idea that men as well as women suffer from restrictive roles. Don had virtually devoured the book, but had distorted the author's meaning to an incredible degree. He had taken the author to mean not simply that men needed to express their feelings more, but that they should stand up for their rights and what they believe in, as Don put. Translation (mine): "Enough of this bullshit about jobs and careers. Your place is in the home."

He had certainly stood up for what he believed, so much so that Gwen became infuriated, packed up the kids and a few belongings, and went to stay with her mother. Don was immovable: If Gwen could not be the kind of wife he wanted, then he didn't want her. And "to hell with this therapy stuff." He had even brought the book with him to the session, and had marked off several sentences as a sort of indirect expert testimony to support his case. I quickly scanned the underlined sentences, and saw how grossly out of context he had latched on to them. My efforts to translate what the author intended to get across were futile. He simply did not want any more of this talk. He'd made up his mind. Gwen was enraged and not about to give up her job, "not for anyone, not for your father, and not for you."

Don calmed down some, after a while. He thanked me for my help in getting him back in touch with his boys, and for my support and suggestions on how to deal with his father. He felt a lot better about those relationships than before we started therapy. And he wanted to be closer to Gwen, but just couldn't accept the idea of her "really moving out into the world." What's more, therapy was expensive (actually, it had cost them nothing, since their insurance policy covered five sessions per family member per year, and this was only our ninth meeting), and money was tight, as he had told me the first time we met. So, this would be our last session. Gwen could see me by herself if she wanted to, and "pay for it with her new job", he added sarcastically, but this was "good bye" for Don.

All my efforts in the next few minutes to connect with Don affectively and discuss the matter of termination failed. He refused to explore his feelings. Rather than challenge him at that point on whether he would actually go through with a divorce, I suggested that if they would go on to divorce, I would like to have just one more meeting with them in order to help them deal with the kinds of issues that would be coming up. I was especially concerned about the boys' welfare in all of this, I said. This seemed to grab him, and he acceded to "just one more meeting." I suggested that we let a little more time go by than our usual 1-week interval, and meet in 2 weeks, right after Christmas, "just to see how things have played themselves out."

Tenth Session

As I'd hoped, Don and Gwen had both backed off somewhat from their positions of two weeks earlier. Maybe the Christmas season had something to do with it. Don had asked Gwen to return, and she had done so, having made it clear to Don that while she appreciated that it was difficult for him to live with the idea of her really going after what she wanted outside the home, she was going to stick with her job.

Their short-lived separation had not been for naught in one other respect, as well. While at her mother's house, and talking to her mother about Gwen and Don's marital problems, Gwen had, as she put it, "*really* told her what's been going on." I took this to be a coded message to me that she had revealed her affair. To Gwen's relief and reassurance, her mother had listened with apparently genuine concern and caring. Mother, perhaps spurred on by Gwen's self-disclosure, told Gwen a great deal about her own marital problems many years earlier. They even hugged each other, "for the first time in years."

Jonathan was still giving them occasional "trouble" at bedtime, but, on the whole, they felt that situation was greatly improved. Nothing was different *between* Don and Mr. Olson, but it seemed to me that there had been at least a moderate beginning of change *within* Don about that relationship.

Since neither Don nor Gwen raised the issue of whether they (Don, especially) had reconsidered continuing in therapy, I decided to respect the decision Don had made two weeks earlier, and did not bring up their returning to see me. We all seemed to drift into a more "social" kind of chitchat after awhile, with them asking me questions about my family, etc. After about a half hour, I suggested that we not "just fill the time just to fill it," and that we should probably just end the session. Looking at Don, I reminded them that I would always be glad to see either or both of them again, should they feel the need to come back.

Follow-Up

About 4 months after our last session, Gwen phoned me to try to straighten out some kind of confusion about their bill, she said. Since the question could have been handled by my billing office easily enough, I was sure that she had used the question about their account as a pretense to call to let me know how life was going for the two of them, so I asked. Don and Mr. Olson were still distant, and not a word of their confrontation the previous fall had been spoken; Jonathan was only occasionally a problem at bedtime, and Don participated in the bedtime routine most nights (and even *had* given the boys their bath a couple of times); Don was reading some more self-help books, mostly on how to be more assertive; Gwen's job was going very well, and was still half-time; Don and Gwen still socialized with other couples rarely, but with a new solution—they invited friends to their home, which made Don feel much more at ease; and Gwen felt she had gotten a bit closer to her mother. I wished her well, and sent my regards to Don.

Coda

As I think back on my several weeks of working with the Olsons, I am mostly pleased by what we accomplished in a relatively brief time: Don had begun to become a real father to his own kids; he had finally, at least once, let Mr. Olson know he had feelings; he had apparently become rather curious about himself and was continuing to help himself with his own bibliotherapy; and he was occasionally venturing out socially. Gwen had stuck with her career aims, and was doing well; she had begun, in a significant way, to heal a major rift of many years with her mother; she was not reflexively jumping into the caretaker role, but seemed to be finding a better balance between taking care of others and attending to her own needs; she had taken a major risk at trusting a man in her life to listen to her pain, and take it seriously. And finally, it seemed that neither of the Olsons was any longer clinically depressed.

At the same time, I am aware of all that we never got to in our work together, or at least did not complete. I still have no idea whether Don and Gwen have gotten any more intimate, other than around the issues we discussed in rather limited ways; I doubt that Don's attitudes about women's role in the family has changed very much; I am still concerned about Don's social isolation and anxiety, and, of course, the gap between him and Mr. Olson; and I am ambivalent, at best, about the limited extent to which Gwen and I were able to work through her feelings about her abortion.

A therapist probably always sees more possibilities for meaningful change than his or her patients. But a therapist also must respect patients' limits on how much they want, or even can tolerate, the help of a therapist. We should not hold on tighter or longer than we are asked to, generally. I have not heard from the Olsons in almost two years, and I suspect I never will. Though a portion of the couples I work with return for either occasional "booster sessions," or for additional short courses of therapy, and some will drop me a note about how they're doing even years after we have stopped meeting, most of them I never hear from again. In these cases, I can only hope that, in our usually short time together, I have done something to help them get on and stay on a new track in their unfolding lives together.

References

Bagarozzi, D. A., & Giddings, C. W. (1984). The role of cognitive constructs and attributional processes in family therapy: Integrating intrapersonal, interpersonal and systems dynamics. In L. Wolberg & M. Aronson (Eds.), *Group and family therapy, 1983*. New York: Brunner/Mazel.

Burns, D. (1981). *Feeling good: The new mood therapy*. New York: Signet.

Doherty, W. J., & Colangelo, N. (1984). The family FIRO model: A modest proposal for organizing family treatment. *Journal of Marital and Family Therapy, 10*, 19–29.

Gurman, A. S. (1978). Contemporary marital therapies: A critique and comparative analysis of psychodynamic, behavioral and systems theory approaches. In T. Paolino & B. McCrady (Eds.), *Marriage and marital therapy*. New York: Brunner/Mazel.

Gurman, A. S. (1980). Behavioral marriage therapy in the 1980's: The challenge of integration. *American Journal of Family Therapy*, *8*, 86-96.

Gurman, A. S. (1981). Integrative marital therapy: Toward the development of an interpersonal approach. In S. Budman (Ed.), *Forms of brief therapy*. New York: Guilford.

Gurman, A. S. (1982a). A rationale for the inclusion of behavioral and paradoxical techniques in psychodynamic marital therapy. *Partnerberatung*, *19*, 1–11.

Gurman, A. S. (1982b). Using paradox in psychodynamic marital therapy. *American Journal of Family Therapy*, *10*(1), 72–74.

Gurman, A. S. (1982c). Changing collusive patterns in marital therapy. *American Journal of Family Therapy*, *10*(4), 71-73.

Gurman, A. S. (1984, September). *Issues in the development of integrative approaches to marital therapy*. Paper presented at the International Symposium on Couples Therapy, Zurich, Switzerland.

Jacobson, N. S., & Margolin, G. (1979). *Marital therapy: Strategies based on social learning and behavioral exchange*. New York: Brunner/Mazel.

Minuchin, S. (1974). *Families and family therapy*. Cambridge, Massachusetts: Harvard University Press.

Sager, C. J. (1981). Couples contracts and marital therapy. In A. Gurman & D. Kniskern (Eds.), *Handbook of family therapy*. New York: Brunner/Mazel.

Whitaker, C. A., & Keith, D. V. (1981). Symbolic–experiential family therapy. In A. Gurman & D. Kniskern (Eds.), *Handbook of family therapy*. New York: Brunner/Mazel.

Willi, J. (1982). *Couples in collusion*. New York: Jason Aronson.

Willi, J. (1984). The concept of collusion: A combined systemic–psychodynamic approach to marital therapy. *Family Process*, *23*, 177–185.

Chapter 13

To Marry or Not: Treating a Living-Together Couple in Midlife

Florence W. Kaslow, PhD

To encapsulate one's philosophy or theory of marital therapy in a few pages is a compressing task that forces the writer to remember that parsimony is a valued asset of the researcher and author. Since it is not an integral aspect of my loquacious expository style, the same kind of discipline is utilized here that I exercise with patients in order to provide them with as much opportunity as possible to tell *their story*, experience and come to know *their feelings*, explore *their options*, and set *their goals* and preferred pathways for achieving them.

First, after perusing the data they have filled out on the intake form, I try sensitively to ascertain what brought them to my office with a request for therapy at this time. Has the discontent and tension mounted over time, or was there a severe precipitating event or argument? Are both troubled about the conflict, or is one perceived as indifferent or engaging in denial by the other? As they respond to these queries, and many more that are likely to follow, I assess their mood, affect, intelligence, interaction, and transactions. Since I try to deal with intrapsychic as well as interpersonal conflicts while treating the individuals *and* their dyadic relationship, my ongoing diagnostic evaluation focuses on understanding each member of the couple as well as their relational system.

Once they have unburdened as to what the internal stresses and/ or external presses are that motivated them to seek treatment at this time, and the presenting problem(s) as they discern them to be, I ask that they tell about their joint history as a couple. This may take several sessions. While they revisit their past, I respond to feelings, raise questions, and make tentative comments regarding patterns of behavior and coping mechanisms. The history sought includes how they met, what attracted them to each other, who took the overt initiative, what were the factors that kept the relationship blossoming, what kinds of things they argued about, how long they dated before making a commitment, and whether they lived together, and if so for how long and how did it go. Other areas of exploration address such questions as, Did either feel "trapped" into the marriage? What were the reactions of both sets of parents and the rest of their respective families of origin to their proposed union? How much had they explored expectations of each other and preferred life styles and objectives? Did they engage in any premarital contracting, and if so, how explicit was it (Sager, 1976)? Do they periodically renegotiate their contract? How did their sexual relationship evolve and what was problematic and what was gratifying? What is the nature of their sexuality now? Questions about finances, in-laws, children, vocational and avocational pursuits, values, frustrations and aspirations, dreams and disappointments, and extra-marital involvements may also be raised if deemed relevant, while the core focus remains on the dilemmas about which they sought treatment. Some interventions geared toward modifications in behavior to bring about changes in the desired direction are also made during this initial period, while a clearer picture of the couple's separate and interactional dynamics and functioning continues to emerge.

As can be deduced from the foregoing, my philosophic orientation is a hybrid that in previous writings I have designated as a *diaclectic* model (Kaslow, 1980, 1981a, 1981b). "Diaclectic" is a term I invented

> to convey the fact that this non-model draws selectively and eclectically from numerous sources and seeks a new, more compelling dialectic synthesis of theoretical formulations conducive to astute analysis of a couple or family's difficulties and to facilitating the resolution of the troubles and dysfunctions. Clinically it makes treatment a continuing challenge in which therapist and patients . . . explore together—tuning into each other's conscious and unconscious processes and verbal and nonverbal communications. (Kaslow, 1981a, pp. 347–348)

One hopes that it fosters a judicious amalgamation of the science and the art of psychotherapy at its highest level.

My theory and practice of therapy reflect my original psychoanalytic heritage, as should be visible in the case presentation that follows. It also incorporates concepts and techniques derived from Bowenian systems theory (Bowen, 1977), from the contextual-relational school of Boszormenyi-Nagy and Spark (1973), and from the experiential approach of Whitaker (1976) and Keith (1981). Some aspects of Epstein and Bishop's (1981) problem-solving approach and other cognitive–behavioral modalities often surface, as do key elements regarding boundaries derived from Minuchin's (1971) work in structural therapy, reframing, and use of paradox from the strategic work of individuals like Haley (1976) and the systemic epistemology of the Milan School (Selvini Palazzoli *et al.*, 1978). Inherent also are key formulations adopted from communication theoreticians such as Satir (1964) and Jackson (1961). There is also an overall humanistic–existential orientation (Maslow, 1968; May, 1969). This "diaclectic" world view has close parallels to the Duhls' integrative approach (Duhl & Duhl, 1981) and to Lazarus's (1981) multimodal theory and practice. To the extent that it is dynamic, expanding, and sometimes deleting of concepts that do not serve to describe accurately or help to alter reality, it is hard to crystallize in static terms, and being in continual flux, is nonpurist and nonorthodox.

The following case reflects the freedom to utilize a diaclectic approach within the carefully structured sanctuary of the therapeutic office. Since the couple in this case were not married, and were in their fifth and sixth decades of life, respectively, having accrued substantial life experiences separately, their individual as well as joint history was elicited in some detail. It is presented here as two separate streams finally merging for purposes of narrative clarity, though in actuality these were interwoven in the sessions and overlapped in terms of treatment focus. The approach encompasses premarital therapy for a couple in which each is contemplating a second marriage.

The World of Cynthia and Don

In early March 1982 Cynthia called for an appointment. She had been referred to me by the therapist she had been seeing in individual treatment. The request was for conjoint relationship therapy for her and Don, the man with whom she was living. She felt that she loved him deeply but was distressed by the fact that the relationship was so turbulent and that there were some difficulties in the area of sexual gratification. They also wanted to deal with their respective "crazies" in couples therapy, and to discontinue their separate individual treatments. She was calling for both of them, and they wanted to be seen quickly. In keeping with the philosophy of my practice to see new patients as soon as possible in order to begin when they are consciously feeling troubled and motivated, an appointment was set for the next week.

Cynthia's Story

At 48 years of age, Cynthia was an attractive, stately, and trim redhead. She always arrived well groomed in a sporty, semitailored mode. She seemed to have good social skills, appearing friendly, considerate, and energetic. She was working as a real estate saleswoman in south Florida, and her competence and ability to earn a good living at this time in her life seemed assured.

As she told her story over the next few months of weekly intense sessions, the following facts emerged: Cindy was born into a staunchly Catholic family. They felt that she had a vocational calling, and so she was sent to live and study at a convent from the time she was 13 years of age until she was 17½ years old. At this juncture she decided she did not want to be a nun and left the convent. She acquired a general education diploma (G.E.D.) in lieu of a regular high school diploma. Within the next few months and after very little prior dating experience, she married her next-door neighbor, a young Catholic male who, like Cindy, was a virgin and sexually inhibited in attitude. The first 15 years of their marriage followed the then traditional pattern, with nothing extraordinary occurring. He worked and came to earn a substantial living, providing well for his family in their New England home. Cindy stayed home to raise their three sons. Sid, now 30 years old, had been born during the first year of marriage when Cindy, at barely 18, was still a new bride. The other two boys were Mickey, 27 years old, and Bob, born many years later, only 18 years of age.

Life changed markedly when Cindy was in her early 30s and Bob only 3 years old. Her husband, at a business function, took his first drink. He rapidly became an alcoholic. When drunk, he was physically abusive and would beat Cindy. After one particularly brutal beating, she went, bloody and bruised, to seek counsel from her priest and her parents. Each told her "to go back home, for it is a wife's duty to stay with her husband under all circumstances," and "to turn the other cheek when necessary." Remonstrated that it is God's will that "marriage is until death do us part," and with her hoped-for support system subjugating her physical and emotional needs for well-being to conformity to church doctrine, she returned home, frightened and dejected. She stayed with her husband for 5 harrowing years of abuse and criticism, trying to find a suitable alternative to the living hell that engulfed her and her sons. She applied to the church for a legal separation, but this was denied, and another avenue of escape was sealed off. Her husband had become a known and respected politician in the Irish Catholic community and a sizable contributor to the church. Even when he got drunk at a local bar or political function, the police merely brought him home. Since drunkenness and wife beating were fairly commonplace in their community, no one understood why Cindy made such a fuss and couldn't roll with the punches as so many others did. Finally, after a particularly vicious attack, she decided she could no longer retain faith in a religion that held marriage to be more sacred than dignity, decency, and life itself and therefore felt she could no longer abide by its dictates.

One day, while her husband was at work, she loaded the three boys and a few possessions into her car, took a thousand dollars from their bank account, and, determined to make a new and better life for them, headed south. As the distance between them and their former home grew greater, they all felt an increasing sense of relief from fear and captivity. The children regretted leaving their dogs and horses behind, but not having left their father. They sang, enjoyed the trip, and planned their future. On arrival in Florida they rented an inexpensive apartment, and Cindy worked three jobs to make ends meet. Despite a greatly reduced standard of living, they felt more relaxed and happier. They had a marvelous time at the beach, whenever time permitted. Cindy's main regret was that she had not had the courage and fortitude to make the break earlier and follow her own internal logic that she should protect herself and the boys from abuse by departing.

Her husband, Jerry, had detectives try to trace her, since she had virtually disappeared, leaving no forwarding address. A year later he appeared at their home, contrite and sober. He indicated that he no longer drank and pleaded to get back together. Since Cindy and the boys had acclimatized to Florida and wanted to remain there, when she agreed to a reconciliation, they sold their elegant house in New England and rented a larger and nicer home in the Miami area than the quarters in which they had been living heretofore. Cindy and Jerry did some traveling during the next 6 months, and the family had fun loafing and being together again. Then Jerry got a job and soon after began drinking again. By the end of the year, he stealthily departed, but not before canceling the lease, without informing Cindy. Not only was she evicted from their home, but she was left saddled with in-numerable unpaid bills. Again, Cindy got a job, moved into a shack given her by her employer, and began to put life back together for herself and the three boys while living in a roach-infested tenement.

Because of her competence, tenacity, and determination, she again did well financially during the next few years. She abhorred being touched or having physical contact with men as a consequence of several factors, including her convent upbringing and the physical abuse she had been subjected to by her ex-husband. Thus, she abstained from any sexual involvement and concentrated on building her career and raising her family. Finally, she met Skip and they dated casually. He was kind to and considerate of her sons. He had been wounded in war by exploding shrapnel, and his entire genital area was scarred, causing impotence. Since Cindy did not want to be bothered by sexual demands, his condition was acceptable to her, and they decided to get married. For 5 years this brother–sister relationship proved reasonably satisfying and stabilizing. He became so devoted to the family that all agreed to his adoption of her youngest son.

Cindy stayed with Skip for 5 years, during which time she became quite successful in her real estate career. The two older boys grew up and moved out. She utilized some of the money she made to purchase antiques and other works of art. Then she had to have a thyroidectomy because of a growth in her throat. Although it was benign, the fear of cancer was great. During the recuperation period, Cindy realized she had been in self-imposed "hiding" in this marriage and that this was no longer satisfying. She saw her recovery as a reprieve to live more fully and decided that she wanted and would seek to find a better relationship than was possible with Skip, who was not very capable of any affectional, sexual involvement, and who, like her first husband, engaged in behaviors that were destructive to Cindy. Thus, she resorted to a second divorce.

In mid-1980, shortly after becoming single again, Cindy met Don at a singles group where both were participating in a "rap group." But before we explore the evolution of their tumultuous relationship, and what finally catapulted them into couples therapy 2 years after they first gravitated toward each other, I will double back and recapitulate Don's equally idiosyncratic and fascinating "story." Like Cindy's, his story unfolded in fragments and nonsequentially over a period of several months. It is reconstructed here in chronological order for purposes of etching a life-size portrait of the man Don was at age 50 when he first appeared at my office.

Don's Story

Don's still hot anger at being born an illegitimate child of a Jewish mother, an unusual happening in a Jewish family in conservative Michigan in the 1930s, surfaced when he recounted the circumstances of his birth. Because it was an uncommon phenomenon, when his mother decided she could not raise an infant alone, there were no Jewish orphanages to which she could take him. Thus he was placed in a Catholic orphanage where he remained until he was 16 years old. Early on, he and his peers were made aware of this religious difference. He was taunted with jeers of being a "Christ Killer" and a "Dirty Jew Boy." Although he did not know what being Jewish really entailed, he knew it was a painful identity. He recalled other odious events of his experience as an orphan—for example, that when he (and the others) wet the bed at night, they were compelled to come to morning flag raising with the wet sheet prominently displayed over their heads. Then punishment was heaped on embarrassment. He developed a tough exterior in order to survive rejection from his family of origin compounded by the degradations bestowed from his environment. To fill the long hours, he also developed a respect for books and became an avid reader. This penchant for learning through reading has continued throughout his life, and although he never was able to acquire a formal college education, I found him to be extremely well versed, scholarly, and perhaps "brilliant." (More on this later in regard to his extensive knowledge of psychoanalytic theory.)

At age 16 he was permitted to leave the orphanage. He went in search of the mother he knew he had somewhere and found her in the environs of the institution in which he had been reared. He spent the next few years "knocking around," getting to know his mother and maternal grandmother. Also, he was determined to find out what it meant to be "a Jew" and to try to find a sense of his own Jewish identity.

By the time he was in his late teens, the many deprivations and degradations he had suffered had contributed to his becoming a pugnacious character. After a brawl, in which someone cast aspersions on both his Jewishness and his masculinity, he was booked on an assault-and-battery charge, found guilty, and sentenced to a year in prison. Young, small in stature, and new to "doing time in a joint," he was already streetwise enough to know that he had to devise a scheme to protect himself from such horrors of prison life as gang rapes and forced homosexual liaisons. He decided not to brush his teeth; the offensive smell of halitosis was noxious enough to deter predators. He voluntarily isolated himself as much as possible and again filled his idle hours with extensive reading. By the time of his release, he had resolved to keep his rage controlled so that he would never again run into difficulty with the law. In this he succeeded admirably well.

By then, Don longed for a respectable way of life and establishing roots with a family and in a community. He harnessed his excellent native intelligence and combined it with his drive to be upwardly mobile and acquire an upper-middle-class life style. Through much determination and hard work over the ensuing 25 years, he built his own thriving business as a sales representative. He recognized his strong need for freedom for doing things in his own way, and so he was careful to be his own boss, at least in the vocational sphere of his existence. He met and married Phyllis, a Jewish woman who came from a "good family" and who shared his desire to have a conventional marriage. They had two children, Saul and Debra. Don became an extremely devoted father, consciously wanting to assure that his children would have the continuity of love and affection and sense of belonging in a stable and secure family that he had lacked. (Unconsciously, in providing this for them, he was also hoping to fill in some of the missing ingredients from his own childhood.) His wife's primary role was homemaker and mother. His sense of self-esteem was integrally entwined with earning a good living, providing all the necessities and some of the luxuries for his family, being an involved father who guided his children toward the pursuit of a fine education and into professions as careers, becoming respected in his community, and living as a person in a family that was proud of and identified with their Jewishness.

The first 10 years of his marriage were reasonably gratifying in all of these aspects. But when he was in his early 30s the "heavy hand of fate" struck ominously once again: His wife had a radical mastectomy. He was told that the cancer had spread and that her years were limited. From then on, the family revolved around her condition, catering to and protecting her. Phyllis became sullen and depressed; she lost all interest in sex and never regained any libidinal drive. Her needs were paramount; the children's came second, and Don's were regarded by all as unimportant. He worked increasingly hard to pay the continuous medical bills, spending more and more time on the road for business purposes. Despite his disappointment with Phyllis and their marital relationship, for 10 years he felt duty-bound to stay with his cancer-stricken wife, who clung to life despite medical predictions that her living this long was overwhelmingly against the odds. He also remained faithful sexually, which meant virtual celibacy for years, accompanied by increasing resentment and frustration.

One day, after sneezing and coughing violently, Don felt severe pain in his neck and right arm. When it persisted, he was X-rayed and diagnosed as having a herniated cervical disk; he was also found to be suffering from polycythemia. The illness produced marked fatigue, inability to sleep, and deterioration in his general health, and was accompanied by severe depression. For a year he was in excruciating pain and almost totally bedridden. Even though he had ministered to his wife's physical needs and done many of the housekeeping chores for so long—for she kept firing the domestic help he hired— she made no effort to nurse him in his time of debilitating crises, and he often had to crawl out of bed to get his own meals. The children, about whom he cared so deeply, also neglected him, as they were too busy with their social activities and studies to do any of the nursing chores or even to spend much quality time with him. He lay in agonizing silence, with only his faithful dog on the foot of his bed for companionship.

Then, to his extreme dismay, his beloved daughter came home with a Syrian boyfriend, who, despite his involvement with Debra, participated in anti-Semitic and anti-Israeli activities. They had met at the university where both were students. Don found this relationship intolerable and saw it as a total rejection of him and the heritage he had labored so diligently to acquire and impart to his children. When Debra decided she would marry Abdul, with or without Don's consent, and Phyllis backed up her daughter's right to choose her own spouse and her own religious and political beliefs, Don became enraged and threatened to disown his daughter. She defied him and eloped with Abdul.

Depressed, disillusioned, and outraged over the horrible state of his marital and family existence, Don finally decided he had to extricate himself and filed for divorce. His bitterness increased markedly during and following the divorce process, since both children sided with their mother and the judge awarded her a disproportionate share of the assets; she had successfully played on the judge's sympathies about her malady and made light of her husband's affliction. She somehow wrested major interest in his business from him, and all he was awarded was a fixed disability allowance of about $30,000 a year, for, in truth, he could no longer work. This was quite a comedown from the $100,000 figure he had been accustomed to earning during the recent peak years of his career. Incapacitated and isolated, he harbored suicidal ideas. The male psychiatrist whom he had been seeing for 5 years suggested that he needed an intensive experience at a human potential growth center to enable him to "find himself" and become more pleasure oriented, so he left the Midwest for the West Coast and spent a year living and exploring himself intrapsychically and in relationships at a well-known "growth center." Here, too, he felt alienated, and although he mastered the concepts, vocabulary, and rhetoric of the human potential movement, he left there still feeling beaten, hopeless, and discouraged. His neck pain had not abated; the frequent group sessions he participated in to decrease his symptoms and worries and the nude marathons in the warm pool had not helped much more than traction had.

Following the mishap, he had tried chiropractors, orthopedists, acupuncture, and cortisone injections in a futile effort to decrease the constant ache. A neurological examination proved negative. At one point, he was on 200 milligrams of Tofranil a day, but this led to severe dizziness and had to be terminated. Next, he took codeine daily.

I received one medical report, written after a myelogram, which read: "*Impression*—that of osteoarthritis of the cervical spine with possible mild spondylosis and a rather major factor of muscular/cutaneous psychophysiological reaction." Another, based on a chest X-ray, reported: "*Impression*—findings suggest mild to moderate chronic obstructive pulmonary disease. No evidence of active pulmonary disease."

Clearly, there was some chronic physical base for his continual physical suffering.

Disheartened and terribly alone, he decided to move to south Florida and rent an inexpensive apartment and live out his remaining days in a warm climate. He son, now in college, spurned him as much as did his daughter. Don brought along and added to his sizable record collection of fine classical music and opera; this was one of the few possessions that afforded him any comfort. He expected, and perhaps wanted, to die soon.

Yet some life force still rippled, albeit mostly underground. As a bachelor in his late 40s, he found himself sought after by women. But he was so frightened that it took the sure encouragement and experienced guidance of a professional prostitute who befriended him for a period of several years to defrost him even slightly—to nurture him, to help him overcome the impotence that had developed and lasted for 2 years from 1977 to 1979, and to teach him how to pleasure and be pleasured by a woman. This was a new and appealing realm of experience for him. He remained grateful to Desirée for helping him regain his masculine pride and continued to relish her friendship.

However, an issue that he talked about early in therapy with me and that remained a paramount concern for many months was that after his indoctrination to the wonderful world of creative sexual experience by Desirée, a pattern had developed that was a mixed blessing. When he had an erection, it lasted for hours. Normal detumescence did not occur. During his bachelor days in Florida, he found this sustaining quality had made him a sought-after lover by women who were more accustomed to sexual partners who reached climax quickly and left them unsatisfied and frustrated. His staying power was prolonged; he did not convey to his partners the physical agony and emotional anguish that his inability to ejaculate caused him because he sought sexual gratification and release but not intimacy or mutual regard in the communication realm. None of the various therapists and other physicians he had consulted had dealt with this dilemma nor succeeded in helping him alleviate his depressed, pessimistic frame of mind.

Woman Meets Man

The evening they met at a church-sponsored singles group, Cindy found Don's incisive comments intriguing. He spoke knowledgeably in a philosophic vein and immediately impressed her with his keen mind and articulate manner. He was markedly different from the previous men in her life. Short of stature and with dark, curly hair, even his looks were the polar opposite of her usual tall, thin, blond husbands and other escorts. Don found soft-spoken, svelte Cindy appealing and viewed her from the first as a "class act." They sought each other out, each longing to fill the emotional void in their lives yet not wanting to risk being badly hurt again. Don introduced Cindy to the glorious world of music; they spent hours listening to his records. She acquired a love and appreciation for music; he was a marvelous teacher–guide to opera and the classics, and she was an apt and eager student. They became lovers, and Don taught Cindy much that he had learned from Desirée. After her many years of sexual starvation, Cindy thoroughly enjoyed the long hours they spent in sexual play; he awakened and fulfilled her sexual appetites, but his inability to reach climax perturbed him greatly, and the accompanying pain persisted.

The Vicissitudes of Life and Therapy

When Cindy and Don first entered my office, I was aware of an immediate visceral reaction to him. His physical resemblance to my father and his brothers was so striking, it was uncanny. In stature, looks, and age there was so much similarity that we might have been brother and sister, perhaps even twins. His caustic, cynical manner and success via gutsy determination without benefit of formal education also was a replay of the personality and modus operandi of several of my paternal uncles. I felt an immediate kinship with and strong desire to help this troubled, tormented man. Mindful of the pitfalls of over-identification and of countertransference reactions, I told them about this response to him by the end of the first session. It facilitated the difficult "joining process" and set the foundation for the precarious therapeutic alliance. Cindy had wanted a female therapist, and Don felt that he had been dragged along. He had not found his previous therapies very helpful, and because of numerous power and control issues in relation to women, definitely did not want to be treated by a female therapist. He felt sufficient acceptance and bonding to agree to a second session.

When they entered therapy, Cindy felt that she had fallen in love with Don and wanted to make a commitment to the relationship and strive to improve it so that they could plan to marry. Don wanted the comforts of a living-together arrangement but said he would never marry and disliked being "nagged" to do so. He felt uncomfortable with Cindy's Florida friends and their life-style, which included sailing, speed boating, fast cars, cocktail parties, and big social bashes. He disliked her having an income that exceeded his and criticized her for being a meticulous housekeeper and her willing and gracious manner of preparing meals and serving him. He was unaccustomed to being catered to; he had been a virtual servant to his wife and had detested it. He could not understand that Cindy did not perceive the homemaker–chef role as demeaning and that, in fact, she enjoyed facets of it. Bringing him a cup of tea and making the apartment attractive and clean actually gave her pleasure. He considered himself unappealing and unlovable (remnants of the self as the grotesque, foul-smelling prisoner) and did not believe Cindy or anyone else could find him desirable and lovable.

Both felt and expressed great empathy for one another's sufferings in the past. They had listened to each other's sad stories and offered comfort and solace, really seeming to have comprehended and touched each other's pain. They had less understanding of how the multiple determinants inherent in life experiences, including prior depriving and/or devastating relationships, came to be embedded in their present personalities, patterns of behavior, and interpersonal transactions.

At the outset, Cindy's goals for therapy were to reduce the amount of unproductive arguing and conflict in the relationship, and to convince Don that he was lovable and that she did love him and would not abandon him as other key women in his life had. Don's spoken objectives were to ascertain if this therapy might be more meaningful for him, and if so, to bring about reduction in his chronic physical pain (he was at that point on 50 milligrams per day of Valium) and alleviation of his depression. He wanted companionship and stabilization of the relationship so that the struggles for power would end—with Cindy acquiescing to his life-style preferences, which included a semipermanent living-together arrangement with no commitment of future marriage. He also wanted more satisfying sex, which for him meant being able to achieve orgasm during intercourse without having to resort to masturbation and delayed, painful postcoital release.

The Process of Therapy

From March through August of 1982 Don and Cindy were usually seen weekly. For the most part, sessions ran 50 minutes; on three or four occasions when the tension level was extremely high, we held double sessions. They had to travel about an hour each way and sometimes, because of Cindy's work commitments or because of an argument, they came in separate cars. When Don drove for long periods of time, his neck and shoulder pain became accentuated.

From the first session on, both participated actively, although Don tended to talk more. Cindy's facial expressions and body gestures showed that she was engaged in the process, and she would enter into the dialogue whenever she had something to say. Some days, when she was bursting with particularly good news about their progress or excessive anxiety over their impasses, she would lead off—rapidly plunging in to share the latest insights, battles, or leaps forward.

Sessions 1 and 2 were largely devoted to getting the outline of the individual and couples history chronicled above. Many of the more personal details and feelings surrounding life events and touchy relationships were recounted in later sessions as they were evoked by my raising questions regarding memories, old feelings surfacing in new situations, and trying to link together and then disrupt dysfunctional patterns of behavior.

Don's earlier therapists had treated him using ego-supportive therapy combined with medication. He had been on antidepressants and pain killers—including Percodan, codeine, and Demerol prior to the current megadose of Valium. Since he had read and voraciously devoured books on psychoanalysis, personality theory, and humanistic psychology, he had been able to spar with them intellectually about his problems. He may even at times have enjoyed being a partner in a therapy game, and may have garnered additional self-knowledge, but neither his feelings toward himself or others nor his behavior had changed in any significant way.

During the second session he indicated that not only had he spent a year at a growth center but had subsequently been "Rolfed" and learned to utilize Transcendental Meditation. He was sophisticated about therapy, well aware of its limitations, and pessimistic about whether this could really be substantially different and better. From the beginning, I felt drawn to this couple and challenged to facilitate their striving toward health.

Therefore, I decided I had to move in a creative pathway and that I would try to cut beneath the verbal sparring and enter the affective realm of his existence. I realized the potential risks inherent in a combined probing and confrontational approach, yet my clinical assessment was that he had both the gutsiness and ego strength to sustain it and that he was functioning at a sufficient level of anxiety and discontent that he might be amenable to some different kind of powerful intervention.

It also appeared that Cindy sensed my therapeutic unconditional acceptance of them and my quick personal liking for them and that, given this, she too might respond to some leading questions and direct interpretations. I indicated, therefore, that therapy would be intense and probably turbulent and that anger was a theme that we would be giving a great deal of attention to. Both agreed that they would give it a try.

Cindy called several days after the second meeting to relate that Don had gone on a horrible 12-hour screaming rampage after the session. He wanted her to leave, told her, "I hate you, your friends, your furniture." She packed, crushed at this turn of events, and planned to leave the next morning. By then he was calmer and assumed she would stay. She was ambivalent, realizing she did not want to be on a roller-coaster and wondering whether she was reverting to her former masochistic self. He wanted to return to a former male therapist–friend who was gentler with him and more supportive of his behavior, but this therapist was not eligible for insurance reimbursement, and I was. He feared "the girls" (Cindy and I) would gang up on him. I listened while Cindy poured out her sadness and hurt, reassured her

I felt I could be of some real help (which I believed at a deep, intuitive level), and asked if it would be O.K. if I called Don. She agreed and I called. He seemed worried that Cindy would leave and abandon him and could not believe I really cared about what would happen to him. He reconfirmed the next appointment. I realized that my candor had contributed to his panic being externalized and directed at Cindy; that he was like a seething cauldron.

In the next session we began to look at his deep-rooted sources of anger. He filled in some of the pitiful aspects of his life in the orphanage and then went on, for the first time with me, to recount the episode that landed him in prison and what it was like for him to "do time." Since I had had experience setting up a correctional psychology internship program, which periodically included walking a cell block, supervising interns in the prison, consulting to prison systems, and much reading and teaching about prison life, I was able to "listen with the third ear" (Reik, 1948). He was amazed and appreciative of my sensitivity to and knowledge about what this terrible period in his life must have been like for him. Fearing rejection, it had taken him many months before he had divulged this part of his background to Cindy. He was also testing me out with this revelation. When he mentioned not brushing his teeth as a way to make himself vile to the other inmates, I told him I thought it an innovative and clever way of handling a difficult situation and that it reflected good reality testing. He was surprised at my interpretation, since prior therapists had told him this was extremely manipulative and one aspect of his character disorder. I countered that perhaps they had never been in prison and were not aware of the need for protective armor to avoid the sexual overtures of other prisoners. He was intrigued and heartened by these comments, yet somewhat uncertain if I could really accept him knowing his prior violence and status as an ex-con.

Also in this session, he reported that the day before he had performed cunnilingus on Cindy. She had enjoyed it immensely and had tactilely stimulated him until he reached orgasm. This was the first time in several years he had been able to achieve orgasm in a dyadic interaction, that is, without strenuous masturbation. He wondered if this was the beginning of a breakthrough; I responded with cautious optimism. He reported that sometimes during the period of abstinence from intercourse with his ex-wife in the last years of his marriage, he had watched pornographic films for arousal and now sometimes looked at pictures in *Playboy* magazine while masturbating. He wanted to know if this was O.K., that is, normal, or if I considered it deviant. We explored if he was seeking information about human sexuality and generally perceived acceptable modes of satisfaction or if he wanted approval. In actuality, he wanted and received both, with my suggesting that healthy sexuality can encompass a broad range of activities, including fantasizing a partner and using pictures and film evocatively. As he felt acceptance and that he was not being labeled "kinky," he relaxed somewhat and articulated his desire for orgastic fulfillment during intercourse. He and Cindy had experienced this only once in their 2½-year relationship, shortly after they became involved with one another. She was due to leave for a business trip to South America, and he was unhappy about her going. Cindy felt perhaps his successfully ejaculating while inside her had been his ultimate seductive effort to show her he could perform wonderfully well and therefore deter her from departing. Whether this was so or not, clearly sexual politics was an ingredient in the relationship stew.

The session culminated with Don saying that he could not understand what she saw in him and why she wanted to keep the relationship going. He felt useless in that he did not earn a living, was frequently in pain, did not perform well sexually, and was not able or willing to live in the showy, fast lane. Cindy tried to explain, but could not convey her feelings. When I suggested that it had little to do with any activities or what he did, rather to what he offered as a person, his way of being in the world, Cindy impulsively said, "That's it—it's what you are—you're a beautiful person to me." She hugged me good-bye; I reciprocated and then turned and following an unexpected impulse, hugged Don and lightly kissed him on the forehead. He was shocked; this was incomprehensible behavior to him for anyone, especially a therapist. Spontaneously, it felt right to me; it proved to be a major milestone. To both of them it came to signify that they really were receiving total unconditional regard, acceptance, and caring. They realized that they could reveal anything, no matter how sordid or seamy, without fear of derision or rejection.

In Session 4, both talked more about their separate families. Cindy's two older sons were living on their own and kept in contact. They seemed to have arrived at a reasonably comfortable relationship with

their mom, and they liked Don. Her youngest, Bob, periodically stayed
with Cindy and Don, and they got along well. Apparently Don was
kind and considerate of her sons and offered counsel and caring appropriately.

His estranged relationship with his children remained a source of
torment for him. He never heard from his daughter; he still detested
her for her major transgression and yet yearned to hear from her and
see her, preferably if he could extract an apology and a renunciation
of her Arab husband. He had maintained some contact with his son,
but this had dwindled; he was hurt and enraged that there was not
so much as a card or phone call for his birthday or Father's Day
anymore. He flatly turned down my suggestion that sometime in the
future we might consider inviting his children to come in with him
for a session or two and see if we could begin to heal some of the
wounds and bring about a rapprochement. He was adamant; he said
he could never forgive either of them and did not care if he never
saw them again. He wanted to close the door on this phase of his life.
I told him my experience has been that this is rarely possible but
affirmed it as his choice.

Therapy notes following Session 5 read as follows:

Cindy arrived without Don. He had asked her to leave and not return
last night, and she finally did. She had hoped that he would meet her
here, but he neither showed up nor called to cancel.

Following their last session, Don went to see a chiropractor. Although
originally he refused to have X-rays taken or a new myleogram, at the
recommendation of the chiropractor he has agreed to do so and made
another appointment.

Don began to act out again within 48 hours of the last session. Although
he has made Cindy his executor and has put many things in her name
since his ex-wife had sued him, he told her that he does not want her to
meet his children or his ex-wife—that they've all been hurt enough. This
must have been a reaction to my suggestion that we have his children
come in at a later date for a therapy session in order to renew ties. It
really stirred him up. He seems very much to want to see them and
reestablish a relationship, yet this is tinged with his usual ambivalence
and negativism.

He was quite distraught on Sunday and was verbally abusing her.
She decided to cool it after putting Easter dinner in to cook, and went
to see some friends. He does not like her wealthy friends and is definitely
uncomfortable with them; he believes them to be anti-Semitic and phony.
He told her to get out and stay out, and when she returned that evening,
he continued to criticize and abuse her. Finally, by Tuesday evening she
could not tolerate it any more and moved out.

We took a look at what she is deriving from the relationship, and she indicates that maybe the first few months before she left to go to South America, Don was on his good behavior. He now says the honeymoon is over and that he can take off his mask and really be himself. We looked at some of the cruelty that she has experienced and again discussed what may have been the nature of his involvement with Desirée. We talked about how much more she was willing to subject herself to and the fact that she sees Don as almost two people—one man who is tender and brillant and who loves music and culture and is extremely sensitive and the other who is abusive and destructive and very, very angry. She loves the former and doesn't find the latter well integrated, and it seems to be in ascendance. Nonetheless, there is a great deal of caring here, and she would probably go back if he would ask her. She doubts if he will call.

Since she was concerned about Don's tendency to hide and withdraw when he is upset, I indicated that I would follow-up with a phone call to him.

I called Don later in the day. I inquired how he was, and he responded with, "Didn't Cindy pay you?" I indicated that she had and that my phone call was to see if he wanted me to keep treatment open for him, and for him to know that I was here if he wished to see me. He was extremely abrupt and said that I should consider treatment terminated and that he would not honor any of the bills; Cindy had to pay me on her own.

I reiterated my availability, and he said he did not care to continue. "Case with Don closed."

A week later, Don showed up without an appointment. He had seen Cindy Friday when she called him about some financial matters regarding his estate. He accused her of using it as a ruse to return to him, and she left again. He had come today to join her for the session without calling her or letting me know. Since he was quite early, he asked to have a session alone with me first.

During this session, he talked about his relationship with Desirée, a woman whom he had cared about deeply. He needed to examine what it had meant for him, to treasure it and realize it could not flourish into a lasting relationship. Hard as it was for him, he admitted to himself that now he derives a great deal from the relationship with Cindy and would like her to come back but not to feel that she is an octopus with tentacles out to trap him into marriage all the time.

He was well under control today and seemed to relate better. His facial expression and eyes rarely softened, but in this session they filled with tears. We talked about the fact that it is not that he does not care but that he is afraid to risk caring.

He indicated that he plans to continue in therapy, at least for now. My notes read: "I suspected that he would as long as he feels that he can hold on to the relationship with Cindy. Although he doesn't say so, he seems very lonesome. He sees himself as a shell of his former being. In the past he had relied on titles and how much money he made for his identity; now that is all gone."

Cindy arrived on time and was shocked to see Don at my office. She seemed somewhat dazed during the session, trying to get her bearings. We looked at their pattern of interaction in terms of Don either verbally attacking or withdrawing when he gets upset and wants to be let alone. Cindy becomes anxious when she feels rejected and pursues him, sitting on the bed when he wants to hide under the covers. We looked at whether he could withdraw less or whether she could back off until such time as he is ready to move toward her. She wanted to know how long this might take, and we made some headway in Don's being able to say, "I don't like it to take a few days, and I will try to come out of my shell more rapidly if you can leave me alone." Cindy indicated that if she goes into another room, she can't listen to television because he's taping on one channel. He immediately volunteered that he could change this and that she could be in any room that she wants, that he doesn't need the bedroom. For him, this was a big concession.

Toward the end of the session, Don was actually able to turn to her and say, "Cindy, I'd like you to come back and I do want to live together. I miss you." This was the first time he had ever actually asked her to come and stay with him. Don left, asking her to meet him for a light dinner. Cindy stayed a few minutes to indicate that she couldn't believe what had transpired and that, of course, she would go back. I tried to explain the distancer–pursuer interaction and support her ability to sit tight and give him space to move toward her. My notes here read: "Although this is a very tumultuous relationship, both parties are quite sane and know what they are doing. Yet he has a good deal of impulsivity and states correctly, 'I want what I want when I want it.' "

My notes continue:

The following week they requested extra time—wanting an hour and a half session. Don has rented a larger apartment, and they will be moving in together. They have put their relationship on a year's trial basis, and if it continues to go well, he's now talking about marriage. Cindy seems surprised that it has developed this far.

They wanted to discuss their sexuality today. I indicated that as long as he is still on 50 mg a day of Valium and other medications that there is little that we can do in terms of sex-therapy techniques. Part of the problem is the vasoconstriction caused by the medications, so I asked that he have his prescribing physician be in touch with me and that I would ask him to consider a gradually diminishing dosage. (At this stage, I was unaware of the extent of the tie-in of these two factors.)

Another issue today was Don really being out of touch with his feelings. I've begun to try to have him label what he is feeling as he deals with emotionally heavy material. Today, he was able to express feelings of sadness, frustration, and even to be sensitive to his anger. It seems that only when he's in a rage does he experience awareness of the anger.

The other main theme was Don's search for his Jewishness. This evolved out of talking about what Cindy sees in him and that this includes his love for culture, music specifically. In addition, she enjoys hearing his Sholom Aleichem tales and other Jewish folklore. She finds a warmth and stability in his sense of a historic civilization and extended family.

He was concerned about her bringing more material goods into the relationship than he can, in terms of her expensive furniture and art collection, and I helped him look at his expensive and extensive tape collection and recording devices. He seems constantly amazed when I interpret the obvious, and he tunes in to looking at why he missed it. As he talked about the collective unconsciousness of Judaism as a civilization, I asked whether perhaps he is violating a tradition and a prohibition in being involved with a non-Jewish woman. This led to an "Aha" phenomenon in which he indicated that this has not been conscious, but of course he connected to it immediately. He turned to Cindy and said, "Deep down, I really am prohibited from marrying a Shiksa." We talked about how he could get his conscious desires to a more rational point because Cindy fulfills many more of his needs than the kind of "Jewish princess" he came to detest does and than his Jewish wife had. I also prodded him as to why it was all right for him to have a non-Jewish partner when he had disowned his daughter for a similar action. He indicated that he disapproved of mixed marriages out of which children would be born.

I gently teased him about his ambivalence to both Catholic and Jewish women and toyed openly with the idea that he grew up with images of both the "bad" Catholic and the "bad" Jewish mother. Now in life and in therapy he had a new pair of women representing the "good" Jewish and Catholic mothers, and this could be a curative and integrating experience. He immediately knew this as an accurate fact and a compelling opportunity. Cindy felt the bonding also.

When they were leaving, for the first time Don thanked me for what he felt was a very productive and enlightening session. They also both indicated they're coming to hear me speak at a local singles group next

week. They seemed to have, at this point, a lot of pride in having me as
their therapist.

At the next session Don seemed more relaxed than usual and even
smiled twice. He and Cindy were obviously in good spirits and had
moved their residence during this time. The place is overcrowded,
but Don feels comfortable about selling his junky furniture and keeping
Cindy's good stuff. This was another step forward.

Most of this session was devoted to a continuation of Cindy's
marital and sexual history (recounted earlier).

Don sat rather quietly, asking only if I had ever heard anything
so horrible. I picked up on the similarity of their backgrounds and
the devastating hatred that both had felt for their first spouses, including
moments of murderous rage. I pondered aloud whether either was
free to love with so much rancor still festering.

The following session they came in reasonably calm; I was, therefore,
able to shift away from the history taking and "crisis of the week"
aspects of some of the earlier sessions and focus on the negative aspect
of their interaction—her need during tense periods for closeness, reassurance, commitment, and resolution of conflict issues and his need
for space and privacy—and when these were invaded, he usually verbally
attacked and then totally isolated himself. This time, they were able
to grasp more fully the repetitive cycle that was triggered, how they
got stuck, as if in quicksand once it did, and to view therapy as a
lifeline to pull them out and help them remain unstuck. They agreed
to try to head off entering these destructive interactional sequences.
Cindy felt she could try to utilize the "I" statements that I demonstrated
and had them enact during this session. These would be alternatives
to the accusatory "you" statements she sometimes made, which she
felt pushed him away. Don agreed to try to respond more rapidly and
fully to Cindy's expressions of feelings and not go into hibernation,
which caused her to become highly anxious and begin to demand
attention. (This kind of strategy reflects my diaclectic orientation; it
looks at the repetitive patterns of each individual and the way they
interrelate as a couple. Based on a psychodynamic assessment, a structural change is sought that is to be brought about here by a behavioral
intervention.)

My other area of concern today was Don's physical condition and
the amount of medication he was taking. I again indicated that I

wanted to talk with his physician to propose a gradual decrease in the Valium dosage. By now he was off antidepressants and had tapered down to 45 mg of Valium. He was planning to return for more acupuncture as soon as he finished his course of treatment with the chiropractor. I recommended that he have one physician in whom he had confidence coordinate the various treatments, but he preferred to keep following his own predilections.

The following week, unforseen circumstances prevented Cindy from coming to the office, and Don had the session alone. He utilized it to recapitulate more about his past relationship with Desirée and why she had meant so much to him. Despite her status as a "pro" sexually (or perhaps because of it), he felt that she had been the "perfect woman" for him, nurturing, understanding, and willing to engage in any kind of sexual behavior. He finally dealt with her un-attainability for anything more than sporadic encounters, and I think, at this session, finished letting go of his fantasy of having Desirée as his own. He had continued to have a great deal of libidinal energy invested in this prior relationship that still was quite alive in his thoughts.

When this segment seemed complete, he began to talk about the strengths in his relationship with Cindy and the many ways in which he found her interesting and attractive. I indicated that it is usually difficult to split one's emotional commitment and now that he seemed ready and able to close the chapter of his life that involved Desirée, he might have much more energy and desire to devote to his relationship to Cindy. Consequently, she might sense the difference and not feel as uncertain or as if something vital was lacking.

His sexual difficulties continued to plague him. I told him I had gone back through a dozen or more of the major books on sex therapy and the closest I had come to finding anything descriptive of his syndrome was data about retarded ejaculation, but that really was not accurate. I indicated I would continue my search. I also commented that sometimes the inability to reach orgasm during intercourse is linked unconsciously to the fear of exploding and losing control—that one holds in instead of being able to let go to contain the sexual explosion because of its perceived similarity to the release of rage in aggressive form. He certainly felt these ideas might be connected for him.

The next few sessions were dramatic, intense, and critical. I felt by now that the therapeutic alliance was strong enough to sustain some concentrated probing and interpretations. I also believed that Don's ego was less fragile and that both he and Cindy were more optimistic about their relationship developing into a solid and satisfying one. Thus, when Don again stated that his shoulder, back, and arm pains were still often excruciating and no amount of medication had decreased the pain, and all the "damn treatments" had failed, I told him I thought that, in addition to the pain caused by the real physical injury sustained, there were also a psychosomatic component. My line of exploration and explanation went as follows:

KASLOW: You are right-handed, and it is your right arm that is sometimes so painful that it is immobilized. Who might you have wanted to hurt and how?

DON: My wife, my daughter. I wanted to kill them at times. [Affect fitted words.]

KASLOW: The body creates its own safety mechanisms—by bringing about semiparalysis, it made this impossible.

DON: Dr. K., you're implying it's partly a conversion hysteria. Nobody believes in that today. It went out with Freud.

KASLOW: Not true. We still see conversion phenomena, and I think this has some elements of it.

(Don and Cindy sat silently a few long seconds.)

DON: Wow, that really makes sense. And I know all about this stuff from the literature and never connected it to my condition.

KASLOW (encouraged): Let's go back to when your [first] wife was hospitalized, had a masectomy, and you were told she had cancer. How did you feel at that time?

DON (flushed—his angry memories flooding back into consciousness; he tries to cover up): I don't want to talk about it!

KASLOW: I think we must. It holds a key to unlocking the anger and maybe diminishing some of the pain.

DON (quietly, eyes tearing): I wanted her to die. (More forcefully.) I hated her and the burden she would become. I didn't want to live through prolonged agony. I hoped she would die, but she didn't. (Angrily, sobbing.)

He was trembling, and Cindy, who was sitting near him, reached out to comfort him. I moved closer and spoke softly but urgently so that we could keep stripping away the layers of guilt, self-recrimination, physical and emotional anguish, and rage, and perhaps help him make peace with himself.

KASLOW: If I recall correctly, you were about 32 or 33 when the surgery occurred and your death wishes toward your wife surfaced.

DON: That's right.

KASLOW: Isn't that the same age Christ was when he was crucified?

DON: Yes, I think so. Oh—yes, I felt crucified, but I had so often been accused in the orphanage of being a Christ Killer! Jung was really right on his ideas about collective unconscious. And I wanted her, not me, to die then. I've never told anyone any of this. How did you put it together?

He was so perceptive in making connections that no further elaboration was needed. Both were fascinated with this sequence, and it struck a responsive chord. It also released some of the pent-up rage.

DON (*with raised voice*): Look at all the years I wasted in therapy! Years of analysis, group therapy, growth centers—every kind of treatment for pain. Why didn't they make connections? (*Turning to Cindy.*) I'm going to sue all of them. They were incompetent. They robbed me of thousands of dollars and never admitted they didn't know what to do.

KASLOW: It's good for you to spill out the wrath. But suing won't give you back the money—it will cost more. No doubt each doctor did his best— we've just had a fortuitous situation here and the pieces have come together. Let's continue to progress in the present.

We all sat quietly for a few minutes, catching our breath after this expedition into the inner reaches of Don's heart and soul. They left in a state of semi-shock; I felt utterly drained and shaken. Yet I knew it was worth the effort, that several deep "Ahas" had been gleaned. I lent them my bataca bats and suggested they "fight" with these to express some of the residual anger safely over the next few weeks.

The momentum continued in the next session. Don was surprised but gratified that neither Cindy nor I had rejected or criticized him for thoughts and feelings he had heretofore considered sordid and unnatural. They were pleased that so many pieces of the puzzle had fit together.

Since they were again ready to work hard in this session, I told Don I had checked with several people regarding his sexual difficulties and that one of them had come up with the possible diagnosis of priapism. I told him I then looked this up in an excellent text, *Clinical Management of Sexual Disorders* (Meyer, 1976), and found the following, which I read to them. Priapism is

a sustained and sometimes painful erection. Presumably drug induced priapism is a function of chemical alterations in the normal autonomic

control of erection and detumescence. Penile erection is a parasympath-
etically . . . controlled function involving vasodilation and engorgement
of the penile vessels. With increased sympathetic activity . . . these vessels
constrict and the erection subsides. (pp. 199–200)

This clicked as a correct diagnosis, and he was pleased with my honesty
in sharing how I searched to find the answer. He also was perturbed
that so many others had missed it.

I again urged him to have his physician call me as I had become
certain that a slow reduction in the Valium dosage would be a decisive
factor in the cure of the priapism.

When they came the next week, they relayed the following:

Don had decided to go "cold turkey" off the Valium and rise to the
challenge. He believed I would need to be "a miracle worker" to cure his
sexual problems, and he wanted to do whatever he could. On Tuesday,
after they left here, he went off all medication, although he had stayed
until then on 45 mg a day. He was in great pain during the week but did
not go into DT's. By Sunday, he found sensation returning as the medication
in his system began to diminish. Sunday, Monday, and Tuesday he was
able to have vaginal intercourse with Cindy and to achieve orgasm and
ejaculate while inside. Both were ecstatic at the return of feeling and a
move toward some sexual normalcy. However, Don is in great physical
pain now that he is off of muscle relaxants and antidepressants. He has
decided to stay off meds for a month and see just how painful it is, and
I have urged him to have his prescribing physician put him on a dosage
that will keep the pain tolerable without impairing his sexual functioning.
Both are in a victorious state of disbelief.

Cindy has stayed home from work to see him through this period.
However, she plans to return to work soon. What has been disclosed is
that during the past year, while Don was able to stay erect for so long,
she often took off from work and their sexual play went on from 6 to 8
hours. In readjusting to their new sexuality, she is feeling somewhat
deprived. During the past, Don had been so intent on pleasuring her,
and she had grown to love their prolonged sexual sessions. Now that he
is over the priapism, he is much more concerned with himself. His new
behavior seems like premature ejaculation to her. She has been very
uptight and overtired and the reaction that seems to be emerging is that
she no longer feels as patient and giving, but is somewhat angry.

When they came the next week:

Don was a little more comfortable as he had been given some codeine
when he had his dental work done. Otherwise, he has not gone back on
medication.

The ongoing theme resurfaced again that their definitions of sharing and commitment are very different. He doesn't mind at all if Cindy goes out with friends after work and seems to be encouraging her to take a job that will take her overseas periodically so that she can have additional experiences. She wants a very close relationship and prefers being with Don to going out alone but feels that he will not come around to that kind of intensity. She seemed downcast today and like she has made a decision to try to cool it and pull out. Don was quite emphatic about wanting the relationship and feeling that although at this time he is not ready to get married, he might be in the future. Cindy, who seemed to hang in during the worst, seems ready to take off now—it seems like her patience is at end. (There seemed to be many similar elements in her behavior to that of the wife of an alcoholic who leaves after he becomes sober.) I suggested to her that she take a couple of weeks vacation just to catch up with herself and think things through. She seems angry with Don—perhaps because he is no longer the "super stud" he was.

Some weeks earlier, Don had written to his children, letting them know he was still alive, cared about them, and would like to resume some relationship with them. He knew his son's whereabouts but not his daughter's, and he went to great lengths to track her down.

In the last minutes of the session Don indicated he wanted to talk about his son's response to the letter. His son had learned that he had been in jail and is very confused about the past. Don wanted to know whether to discuss that with him and whether to reveal what his wife's cancer had meant to him. I indicated that the time seems to have come for him to have much more open and honest communication and that his son certainly has a right to ask these probing questions, but that sharing his thoughts of homicide was probably not wise outside of therapy.

The summary comment in my notes reads, "Each session with them is gripping. There seems to be a good deal of progress—but it is not always in complementary directions."

The next entry in my notes read:

When I returned to the office on 8/27 after having been away for several days, there was a message awaiting me that Cindy had called to cancel their next appointment. I called her back and learned that she had moved out from Don's apartment after taking a brief vacation alone. She did not feel that she could continue on the topsy-turvy merry-go-round any longer and that although she loved him, she no longer liked him enough to continue the relationship and the hassling. She wants a more steadfast, smooth, and definitely committed relationship than he does. Living together still doesn't feel respectable to her. She was looking for a place to live and sounded quite definite in her decision. I indicated that I felt that therapy was far from complete and that she should, if possible, continue until she felt that she had integrated the experience with Don and reached a new level of stabilization in herself. She felt that she could not make an appointment at this time but would get back to me in a few weeks after her living situation is settled. She asked that I call Don, since she felt that he would be quite upset and feel very alone and desolated. I indicated I would think about it and hoped that perhaps he would call me first.

A few days later, as I hadn't heard from him, I called Don. He said it was "splitsville" for him and Cindy, final and definite and for the best. He felt fine, felt treatment was extremely helpful, and "liked me." He did not care to continue treatment right now. He had many loose ends to wrap up. He would call when and if he wanted to resume.

I was slightly taken aback at this turn of events. Why now? It had seemed progress was fairly steady, sometimes with major breakthroughs. Don's rages had decreased in frequency and severity, his medication was greatly reduced and the pain slightly diminished. His sexual dysfunction had been successfully treated, and he felt more whole. His son had responded to his letter, so that door was still ajar, even though his daughter had not. Both he and Cindy seemed to have resolved much about their troubled backgrounds, become much less self-critical, and begun to live in the here and now. They cared for each other immensely. As I thought about it more, I realized that perhaps Don, the more outspoken and demanding, had received much more of the therapeutic attention, and maybe Cindy was in much more pain than I had realized. Perhaps she had derived so much from the sexual relationship while he had priapism that his improvement really represented severe denial and loss for her. Perhaps she could not hold down the intensity of her need for immediate response and reassurance, and she could no longer believe that some nebulous day in the future he might decide on marriage. Since she wanted a committed and legalized relationship with certainty and predictability, and could not have them with Don at this time, her move out made sense. For her, it could well have been a manifestation of her stronger self-image and not wanting to continue to live on an emotional roller-coaster. She had certainly become less masochistic. I wondered how long the separation would last and how each of them would fare. I did not think the separation would be permanent.

Aftermath and Retrospective

Four months later, I received a Christmas card from Cindy. A few weeks later, it was followed by a jubilant phone call. During their separation of several months' duration, each had done a great deal of soul searching and solidifying the gains made in therapy. They missed each other immensely and decided to get married during the holiday season, convinced they could now make a go of it. Don was by then ready to make a commitment, so they had a small wedding. They were planning a dinner–dance as a reception to celebrate their joy, and since I had become so special to them both, they hoped I would attend. I did attend, and both were glowing. Don seemed pleased with his choice and proud of his lovely bride. Shortly thereafter, I received a note from them, which stated in part: "It meant a lot to both of us that you were there. Our present happiness now is directly related to your care, concern and love."

In spring 1983 I decided I would like to write about this case for this Casebook, since it illustrates the kind of in-depth work sometimes required with couples who are dealing with (*a*) whether they want to make another definite commitment; (*b*) whether they can allow the narcissistic wounds from past relationships to heal; (*c*) whether they can work through the anger and outrage sufficiently for tender feelings to be in the ascendance; (*d*) whether they are willing to and can risk, trust and compromise in a relationship without fear of loss of individuality, since true intimacy can be obtained only when one's identity is clear and comfortable.

I contacted Cindy and Don to seek permission to recount aspects of their story in print. Both concurred. Halfway through the writing, I decided to contact them for some input and wrote raising several questions. They called in response to my letter. The following is a summation of their remarks during a three-way phone conversation:

KASLOW: What aspects of your therapy with me were most meaningful? How did it differ from previous therapies?
CINDY: I found my earlier group therapist too provocative and confrontational. He triggered too much acting out, was verbally abusive. You were always considerate and quite gentle even though you were always thought-provoking. . . . We felt safe with you. You were honest, up front, clear on the ground rules of therapy with you. It had none of the feel of "pop psych"—you were much more skilled.

DON: Other therapists were afraid of my anger and never attempted to touch it. You weren't afraid of it or of me. I couldn't con you. You hung in and took me through it. They did supportive therapy—patted me on the head and gave me drugs. It didn't work. Talking it out and using the batacas both helped.

CINDY: We knew from the beginning that you really cared what happened to us. We came to trust you and were often astonished at your perceptiveness. When I was struggling to say something, you could help me formulate my feelings and needs with such accuracy and sensitivity. I really came to know myself much better.

DON: I appreciated your immediate zeroing in with new slants [reframing], the rapid connections and straightforward interpretations. Most frequently you were "right on" and it hit like "pow." When it didn't fit, we could say "bullshit," and you not only accepted it but gave credence to our intelligence and interpretations too. It was startling when you indicated part of the pain in my arm was a conversion phenomenon and it rang true—forcing me to know I had to come to grips at long last with my repressed rage.

CINDY: For me it was important that we were seeing a woman therapist. The rapport was better. When I talked about washing the floor and liking to have things very clean—you understood my wanting the apartment to look nice—but also knew it was excessive and asked, "Who are you trying to please?"—out came an immediate "My mother." That was an important key to my dawning self-awareness. Now I only try to please us; I still scrub, but less so, and I know why I do it. You always seemed to be on the same wavelength with us. My previous male therapists weren't.

DON: Initially I didn't want to see a female therapist, but Cindy insisted because you came highly recommended. From the first I found you warm, gentle, and strong—strong enough to open up and take me through some rough spots. I always sensed that we were all really working together and that you were attuned to our uniqueness. For me, your Jewishness was important. You responded to and understood my idiomatic expressions and that felt good. You touched my *neshuma* [Yiddish for "guts" and "soul"]; you shared my heritage and collective unconscious—no one else had done that. You even cried with us—we knew we mattered to you, and that was very significant.

Thus, 16 months after termination of 6 months of intensive couples therapy, Cindy and Don have been married a year. They seem highly committed to the relationship, yet would like to join a therapy group to learn how to fight fairly and productively. Otherwise, both are much happier than last year at this time and, as a tangible sign of this, they recently bought a home together and have moved into more spacious permanent quarters.

From the therapist's retrospective perspective, there seem to have been some other salient features in the treatment. Don was in such excruciating emotional and physical pain that despite his cynicism, he was highly motivated to change if this could provide relief from despair. He captured my sympathy right from the first—the pathos of his background as an unwanted, abandoned child placed in an orphanage, although his mother and grandmother were alive. My empathy with his quest for his Jewish identity and his resemblance to my paternal family of origin seemed to help us establish a special bonding, strong enough to sustain him through testing out whether he could trust his therapist and find herein the acceptance and regard he never had had and durable enough to help him confront and release his pent-up rage. My admiration for his self-acquired brilliance, his love for and knowledge of classical music, his philosophic bent, and his compassion for other wounded individuals was perceived correctly by him. Cindy basked in my understanding of why she found him lovable and worthwhile, even though to others he seemed like a volatile, selfish, borderline personality who was a poor risk for a marital partner. There were sessions in which we both sat very near him, almost physically holding him together and containing him while the hurt and venom poured out. His having the collaboration of a good Jewish mother (the therapist) and a good Catholic mother (Cindy) in the service of his restoration diminished his hatred of the former bad personifications of each prototype and enabled him to trust his dawning awareness that not all of the key women in his life were destined to desert him because he was too flawed to be wanted. As he internalized the esteem in which he was held, his sense of self improved markedly, and some of the borderline characteristics receded, to be replaced by a healthier personality integration. Consequently, Cindy was able to feel more secure and rooted in the relationship, and her fears of rejection and making another poor choice of partners diminished.

I have seen them recently, and both indicate that their marriage has worked out far better than either anticipated. Behavioral indicators of their marital well-being (Kaslow, 1982) include more flexibility, adaptability, and expansiveness regarding life style and decision making and the ability to incorporate respect for each other's heritage so that, for instance, both Hanukkah and Christmas are celebrated. Each seems calmer, more content, and secure—and grateful that they are married to each other.

References

Boszormenyi-Nagy, I., & Spark, G. (1973). *Invisible loyalties*. New York: Harper & Row.

Bowen, M. (1978). *Family therapy in clinical practice*. New York: Jason Aronson.

Duhl, B. S., & Duhl, F. J. (1981). Integrative family therapy. In A. S. Gurman & D. P. Kniskern (Eds.), *Handbook of family therapy*. New York: Brunner/Mazel.

Epstein, N. B., & Bishop, D. S. (1981). Problem centered systems therapy of the family. In A. S. Gurman & D. P. Kniskern (Eds.), *Handbook of family therapy*. New York: Brunner/Mazel.

Haley, J. (1976). *Problem solving therapy*. San Francisco: Jossey-Bass.

Jackson, D., & Weakland, J. (1961). Conjoint family therapy: Some considerations on theory, technique and results. *Psychiatry Supplement, 2*, 30–45.

Kaslow, F. W. (1980). Stages in the divorce process: A psychological perspective. *Villanova Law Review, 25*(4-5), 718–751.

Kaslow, F. W. (1981a). A diaclectic approach to family therapy and practice: Selectivity and synthesis. *Journal of Marital and Family Therapy, 1*, 345–351.

Kaslow, F. W. (1981b). Divorce and divorce therapy. In A. S. Gurman & D. P. Kniskern (Eds.), *Handbook of family therapy*. New York: Brunner/Mazel.

Kaslow, F. W. (1982, December). Portrait of a healthy couple. *Psychiatric Clinics of North America, 5*(3), 519–527.

Keith, D. V., & Whitaker, C. A. (1981). Play therapy: A paradigm for work with families. *Journal of Marital and Family Therapy, 7*(3), 243–254.

Lazarus, A. (1981). *The practice of multimodal therapy*. New York: McGraw-Hill.

Maslow, A. (1968). *Toward a psychology of being*. New York: Van Nostrand.

May, R. (1969). *Love and will*. New York: Norton.

Meyer, J. K. (1976). *Clinical management of sexual disorders*. Baltimore: Williams and Wilkins.

Minuchin, S. (1974). *Families and family therapy*. Cambridge, MA: Harvard University Press.

Reik, T. (1948). *Listening with the third ear*. New York: Grove Press.

Sager, C. J. (1976). *Marriage contracts and couples therapy: Hidden forces in intimate relations*. New York: Brunner/Mazel.

Satir, V. (1964). *Conjoint family therapy*. Palo Alto: Science and Behavior Books.

Selvini Palazzoli, M., Boscolo, L., Cecchin, G., & Prata, G. (1978). *Paradox and counterparadox*. New York: Jason Aronson.

Whitaker, C. (1976). Hindrance of theory in clinical work. In P. J. Guerin (Ed.), *Family therapy: Theory and practice*. New York: Gardner Press.

Chapter 14
"We've Got a Secret!"
A Nonmarital Marital Therapy

Evan Imber Coppersmith, PhD

Principles of Systemic Practice with Couples: An Overview

Although a growing literature exists regarding systemic therapy with families (e.g., Hoffmann, 1981; Selvini Palazzoli, Boscolo, Cecchin, & Prata, 1978; Tomm, 1982, 1984a, 1984b), there is little in the family therapy literature specific to systemic practice with couples. Many of the major principles of systemic thought and practice obtain whether one is working with an entire family or with a couple. For instance, the now-familiar concepts of hypothesizing regarding the salient features of the system and the potential function of the problem or symptom, utilizing the interview to ask questions that yield circular rather than linear information, and the therapist's stance of neutrality toward persons and ideas all pertain to systemic couples therapy.

Several additional notions are crucial when the unit of assessment and intervention is a couple. The first idea pertinent to the therapist is a contradictory one: A couple is never a couple. That is, for purposes of therapy the couple becomes understandable and amenable to intervention when the therapist searches for "the couple in relationship to. . . ." It may be the couple in relationship to children, extended family, community, work, a third person, another helper, an idea, a myth or belief, etc. The therapist who adopts the stance that a couple never exists in isolation is able to avoid a common trap of couples

369

therapy in which the focus becomes more and more narrowly defined by the boundaries of the couple, and the therapist becomes the third leg of the triangle. Since many troubled couples have become increasingly so by turning in on themselves and rigidly repeating the same interactional dance over and over again, the therapist who views the couple in context potentially is able to counter this tendency rather than reify it further.

Viewing the couple this way opens many avenues for circular interviewing that would otherwise be lost to the therapist. Querying about the attitudes, beliefs, and actions of others toward the couple, and vice-versa, has the effect of expanding rather than limiting the couple's world. Examination of the potential effects of change in the couple's relationship on their wider network informs both the couple and their therapist of arenas of support and constraint. The questions per se may reframe the couple's experience of an isolated and disconnected dyadic repertoire to a sense of connection to issues of loyalty and relatedness beyond their own unit.[1]

Questions to the couple, based on the therapist's and team's continually developing hypotheses, span meanings of the past as interpreted by the couple in the present, current interaction and beliefs, and strongly held fantasies of the future. Such questions and responses contribute to the therapist's ongoing hypothesizing process and serve as interventions per se, highlighting information to couples regarding their organization.

The therapist searches for avenues of permission with the couple. Many couples are frightened to discuss their relationship. They may have tried and failed many times. A variety of toxic issues or relationships may initially be off-limits to the therapist's inquiry, as indicated by abrupt subject changes, increased vagueness, or an outright refusal to engage. The systemic therapist notes this as potentially important information but does not engage in direct confrontation with the couple. Instead, she adopts a complementary stance and then searches for unexpected modes of entry.

---

1. Evidence of this can be gleaned from our practice in the Family Therapy Program at the University of Calgary. Couples filling out our Demographic Form often do not indicate connections to extended family or the outside world in general, although questions are asked about these areas on the form. The couple's own problem is most often seen in isolation from other family or community issues. Only when the therapist frames questions that examine this dimension do the couple discover the connections.

Neutrality in couples therapy includes accepting each member of the couple, not taking sides with either person, searching for the context in which a couple's ways of being together make sense, and remaining free of a moralistic framework that judges the couple's ideas and beliefs or prescribes the "correct" way to be a couple. Such neutrality does not imply coldness or lack of concern on the part of the therapist. Instead, it implies a stance of curiosity and openness to the particular couple and a deep respect for the couple's decision-making capacity, once freed from overriding systemic constraints.

The notion that "a couple is never a couple" leads naturally to the importance of recognizing and utilizing the formation of the therapist–couple system. It is likely that the couple will attempt to relate to the therapist in ways that are familiar. Invitations to ally with one or the other member and subtle cues regarding forbidden topics will emerge. Couples who have had prior therapy (as in the case discussed here) or with long-standing histories with professional helpers often come to the new therapy with covert expectations of a similar relationship (Imber Coppersmith, 1983). The therapist must assess the new therapist–couple system in which she is an active participant and generate un-expected interactional possibilities. Such assessment is ongoing as the therapist–couple system develops over the course of therapy and may often entail the use of a team, supervisory input, or consultation.

The concepts of complementarity and symmetry (Jackson & Led-erer, 1968; Watzlawick, Beavin, & Jackson, 1967) continue to be useful to the systemic therapist. In their original application these concepts effectively described dyadic interaction. At present, the systemic therapist utilizes these concepts as a lens to view the couple in relationship to their problem, to assess the therapist–couple system, and to intervene appropriately. For example, if the therapist–couple system becomes riddled with struggles over "who knows best," the therapist can un-expectedly adopt a complementary one-down stance and alter the symmetrical pattern. On the other hand, if the couple pretend to helplessness, inviting direct advice and interminable therapy, the therapist may move to introduce greater symmetry in the therapist–couple system.

It is not unusual for patterns to develop in the therapist–couple system that mirror patterns in the couple. When unrecognized, such patterns may be mirrored in the therapist–team or therapist–supervisor relationship (Wright & Imber Coppersmith, 1983). The recognition of this phenomenon frequently expands assessment and intervention possibilities. Since information to a system is "news of a difference," it is important that the therapist not adopt a relational stance with the couple that mirrors their relationship to one another.

Finally, the systemic therapist does not search for pathology in couples. She avoids diagnostic labels and the usual blinders on treatment and life possibilities that these imply. Instead, she searches for strengths, affirms natural resources in the couple, and designs interventions that remove constraints in ways that allow the couple both to elaborate further changes and attribute new patterns to themselves. This stance often means that therapy is short and that, in fact, one intervention may trigger complex changes in a variety of areas. When the couple begin to show and report changes, many may be in areas that were either never discussed or were touched on lightly in therapy. Such changes are viewed as evidence of greater complexity and flexibility in the couple system. The therapist and couple may then negotiate a much longer interval until the next session, redefine the next session as follow-up, or terminate therapy.

The Context of Treatment

If one attends to the importance of the evolving therapist–couple system, then the larger treatment context in which that system is embedded becomes salient. The case to be discussed in this chapter was seen in the larger context of a university-based training clinic. Clients paid fees for therapy on a sliding-scale basis. Couples and families were either self-referred or referred by another professional.

I was the supervisor of a team composed of five doctoral students from two different doctoral programs. I deliberately designed the team to take advantage of the differences among the members, highlighting strengths and competencies and hence mirroring what trainees were expected to do with clients. The team was defined as a collaborative team (Roberts, 1983a, 1983b), and every case was considered to be the responsibility of the entire team.[2]

As a supervisor, I saw my role as multifaceted, ranging from a central and more hierarchical position early on in the year to a less

2. The reader is directed to Dr. Janine Roberts's research and theoretical exposition of collaborative teams.

central and more collaborative position later in the year. This supervisory shift may be seen as isomorphic to the shift in therapist position over the course of treatment in the models we practiced. I saw my responsibility to be facilitating collaborative relationships on the team such that each member's contributions were valued and linked in ways that appropriate plans for clients emerged. The case to be examined here was seen in the the first half of the year when my own input on cases was more central and directive.

In the wider context of the entire clinic, our team had strong support from the clinic director and at the same time was regarded with more than a touch of suspicion by other trainees. In retrospect, I believe that this unusual combination of confirmation and doubt contributed mightily to our determination to do good work and our willingness to take risks.

It is important to note that the work to be discussed here was seen at a time when the work of the Milan team was first appearing in North America. Our team had practiced structural and strategic therapies, and we were just beginning to study and utilize Milan systemic thought and practice. The prescribed nature of the team was highly experimental. As such, the systemic model was inviting. As supervisor, I encouraged innovation and unusual approaches providing a rational and sound assessment was available. This resulted in a team whose working methods were highly creative and whose morale, even in the face of difficult situations, was very strong.

The Therapy

Entry and Early Formation
of the Therapist–Couple System

Mrs. Wilson contacted the clinic for therapy for the entire family, which consisted of Mr. Wilson, age 35, a truck driver; Mrs. Wilson, age 30, a homemaker; and three children, Ellen, age 11, Janice, age 8, and Joey, age 4. In the initial telephone call Mrs. Wilson complained about temper tantrums in Janice but hinted vaguely at general unhappiness in the family and an inability to cooperate on parenting issues between her and her husband. No other mention was made of marital issues in this phone call.

The family arrived for the first interview. The parents looked frankly worn out and older than their years. Mrs. Wilson looked haggard and presented herself as extremely anxious. Mr. Wilson appeared depressed. The oldest and youngest children also seemed tired out. Only the middle child, the girl with tantrums, looked energetic at this time.

During the initial session a number of complaints emerged including child-focused complaints regarding Janice's tantrums at home and general bickering among the siblings; child–parent relationship complaints that took the form of the children's nagging and pestering their mother continually; parental complaints regarding each one's handling of the children; and complaints by each adult about their general dissatisfaction with life. Both adults experienced themselves as overworked and felt that little in daily life provided a sense of well-being. All of the therapist's initial inquiries into the family's view of itself and its difficulties were responded to in a tone of despair by the mother and cynicism by the father. An air of hopelessness permeated the interview. Significant by its absence in a family that highlighted complaints about every other possible configuration was any direct complaint about the marital relationship.

In response to the therapist's inquiries about a typical day in the life of the family at home, a picture emerged in which Mrs. Wilson interacted intensely and constantly with the children, while Mr. Wilson was either away driving the truck or at home sleeping. The couple appeared to avoid any direct involvement with each other that did not include the children. When the father came home after driving for 2 or 3 days, his contact with his wife involved listening to her exhausted complaints about the children. She expected him to discipline them for their misbehavior in his absence; he, in turn, felt she should not wait for him and frequently refused her requests, leading to her feelings of frustration, nonsupport, and disappointment. This parental sequence permeated a number of relationships in a circular fashion. The mother, feeling let down by husband, would turn back to the children. The children, sensing her depressed air and knowing there would be no consequences for misbehavior, seemed intent on distracting their mother with nagging and tantrums. The nagging and bickering appeared to mirror the wife's nagging of her husband and the parental bickering regarding the children. The husband withdrew farther and farther from his wife and children, leading to the wife's next attempts to involve him.

In those brief moments when the husband and wife did interact on topics other than the children, all three children felt free to intrude and were not stopped from doing so. One had the sense of children who felt that it was somehow unsafe for their parents to be alone together, and much of the children's time and energy was spent overinvolved in their parents' lives. In the first session the husband and wife described that they did not have a door on their bedroom and that the children were constantly in their room. It did not seem to occur to the couple to put a door on their bedroom; instead, they spent a lot of time and energy complaining ineffectually to the children for running in and out of their parents' room.

Exploration of Janice's tantrums revealed interaction patterns similar to those described above wherein Mrs. Wilson would warn her daughter that Mr. Wilson would discipline her, he would refuse to become involved after the fact, Mrs. Wilson would grow more frustrated and overwrought, and the couple would distance from each other. The tantrums appeared to be the only overt expression of anger in the family and were hypothesized by the therapeutic team to be a metaphor for suppressed anger between husband and wife. The tantrums seemed to function like small volcanic eruptions, preventing a more major blow-up in the marital system.

After receiving a lot of information about a variety of issues and relationships, the therapist inquired directly about the marriage. At this point the children, who had been generally cooperative in the session, began to misbehave, and the husband and wife were adamant in denying marital problems. The couple saw themselves as having difficulties with the children and placed direct blame for this on the children. They willingly verbalized dissatisfaction with each other's parenting but denied any connection between this and marital issues. Their marriage was defined as off-limits to the therapist. As the session drew to a close Mr. Wilson volunteered to the therapist, "We were in therapy before, you know, and that therapist *made* us talk about things from the past and it made things worse!"

REFLECTIONS ON ENTRY AND EARLY FORMATION
OF THE THERAPIST–COUPLE SYSTEM

The case presented several difficulties, many of which were common but required careful analysis by the team in order to facilitate relevant therapy and obviate against errors. First, Mr. and Mrs. Wilson presented lots of problems while denying any marital issues. Our initial thinking was that these problems provided safe distractions, ones that absorbed the couple. The problems were fairly noisy and dramatic, e.g., tantrums, constant bickering, nagging, and seemed to feed a sense that life was overwhelming the adults. The couple's jointly held beliefs about life that emerged in the first session included the fatalistic notion that "things just are the way they are"; their sense of personal empowerment seemed to be quite depleted. The focus of blame shifted rapidly, but there seemed to be little expectation that anyone could or would change.

It was clear at the end of the first session that, for the time being, the therapist and team had no permission to frame this as a marital therapy and explore marital issues directly, even though the couple provided ample evidence of severe marital strife. We assessed the couple as engaged in a symmetrically escalating battle regarding handling of the children, and we had hints that this symmetrical pattern pervaded other aspects of their marital relationship. The team recognized the danger that the treatment context would replicate the couple's pattern if the therapist assumed a symmetrical stance in interaction with the couple by insisting on a marital focus. The couple's protests about their marriage in the face of overwhelming interactional evidence in the first session seemed almost to be an invitation to engage symmetrically with them by pursuing marital issues. Instead, it was decided that marital issues would be explored indirectly and metaphorically, at least until the couple invited a more direct focus. It was hypothesized that successful resolution of the various problems presented would either lead to resolution of the marital conflict by proxy or would force a focus on the marriage in therapy.

Finally, this case contained a potential pitfall of crucial importance: a prior unsuccessful therapy. It was our standard practice to inquire about prior treatment, coming from a belief that people frequently totalize their experiences with professional helpers. In this case the husband brought up the information before our inquiry and under-scored both the failure of previous therapy and his beliefs regarding the reasons for such failure. Indeed, not only did the first therapy fail, it "made things worse." Unsolicited information of this nature seemed very important to our team, for it carried the quality of a warning and a challenge. It was decided to explore their views of the prior treatment in greater depth in order to design a therapy that would utilize the unexpected.

Establishing the Meaningful System for Intervention

The next three sessions were spent establishing the meaningful system for intervention, including an examination of relationships with families of origin, interventions designed to deal with the child-focused complaints, and further exploration of the prior treatment failure.

Mr. and Mrs. Wilson lived a block away from Mr. Wilson's parents. Mrs. Wilson's parents lived about an hour's drive away. Establishing a frame of family development, the therapist gained the couple's permission to inquire about their courtship and early marriage. Both families of origin supported the couple's getting together and getting married. Careful exploration indicated that loyalty issues were not salient in understanding the couple's current dilemmas. The children interacted comfortably with both sets of grandparents. That they saw the husband's parents more frequently was the result of proximity and not favoritism or any estrangement from Mrs. Wilson's parents. The grandparents all knew that their adult children were having difficulty parenting but were in agreement with the view that these were just normal problems connected to raising three children. Hence, the families of origin did not appear to be part of the meaningful system for our attention, except in one regard. Mr. and Mrs. Wilson both agreed that coming to therapy would *not* be a way that their parents would handle problems.

We decided to deal with the child-focused and parent–child concerns, as these were the entry points provided by Mr. and Mrs. Wilson. The parents were given simple paradoxical instructions to work first with Janice's tantrums. The intervention was designed with an action orientation requiring that both parents be present and participating. Not surprisingly, when instructed by her parents to have a tantrum, Janice refused. Of greater importance to the development of the therapy is that the parents came back complaining even more strongly about the nagging and bickering behavior of all three children. Relief regarding the cessation of Janice's tantrums was very brief, and Mrs. Wilson seemed even more distraught than she had initially as she described how all three children were "driving her crazy." Mr. Wilson appeared more withdrawn and depressed following the end of Janice's tantrums. He agreed with his wife, however, that all three children and their nagging were now the main issue. An intervention basically replicating the one regarding Janice's tantrums was offered. Once again the parents were put together, this time to instruct the children to have "pestering time," a prescribed time each day to nag. The effect was similar. The children ceased nagging; the wife became more anxious and the husband more withdrawn and depressed. Cleared of the various child-related distractions, the therapy was about to reach a significant turning point.

At this time, the earlier treatment was explored again. What emerged was the description of an initially individual therapy for the husband because of his feelings of depression. The therapist invited the wife to the sessions and, according to the couple, insisted that they discuss their marriage, although they did not want to do so. The couple then indicated that they had some event or situation in the past that occurred early in their marriage. They insisted in the present therapy that they did not want to talk about it and that the previous therapist had, according to Mr. Wilson, "made us talk about it, and everything got much worse and we quit."

We asked the couple to leave the children at home for the next session.

REFLECTIONS ON ESTABLISHING
THE MEANINGFUL SYSTEM

Three important dimensions emerged during this phase of therapy. First, hypotheses regarding family-of-origin involvement proved to be largely inappropriate, except for the discovery of their families' lack of belief in the efficacy of therapy. Our team hypothesized that this gave further weight to the first failed treatment and provided an added burden to our present work, since if it was seen that the therapy succeeded, then the couple had to prove their families wrong. Hence it was important that the couple be able to own any changes, rather than credit them to therapy.

Second, intervening in the child-related issues seemed to have the effect of putting more and more pressure on the couple. While they verbalized relief, they appeared more distraught. Neither suggested terminating at this point. Each complained more about self. No clear marital focus had emerged as yet. Our team's view was that the couple was confused at this point. On the one hand, they trusted the therapist a bit because her suggestions had led to an alteration in the children's behavior. On the other hand, each adult was feeling more miserable. The safety valve of distractions was disappearing.

Finally, the discussion of the earlier failed treatment indicated the very symmetrical battle we were hoping and planning to avoid: "He *made* us talk" and "we quit." As well, a secret was now being tantalizingly dangled in front of the therapist. The invitation to do "more of the same" as the prior therapist was blatant. If we pursued the secret in a similar manner, which the couple expected we would, therapy would again fail.

Focus on the Couple and the Roles of the Secret

The couple came alone to the fifth session. At first they insisted that they did not want to deal with their marriage and then they proceeded to complain bitterly about fights they had been having. A picture emerged of 8 years of fighting with no resolution of issues. These fights, which did not involve the children, had not been mentioned at prior sessions, despite the therapist's invitation that the couple list all their problems.

The repetitive nature of the fight was as follows: One or the other would raise a current issue of dispute, and a fight would ensue. Soon, one or the other would "bring up the past." The couple would fight bitterly about the past and reach no resolution of the current issue. They would then part in anger and avoid each other. After describing this sequence, and after both agreed to its accuracy, the husband stated, "But we don't want to talk about the past in here!" Thus the secret issue was presented as the key to unlock current difficulties, but the therapist was in essence told that she would have to find entry through some other door.

The therapist then surprised the couple by agreeing with them that it would be a mistake to discuss the secret and whatever happened in the past. Instead, she encouraged them to keep it to themselves and not share it with her, since that would "probably make things worse." The couple looked quite startled, and the session ended.

REFLECTIONS ON WORKING WITH SECRETS
IN MARITAL THERAPY

Many couples come to marital therapy with secrets. Our team's view was that secrets are messages that define and calibrate relationships and that it is this quality about secrets that is more important than the actual content. In the case under discussion, the secret was a major part of the couple's definition of itself. It functioned to maintain myths of villains and victims. It supported a repetitive pattern of intense conflictual engagement, nonresolution of conflict, leading to mutual avoidance until the next round of intense conflictual engagement. Further, the secret defined the couple as a couple. Only they knew its content. Outsiders who broke in "made things worse." Thus the secret functioned as a message to helpers, preventing effective entry into the couple's domain. By highlighting the existence of the secret, the couple invited intrusion and then refused access. Thus, a similar "come here—go away" dance that permeated the couple's interaction with each other also infused the couple's relationship with the therapist.

Viewing secrets as interactional messages frees the therapist from the need to pursue the content of the secret. Here, the notion that "bringing something out into the open" will resolve it drops away. The couple is instead encouraged to keep their secret; this gives the therapist the leverage of utilizing the unexpected. Remaining outside the content of the secret also facilitates the therapist's position of neutrality, since the content often involves blame. Maintaining neutrality, the therapist communicates acceptance of the system as it currently is organized. This acceptance, when the couple expects disapproval, operates to free the system to explore other options. Further, in agreeing with the couple not to reveal the content of the secret, the therapist affirms the couple as knowing best about themselves, facilitating exploration of their own resources. Finally, as the couple is freed from having to struggle with the therapist regarding the secret, they are potentially able to examine their own strongly held beliefs about the secret.

Instead of engaging in a symmetrical battle of pursuit of the content, the therapist adopts a complementary one-down stance and agrees with the couple's decision to keep the secret a secret. From this vantage point, the therapist is able to explore how the secret works in the system, who knows about it, who is closer and who farther apart because of it, what life was like before the secret, what life would be like without the secret, etc. Freed from the struggle over content, the therapist can focus on relationships. Once an understanding is generated regarding how the secret works in the system, then the therapist is in a position to recontextualize it and facilitate the alteration of patterns.

The In-Session Ritual

The team met at length to discuss possible ways to deal with the "secret" issue that would not repeat the error of the previous therapy and that would provide Mr. and Mrs. Wilson with the opportunity to live more fully in the present, negotiate conflicts with each other, and derive more satisfaction in their marriage. As a team, we had been impressed with the efficacy of a burial ritual described by the Milan team (Selvini Palazzoli *et al.*, 1974). Since we were searching for ways to make this therapy very different from the Wilson's earlier treatment, it was decided to plan and implement a burial ritual of the secret past event *in the session*, rather than assign it as a homework task.

Mr. and Mrs. Wilson arrived for the sixth session and began immediately to complain about their fights, their inability to negotiate, and the place of the past secret in their present fighting. Since the therapist had urged them previously to keep the content of the secret to themselves, this manner of opening the session was viewed as a symmetrical response to the therapist. The quality of their report had elements of an inviting trap. The therapist responded: "You know, tonight I thought we'd try something to put a boundary on the past, to mark it off, to put it in its proper place." The couple seemed intrigued. The therapist handed each a piece of paper and a pencil and asked them to spend a few minutes separately writing down the past event that was affecting them so profoundly in the present. At first, the couple seemed confused.

MR. WILSON: How can you write down the past? To me, the past just is, and it should never have happened.
MRS. WILSON: Is this so you'll know we're both talking about the same thing?"
THERAPIST: No. I'm not going to look at these. It's to mark off the past, put it in its proper place.
MR. WILSON: To me there is no past—it's just everything since *that time*.
THERAPIST: Yes—that time. Whatever happened at that time.
MR. WILSON: That's what you want us to write down?
THERAPIST: Yes.

The couple then wrote intently for several minutes. Every so often, one or the other would murmur that they didn't know what this was for, but their curiosity grew. When they finished writing, the therapist asked them to fold the papers. She then gave them a very small box to put the papers in, symbolically indicating that perhaps this issue could be made smaller. She gave fancy wrapping paper to the husband and asked him to wrap the box. Then she gave ribbon to the wife to tie it. As Mrs. Wilson was tying a bow, she stopped and said, "I ain't gonna put no pretty ribbon on *that* thing!" Clearly, the couple had accepted the symbolic act that indicated the secret was now in this little box.

THERAPIST: Well, as I said, you can't really bury the past, but you can put it in it's rightful place.
MRS. WILSON: Right—I don't want to bury the past. I just want it to stop coming up all the time!
THERAPIST: I thought we'd go put this in the ground outside.

The couple seemed very startled and protested that it was January and the ground was hard. The frozen ground served as a further metaphor for their currently frozen relationship.

THERAPIST: I know, but I have a shovel and I think you two can dig.

At that moment, with no further discussion, the therapist got up and put on her coat. The couple followed suit. Mrs. Wilson carried the box, and Mr. Wilson took the shovel from the therapist. Outside, the couple took turns digging, opening the "frozen ground" together. They placed the box in the ground and became very solemn. Each spontaneously said some words over the box as he or she covered it. Then they reentered the clinic.

THERAPIST: I'd like to see you in a month. During that time, I'm sure you'll have many fights, and that's O.K. The only difference is that the past is over here now. So when you fight about the past, you must get in your car and drive over here and go to the hill behind the clinic where the past is buried and finish your fight there.

The couple lived a 25-minute drive from the clinic. They chuckled for the first time, agreed, and left the session.

REFLECTIONS ON THE IN-SESSION RITUAL

The in-session ritual utilizes the capacity of the session itself for intervention possibilities. Instead of sending a couple home to perform a ritual, the session is transformed temporarily into an arena of dramatic and metaphorical action. The in-session ritual in this case was designed to unite the couple vis-à-vis their past secret. No longer an issue to fight over, the secret became the subject of an unusual shared enterprise.

Definitions of "villain" and "victim" were cast aside. Humor was introduced into an otherwise deadly serious struggle, for burying the secret in the frozen ground highlighted the absurdity of the entire matter. Also, the possibility of breaking new ground together was expressed symbolically.

The therapist utilized two roles, that of director of the ritual initially and that of neutral witness during the writing and actual burial. Her role as therapist vis-à-vis the secret bore no resemblance to the couple's earlier therapy experience and hence was unexpected in ways that heightened the couple's curiosity and openness to new information.

The in-session ritual was then combined with an at-home ritual designed to heighten the effects of the burial of the secret. In effect, the couple were told: "You will have to make an effort to maintain the negative place of this secret in your lives now." The ritual provided a choice of doing the same old thing or discovering something new. The month-long interval was utilized to enable the couple to experience the effects of the ritual without being able to "talk it away" with the therapist. The time break also communicated in action that the therapist saw them as capable of making their own sense of the ritual.

Feedback of the Ritual and Termination

The couple returned in a month. Each looked physically different. Mrs. Wilson's haggard appearance was gone, and Mr. Wilson's depressed air had disappeared. They looked younger as they walked, arm-in-arm, into the therapy room.

The therapist began by asking them how many times they had driven over to the clinic in the past month.

MR. WILSON: Oh, we weren't over here at all.
THERAPIST: You weren't over here at all? Do you mean you had *no* fights in the past month?
MRS. WILSON: Oh, we had plenty of fights! But as soon as one of us would bring up the past, the other one would say, "Take a trip!" and then we would laugh and settle the argument.

The couple then related several issues they had negotiated to each one's satisfaction in the preceding month. These were issues that they previously could not resolve because of the pattern of fighting about the past. In addition, the husband volunteered that he had put a door on their bedroom! The wife had attended a party from work with her husband, and he went to the ballet at her request. Previously, each would angrily refuse such requests from the other. Mr. Wilson had altered his work schedule to be home more often. Both reported that the children were doing well. Except for the children's behavior, none of these other issues had been a major focus in therapy, and, in fact, most had been defined by the couple as off-limits.

The couple were very proud of themselves and took credit for the changes. Together the therapist and couple agreed that no further therapy was needed.

REFLECTIONS ON THE EFFECTS OF THE RITUAL
AND TERMINATION

The burial ritual had a variety of effects in this case. It served to re-contextualize an old event in ways that interdicted an escalating, repetitive struggle. It provided the possibility of healing old hurts and bitterness in a way that the couple had not previously been able to do. Freed from the over-and-over-again pattern of fights that only provoked unhappy memories, the couple were able to begin to solve problems, to be creative, to see new possibilities, to utilize humor. Latent abilities in their system became available. The secret had lost its value as a message of hostility and distance for the couple and as something that functioned to preclude effective outside help.

The decision to terminate may seem abrupt. However, it was our team's assessment that a major constraint had been removed from the system and that the couple showed ample evidence of being more flexible, more expansive, more creative. Additionally, the couple were owning the changes as their own, instead of attributing them to the therapist. To continue therapy at this juncture was seen as a potential way to undermine the couple's new-found confidence in their problem-solving abilities. To terminate was in keeping with our belief that, freed from overriding systemic constraints, people are their own best resources.

One-Year Follow-Up

The Wilsons were phoned a year after the therapy's termination. They reported continued satisfaction in their lives. All three children were doing well at home and school. Janice was channeling her energies into becoming an excellent gymnast. The nagging had not reappeared. Mr. and Mrs. Wilson no longer fought about the past. They felt that they had some good fights about present issues and were able to resolve them satisfactorily.

Conclusion

The systemic therapy described in this chapter was brief; it was concluded in six sessions. Through utilizing a team approach, the therapy was able to combine careful assessment of the salient features of the couple's system with creative and unusual interventions. The rational and the slightly absurd were brought together to effect therapeutic change.

The central intervention in the case was the in-session ritual. But this intervention did not stand alone. It was embedded in a therapeutic relationship that attended to issues of prior treatment, working with secrets, and the crucial importance of the evolving therapist–couple system.

Acknowledgments

The author expresses her deep appreciation to Dr. Lee Bell, Dr. Linda Webb-Woodard, Dr. Mary Haake, Dr. Lauren Kaplan, and Scott Nielson, whose creative efforts as members of the 1979–1980 family therapy team in this case are detailed here.

References

Hoffman, L. (1981). *Foundations of family therapy: A conceptual framework for systems change*. New York: Basic Books.

Imber Coppersmith, E. (1983). The family and public service systems: An assessment method. In B. Keeney (Ed.), *Diagnosis and assessment in family therapy*. Rockville, MD: Aspen Systems.

Jackson, D., & Lederer, W. (1968). *Mirages of marriage*. New York: Norton.

Roberts, J. (1983a). Collaborative training teams in live supervision. *Family Therapy Networker, 7*(2), 30, 60–61.

Roberts, J. (1983b). Two models of live supervision: Collaborative team and supervisor guided. *Journal of Strategic and Systemic Therapies, 2*, 68–83.

Selvini Palazzoli, M., Boscolo, L., Cecchin, G., & Prata, G. (1974). The treatment of children through brief treatment of their parents. *Family Process, 13,* 429–442.

Selvini Palazzoli, M., Boscolo, L., Cecchin, G., & Prata, G. (1978). *Paradox and counterparadox.* New York: Jason Aronson.

Tomm, K. (1982). Circularity: A preferred orientation in family therapy. In A. Gurman (Ed.), *Questions and answers in the practice of family therapy.* New York: Brunner/Mazel.

Tomm, K. (1984a). One perspective on the Milan systemic approach: I. Overview of development, theory and practice. *Journal of Marital and Family Therapy, 10,* 113–125.

Tomm, K. (1984b). One perspective on the Milan systemic approach: II. Description of session format, interviewing style and interventions. *Journal of Marital and Family Therapy, 10,* 253–271.

Watzlawick, P., Beavin J., & Jackson, D. (1967). *Pragmatics of human communication: A study of interactional patterns, pathologies and paradoxes.* New York: Norton.

Wright, L., & Imber Coppersmith, E. (1983). Supervision of supervision: How to be "meta" to a metaposition. *Journal of Strategic and Systemic Therapies, 2,* 40–50.

Index